FOUNDATION CENTER

Knowledge to build on.

Grant Guides · **2006 / 2007**

GRANTS FOR LIBRARIES & INFORMATION SERVICES

CONTENTS

D1510653

FOUNDATION CENTER

Knowledge to build on.

The Foundation Center's mission is to advance knowledge of U.S. philanthropy.

Established in 1956, and today supported by more than 600 foundations, the Foundation Center is the nation's leading authority on organized philanthropy, connecting nonprofits and the grantmakers supporting them to tools they can use and information they can trust. The Center maintains the most comprehensive database on U.S. grantmakers and their grants and conducts research on trends in foundation growth and giving. It also operates education and outreach programs that help nonprofit organizations obtain the resources they need. Its web site receives more than 40,000 visits each day, and thousands of people are served in its five regional learning centers and through its national network of more than 280 Cooperating Collections. For more information, visit foundationcenter.org or call (212) 620-4230.

Copyright © 2006 by the Foundation Center

ISBN 1-59542-117-3

$75.00

INTRODUCTION

Grants for Libraries & Information Services lists 2,613 grants of $10,000 or more with a total value of $358,330,360 made by 651 foundations, mostly in 2004 or 2005. It covers grants to public, academic, research, school, and special libraries, and to archives and information centers for construction, operations, equipment, acquisitions, computerization, and library science education. Also included are grants for citizen information and philanthropy information centers.

Grants for Libraries & Information Services is one of 12 topic-oriented publications included in the Foundation Center's *Grant Guides* series (see page v for a list of titles in the series). The *Grant Guides* are derived from the Center's grants database, which includes the grants from more than 1,150 U.S. foundations annually, including the largest foundations by total giving and the top funders in every state. Many of these foundations report their grants directly to the Foundation Center by way of grant reporting forms, electronic files, newsletters, annual reports, or other grants lists. Each volume in the *Grant Guides* series provides a general overview of foundation giving in a particular field of nonprofit activity.

The grants listed in the *Grant Guides* series are also published in *The Foundation Directory Online* subscription-based service, along with profiles of the foundations making the grants.

ARRANGEMENT

Within this volume, grants are arranged alphabetically by state, then by foundation name and recipient name within each foundation listing. For each grant you will find the following information: the name, city, and location (state or foreign country) of the recipient organization; the amount awarded; the fiscal year of grant authorization (or payment); and a description of the activity funded.

Access to the grants is available through three indexes:

◆ an index of recipient names;

◆ a geographic index (arranged by recipient state or foreign country location, then recipient name); and

◆ an index of subject key words.

Numeric references in the indexes are to grant identification numbers, *not* page numbers.

Sample Entry

Foundation location —— **GEORGIA**

Foundation name —— **Jencks Foundation**

Limitations —— *Limitations:* Grants limited to GA, with primary consideration given to youth agencies and community organizations.

Grant Identification number —— **2055.** Friendship Community
Recipient name & location —— Center, Atlanta, GA,
Amount —— $15,000, 2004. 2-year
Year authorized —— grant. For program
Duration —— development and planning
Description —— of capital campaign.

Statistical tables analyzing the grants in this volume follow this introduction. These tables provide information on the dollar amount and number of grants according to the following breakdowns: foundation name; recipient state (or foreign country); primary subject; type of support (capital, general, research, etc.); recipient type; and population group served. Additionally, a list of the top 15 recipients by highest grant dollar amount and a list of the top 25 foundations awarding grants in this subject area are included with the statistics.

A list of foundation addresses and geographic limitations can be found at the back of this volume.

RESEARCH USING THIS GUIDE

In developing your basic list of potential funding sources, you should scan the grant listings in the category or categories closest to your field. Depending on the nature of your search, you will add to your list of possibilities the names of those foundations whose recent grants seem to indicate a potential interest in your organization or project. You should be looking for foundations that have funded an organization or project like yours, that are located or seem to award grants in your geographic area, and/or that have made grants in dollar amounts similar to the amount you are seeking. If you are new to grantseeking research, we recommend reading the Foundation Center's *Foundation Fundamentals* and visiting the Get Started section of our web site at foundationcenter.org.

PLEASE REMEMBER: IF YOU DO NOT QUALIFY, DO NOT APPLY.

Comprehensive research using all available resources will help the grantseeker determine the overall giving interests of a particular foundation and decide on appropriate foundations to apply to for funding. It is essential to remember that many foundations place limitations on their giving, including by subject area, recipient type, and geographic location. Finding out about any limitations before submitting grant proposals will save you time, decrease the number of rejections you receive, and demonstrate to the foundations you target that you know your field. The restrictions to giving under which some foundations operate appear in two places in this volume: in the "Grant Listings" section and in the "List of Foundations" section. If you do not fall within a funder's giving guidelines, do not apply for a grant. For *all* foundations, however, it is vitally important that you do further research before applying for funding.

After developing a list of foundations with a funding history in your field, it is imperative that you learn more about each one by consulting additional reference sources. These sources include annual reports (over 1,500 foundations publish one); IRS information returns (Forms 990 or 990-PF are available at the Foundation Center's web site); and foundation profiles published in the Foundation Center's print *Foundation Directory, FC Search: The Foundation Center's Database on CD-ROM,* and *The Foundation Directory Online.*

For current information, expert librarian assistance is available at one of our five Library/Learning Centers or more than 280 Cooperating Collections nationwide. Visitors enjoy free access to the Center's online databases, CD-ROMs, and directories—plus books, periodicals, and research findings on foundations and philanthropy. A list of Cooperating Collections is provided in this publication, or you can call (800) 424-9836 or visit foundationcenter.org/collections/ for the collection nearest you.

LOG ON TO FOUNDATIONCENTER.ORG

Continuously updated, the Foundation Center's web site is visited daily by tens of thousands of grantseekers, grantmakers, and others interested in the world of philanthropy. Find the latest philanthropy news, job listings, requests for proposals, and research reports. Many visitors also turn to us for online learning and immediate access to our free and subscription-based databases.

GRANT GUIDES:
TITLES IN THE SERIES

#1 — Arts, Culture & the Humanities

#2 — Children & Youth

#3 — Elementary & Secondary Education

#4 — Environmental Protection & Animal Welfare

#5 — Foreign & International Programs

#6 — Higher Education

#7 — Libraries & Information Services

#8 — Mental Health, Addictions & Crisis Services

#9 — Minorities

#10 — People with Disabilities

#11 — Religion, Religious Welfare & Religious Education

#12 — Women & Girls

To order, call (800) 424-9836 or visit
foundationcenter.org/marketplace/

TWO-LETTER STATE AND U.S. TERRITORY ABBREVIATIONS

AL = Alabama	**KY** = Kentucky	**OK** = Oklahoma
AK = Alaska	**LA** = Louisiana	**OR** = Oregon
AS = American Samoa	**ME** = Maine	**PA** = Pennsylvania
AZ = Arizona	**MD** = Maryland	**PR** = Puerto Rico
AR = Arkansas	**MA** = Massachusetts	**RI** = Rhode Island
CA = California	**MI** = Michigan	**SC** = South Carolina
CO = Colorado	**MN** = Minnesota	**SD** = South Dakota
CT = Connecticut	**MS** = Mississippi	**TN** = Tennessee
DE = Delaware	**MO** = Missouri	**TX** = Texas
DC = District of Columbia	**MT** = Montana	**UT** = Utah
FL = Florida	**NE** = Nebraska	**VT** = Vermont
GA = Georgia	**NV** = Nevada	**VA** = Virginia
GU = Guam	**NH** = New Hampshire	**VI** = Virgin Islands
HI = Hawaii	**NJ** = New Jersey	**WA** = Washington
ID = Idaho	**NM** = New Mexico	**WV** = West Virginia
IL = Illinois	**NY** = New York	**WI** = Wisconsin
IN = Indiana	**NC** = Noth Carolina	**WY** = Wyoming
IA = Iowa	**ND** = North Dakota	
KS = Kansas	**OH** = Ohio	

STATISTICAL ANALYSIS

TABLE 1. Grants for libraries & information services by foundation

Foundation	Amount	No.
3M Foundation	$10,000	1
Abbott Laboratories Fund	10,000	1
Abell Foundation, Inc., The	104,000	2
Abell-Hanger Foundation	140,000	4
Abrons Foundation, Inc., Louis and Anne	25,000	1
AEGON Transamerica Foundation	10,000	1
Aflac Foundation, Inc., The	250,000	1
Ahmanson Foundation, The	3,730,000	27
Akron Community Foundation	10,000	1
Alabama Power Foundation, Inc.	100,000	1
Alcoa Foundation	563,200	16
Alden Trust, George I., The	30,000	2
Allen Charitable Foundation, Andrew, The	10,000	1
Altman Foundation	1,441,000	8
Amarillo Area Foundation, Inc.	10,000	1
American Express Foundation	258,725	9
Amgen Foundation, Inc.	300,000	1
Andersen Foundation, Fred C. and Katherine B.	126,000	2
Anderson Foundation, M. D.	250,000	2
Anheuser-Busch Foundation	30,000	1
Annenberg Foundation, The	5,274,307	20
Aon Foundation	75,000	2
Applebaum Family Foundation, Eugene, The	87,500	1
Applied Materials Foundation, The	25,000	1
Arcadia Foundation, The	46,200	3
Archstone Foundation	326,989	5
Arcus Foundation	65,000	1
Arizona Community Foundation	20,000	2
Arkansas Community Foundation, Inc.	30,000	1
Assisi Foundation of Memphis, Inc., The	250,700	6
AT&T Foundation	1,981,841	34
Avenir Foundation, Inc.	100,000	1
AVI CHAI Foundation, The	35,198	1
Bader Foundation, Inc., Helen	211,700	8
Bakken Foundation, Earl & Doris, The	175,000	2
Balfour Foundation, L. G.	56,000	1
Ball Foundation, George and Frances	90,000	2
Baltimore Community Foundation, The	118,000	4
Bank of America Charitable Foundation, Inc., The	432,500	11
Baptist Community Ministries	379,908	1
Barr Foundation	50,000	2
Baton Rouge Area Foundation	278,757	4
Bauman Family Foundation, Inc.	310,000	3
BB&T Charitable Foundation	10,000	1
Bean Foundation, Norwin S. and Elizabeth N.	34,450	2
Bechtel, Jr. Foundation, S. D.	40,000	3
Beckman Foundation, Arnold and Mabel	10,000	1
Bedsole Foundation, J. L., The	64,400	3
Beldon Fund	50,000	1
Benedum Foundation, Claude Worthington	180,000	2
Beren Charitable Trust, Israel Henry	68,000	2
Berger Foundation, H. N. & Frances C.	70,000	1
Berkshire Taconic Community Foundation	70,000	2
Best Buy Children's Foundation	20,000	1
Bigelow Foundation, F. R.	30,000	1
Bing Fund Corporation	60,000	2
Blandin Foundation, The	84,000	2
Blank Family Foundation, Arthur M., The	30,000	1
Blaustein Foundation, Inc., Jacob and Hilda, The	10,000	1
Bodman Foundation, The	15,000	1
Boehringer Ingelheim Cares Foundation, Inc.	20,000	1

TABLE 1. (continued)

Foundation	Amount	No.
Boettcher Foundation	100,000	4
Booth Ferris Foundation	430,000	4
Boston Foundation, Inc.	261,000	7
Bothin Foundation, The	15,000	1
BP Foundation, Inc.	3,162,444	3
Bradley Foundation, Inc., Lynde and Harry, The	990,000	8
Bradley-Turner Foundation, Inc.	125,000	1
Bremer Foundation, Otto	363,695	13
Bristol-Myers Squibb Foundation, Inc., The	100,000	2
Broad Foundation	5,000,000	1
Broad Foundation, Eli & Edythe L.	570,000	2
Brown Foundation, Inc., The	100,000	3
Bruening Foundation, Eva L. and Joseph M.	90,000	3
Bucksbaum Family Foundation, Martin	25,000	1
Buell Foundation, Temple Hoyne	117,200	6
Buffett Foundation, Susan Thompson, The	50,000	1
Burlington Northern Santa Fe Foundation	10,000	1
Burnett Foundation, The	1,300,000	3
Burns Foundation, Fritz B.	10,000	1
Burroughs Wellcome Fund	10,000	1
Bush Foundation	256,000	4
Butler Foundation, Inc., J. E. & Z. B.	35,000	1
Byrne Foundation, Inc., The	45,050	2
C.E. and S. Foundation, Inc., The	185,000	3
C.I.O.S.	20,000	1
Cafritz Foundation, Morris and Gwendolyn, The	60,000	3
Cain Foundation, Effie and Wofford, The	13,000	1
Cain Foundation, Gordon and Mary, The	10,000	1
Calder Foundation, Louis, The	490,000	7
California Community Foundation	280,000	2
California Endowment, The	239,883	5
California Wellness Foundation, The	1,200,000	7
Cannon Foundation, Inc., The	40,000	2
Capital Group Companies Charitable Foundation, The	95,000	6
Capitol Federal Foundation	10,000	1
Cargill Foundation, The	250,000	1
Carls Foundation, The	30,000	1
Carnegie Corporation of New York	5,213,400	19
Carpenter Foundation, E. Rhodes & Leona B.	690,000	4
Carson Family Charitable Trust, The	50,000	1
Carter Family Charitable Trust, The	25,000	1
Carter Foundation, Amon G.	240,000	3
Carver Charitable Trust, Roy J.	977,137	18
Case Foundation, The	50,000	1
Casey Foundation, Annie E., The	1,701,097	19
Casey Foundation, Marguerite	650,000	6
Castle Foundation, Harold K. L.	220,000	2
Caterpillar Foundation	236,000	3
Central New York Community Foundation, Inc.	75,000	3
Champlin Foundations, The	2,160,973	22
Chartwell Charitable Foundation	175,000	4
Chase Foundation	213,234	6
Chatlos Foundation, Inc., The	68,600	3
CHC Foundation	20,000	1
Cheney Foundation, Ben B.	50,000	1
Chicago Community Trust, The	458,990	10
Chichester duPont Foundation, Inc.	30,000	1
Christy-Houston Foundation, Inc.	50,000	1
Cincinnati Foundation, Greater, The	85,000	3
Cinnabar Foundation, The	15,000	1
Cisco Systems Foundation	659,379	3
Citigroup Foundation	3,709,900	44

TABLE 1. Grants for libraries & information services by foundation

Foundation	Amount	No.
Citizens Charitable Foundation	75,000	5
Clark Foundation, Edna McConnell, The	65,000	2
Clark Foundation, Inc., Robert Sterling	235,000	4
Clark Foundation, The	80,000	1
Cleveland Foundation, The	2,030,609	15
Clowes Charitable Foundation, Inc., Allen Whitehill	4,000,000	1
Cogswell Benevolent Trust	25,000	1
Cohen Foundation, Naomi and Nehemiah	25,000	1
Cohen Foundation, Sam L.	32,500	1
Collins Foundation, The	450,000	9
Colorado Trust, The	30,196	1
Columbus Foundation and Affiliated Organizations, The	250,800	10
Comcast Foundation, The	195,000	10
Comerica Foundation	12,500	1
Commonwealth Fund, The	116,518	3
Communities Foundation of Texas, Inc.	122,000	3
Community Foundation for Greater Atlanta, Inc.	44,045	2
Community Foundation for Monterey County	10,000	1
Community Foundation for Muskegon County	50,000	2
Community Foundation for Palm Beach and Martin Counties, Inc.	105,306	2
Community Foundation for Southeast Michigan	95,000	2
Community Foundation for the National Capital Region, The	1,229,306	9
Community Foundation in Jacksonville, The	51,500	2
Community Foundation of Greater Lorain County, The	35,800	2
Community Foundation of Greater Memphis	20,000	2
Community Foundation of Sarasota County, Inc., The	25,500	1
Community Foundation of Western Massachusetts	10,000	1
Community Foundation of Western North Carolina, Inc., The	50,000	1
Community Foundation Serving Richmond & Central Virginia, The	60,000	3
Community Foundation Silicon Valley	1,482,730	16
Compton Foundation, Inc.	105,000	3
ConAgra Foods Foundation	10,000	1
Connell Charitable Trust, William F., The	50,000	1
Connelly Foundation	140,000	5
Corzine Foundation, Jon S., The	250,000	1
Cowell Foundation, S. H.	12,000	1
Credit Suisse Americas Foundation	25,000	1
Crown Memorial, Arie and Ida	74,300	2
Crystal Trust	500,000	1
Cullman Foundation, Inc., Lewis B. & Dorothy	1,882,820	5
Cummings Foundation, Nathan, The	104,500	4
CVS/pharmacy Charitable Trust, Inc.	20,000	1
D & DF Foundation	25,000	1
Dade Community Foundation, Inc.	35,000	1
DaimlerChrysler Corporation Fund	45,000	3
Dallas Foundation, The	117,000	4
Dana Foundation, The	83,000	4
Danforth Foundation, The	1,233,000	2
Daniel Foundation of Alabama, The	20,000	2
Daniels Fund	140,000	6
Davis Foundation, Shelby Cullom, The	150,000	3
Davis Foundations, Arthur Vining, The	678,000	4
Daywood Foundation, Inc., The	60,000	2
DeCamp Foundation, Ira W., The	65,000	1
Deere Foundation, John	200,000	1
Degenstein Foundation, 1994 Charles B., The	235,000	6
Dekko Foundation, Inc.	1,026,111	8
Delany Charitable Trust, Beatrice P.	10,000	1
Dell Foundation, Michael and Susan, The	50,251	1
Denver Foundation, The	45,000	4
Deutsche Bank Americas Foundation	848,500	9
DeVos Foundation, Richard and Helen, The	30,000	2
Diamond Fund, Irene	50,000	1
Dibner Fund, Inc., The	648,412	6
Dillon Foundation	33,100	1
Dodge Foundation, Inc., Geraldine R.	140,000	2
Dodge Jones Foundation	32,500	1
Doheny Foundation, Carrie Estelle	10,000	1
Dominion Foundation	167,500	7
Donner Foundation, William H., The	10,000	1

TABLE 1. (continued)

Foundation	Amount	No.
Dorot Foundation	241,667	3
Doss Foundation, Inc., M. S., The	25,000	1
Dow Chemical Company Foundation, The	10,000	1
Dow Foundation, Herbert H. and Grace A., The	227,094	3
Drown Foundation, Joseph	120,000	5
Duke Charitable Foundation, Doris	1,284,440	3
Duke Endowment, The	2,342,376	13
duPont Fund, Jessie Ball	69,573	3
Dyson Foundation	5,185,000	5
E.ON U.S. Foundation	13,500	1
Earhart Foundation	130,100	3
Eaton Charitable Fund, The	36,000	2
Eccles Foundation, George S. and Dolores Dore	486,227	7
Eden Hall Foundation	581,000	5
Educational Foundation of America, The	100,000	2
Eisner Foundation, Inc., The	15,000	1
El Pomar Foundation	65,000	3
Ellison Foundation, The	20,000	1
Emerson Charitable Trust	30,000	3
Energy Foundation	215,000	6
Engelhard Foundation, Charles, The	211,000	7
Englander Foundation, Inc.	18,000	1
English-Bonter-Mitchell Foundation	75,000	1
Enterprise Rent-A-Car Foundation	10,000	1
ExxonMobil Foundation	260,000	4
Fairbanks Foundation, Inc., Richard M.	2,000,000	1
Fairchild Foundation, Inc., Sherman, The	857,956	1
Fannie Mae Foundation	160,000	2
Feinberg Foundation, Joseph and Bessie	15,300	1
Fidelity Foundation	50,000	1
Fifth Third Foundation, The	200,000	2
Figge Charitable Foundation, V. O. Figge and Elizabeth Kahl	10,000	1
Fikes Foundation, Inc., Leland	85,000	2
First Data Western Union Foundation	130,000	3
First Interstate BancSystem Foundation, Inc.	16,500	1
FirstEnergy Foundation	10,000	1
Flight Attendant Medical Research Institute, Inc.	227,873	1
Flora Family Foundation	70,000	3
Fondren Foundation, The	150,000	1
Ford Family Foundation, The	1,515,000	13
Ford Foundation, The	13,432,339	58
Ford Motor Company Fund	60,000	2
Forest City Enterprises Charitable Foundation, Inc.	25,000	1
Foundation for Child Development	10,000	1
Foundation for the Carolinas	46,000	1
Freedom Forum, Inc., The	20,000	2
Freeman Foundation	1,666,000	7
Freeman Foundation, Ella West, The	10,000	1
Fremont Area Community Foundation	295,765	10
Frey Foundation	93,000	3
Frueauff Foundation, Inc., Charles A.	60,000	2
Fry Foundation, Lloyd A.	58,539	3
Gannett Foundation, Inc.	65,000	5
GAR Foundation, The	155,000	2
Garland Foundation, John Jewett & Helen Chandler	850,000	3
Gates Family Foundation	125,000	3
Gates Foundation, Bill & Melinda	18,342,554	93
GE Foundation	303,000	6
Gellert Foundation, Carl Gellert and Celia Berta, The	850,000	3
General Mills Foundation	40,000	3
Georgia-Pacific Foundation, Inc.	10,000	1
Gerbode Foundation, Wallace Alexander	10,000	1
Gerstacker Foundation, Rollin M., The	60,000	2
Getty Foundation, Ann and Gordon, The	10,000	1
Getty Trust, J. Paul	1,584,400	14
Gibbs Charitable Foundation	15,229	1
Gilder Foundation, Inc.	1,218,290	2
Gilhousen Family Foundation	25,000	1
Gill Foundation, The	153,000	5
Gleason Foundation	1,220,000	3
Glick Foundation Corporation, Eugene and Marilyn	33,334	1
Goldman Fund, Lisa and Douglas	110,000	2
Goldman Fund, Richard and Rhoda	285,000	6

TABLE 1. (continued)

Foundation	Amount	No.
Goldsmith Foundation, Horace W.	860,000	7
Gottesman Fund, The	82,500	3
Gottstein Family Foundation	10,000	1
Gould Foundation, Florence, The	754,765	12
Grable Foundation, The	271,950	9
Graham Fund, Philip L.	120,000	2
Grand Rapids Community Foundation	65,000	2
Grand Victoria Foundation	173,283	5
Grant Foundation, William T.	149,115	1
Greenwall Foundation, The	30,000	2
Gruss-Lipper Family Foundation, The	677,622	2
Guenther Foundation, Henry L.	25,000	1
Gund Foundation, George, The	65,000	3
Haas Fund, Miriam and Peter	110,000	2
Haas Fund, Walter and Elise	293,000	5
Haas, Jr. Fund, Evelyn and Walter	305,000	5
Hall Family Foundation	350,000	3
Hall-Perrine Foundation, Inc., The	16,000	1
Hamill Foundation, The	250,000	2
Hamilton-White Foundation, The	40,000	1
Hanson Foundation, John K. & Luise V., The	975,000	2
Harman Family Foundation	125,000	2
Harriman Foundation, Gladys and Roland	65,000	2
Harris Foundation, Irving, The	14,577	1
Hartford Foundation for Public Giving	419,510	11
Hartford Foundation, Inc., John A., The	5,279,908	3
Hawaii Community Foundation	25,000	1
Hayden Foundation, Charles	178,000	2
HCA Foundation, The	111,000	5
Healthcare Georgia Foundation, Inc.	65,000	2
Hearst Foundation, Inc., The	125,000	2
Heinz Endowment, Howard	1,215,000	5
Heinz Endowment, Vira I.	450,000	3
Heritage Mark Foundation	25,000	1
Heron Foundation, F. B., The	50,000	2
Herrick Foundation	50,000	1
Hewlett Foundation, William and Flora, The	12,986,000	27
Highland Street Connection, The	60,000	2
Hillcrest Foundation	235,000	6
Hilton Foundation, Conrad N.	275,000	1
HMSA Foundation	178,147	2
Horn Foundation, Mildred V.	66,035	1
Houston Endowment Inc.	945,700	8
Hubbard Foundation, R. D. & Joan Dale, The	25,000	1
Hudson-Webber Foundation	310,000	2
Humana Foundation, Inc., The	365,000	3
Hume Foundation, Jaquelin	25,000	1
Hunt Foundation, Roy A.	107,000	5
Hyams Foundation, Inc., The	40,000	1
Hyde and Watson Foundation, The	40,000	3
Hyde Family Foundations	95,000	4
Illinois Tool Works Foundation	10,000	1
Inasmuch Foundation	15,000	1
Independence Community Foundation	205,000	6
Intel Foundation	55,000	2
Iowa West Foundation	91,000	4
Irvine Foundation, James, The	913,500	10
J & L Foundation, The	15,000	1
Janirve Foundation	600,000	3
Jeld-Wen Foundation, The	121,500	1
Jerome Foundation	77,000	1
Johnson & Johnson Family of Companies Contribution Fund	280,000	9
Johnson Endeavor Foundation, Christian A.	20,000	1
Johnson Foundation, Robert Wood, The	6,111,224	37
Johnston Trust for Charitable and Educational Purposes, James M., The	30,000	1
Jones Foundation, Fletcher, The	150,000	2
Jones Foundation, Inc., Helen	15,000	1
Joyce Foundation, The	354,300	8
JPMorgan Chase Foundation, The	311,779	12
Kade Foundation, Inc., Max	300,000	1
Kahle/Austin Foundation	2,928,000	1
Kalamazoo Community Foundation	153,729	2

TABLE 1. (continued)

Foundation	Amount	No.
Kansas Health Foundation	1,060,000	6
Kaplan Fund, Inc., J. M., The	40,000	2
Kaplen Foundation, The	485,000	2
Kauffman Foundation, Ewing Marion	390,907	5
Kauffman Foundation, Muriel McBrien	10,000	1
Kaul Foundation, Hugh, The	25,000	1
Kellen Foundation, Inc., Anna Maria & Stephen	30,000	2
Kellogg Foundation, W. K.	1,664,772	9
Kellogg's Corporate Citizenship Fund	25,000	1
Kemper Foundation, William T.	70,047	3
Key Foundation	15,000	1
Kiewit Foundation, Peter	493,800	6
Kimberly-Clark Foundation, Inc.	10,000	1
Kimmel Foundation, Sidney, The	10,000	1
Kinder Foundation	25,000	1
King Foundation, Inc., Stephen and Tabitha	463,000	16
Kirby Foundation, Inc., F. M.	202,500	7
Kleberg Foundation, Robert J. Kleberg, Jr. and Helen C.	500,000	1
Klingenstein Fund, Inc., Esther A. & Joseph, The	50,000	1
Kluge Foundation, John W., The	2,074,635	6
Knight Foundation, John S. and James L.	530,000	4
Kohlberg Foundation, Inc., The	54,000	2
Koret Foundation	165,000	3
Kravis Foundation, Inc., Henry R.	160,833	4
Kresge Foundation, The	1,400,000	3
Kress Foundation, Samuel H.	117,500	8
Kronkosky Charitable Foundation, Albert & Bessie Mae	50,000	1
Lannan Foundation	370,000	7
Lattner Foundation, Inc., Forrest C.	323,300	4
Lavelle Fund for the Blind, Inc.	105,000	1
Lazarus Foundation, Inc., The	1,000,000	1
Leach Foundation, Inc., Tom and Frances	43,750	1
Lennar Foundation, Inc., The	25,000	1
Lennon Charitable Trust, Fred A., The	100,000	1
Libra Foundation	155,000	7
Lied Foundation Trust	358,191	2
Lilly and Company Foundation, Eli	360,000	4
Lilly Endowment Inc.	17,178,208	11
Lincoln Financial Group Foundation	50,000	2
Lloyd Foundation, John M., The	15,000	1
Lockheed Martin Corporation Foundation	30,000	2
Long Foundation, Thomas J., The	10,000	1
Longwood Foundation, Inc.	20,000	1
Lowenstein Foundation, Inc., Leon	42,300	2
LSR Fund	10,000	1
Luce Foundation, Inc., Henry, The	730,000	6
Lucent Technologies Foundation	49,800	1
Lumina Foundation for Education, Inc.	833,100	4
Lurie Foundation, Ann and Robert H.	50,000	1
M & T Charitable Foundation, The	162,951	1
MacArthur Foundation, John D. and Catherine T.	4,245,000	15
Macy, Jr. Foundation, Josiah	1,443,796	4
Madison Community Foundation	80,000	2
Maine Community Foundation, Inc., The	25,000	1
Maine Health Access Foundation	387,281	5
Marcus Foundation, Inc., The	25,000	1
Marin Community Foundation	797,400	6
Marisla Foundation, The	110,000	4
Marriott Foundation, J. Willard and Alice S., The	333,333	1
Mathers Charitable Foundation, G. Harold & Leila Y., The	20,000	1
Mathile Family Foundation	1,200,000	4
May Department Stores Foundation, The	1,527,502	13
MBNA Foundation, The	1,885,306	13
McCabe Foundation, B. C.	262,000	3
McConnell Foundation, The	12,917	1
McCune Charitable Foundation	45,000	3
McCune Foundation	685,000	3
McDermott Foundation, Eugene, The	131,000	3
McDonough Foundation, Inc., Bernard	10,000	1
McGovern Foundation, John P.	540,010	16
McGregor Fund	600,000	1
MCJ Foundation, The	10,000	1
McKnight Foundation, The	1,500,000	4
MDU Resources Foundation	10,000	1

TABLE 1. Grants for libraries & information services by foundation

Foundation	Amount	No.
Meadows Foundation, Inc., The	339,000	5
Medina Foundation	60,000	1
Medtronic Foundation, The	220,000	6
Mellon Financial Corporation Fund	50,000	1
Mellon Foundation, Andrew W., The	41,287,000	75
Mellon Foundation, Richard King	1,125,000	4
Melville Charitable Trust, The	382,200	3
Merck Company Foundation, The	10,000	1
Merck Fund, John, The	280,000	3
Merrill Lynch & Co. Foundation, Inc.	415,000	3
Mertz Gilmore Foundation	40,000	1
Messengers of Healing Winds Foundation	10,000	1
MetLife Foundation	168,200	5
Meyer Foundation, Eugene and Agnes E.	43,500	2
Meyer Memorial Trust	2,380,952	18
Milgard Family Foundation, Gary E.	17,148	1
Milstein Foundation, Paul and Irma	50,000	1
Milwaukee Foundation, Greater	477,004	8
Minneapolis Foundation, The	255,000	5
Monell Foundation, Ambrose, The	320,000	7
Monterey Fund, Inc.	29,800	2
Moore Foundation, Gordon and Betty	11,388,512	12
Morgan Stanley Foundation	12,500	1
Moriah Fund	126,000	4
Mott Foundation, Charles Stewart	4,619,179	28
Mott Foundation, Ruth	144,095	5
Murdock Charitable Trust, M. J.	662,000	3
Murphy Foundation, Dan	60,000	2
Murphy Foundation, The	15,000	1
Nash Family Foundation, Inc., The	387,585	9
Nationwide Foundation	130,000	2
NCC Charitable Foundation	87,000	5
New Hampshire Charitable Foundation, The	85,000	4
New Mexico Community Foundation, The	15,000	1
New York Community Trust, The	2,211,318	57
New York Foundation	107,385	4
New York Life Foundation	700,000	2
New York Times Company Foundation, Inc., The	105,000	5
Newhouse Foundation, Inc., Samuel I.	35,000	2
NIKE Foundation	1,000,000	1
Noble Foundation, Inc., Samuel Roberts, The	66,000	3
Norcliffe Foundation, The	30,000	2
Norfolk Foundation, The	10,325	1
Norris Foundation, Kenneth T. and Eileen L., The	465,000	5
Northwest Area Foundation	12,500	1
Northwestern Mutual Foundation	124,000	4
Norton Family Foundation, Peter	50,000	1
Noyes Foundation, Inc., Jessie Smith	150,000	3
O'Shaughnessy Foundation, Inc., I. A.	50,000	1
Oakwood Foundation Charitable Trust	10,000	1
Offield Family Foundation, The	10,000	1
Open Society Institute	465,000	9
Oregon Community Foundation, The	239,600	12
Osteopathic Heritage Foundations	94,997	1
Overbrook Foundation, The	60,000	2
PacifiCare Health Systems Foundation	30,000	3
Packard Foundation, David and Lucile, The	2,193,241	14
Packard Humanities Institute, The	1,466,345	5
Park Foundation, Inc.	75,000	3
Parsons Foundation, Mary Morton, The	20,000	1
Parsons Foundation, Ralph M., The	250,000	4
Paso del Norte Health Foundation	15,000	1
Payne Foundation, Frank E. Payne and Seba B.	148,365	1
Peninsula Community Foundation	5,860,382	16
Penn Foundation, William, The	305,199	3
Pennington Foundation, Irene W. & C. B.	10,000	1
PepsiCo Foundation, Inc., The	865,500	2
Perelman Family Foundation	68,000	3
Perot Foundation, The	15,000	1
Pettit Foundation, Jane Bradley	10,000	1
Pfaffinger Foundation	10,000	1
Pfizer Foundation, Inc., The	100,000	1
Pforzheimer Foundation, Inc., Carl and Lily, The	675,000	6

TABLE 1. (continued)

Foundation	Amount	No.
Philadelphia Foundation, The	108,000	5
Phillips Family Foundation, Jay and Rose, The	390,000	4
Picower Foundation, The	1,023,500	1
Pincus Family Fund, The	1,121,700	4
Pinkerton Foundation, The	70,000	3
Piper Charitable Trust, Virginia G., The	325,660	3
Pittsburgh Foundation, The	277,366	4
Plough Foundation	55,000	1
PNC Foundation, The	10,000	1
Pohlad Family Foundation, Carl and Eloise	250,000	1
Polk Bros. Foundation, Inc.	144,300	5
Prim Foundation, Wayne L.	1,097,550	1
Prince Charitable Trusts	115,000	3
Principal Financial Group Foundation, Inc.	300,000	1
Procter & Gamble Fund, The	51,388	3
Prudential Foundation, The	40,000	1
Public Welfare Foundation, Inc.	318,500	7
Publix Super Markets Charities	16,667	1
Pulliam Charitable Trust, Nina Mason	230,000	2
Raskob Foundation for Catholic Activities, Inc.	25,000	2
Rasmuson Foundation	93,542	5
Rasmussen Foundation, V. Kann	107,000	1
Redfield Foundation, Nell J.	110,833	2
Reese Health Trust, Michael	100,000	4
Reiman Foundation, Inc.	10,000	1
Reinberger Foundation, The	75,000	1
Retirement Research Foundation, The	737,885	8
Revson Foundation, Inc., Charles H.	625,000	4
Reynolds Charitable Trust, Kate B.	454,258	3
Reynolds Foundation, Donald W.	154,713	2
Reynolds Foundation, Inc., Z. Smith	80,000	2
Rhode Island Foundation, The	95,000	2
Richardson Foundation, Inc., Smith	689,487	4
Richardson Foundation, Sid W.	365,000	3
Riley Foundation, The	20,000	1
Rochester Area Community Foundation	71,500	3
Rockefeller Brothers Fund, Inc.	143,543	4
Rockefeller Foundation, The	3,027,874	11
Rockefeller Foundation, Winthrop, The	35,250	1
Rockwell Collins Charitable Corporation	45,000	2
Rockwell Fund, Inc.	150,000	2
Rose Foundation, Frederick P. & Sandra P.	195,000	4
Rosenberg Foundation, Murray & Sydell	11,500	1
Ross Foundation, Inc., Arthur	60,000	1
Rubinstein Foundation, Inc., Helena	20,000	1
Saint Luke's Foundation of Cleveland, Ohio	20,000	1
Saint Paul Foundation, Inc., The	660,143	10
Samberg Family Foundation	100,000	1
Samuels Foundation, Inc., Fan Fox and Leslie R., The	79,700	2
San Diego Foundation, The	411,409	8
San Francisco Foundation, The	603,544	27
Sandy River Charitable Foundation, The	40,000	1
Santa Barbara Foundation	55,063	2
Sara Lee Foundation	205,000	6
Scaife Family Foundation	37,368	1
Scherman Foundation, Inc., The	160,000	2
Scholl Foundation, Dr.	10,000	1
Schumann Center for Media and Democracy, Inc., The	920,000	2
Schwab Foundation, Charles and Helen	150,000	3
Scott Foundation, Homer A. & Mildred S.	165,000	2
Scripps Howard Foundation	35,000	2
Seattle Foundation, The	427,845	14
Seaver Institute, The	37,500	2
Sharp Foundation, Peter Jay, The	1,550,000	6
Shubert Foundation, Inc., The	40,000	1
SI Bank & Trust Foundation	20,000	1
Siebert Lutheran Foundation, Inc.	10,000	1
Silverman Foundation, Marty and Dorothy	35,000	2
Simon Foundation, Inc., William E.	135,000	3
Simons Foundation, The	10,000	1
Simpson PSB Fund	510,000	2
Skillman Foundation, The	155,000	6
Skirball Foundation	25,000	1
Skoll Foundation, The	375,000	3

TABLE 1.   (continued)

Foundation	Amount	No.
Slifka Foundation, Inc., Alan B.	11,000	1
Sloan Foundation, Alfred P.	6,358,813	17
Smart Family Foundation, The	245,000	4
Smith Fund, Inc., George D.	600,000	1
Soda Foundation, Y & H	25,000	2
Southern Oklahoma Memorial Foundation	175,000	3
Spangler Foundation, Inc., C. D.	125,000	1
Spencer Foundation, The	74,500	3
Speyer Family Foundation, Inc., The	33,000	1
St. Paul Travelers Foundation	125,000	6
Stark Community Foundation	20,000	1
Starr Foundation, The	2,335,000	8
State Farm Companies Foundation	10,000	1
State Street Foundation	90,000	3
Steelcase Foundation	25,000	1
Stockman Family Foundation Trust	12,000	1
Strauss Foundation, Levi	580,000	3
Stuart Foundation	500,000	3
Sunshine Lady Foundation, Inc., The	32,000	2
Surdna Foundation, Inc.	545,000	9
Swindells Charitable Trust, Ann and Bill	123,253	4
Taylor Foundation for Children, Inc., Carl Gary	30,000	1
TD Banknorth Charitable Foundation	30,000	3
Teagle Foundation, The	120,000	3
Temple Foundation, T. L. L.	631,417	6
Temple-Inland Foundation	69,450	1
Templeton Foundation, John	20,000	2
Tenet Healthcare Foundation	45,000	2
Textron Charitable Trust, The	83,333	1
Thaw Charitable Trust, Eugene V. & Clare E.	532,500	3
Tiger Foundation	150,000	1
Timken Foundation of Canton	150,000	1
Tisch Foundation, Inc.	50,000	1
Topfer Family Foundation	110,000	3
Trexler Trust, Harry C.	210,000	3
Triad Foundation, Inc.	150,000	1
Triangle Community Foundation	68,000	2
Trinity Foundation	100,000	1
Trust for Mutual Understanding, The	80,000	3
Tulsa Community Foundation	25,435	1
Turner Foundation, The	12,000	1
Turrell Fund	82,000	5
U.S. Bancorp Foundation, Inc.	33,000	3
UBS Foundation U.S.A.	14,500	1
UniHealth Foundation	150,000	2
Unilever United States Foundation	93,800	1
Union Pacific Foundation	22,500	2
UPS Foundation, The	27,500	2
Valero Energy Foundation	50,000	3
Valley Foundation, The	50,000	2
Valley Foundation, Wayne & Gladys	186,961	2
van Ameringen Foundation, Inc.	36,000	1
Van Andel Foundation, Jay and Betty	25,000	1
van Beuren Charitable Foundation, Inc.	776,000	3
Verizon Foundation	561,326	29
Victoria Foundation, Inc.	45,000	2
Vulcan Materials Company Foundation	10,000	1
Wachenheim Foundation, Sue and Edgar	2,375,000	5
Waitt Family Foundation	35,932	1
Wal-Mart Foundation	4,850,302	10
Wallace Foundation, The	115,000	1
Wallace Genetic Foundation, Inc.	95,000	4
Wallace Global Fund	285,679	5
Wallis Foundation	45,000	3
Walton Family Foundation, Inc.	502,940	3
Wang Foundation, Charles B.	100,000	1
Warhol Foundation for the Visual Arts, Andy, The	10,000	1
Wasserman Foundation	310,000	3
Wean Foundation, Raymond John, The	188,156	5
Wege Foundation	13,800	1
Weinberg Foundation, Inc., Harry and Jeanette, The	195,000	2
Weingart Foundation	357,500	9
Welfare Foundation, Inc.	250,000	2
Wells Fargo Foundation, The	368,000	17

TABLE 1.   (continued)

Foundation	Amount	No.
WEM Foundation	25,000	1
Wendt Foundation, Margaret L., The	190,000	2
Whitaker Foundation, The	60,000	6
Wiegand Foundation, E. L.	285,643	3
Wiener Foundation, Inc., Malcolm Hewitt	10,000	1
Wilburforce Foundation, The	225,000	3
Wilson Charitable Trust, Robert W., The	3,000,000	3
Winnick Family Foundation, The	460,000	3
Winston Foundation, Inc., Norman and Rosita, The	70,000	3
Wisconsin Energy Corporation Foundation, Inc.	37,500	2
Wolf Creek Charitable Foundation, The	10,000	1
Wood-Claeyssens Foundation	160,000	3
Woodruff Foundation, Inc., Robert W.	550,000	2
Wyoming Community Foundation	25,000	1
Xcel Energy Foundation	10,000	1
Yawkey Foundation II	55,000	2
Yum! Brands Foundation	25,025	1
Zarrow Foundation, Anne and Henry, The	74,175	3
TOTAL	**$358,330,360**	**2,613**

TABLE 2.   Grants for libraries & information services by recipient location

Recipient location	Amount	No.
Alabama	$455,750	9
Alaska	188,862	10
Argentina	415,000	2
Arizona	835,110	13
Arkansas	8,468,002	28
Australia	23,000	1
Austria	100,000	1
Azerbaijan	20,500	1
Bahamas	10,000	1
Belgium	1,785,400	15
Bulgaria	60,000	1
California	52,178,169	370
Canada	2,635,338	10
Chile	38,000	2
China	294,900	4
Colorado	2,871,716	37
Connecticut	4,141,996	35
Costa Rica	100,000	1
Croatia	60,000	1
Czech Republic	113,000	1
Delaware	884,950	8
Denmark	45,000	1
District of Columbia	29,342,623	179
Egypt	100,000	1
England	11,232,503	25
Florida	1,982,473	20
France	728,500	9
Georgia	8,191,470	21
Germany	1,890,000	7
Hawaii	648,147	9
Hong Kong	150,000	2
Hungary	42,000	1
Idaho	290,000	2
Illinois	6,848,102	84
India	597,465	4
Indiana	17,607,128	31
Indonesia	131,000	1
Iowa	2,866,087	37
Ireland	180,000	2
Israel	281,667	5
Italy	55,000	1
Jamaica	60,000	2
Kansas	1,368,187	12
Kentucky	2,803,785	21

TABLE 2. (continued)

Recipient location	Amount	No.
Kenya	1,093,539	6
Lebanon	275,000	2
Louisiana	1,832,078	14
Maine	2,229,037	48
Maryland	2,874,000	31
Massachusetts	9,626,523	73
Mauritius	25,000	1
Mexico	1,105,000	9
Michigan	5,659,498	63
Minnesota	4,343,738	60
Mississippi	80,000	3
Missouri	4,140,029	32
Montana	665,594	11
Namibia	80,000	1
Nebraska	934,441	11
Nepal	12,917	1
Netherlands	134,000	1
Nevada	1,509,082	5
New Hampshire	134,500	8
New Jersey	1,168,982	28
New Mexico	1,006,650	14
New York	72,885,962	418
Nigeria	75,000	2
North Carolina	6,391,561	34
North Dakota	140,250	5
Ohio	12,913,110	77
Oklahoma	758,518	13
Oregon	4,756,305	57
Pennsylvania	9,944,463	94
Peru	10,000	1
Philippines	443,543	3
Puerto Rico	151,780	4
Rhode Island	4,083,923	44
Romania	25,000	1
Russia	1,119,000	6
Slovakia	60,000	1
South Africa	5,198,500	14
South Carolina	376,192	6
South Dakota	268,133	4
Spain	29,200	1
Sweden	180,000	2
Switzerland	215,000	2
Tanzania	50,000	1
Tennessee	1,119,315	26
Texas	10,871,401	121
Ukraine	30,000	1
Utah	2,717,457	12
Venezuela	45,000	1
Vermont	1,842,000	8
Vietnam	350,200	1
Virginia	13,429,333	117
Washington	2,832,409	30
West Virginia	360,850	7
Wisconsin	2,317,517	44
Wyoming	205,000	4
Zimbabwe	84,000	1
TOTAL	**$358,330,360**	**2,613**

TABLE 3. Grants for libraries & information services by primary subject

Subject	Amount	%	No.
Animals/wildlife	$1,407,140	0.4	4
Arts/culture/humanities	24,166,016	6.7	232
Civil rights	3,044,541	0.8	23
Community improvement/development	5,660,231	1.6	59
Crime/courts/legal services	1,549,700	0.4	22
Education	192,144,491	53.6	1,306
Employment	634,477	0.2	20
Environment	12,264,112	3.4	99
Food/nutrition/agriculture	320,712	0.1	8
Health—general	20,123,613	5.6	157
Health—specific diseases	8,496,324	2.4	34
Housing/shelter	2,221,000	0.6	28
Human services—multipurpose	13,695,103	3.8	194
International affairs/development	7,412,047	2.1	57
Medical research	360,000	0.1	3
Membership benefit groups	81,000	0.0	2
Mental health/substance abuse	1,618,809	0.5	19
Philanthropy/voluntarism	22,332,705	6.2	227
Public affairs/government	10,574,739	3.0	46
Recreation/sports/athletics	1,512,650	0.4	4
Religion	16,566,208	4.6	12
Safety/disaster relief	178,900	0.0	4
Science	9,535,745	2.7	29
Social sciences	1,868,597	0.5	15
Youth development	561,500	0.2	9
TOTAL	**$358,330,360**	**100.0**	**2,613**

TABLE 4. Grants for libraries & information services by type of support

Type of support	Amount	No.
Annual campaigns	$284,600	3
Awards/prizes/competitions	707,301	12
Building/renovation	43,554,639	237
Capital campaigns	5,930,562	48
Collections acquisition	8,448,741	77
Collections management/preservation	10,605,457	48
Commissioning new works	11,000	1
Computer systems/equipment	16,558,785	135
Conferences/seminars	6,757,864	54
Continuing support	92,411,879	668
Curriculum development	10,827,326	26
Debt reduction	35,000	2
Electronic media/online services	59,428,257	251
Emergency funds	530,000	5
Endowments	4,232,090	20
Equipment	2,160,010	56
Exhibitions	1,927,400	22
Faculty/staff development	3,386,843	46
Fellowships	2,395,500	12
Film/video/radio	1,558,510	11
General/operating support	71,918,482	503
Internship funds	251,046	3
Land acquisition	861,710	5
Management development/capacity building	7,202,747	42
Matching or challenge grants	4,471,752	25
Performance/productions	499,600	9
Professorships	10,000	1
Program development	107,075,406	802
Program evaluation	1,888,630	13
Publication	7,090,806	61
Research	21,680,077	92
Scholarship funds	347,385	7
Seed money	1,301,199	14
Student aid	25,000	1
Technical assistance	5,481,113	22
Not specified	17,786,586	253

Grants may be for multiple types of support, and would thereby be counted twice.

TABLE 5. Grants for libraries & information services by recipient type

Recipient Type	Amount	No.
Animal/Wildlife Agencies	$440,000	5
Arts/Humanities Organizations	31,798,926	167
Churches/Temples/Mosques	11,219,532	23
Civil Rights Groups	2,405,957	25
Colleges & Universities	53,569,145	217
Community Improvement Organizations	8,563,984	89
Disease-Specific Health Associations	1,146,987	19
Educational Support Agencies	51,570,641	214
Environmental Agencies	10,536,179	76
Government Agencies	7,614,865	64
Graduate Schools	9,818,580	32
Hospitals/Medical Care Facilities	5,727,867	46
Human Service Agencies	19,024,013	307
Information/Public Education Centers	77,583,237	764
International Organizations	8,499,641	59
Junior/Community Colleges	1,988,188	9
Libraries	150,871,042	1,128
Media Organizations	2,820,237	33
Medical Research Organizations	1,717,972	8
Mental Health Agencies/Hospitals	673,368	15
Museums/Historical Societies	17,815,099	145
Performing Arts Groups	2,650,000	19

TABLE 5. (continued)

Recipient Type	Amount	No.
Philanthropy Organizations	32,491,870	315
Professional Societies & Associations	22,492,390	148
Public Administration Agencies	24,256,394	122
Public Policy Institutes	2,873,839	23
Public/General Health Organizations	19,346,126	132
Recreation Organizations	58,750	2
Reform Organizations	771,155	4
Research Institutes	6,656,527	35
Schools	18,972,846	91
Science Organizations	7,424,850	19
Single Organization Support	37,309,766	394
Social Science Organizations	455,321	10
Technical Assistance Centers	39,680,536	122
Volunteer Bureaus	141,497	4
Youth Development Organizations	190,500	8
Not Specified	10,000	1

Grants may support multiple recipient types, and would thereby be counted twice.

TABLE 6. Grants for libraries & information services by population group served

Population group	Amount	No.
African Americans/Blacks	$2,281,300	27
Aging	10,106,524	65
AIDS, people with	1,382,000	13
Alcohol or drug abusers	787,828	9
Asians/Pacific Islanders	722,654	11
Children & youth	24,848,014	326
Crime/abuse victims	1,036,000	17
Disabilities, people with	2,867,256	60
Economically disadvantaged	15,019,091	197
Hispanics/Latinos	3,045,488	19
Homeless	1,354,379	21
Immigrants & refugees	2,835,554	31
Indigenous people	100,000	1
LGBTQ	235,000	6
Men & boys	366,000	10
Migrant workers	215,000	3
Military/veterans	734,060	7
Minorities, general	4,861,114	65
Native Americans/American Indians	335,945	9
Offenders/ex-offenders	223,891	4
Single parents	75,000	4
Women & girls	3,901,691	64
Not specified	300,371,315	1,953

Grants may support multiple population groups, and would thereby be counted twice.

TABLE 7. Top 15 recipients in libraries & information services by single highest grant amount

	Recipient name	Donor	Grant amount	Entry
1.	Indianapolis Center for Congregations	Lilly Endowment Inc., IN	$8,171,433	734
2.	ARTstor	The Andrew W. Mellon Foundation, NY	6,500,000	1591
3.	Ithaka Harbors	The Andrew W. Mellon Foundation, NY	6,000,000	1617
4.	Fund for Theological Education	Lilly Endowment Inc., IN	5,999,075	731
5.	New York Academy of Medicine	The John A. Hartford Foundation, Inc., NY	5,119,908	1525
6.	Council of Chief State School Officers	Broad Foundation, CA	5,000,000	79
7.	Marietta College	Dyson Foundation, NY	5,000,000	1414
8.	Long Now Foundation	Peninsula Community Foundation, CA	4,500,000	302
9.	Public Library of Science	Gordon and Betty Moore Foundation, CA	4,150,000	258
10.	Indianapolis-Marion County Public Library Foundation	Allen Whitehill Clowes Charitable Foundation, Inc., IN	4,000,000	711
11.	Ithaka Harbors	The Andrew W. Mellon Foundation, NY	3,700,000	1618
12.	NewSchools Venture Fund	Bill & Melinda Gates Foundation, WA	3,327,879	2505
13.	Massachusetts Institute of Technology	The William and Flora Hewlett Foundation, CA	3,000,000	198
14.	Internet Archive	Kahle/Austin Foundation, CA	2,928,000	232
15.	Charities Aid Foundation (UK)	BP Foundation, Inc., IL	2,899,944	614

TABLE 8. Top 25 foundations in libraries & information services

	Foundation	State	Amount	No.
1.	The Andrew W. Mellon Foundation	NY	$41,287,000	75
2.	Bill & Melinda Gates Foundation	WA	18,342,554	93
3.	Lilly Endowment Inc.	IN	17,178,208	11
4.	The Ford Foundation	NY	13,432,339	58
5.	The William and Flora Hewlett Foundation	CA	12,986,000	27
6.	Gordon and Betty Moore Foundation	CA	11,388,512	12
7.	Alfred P. Sloan Foundation	NY	6,358,813	17
8.	The Robert Wood Johnson Foundation	NJ	6,111,224	37
9.	Peninsula Community Foundation	CA	5,860,382	16
10.	The John A. Hartford Foundation, Inc.	NY	5,279,908	3
11.	The Annenberg Foundation	PA	5,274,307	20
12.	Carnegie Corporation of New York	NY	5,213,400	19
13.	Dyson Foundation	NY	5,185,000	5
14.	Broad Foundation	CA	5,000,000	1
15.	Wal-Mart Foundation	AR	4,850,302	10
16.	Charles Stewart Mott Foundation	MI	4,619,179	28
17.	John D. and Catherine T. MacArthur Foundation	IL	4,245,000	15
18.	Allen Whitehill Clowes Charitable Foundation, Inc.	IN	4,000,000	1
19.	The Ahmanson Foundation	CA	3,730,000	27
20.	Citigroup Foundation	NY	3,709,900	44
21.	BP Foundation, Inc.	IL	3,162,444	3
22.	The Rockefeller Foundation	NY	3,027,874	11
23.	The Robert W. Wilson Charitable Trust	NY	3,000,000	3
24.	Kahle/Austin Foundation	CA	2,928,000	1
25.	Meyer Memorial Trust	OR	2,380,952	18
	TOTAL		**198,551,298**	**555**

FOUNDATION CENTER
Knowledge to build on.

COOPERATING COLLECTIONS

Free Funding Information Centers

The Foundation Center's mission is to strengthen the nonprofit sector by advancing knowledge about U.S. philanthropy. An authoritative source of information on grantmaker and corporate giving, we ensure free public access to a wide variety of services and comprehensive resources on grantmakers and grants through our five library/learning centers and a national network of Cooperating Collections. Cooperating Collections are libraries, community foundations, and other nonprofit agencies that make accessible a collection of Foundation Center print and electronic resources, as well as a variety of supplementary materials and educational programs in areas useful to grantseekers. The collection includes:

- Foundation Directory Online Professional or FC Search: The Foundation Center's Database on CD-ROM
- The Foundation Directory, Part 2, and Supplement
- Foundation Fundamentals
- The Foundation 1000

- Foundations Today Series
- Foundation Grants to Individuals
- Foundation Grants to Individuals Online
- The Foundation Center's Guide to Proposal Writing

- The Foundation Center's Guide to Winning Proposals
- Guide To U.S. Foundations, Their Trustees, Officers, and Donors
- National Directory of Corporate Giving
- Guide to Funding for International & Foreign Programs

All five Foundation Center libraries provide free access to both *The Foundation Directory Online* and *FC Search: The Foundation Center's Database on CD-ROM*. All Cooperating Collections provide access to either the online service or the CD-ROM, and all provide Internet access. Those seeking information on fundraising and nonprofit management can also refer to our web site (foundationcenter.org) for a wealth of data and advice on grantseeking, including links to grantmaker IRS information returns (990s and 990-PFs). Because the Cooperating Collections vary in their hours, it is recommended that you call a collection in advance of a visit. To check on new locations or current holdings, call toll-free (800) 424-9836 or visit foundationcenter.org/collections/.

FOUNDATION CENTER LIBRARY/LEARNING CENTERS

THE FOUNDATION CENTER
79 Fifth Ave., 2nd Floor
New York, NY 10003
(212) 620-4230

THE FOUNDATION CENTER
312 Sutter St., Suite 606
San Francisco, CA 94108
(415) 397-0902

THE FOUNDATION CENTER
1627 K St., NW, 3rd floor
Washington, DC 20006
(202) 331-1400

THE FOUNDATION CENTER
Kent H. Smith Library
1422 Euclid Ave., Suite 1600
Cleveland, OH 44115
(216) 861-1934

THE FOUNDATION CENTER
Hurt Bldg., 50 Hurt Plaza
Suite 150, Grand Lobby
Atlanta, GA 30303
(404) 880-0094

COOPERATING COLLECTIONS

ALABAMA

BIRMINGHAM PUBLIC LIBRARY
2100 Park Place
Birmingham 35203
(205) 226-3620

HUNTSVILLE PUBLIC LIBRARY
915 Monroe St.
Huntsville 35801
(256) 532-5940

MOBILE PUBLIC LIBRARY
West Regional Library
5555 Grelot Rd.
Mobile 36609
(251) 340-8555

AUBURN UNIVERSITY AT
MONTGOMERY LIBRARY
74-40 E. Dr.
Montgomery 36117-3596
(334) 244-3200

ALASKA

CONSORTIUM LIBRARY
3211 Providence Dr.
Anchorage 99508
(907) 786-1848

JUNEAU PUBLIC LIBRARY
292 Marine Way
Juneau 99801
(907) 586-5267

ARIZONA

FLAGSTAFF CITY-COCONINO COUNTY
PUBLIC LIBRARY
300 W. Aspen Ave.
Flagstaff 86001
(928) 779-7670

PHOENIX PUBLIC LIBRARY
1221 N. Central Ave.
Phoenix 85004
(602) 262-4636

TUCSON PIMA PUBLIC LIBRARY
101 N. Stone Ave.
Tucson 87501
(520) 791-4393

ARKANSAS

UNIVERSITY OF ARKANSAS—FORT SMITH
Boreham Library
5210 Grand Ave.
Fort Smith 72913
(479) 788-7204

CENTRAL ARKANSAS LIBRARY SYSTEM
100 Rock St.
Little Rock 72201
(501) 918-3000

CALIFORNIA

KERN COUNTY LIBRARY
Beale Memorial Library
701 Truxtun Ave.
Bakersfield 93301
(661) 868-0701

HUMBOLDT AREA FOUNDATION
Rooney Resource Center
373 Indianola
Bayside 95524
(707) 442-2993

VENTURA COUNTY COMMUNITY FOUNDATION
Resource Center for Nonprofit Management
1317 Del Norte Rd., Suite 150
Camarillo 93010
(805) 988-0196

FRESNO NONPROFIT ADVANCEMENT COUNCIL
1752 L St.
Fresno 93721
(559) 264-1513

CENTER FOR NONPROFIT MANAGEMENT
Nonprofit Resource Library
Center for Healthy Communities
1000 N. Alameda St.
Los Angeles 90012
(213) 687-9511

LOS ANGELES PUBLIC LIBRARY
Mid-Valley Regional Branch Library
16244 Nordhoff St.
North Hills 91343
(818) 895-3654

FLINTRIDGE FOUNDATION
Philanthropy Resource Center
1040 Lincoln Ave., Suite 100
Pasadena 91103
(626) 449-0839

SHASTA REGIONAL COMMUNITY FOUNDATION
Center for Nonprofit Resources
2280 Benton Dr.
Bldg. C, Suite A
Redding 96003
(530) 244-1219

RICHMOND PUBLIC LIBRARY
352 Civic Center Plaza
Richmond 94804
(510) 620-6561

RIVERSIDE CITY PUBLIC LIBRARY
3581 Mission Inn Ave.
Riverside 92501
(909) 826-5201

NONPROFIT RESOURCE CENTER
828 I St., 2nd Floor
Sacramento 95814
(916) 264-2772

SAN DIEGO FOUNDATION
Funding Information Center
1420 Kettner Blvd., Suite 500
San Diego 92101
(619) 235-2300

COMPASSPOINT NONPROFIT SERVICES
Nonprofit Development Library
1922 The Alameda, Suite 212
San Jose 95126
(408) 248-9505

LOS ANGELES PUBLIC LIBRARY
San Pedro Regional Branch
931 S. Gaffey St.
San Pedro 90731
(310) 548-7779

VOLUNTEER CENTER ORANGE COUNTY
Nonprofit Resource Center
1901 E. 4th St., Suite 100
Santa Ana 92705
(714) 953-5757

SANTA BARBARA PUBLIC LIBRARY
40 E. Anapamu St.
Santa Barbara 93101-1019
(805) 962-7653

SANTA MONICA PUBLIC LIBRARY
601 Santa Monica Blvd
Santa Monica 90401
(310) 458-8600

SONOMA COUNTY LIBRARY
3rd & E. Sts.
Santa Rosa 95404
(707) 545-0831

SEASIDE BRANCH LIBRARY
550 Harcourt Ave.
Seaside 93955
(831) 899-2055

SIERRA NONPROFIT SUPPORT CENTER
39 N. Washington St. #F
Sonora 95370-0905
(209) 533-1093

COLORADO

EL POMAR NONPROFIT RESOURCE CENTER
Penrose Library
20 N. Cascade Ave.
Colorado Springs 80903
(719) 531-6333

DENVER PUBLIC LIBRARY
10 W. 14th Ave. Pkwy.
Denver 80204
(720) 865-1111

DURANGO PUBLIC LIBRARY
1188 E. 2nd Ave.
Durango 81301
(970) 375-3380

PUEBLO CITY-COUNTY LIBRARY DISTRICT
100 E. Abriendo Ave.
Pueblo 81004-4232
(719) 562-5600

CONNECTICUT

GREENWICH LIBRARY
101 W. Putnam Ave.
Greenwich 06830
(203) 622-7900

HARTFORD PUBLIC LIBRARY
500 Main St.
Hartford 06103
(860) 695-6300

NEW HAVEN FREE PUBLIC LIBRARY
133 Elm St.
New Haven 06510-2057
(203) 946-7431

DELAWARE

UNIVERSITY OF DELAWARE
Hugh Morris Library
181 S. College Ave.
Newark 19717-5267
(302) 831-2432

FLORIDA

BARTOW PUBLIC LIBRARY
2151 S. Broadway Ave.
Bartow 33830
(863) 534-0931

VOLUSIA COUNTY LIBRARY CENTER
City Island
105 E. Magnolia Ave.
Daytona Beach 32114-4484
(386) 257-6036

NOVA SOUTHEASTERN UNIVERSITY
Alvin Sherman Library, Research, and
Information Technology Center
3100 Ray Ferrero Jr. Blvd.
Fort Lauderdale 33314
(954) 262-4613

INDIAN RIVER COMMUNITY COLLEGE
Learning Resources Center
3209 Virginia Ave.
Fort Pierce 34981-5596
(772) 462-4757

JACKSONVILLE PUBLIC LIBRARY
Nonprofit Resources
303 N. Laura St.
Jacksonville 32202
(904) 630-2665

MIAMI-DADE PUBLIC LIBRARY
101 W. Flagler St.
Miami 33130
(305) 375-5575

ORANGE COUNTY LIBRARY SYSTEM
101 E. Central Blvd.
Orlando 32801
(407) 835-7323

SELBY PUBLIC LIBRARY
1331 1st St.
Sarasota 34236
(941) 861-1100

STATE LIBRARY OF FLORIDA
R.A. Gray Bldg.
500 S. Bronough St.
Tallahassee 32399-0250
(850) 245-6600

HILLSBOROUGH COUNTY PUBLIC LIBRARY
COOPERATIVE
John F. Germany Public Library
900 N. Ashley Dr.
Tampa 33602
(813) 273-3652

COMMUNITY FOUNDATION OF PALM BEACH &
MARTIN COUNTIES
700 S. Dixie Hwy., Suite 200
West Palm Beach 33401
(561) 659-6800

GEORGIA

HALL COUNTY LIBRARY SYSTEM
127 Main St. NW
Gainesville 30501
(770) 532-3311

METHODIST HOME FOR CHILDREN AND YOUTH
Rumford Center
304 Pierce Ave., 1st floor
Macon 31203
(478) 751-2800

THOMAS COUNTY PUBLIC LIBRARY
201 N. Madison St.
Thomasville 31792
(229) 225-5252

HAWAII

UNIVERSITY OF HAWAII AT MĀNOA
Hamilton Library
2550 The Mall
Honolulu 96822
(808) 956-7214

IDAHO

BOISE PUBLIC LIBRARY
Funding Information Center
715 S. Capitol Blvd.
Boise 83702
(208) 384-4024

CALDWELL PUBLIC LIBRARY
1010 Dearborn St.
Caldwell 83605
(208) 459-3242

MARSHALL PUBLIC LIBRARY
113 S. Garfield
Pocatello 83204
(208) 232-1263

ILLINOIS

CARBONDALE PUBLIC LIBRARY
405 W. Main St.
Carbondale 62901
(618) 457-0354

DONORS FORUM OF CHICAGO LIBRARY
208 S. LaSalle, Suite 740
Chicago 60604
(312) 578-0175

EVANSTON PUBLIC LIBRARY
1703 Orrington Ave.
Evanston 60201
(847) 866-0300

ROCK ISLAND PUBLIC LIBRARY
401 19th St.
Rock Island 61201-8143
(309) 732-7323

CENTRAL ILLINOIS NONPROFIT
RESOURCE CENTER
Brookens Library
University of Illinois at Springfield
One University Plaza, MS Lib 140
Springfield 62703-5407
(217) 206-6633

INDIANA

EVANSVILLE–VANDERBURGH PUBLIC LIBRARY
200 SE Martin Luther King Jr. Blvd.
Evansville 47708
(812) 428-8200

ALLEN COUNTY PUBLIC LIBRARY
200 East Berry St.
Fort Wayne 46802
(260) 421-1238

INDIANAPOLIS–MARION COUNTY PUBLIC
LIBRARY
202 N. Alabama St.
Indianapolis 46206
(317) 269-1700

VIGO COUNTY PUBLIC LIBRARY
One Library Square
Terre Haute 47807
(812) 232-1113

VALPARAISO UNIVERSITY
Christopher Center Library Services
1410 Chapel Dr.
Valparaiso 46383
(219) 464-5364

IOWA

CEDAR RAPIDS PUBLIC LIBRARY
500 1st St., SE
Cedar Rapids 52401
(319) 398-5123

SOUTHWESTERN COMMUNITY COLLEGE
Learning Resource Center
1501 W. Townline Rd.
Creston 50801
(641) 782-7081

DES MOINES PUBLIC LIBRARY
1000 Grand Ave.
Des Moines 50309-3027
(515) 283-4152

SIOUX CITY PUBLIC LIBRARY
Siouxland Funding Research Center
529 Pierce St.
Sioux City 51101-1203
(712) 255-2933

KANSAS

PIONEER MEMORIAL LIBRARY
375 West 4th St.
Colby 67701
(785) 460-4470

DODGE CITY PUBLIC LIBRARY
1001 2nd Ave.
Dodge City 67801
(620) 225-0248

KEARNY COUNTY LIBRARY
101 E. Prairie
Lakin 67860
(620) 355-6674

SALINA PUBLIC LIBRARY
301 W. Elm
Salina 67401
(785) 825-4624

TOPEKA AND SHAWNEE COUNTY
PUBLIC LIBRARY
1515 SW 10th Ave.
Topeka 66604
(785) 580-4400

WICHITA PUBLIC LIBRARY
223 S. Main St.
Wichita 67202
(316) 261-8500

KENTUCKY

WESTERN KENTUCKY UNIVERSITY
Helm-Cravens Library
110 Helm Library
Bowling Green 42101-3576
(270) 745-6163

LEXINGTON PUBLIC LIBRARY
140 E. Main St.
Lexington 40507-1376
(859) 231-5520

LOUISVILLE FREE PUBLIC LIBRARY
301 York St.
Louisville 40203
(502) 574-1617

LOUISIANA

COMMUNITY DEVELOPMENT WORKS LEARNING
LAB
The Rapides Foundation Building
1101 4th St., Suite 101B
Alexandria 71301
(318) 443-7880

EAST BATON ROUGE PARISH LIBRARY
River Center Branch
120 St. Louis St.
Baton Rouge 70802
(225) 389-4967

BEAUREGARD PARISH LIBRARY
205 S. Washington Ave.
DeRidder 70634
(337) 463-6217

OUACHITA PARISH PUBLIC LIBRARY
1800 Stubbs Ave.
Monroe 71201
(318) 327-1490

NEW ORLEANS PUBLIC LIBRARY
219 Loyola Ave.
New Orleans 70112
(504) 596-2580

SHREVE MEMORIAL LIBRARY
424 Texas St.
Shreveport 71120-1523
(318) 226-5894

MAINE

MAINE PHILANTHROPY CENTER
University of Southern Maine
Glickman Family Library
314 Forest Ave.
Portland 04104-9301
(207) 780-5039

MARYLAND

ENOCH PRATT FREE LIBRARY
400 Cathedral St.
Baltimore 21201
(410) 396-5320

MASSACHUSETTS

ASSOCIATED GRANT MAKERS
55 Court St.
Suite 520
Boston 02108
(617) 426-2606

BOSTON PUBLIC LIBRARY
700 Boylston St.
Boston 02116
(617) 536-5400

BERKSHIRE ATHENAEUM
1 Wendell Ave.
Pittsfield 01201-6385
(413) 499-9480

WESTERN MASSACHUSETTS FUNDING
RESOURCE CENTER
65 Elliot St.
Springfield 01101-1730
(413) 452-0697

WORCESTER PUBLIC LIBRARY
Grants Resource Center
3 Salem Square
Worcester 01608
(508) 799-1655

MICHIGAN

ALPENA COUNTY LIBRARY
211 N. 1st St.
Alpena 49707
(989) 356-6188

UNIVERSITY OF MICHIGAN
Graduate Library
209 Hatcher N.
Ann Arbor 48109-1205
(734) 763-1539

WILLARD PUBLIC LIBRARY
Nonprofit & Funding Resource Collection
7 W. Van Buren St.
Battle Creek 49017
(269) 969-2100

WAYNE STATE UNIVERSITY
Purdy/Kresge Library
5265 Cass Ave.
Detroit 48202
(313) 577-6424

MICHIGAN STATE UNIVERSITY LIBRARIES
Main Library
Funding Center
100 Library
East Lansing 48824-1048
(517) 432-6123

FARMINGTON COMMUNITY LIBRARY
32737 W. 12 Mile Rd.
Farmington Hills 48334
(248) 553-0300

FLINT PUBLIC LIBRARY
1026 E. Kearsley St.
Flint 48502-1994
(810) 232-7111

GRAND RAPIDS PUBLIC LIBRARY
111 Library St. NE
Grand Rapids 49503-3268
(616) 988-5400

MICHIGAN TECHNOLOGICAL UNIVERSITY
Corporate Services
ATDC Bldg, Suite 200
1402 E. Sharon Ave.
Houghton 49931-1295
(906) 487-2228

WEST SHORE COMMUNITY COLLEGE LIBRARY
3000 N. Stiles Rd.
Scottville 49454-0277
(231) 845-6211

TRAVERSE AREA DISTRICT LIBRARY
610 Woodmere Ave.
Traverse City 49686
(231) 932-8500

MINNESOTA

BRAINERD PUBLIC LIBRARY
416 S. 5th St.
Brainerd 56401
(218) 829-5574

DULUTH PUBLIC LIBRARY
520 W. Superior St.
Duluth 55802
(218) 723-3802

SOUTHWEST STATE UNIVERSITY
University Library
N. Hwy. 23
Marshall 56253
(507) 537-6108

MINNEAPOLIS PUBLIC LIBRARY
Hosmer Library
347 E. 36th St.
Minneapolis 55408

ROCHESTER PUBLIC LIBRARY
101 2nd St. SE
Rochester 55904-3777
(507) 285-8002

SAINT PAUL PUBLIC LIBRARY
90 W. 4th St.
Saint Paul 55102
(651) 266-7000

MISSISSIPPI

LIBRARY OF HATTIESBURG, PETAL
AND FORREST COUNTY
329 Hardy St.
Hattiesburg 39401-3824
(601) 582-4461

JACKSON/HINDS LIBRARY SYSTEM
300 N. State St.
Jackson 39201
(601) 968-5803

MISSOURI

COUNCIL ON PHILANTHROPY
University of Missouri—Kansas City
4747 Troost, Rm. 207
Kansas City 64110
(816) 235-6259

KANSAS CITY PUBLIC LIBRARY
14 W. 10th St.
Kansas City 64105-1702
(816) 701-3400

ST. LOUIS PUBLIC LIBRARY
1301 Olive St.
St. Louis 63103
(314) 241-2288

SPRINGFIELD-GREENE COUNTY LIBRARY
The Library Center
4653 S. Campbell
Springfield 65810
(417) 874-8110

MONTANA

FALLON COUNTY LIBRARY
6 W. Fallon Ave.
Baker 59313-1037
(406) 778-7160

MONTANA STATE UNIVERSITY—BILLINGS
1500 N. 30TH ST.
BILLINGS 59101
(406) 657-2262

BOZEMAN PUBLIC LIBRARY
220 E. Lamme
Bozeman 59715
(406) 582-2402

LINCOLN COUNTY PUBLIC LIBRARIES
Libby Public Library
220 W. 6th St.
Libby 59923
(406) 293-2778

MANSFIELD LIBRARY
University of Montana
32 Campus Dr.
Missoula 59812-9936
(406) 243-6800

NEBRASKA

BUTLER MEMORIAL LIBRARY
621 Penn St.
Cambridge 69022
(308) 697-3836

UNIVERSITY OF NEBRASKA—LINCOLN
University Libraries
14th & R Sts.
Lincoln 68588-2848
(402) 472-2848

OMAHA PUBLIC LIBRARY
W. Dale Clark Library
215 S. 15th St.
Omaha 68102
(402) 444-4826

NEVADA

GREAT BASIN COLLEGE LIBRARY
1500 College Pkwy.
Elko 89801
(775) 753-2222

CLARK COUNTY LIBRARY
1401 E. Flamingo
Las Vegas 89119
(702) 507-3400

WASHOE COUNTY LIBRARY
301 S. Center St.
Reno 89501
(775) 327-8300

NEW HAMPSHIRE

CONCORD PUBLIC LIBRARY
45 Green St.
Concord 03301
(603) 225-8670

PLYMOUTH STATE UNIVERSITY
Herbert H. Lamson Library
Plymouth 03264
(603) 535-2258

NEW JERSEY

FREE PUBLIC LIBRARY OF ELIZABETH
11 S. Broad St.
Elizabeth 07202
(908) 354-6060

COUNTY COLLEGE OF MORRIS
Learning Resource Center
214 Center Grove Rd.
Randolph 07869
(973) 328-5296

NEW JERSEY STATE LIBRARY
185 W. State St.
Trenton 08625-0520
(609) 292-6220

NEW MEXICO

ALBUQUERQUE/BERNALILLO COUNTY
LIBRARY SYSTEM
501 Copper Ave. NW
Albuquerque 87102
(505) 768-5141

NEW MEXICO STATE LIBRARY
1209 Camino Carlos Rey
Santa Fe 87507
(505) 476-9702

NEW YORK

NEW YORK STATE LIBRARY
Cultural Education Center, 6th Floor
Empire State Plaza
Albany 12230
(518) 474-5355

BROOKLYN PUBLIC LIBRARY
Grand Army Plaza
Brooklyn 11238
(718) 230-2122

BUFFALO & ERIE COUNTY PUBLIC LIBRARY
1 Lafayette Square
Buffalo 14203-1887
(716) 858-7097

SOUTHEAST STEUBEN COUNTY LIBRARY
300 Nasser Civic Center Plaza
Corning 14830
(607) 936-3713

HUNTINGTON PUBLIC LIBRARY
338 Main St.
Huntington 11743
(631) 427-5165

QUEENS BOROUGH PUBLIC LIBRARY
89-11 Merrick Blvd.
Jamaica 11432
(718) 990-0700

LEVITTOWN PUBLIC LIBRARY
1 Bluegrass Ln.
Levittown 11756
(516) 731-5728

ADRIANCE MEMORIAL LIBRARY
93 Market St.
Poughkeepsie 12601
(845) 485-3445

RIVERHEAD FREE LIBRARY
330 Court St.
Riverhead 11901
(631) 727-3228

ROCHESTER PUBLIC LIBRARY
115 S. Ave.
Rochester 14604
(585) 428-8130

ONONDAGA COUNTY PUBLIC LIBRARY
447 S. Salina St.
Syracuse 13202-2494
(315) 435-1900

UTICA PUBLIC LIBRARY
303 Genesee St.
Utica 13501
(315) 735-2279

WHITE PLAINS PUBLIC LIBRARY
100 Martine Ave.
White Plains 10601
(914) 422-1480

YONKERS PUBLIC LIBRARY
Riverfront Library
One Larkin Center
Yonkers 10701
(914) 337-1500

NORTH CAROLINA

COMMUNITY FOUNDATION OF WESTERN
NORTH CAROLINA
Pack Memorial Library
67 Haywood St.
Asheville 28802
(828) 254-4960

THE DUKE ENDOWMENT
100 N. Tryon St., Suite 3500
Charlotte 28202-4012
(704) 376-0291

DURHAM COUNTY PUBLIC LIBRARY
300 N. Roxboro St.
Durham 27702
(919) 560-0100

CAMERON VILLAGE REGIONAL LIBRARY
1930 Clark Ave.
Raleigh 27605
(919) 856-6710

NEW HANOVER COUNTY PUBLIC LIBRARY
201 Chestnut St.
Wilmington 28401-3942
(910) 798-6301

FORSYTH COUNTY PUBLIC LIBRARY
660 W. 5th St.
Winston-Salem 27101
(336) 727-2264

NORTH DAKOTA

BISMARCK PUBLIC LIBRARY
515 N. 5th St.
Bismarck 58501-4081
(701) 222-6410

FARGO PUBLIC LIBRARY
102 N. 3rd St.
Fargo 58102
(701) 241-1491

MINOT PUBLIC LIBRARY
516 2nd Ave. SW
Minot 58701-3792
(701) 852-1045

OHIO

STARK COUNTY DISTRICT LIBRARY
715 Market Ave. N.
Canton 44702
(330) 452-0665

PUBLIC LIBRARY OF CINCINNATI & HAMILTON
COUNTY
800 Vine St.
Cincinnati 45202-2071
(513) 369-6000

COLUMBUS METROPOLITAN LIBRARY
96 S. Grant Ave.
Columbus 43215
(614) 645-2590

DAYTON METRO LIBRARY
215 E. 3rd St.
Dayton 45402
(937) 227-9500

MANSFIELD/RICHLAND COUNTY PUBLIC
LIBRARY
43 W. 3rd St.
Mansfield 44902
(419) 521-3110

PORTSMOUTH PUBLIC LIBRARY
1220 Gallia St.
Portsmouth 45662
(740) 354-5688

TOLEDO–LUCAS COUNTY PUBLIC LIBRARY
325 N. Michigan St.
Toledo 43624
(419) 259-5207

PUBLIC LIBRARY OF YOUNGSTOWN &
MAHONING COUNTY
305 Wick Ave.
Youngstown 44503
(330) 744-8636

OKLAHOMA

OKLAHOMA CITY UNIVERSITY
Dulaney Browne Library
2501 N. Blackwelder
Oklahoma City 73106
(405) 521-5822

TULSA CITY–COUNTY LIBRARY
400 Civic Center
Tulsa 74103
(918) 596-7977

OREGON

OREGON INSTITUTE OF TECHNOLOGY
3201 Campus Dr.
Klamath Falls 97601-8801
(541) 885-1772

JACKSON COUNTY LIBRARY SERVICES
205 S. Central Ave.
Medford 97501
(541) 774-8689

MULTNOMAH COUNTY LIBRARY
801 SW 10th Ave.
Portland 97205
(503) 988-5123

OREGON STATE LIBRARY
250 Winter St. NE
Salem 97301-3950
(503) 378-4243

PENNSYLVANIA

NORTHAMPTON COMMUNITY COLLEGE
Paul and Harriett Mack Library
3835 Green Pond Rd.
Bethlehem 18020
(610) 861-5359

ERIE COUNTY LIBRARY SYSTEM
160 E. Front St.
Erie 16507
(814) 451-6927

DAUPHIN COUNTY LIBRARY SYSTEM
East Shore Area Library
4501 Ethel St.
Harrisburg 17109
(717) 652-9380

HAZLETON AREA PUBLIC LIBRARY
55 N. Church St.
Hazleton 18201
(570) 454-2961

LANCASTER PUBLIC LIBRARY
125 N. Duke St.
Lancaster 17602
(717) 394-2651

FREE LIBRARY OF PHILADELPHIA
1901 Vine St., 2nd Fl.
Philadelphia 19103-1189
(215) 686-5423

CARNEGIE LIBRARY OF PITTSBURGH
612 Smithfield St.
Pittsburgh 15222
(412) 281-7143

COOPERATING COLLECTIONS

NONPROFIT & COMMUNITY
RESOURCE CENTER
1151 Oak St.
Pittston 18640
(570) 655-5581

READING PUBLIC LIBRARY
100 S. 5th St.
Reading 19602
(610) 655-6355

JAMES V. BROWN LIBRARY
19 E. 4th St.
Williamsport 17701
(570) 326-0536

MARTIN LIBRARY
159 E. Market St.
York 17401
(717) 846-5300

RHODE ISLAND

PROVIDENCE PUBLIC
LIBRARY
150 Empire St.
Providence 02903
(401) 455-8088

SOUTH CAROLINA

ANDERSON COUNTY LIBRARY
300 N. McDuffie St.
Anderson 29622
(864) 260-4500

CHARLESTON COUNTY LIBRARY
68 Calhoun St.
Charleston 29401
(843) 805-6930

SOUTH CAROLINA STATE LIBRARY
1500 Senate St.
Columbia 29211
(803) 734-8026

GREENVILLE COUNTY LIBRARY SYSTEM
25 Heritage Green Place
Greenville 29601-2034
(864) 242-5000

SOUTH DAKOTA

DAKOTA STATE UNIVERSITY
Nonprofit Management Institute
820 N. Washington
Madison 57042
(605) 367-5382

SOUTH DAKOTA STATE LIBRARY
800 Governors Dr.
Pierre 57501-2294
(605) 773-3131
(800) 423-6665 (SD residents)

E.Y. BERRY LIBRARY-LEARNING CENTER
Black Hills State University
1200 University St. Unit 9676
Spearfish 57799-9676
(605) 642-6834

TENNESSEE

UNITED WAY OF GREATER CHATTANOOGA
Center for Nonprofits
630 Market St.
Chattanooga 37402
(423) 752-0300

KNOX COUNTY PUBLIC LIBRARY
500 W. Church Ave.
Knoxville 37902
(865) 215-8751

MEMPHIS & SHELBY COUNTY PUBLIC LIBRARY
3030 Poplar Ave.
Memphis 38111
(901) 415-2734

NASHVILLE PUBLIC LIBRARY
615 Church St.
Nashville 37219
(615) 862-5800

TEXAS

AMARILLO AREA FOUNDATION NONPROFIT
SERVICE CENTER
801 S. Filmore, Suite 700
Amarillo 79101
(806) 376-4521

HOGG FOUNDATION FOR MENTAL HEALTH
Regional Foundation Library
3001 Lake Austin Blvd., Suite 400
Austin 78703
(512) 471-5041

BEAUMONT PUBLIC LIBRARY
801 Pearl St.
Beaumont 77704-3827
(409) 838-6606

CORPUS CHRISTI PUBLIC LIBRARY
805 Comanche St.
Corpus Christi 78401
(361) 880-7000

DALLAS PUBLIC LIBRARY
1515 Young St.
Dallas 75201
(214) 670-1487

SOUTHWEST BORDER NONPROFIT
RESOURCE CENTER
1201 W. University Dr.
Edinburg 78539-2999
(956) 384-5920

UNIVERSITY OF TEXAS AT EL PASO
500 W. University, Benedict Hall, Rm. 103
El Paso 79968-0547
(915) 747-5643

FUNDING INFORMATION CENTER OF
FORT WORTH
329 S. Henderson St.
Fort Worth 76104
(817) 334-0228

HOUSTON PUBLIC LIBRARY
500 McKinney Ave.
Houston 77002
(832) 393-1313

LAREDO PUBLIC LIBRARY
Nonprofit Management and
Volunteer Center
1120 E. Calton Rd.
Laredo 78041
(956) 795-2400

LONGVIEW PUBLIC LIBRARY
222 W. Cotton St.
Longview 75601
(903) 237-1350

LUBBOCK AREA FOUNDATION, INC.
1655 Main St., Suite 209
Lubbock 79408
(806) 762-8061

NONPROFIT RESOURCE CENTER OF TEXAS
Davidson Bldg.
7404 US Hwy. 90 W., Suite 120
San Antonio 78212-8270
(210) 227-4333

WACO-MCLENNAN COUNTY LIBRARY
1717 Austin Ave.
Waco 76701
(254) 750-5941

NONPROFIT MANAGEMENT CENTER OF
WICHITA FALLS
2301 Kell Blvd., Suite 218
Wichita Falls 76308
(940) 322-4961

UTAH

GRAND COUNTY PUBLIC LIBRARY
25 South 100 E.
Moab 84532
(435) 259-5421

SALT LAKE CITY PUBLIC LIBRARY
210 E. 400 S.
Salt Lake City 84111
(801) 524-8200

VERMONT

ILSLEY PUBLIC LIBRARY
75 Main St.
Middlebury 05753
(802) 388-4095

VERMONT DEPT. OF LIBRARIES
109 State St.
Montpelier 05609
(802) 828-3261

VIRGINIA

WASHINGTON COUNTY PUBLIC LIBRARY
205 Oak Hill St.
Abingdon 24210
(276) 676-6222

HAMPTON PUBLIC LIBRARY
4207 Victoria Blvd.
Hampton 23669
(757) 727-1314

RICHMOND PUBLIC LIBRARY
325 Civic Center Plaza
Richmond 94804
(804) 620-6561

ROANOKE PUBLIC LIBRARY SYSTEM
Main Library
706 S. Jefferson St.
Roanoke 24016
(540) 853-2473

WASHINGTON

MID-COLUMBIA LIBRARY
1620 S. Union St.
Kennewick 99338
(509) 783-7878

REDMOND REGIONAL LIBRARY
Nonprofit and Philanthropy Resource
Center
15990 NE 85th
Redmond 98052
(425) 885-1861

SEATTLE PUBLIC LIBRARY
1000 4th Ave.
Seattle 98104
(206) 386-4636

SPOKANE PUBLIC LIBRARY
906 W. Main Ave.
Spokane 99201
(509) 444-5300

UNIVERSITY OF WASHINGTON TACOMA
LIBRARY
1902 Commerce St.
Tacoma 98402
(253) 692-4440

WEST VIRGINIA

KANAWHA COUNTY PUBLIC LIBRARY
123 Capitol St.
Charleston 25301
(304) 343-4646

WEST VIRGINIA UNIVERSITY AT
PARKERSBURG LIBRARY
300 Campus Dr.
Parkersburg 26101
(304) 424-8260

SHEPHERD UNIVERSITY
Scarborough Library
King St.
Shepherdstown 25443-3210
(304) 876-5420

WISCONSIN

UNIVERSITY OF WISCONSIN—MADISON
Memorial Library
728 State St.
Madison 53706
(608) 262-3242

MARQUETTE UNIVERSITY
Raynor Memorial Libraries
1355 W. Wisconsin Ave.
Milwaukee 53201-3141
(414) 288-1515

UNIVERSITY OF WISCONSIN—
STEVENS POINT
University Library
900 Reserve St.
Stevens Point 54481-3897
(715) 346-2540

WYOMING

LARAMIE COUNTY COMMUNITY COLLEGE
Instructional Resources Center
1400 E. College Dr.
Cheyenne 82007
(307) 778-1206

CAMPBELL COUNTY PUBLIC LIBRARY
2101 4-J Rd.
Gillette 82718
(307) 687-0115

TETON COUNTY LIBRARY
125 Virginian Ln.
Jackson 83001
(307) 733-2164

SHERIDAN COUNTY FULMER PUBLIC LIBRARY
335 W. Alger St.
Sheridan 82801
(307) 674-8585

PUERTO RICO

UNIVERSIDAD DEL SAGRADO CORAZON
M.M.T. Guevara Library
Santurce 00914
(787) 728-1515

Participants in the Foundation Center's Cooperating Collections network are libraries or nonprofit information centers that provide fundraising information and other funding-related technical assistance in their communities. Cooperating Collections agree to provide free public access to a basic collection of Foundation Center resources during a regular schedule of hours, along with free funding research guidance to all visitors. Many also provide a variety of services for local nonprofit organizations, using staff or volunteers to prepare special materials, organize workshops, or conduct orientations.

A key initiative of the Foundation Center is to reach under-resourced and underserved populations throughout the United States who are in need of useful information and training to become successful grantseekers. One of the ways we accomplish this goal is by designating new Cooperating Collection libraries in regions that have the ability to serve the nonprofit communities most in need of Foundation Center resources. We are seeking proposals from qualified institutions (e.g., public, academic, or special libraries, community foundations, nonprofit resource centers, and other technical assistance providers) that can help us carry out this important initiative.

If you are interested in establishing a funding information library in your area, or would like to learn more about the program, please contact: Coordinator of Cooperating Collections, The Foundation Center, 79 Fifth Avenue, New York, NY 10003 (E-mail: ccmail@foundationcenter.org).

SECTION 1—GRANT LISTINGS

ALABAMA

Alabama Power Foundation, Inc.
Limitations: Giving limited to AL. No support for religious organizations or fraternal, athletic, or veterans' organizations. No grants to individuals (except for employee-related scholarships), or for fundraising or general operating support for United Way-supported organizations.
1. Alabama Archives and History Foundation, Montgomery, AL. $100,000, 2005. For capital support.

The J. L. Bedsole Foundation
Limitations: Giving limited to Mobile, Baldwin, Clarke, Monroe, and Washington counties, AL. No grants to individuals (except for J.L. Bedsole Scholarships and awards).
2. Alabama Department of Archives and History, Montgomery, AL. $29,400, 2004. For operating support.
3. Fairhope Public Library, Fairhope, AL. $25,000, 2004. For operating support.
4. Monroe County Public Library, Monroeville, AL. $10,000, 2004. For operating support.

The Daniel Foundation of Alabama
Limitations: Giving primarily in the southeastern U.S., with emphasis on AL.
5. Nonprofit Resource Center of Alabama, Birmingham, AL. $10,000, 2005.
6. North Shelby County Public Library, Birmingham, AL. $10,000, 2005.

The Hugh Kaul Foundation
Limitations: Giving limited to Jefferson, Clay and Coosa counties, and the greater metropolitan Birmingham, AL, area. No support for religious organizations. No grants to individuals.
7. Nonprofit Resource Center of Alabama, Birmingham, AL. $25,000, 2005.

Vulcan Materials Company Foundation
Limitations: Giving on a national basis in areas of company operations. No support for political organizations, athletic, labor, fraternal, or veterans' organizations, or discriminatory organizations. No grants to individuals (except for employee-related scholarships), or for telephone or mass mail appeals, testimonial dinners, or sectarian religious activities.
8. El Progreso Library, Uvalde, TX. $10,000, 2005.

ALASKA

Gottstein Family Foundation
9. Anchorage Library Foundation, Anchorage, AK. $10,000, 2004.

Rasmuson Foundation
Limitations: Giving limited to AK. No support for K-12 education or religious organizations. No grants to individuals, scholarships, endowments, deficits or debt reduction, fundraising events, indirect or overhead costs; or for operating funds.
10. Anchorage Library Foundation, Anchorage, AK. $25,000, 2005. To replace furnishings and refurbish panels within youth and adult areas of Z.J. Loussac Public Library.
11. Dillingham, City of, Dillingham Public Library, Dillingham, AK. $11,299, 2005. For technology to provide improved Internet access for patrons and to network computers.
12. Nenana, City of, Nenana Public Library, Nenana, AK. $11,040, 2005. To replace worn and outdated books in easy and juvenile collections.
13. Petersburg, City of, Petersburg Public Library, Petersburg, AK. $24,953, 2005. For library furnishings, display shelving, and computer equipment.
14. University of Alaska Fairbanks, Kuskokwim Consortium Library, Fairbanks, AK. $21,250, 2005. For collection enhancement (acquisition of books).

ARIZONA

Arizona Community Foundation
Limitations: Giving limited to AZ. No support for religious organizations for religious purposes. No grants to individuals (except for scholarships), travel to or support of conferences, fundraising campaigns and expenses, debt reduction, or capital grants; generally, no loans.
15. Junior Achievement of Arizona, Tempe, AZ. $10,000, 2005. For Digital Video Library.
16. Yuma County Library District, Yuma, AZ. $10,000, 2005. For computer vend system.

The Virginia G. Piper Charitable Trust
Limitations: Giving primarily in Maricopa County, AZ. No support for private foundations, or for start-ups. No grants to individuals.
17. Chandler Public Library, Chandler, AZ. $255,660, 2005. For implementation of Life Options/Next Chapter project for older adults to explore options including health, wellness, education, volunteer and paid opportunities.
18. Community Information and Referral Services, Phoenix, AZ. $20,000, 2005. To further develop Homeless Management Information System (HMIS) for agencies serving homeless children, adults, families, and older adults.
19. Scottsdale Public Library, Friends of, Scottsdale, AZ. $50,000, 2005. To create after-school teen center at Civic Center Branch of Scottsdale Public Library.

ARKANSAS

Arkansas Community Foundation, Inc.
Limitations: Giving limited to AR. No support for multi-year commitments. No grants to individuals, or for operating expenses, debt elimination, capital improvements, building, property, computer systems or emergency.
20. Central Arkansas Library System, Little Rock, AR. $30,000, 2005. For development of Arkansas Studies Curriculum at Butler Center, particularly to finalize materials for 2nd, 3rd, and 4th grades.

Charles A. Frueauff Foundation, Inc.
Limitations: Giving limited to the U.S. with emphasis on east of the Rockies, the South, and Northeast. No grants to individuals, primary or secondary schools, colleges and universities, churches, multi-year grants, fundraising drives, or special events.
21. Foundation Center, New York, NY. $10,000, 2005. For general support.
22. Millsaps College, Jackson, MS. $50,000, 2005. For library equipment.

The Murphy Foundation
Limitations: Giving primarily in southern AR for grants to organizations; giving limited to the southern AR area for educational grants.
23. Barton Library, El Dorado, AR. $15,000, 2005. For operating support.

The Winthrop Rockefeller Foundation
Limitations: Giving limited to AR, or for projects that benefit AR. No grants to individuals, or for capital expenditures, fundraising campaigns, scientific research, or endowments; no loans (except program-related investments).
24. Arkansas Student Loan Authority, Little Rock, AR. $35,250, 2004. For planning grant and strategy for developing financial aid information clearinghouse for Arkansas.

Trinity Foundation
Limitations: Giving primarily in central AR. No grants to individuals directly.
25. William J. Clinton Presidential Foundation, Little Rock, AR. $100,000, 2005. For general support.

Wal-Mart Foundation
(also known as SAM'S CLUB Foundation)
Limitations: Giving primarily in areas of company operations. No support for faith-based organizations not of direct benefit to the entire community or political organizations. No grants for research, endowments, annual meetings, capital campaigns, conferences, travel, fundraising dinners or galas, cultural performances, or film or video projects.
26. Bentonville Library Foundation, Bentonville, AR. $2,000,000, 2005.
27. Bentonville Library Foundation, Bentonville, AR. $1,000,000, 2005.
28. Fayetteville Public Library Foundation, Fayetteville, AR. $250,000, 2005.
29. Fayetteville Public Library Foundation, Fayetteville, AR. $25,000, 2005.
30. Gentry Public Library, Gentry, AR. $25,000, 2005.
31. Prairie Grove Public Library, Prairie Grove, AR. $25,000, 2005.
32. Rogers Public Library Foundation, Rogers, AR. $250,000, 2005.
33. Rogers Public Library Foundation, Rogers, AR. $16,430, 2005.
34. Springdale Public Library Foundation, Springdale, AR. $258,872, 2005.
35. William J. Clinton Presidential Foundation, Little Rock, AR. $1,000,000, 2005.

Walton Family Foundation, Inc.
Limitations: Giving primarily in AR, with emphasis on the Mississippi River's delta region of AR and MS. No support for non-established medical research programs. No grants to individuals (except for scholarships for children of Wal-Mart associates), or for endowments for operations, church-related construction projects, travel expenses for groups to compete or perform, or start-up funds.
36. Bentonville Library Foundation, Bentonville, AR. $15,000, 2004.
37. Greatschools.net, San Francisco, CA. $207,940, 2004.
38. School Choice Wisconsin, Milwaukee, WI. $280,000, 2004.

CALIFORNIA

The Ahmanson Foundation
Limitations: Giving primarily in southern CA, with emphasis on the Los Angeles area. No support for religious organizations for sectarian purposes, or advocacy or political organizations. No grants to individuals, or generally for continuing support, endowed chairs, annual campaigns, deficit financing, professorships, internships, fellowships, film production, media projects, seminars, general research and development, workshops, studies, surveys, operational support of regional and national charities, underwriting, or exchange programs; no loans.
39. American Antiquarian Society, Worcester, MA. $50,000, 2005. Toward Senior Scholar in Residence Endowment Fund.
40. American Film Institute, Los Angeles, CA. $100,000, 2005. Toward publication of AFI Catalog of Feature Films, 1970-1979.
41. BookEnds, West Hills, CA. $10,000, 2005. Toward program support.
42. Braille Institute of America, Los Angeles, CA. $50,000, 2005. Toward Library Services Improvement Project.
43. Brown University, Providence, RI. $50,000, 2005. Toward cataloging support at John Carter Brown Library.
44. Foundation Center, New York, NY. $30,000, 2005. Toward general support and for FC Online activities.
45. Fuller Theological Seminary, Pasadena, CA. $50,000, 2005. Toward development of music archive in McAlister Library.
46. Healthcare and Elder Law Programs Corporation, Torrance, CA. $20,000, 2005. Toward costs for increased distribution of newsletter and publication of Nuts and Bolts.
47. Huntington Library, Art Collections and Botanical Gardens, San Marino, CA. $1,000,000, 2005. Toward renovation of original Mansion.
48. Huntington Library, Art Collections and Botanical Gardens, San Marino, CA. $50,000, 2005. Toward book acquisitions.
49. Huntington Library, Art Collections and Botanical Gardens, San Marino, CA. $50,000, 2005. Toward Chinese Gardens project.
50. Huntington Library, Art Collections and Botanical Gardens, San Marino, CA. $50,000, 2005. For general support.
51. Library Foundation of Los Angeles, Los Angeles, CA. $300,000, 2005. For additional support toward New Information Technologies Project.
52. Library Foundation of Los Angeles, Los Angeles, CA. $25,000, 2005. Toward Hispanic Program.
53. Museum Associates, Los Angeles, CA. $25,000, 2005. Toward book acquisitions for Balch Research Library, for purchases on behalf of Center for European Art, and for other departments.
54. Occidental College, Los Angeles, CA. $1,000,000, 2005. Toward renovation of Library Reading Room.
55. Philanthropic Research, Inc., Williamsburg, VA. $25,000, 2005. Toward development of GuideStar's information resources.
56. Saint Matthews Parish School, Pacific Palisades, CA. $500,000, 2005. Toward construction of Library and classrooms.
57. San Marino Public Library Foundation, San Marino, CA. $100,000, 2005. Toward capital campaign for new library building.
58. Southern California Institute of Architecture, Los Angeles, CA. $25,000, 2005. Toward Library Book Acquisition Fund.
59. Thurgood Marshall Academy Public Charter High School, DC. $10,000, 2005. Toward charter school's library construction.
60. UCLA Foundation, University Research Library, Los Angeles, CA. $75,000, 2005. Toward acquisitions for Ahmanson-Murphy Aldine collection.
61. UCLA Foundation, William Andrews Clark Memorial Library, Los Angeles, CA. $50,000, 2005. Toward book acquisitions.
62. UCLA Foundation, William Andrews Clark Memorial Library, Los Angeles, CA. $40,000, 2005. For Post-doctoral Fellowship, for Undergraduate Fellowships and for Clark Music Series.
63. University of Richmond, Richmond, VA. $10,000, 2005. Toward acquisition of materials on history, staging and performance of opera for Parsons Music Library.
64. Vistamar School, El Segundo, CA. $10,000, 2005. Toward acquisition of reference materials for establishment of School Library.
65. Whittier Area First Day Coalition, Whittier, CA. $25,000, 2005. Toward Human Services programs.

Amgen Foundation, Inc.

Limitations: Giving primarily in areas of company operations in CA, CO, PR, RI, and WA; giving also to regional and national organizations. No support for religious organizations not of direct benefit to the entire community, political organizations, labor unions or fraternal, service, or veterans' organizations, international organizations, private foundations, or discriminatory organizations. No grants to individuals, or for fundraising or sports-related events, corporate sponsorships, or lobbying activities.

66. National Coalition for Cancer Survivorship, Silver Spring, MD. $300,000, 2004.

The Applied Materials Foundation

Limitations: Giving primarily in CA. No grants to individuals.

67. Santa Clara City Library Foundation, Santa Clara, CA. $25,000, 2004. For challenge grant for summer reading program.

Archstone Foundation

Limitations: Giving primarily in southern CA. No support for biomedical research. No grants to individuals, or for capital expenditures, or bricks and mortar, or building campaigns, endowments or for fundraising.

68. Adult Day Services Orange County, Huntington Beach, CA. $41,310, 2005. For continuation of Dementia Education Collaborative to provide education and outreach to multiethnic communities.
69. Community Hospital of Long Beach, Long Beach, CA. $112,365, 2005. To continue Intergenerational Resource Center.
70. Disability Funders Network, Falls Church, VA. $13,500, 2005. For development of resource materials for funders on emergency preparedness for disabled elders.
71. Info Link Orange County, Costa Mesa, CA. $36,000, 2005. For development of information and referral services for older adults in Orange County.
72. LifeLong Medical Care, Berkeley, CA. $123,814, 2005. To support access to insurance benefits for low-income seniors in Alameda and Contra Costa counties through community outreach and use of BenefitsCheckUp software program.

S. D. Bechtel, Jr. Foundation

(formerly Elizabeth and Stephen Bechtel, Jr. Foundation)

Limitations: Giving primarily in the San Francisco Bay Area and northern CA. No grants to individuals, or for tenured or contract positions, endowment activities, or underwriting/sponsoring events.

73. EdSource, Mountain View, CA. $10,000, 2004. For program support.
74. MentorNet, San Jose, CA. $10,000, 2004. For program support.
75. Oakland Public Library Foundation, Oakland, CA. $20,000, 2004. For program support.

Arnold and Mabel Beckman Foundation

Limitations: Giving primarily in the U.S. No support for political or religious purposes, or for research that does not fall within the foundation's areas of interest. No grants to individuals (except for Beckman Young Investigator's Program), or for dinners, mass mailings, or fundraising campaigns; no loans.

76. Richard Nixon Library and Birthplace Foundation, Yorba Linda, CA. $10,000, 2005. For general operating support.

H. N. & Frances C. Berger Foundation

Limitations: Giving primarily in CA.

77. Women at Work, Pasadena, CA. $70,000, 2004. For general operating support for job preparation programs.

The Bothin Foundation

Limitations: Giving primarily in CA, with emphasis on San Francisco, Marin, Sonoma and San Mateo counties. No support for religious organizations, or educational institutions (except those directly aiding the developmentally or learning disabled). No grants to individuals, or for general operating funds, endowment funds, program support, scholarships, fellowships, medical research conferences or for production or distribution of films or other media presentations; no loans.

78. Homeless Prenatal Program, San Francisco, CA. $15,000, 2005. To purchase computer and office equipment for agency serving homeless pregnant women and mothers with young children.

Broad Foundation

Limitations: Giving on a national basis. No grants to individuals.

79. Council of Chief State School Officers, DC. $5,000,000, 2004. To develop and implement SchoolMatters.com, national education data website.

Eli & Edythe L. Broad Foundation

80. Kenter Canyon School Parents Support Group, Los Angeles, CA. $70,000, 2004. For school library.
81. William J. Clinton Presidential Foundation, Little Rock, AR. $500,000, 2004. For Clinton Presidential library.

Fritz B. Burns Foundation

Limitations: Giving primarily in the Los Angeles, CA, area. No support for private foundations. No grants to individuals.

82. Library Foundation of Los Angeles, Los Angeles, CA. $10,000, 2005.

California Community Foundation

Limitations: Giving limited to Los Angeles County, CA. No support for sectarian purposes. No grants to individuals (except fellowships for artists or scholarships), or for annual campaigns, equipment, endowment funds, debt reduction, operating budgets, re-granting, fellowships, films, conferences, dinners, or special events.

83. Korean Health Education Information and Referral Center, Los Angeles, CA. $250,000, 2005. To expand community clinic in Koreatown.
84. Social and Public Art Resource Center, Venice, CA. $30,000, 2005. For general operating support.

The California Endowment

Limitations: Giving primarily in CA. No support for political purposes, medical or scientific research, or uncompensated care for direct clinical services. No grants to individuals for scholarships; fellowships or grants, or for endowments, operating deficits or retirement of debt, media projects not part of a broader project or strategy, medical supplies, laboratory fees, X-ray services, medications, vaccines or prescriptions; capital funding for purchase, construction or renovation of facilities or other physical infrastructure; indirect costs that exceed 15% of the total of requested personnel and operating costs.

85. Foundation Center, New York, NY. $45,000, 2006. For Services for Grant Makers and Grant Seekers Interested in Health, publications, convenings, and other activities enhancing effectiveness of philanthropy and nonprofits in CA health sector.
86. Korean Health Education Information and Referral Center, Los Angeles, CA. $50,000, 2006. For Outreach and Enrollment Project, expanding retention of coverage among immigrants in central Los Angeles.
87. San Diego County Cancer Navigator, San Diego, CA. $49,729, 2006. For Latino Outreach Project, linking uninsured and underinsured Latinos to resources.
88. Thai Health and Information Services, Los Angeles, CA. $45,154, 2006. For Thai Senior Healthy Heart Phase II, nutrition and exercise program raising awareness and reducing incidence of heart conditions.
89. Whittier Area First Day Coalition, Whittier, CA. $50,000, 2006. For Health and Wellness Clinic Health Needs Assessment Program and Future Program Development.

The California Wellness Foundation

Limitations: Giving limited to CA; national organizations providing services in CA are also considered. No support for religious or sectarian organizations. No grants to individuals (except for research fellowships and awards), or for annual fund drives, building campaigns, major equipment, or biomedical research.

90. Bear Valley Unified School District, Big Bear Lake, CA. $150,000, 2005. 3-year grant. For core operating support for Bear Valley Healthy Start program to continue to provide school-based health screenings and outreach services, linking children and families to local health, mental health and social services.
91. Creating Healthy Lives, Ridgecrest, CA. $165,000, 2005. 3-year grant. For core operating support to continue to provide workplace wellness

programs, health education, information and referrals to low-wage workers in Indian Wells Valley.

92. DataCenter, Oakland, CA. $150,000, 2005. 3-year grant. For core operating support to continue to conduct research and provide research training and technical assistance to California organizations working to improve health of low-wage workers.

93. Grandparents as Parents (GAP), Lakewood, CA. $100,000, 2005. 2-year grant. For core operating support to continue to provide crisis counseling, support groups, respite and other kinship caregiving services in Los Angeles County for grandparents and other relatives who are raising children.

94. Imperial Valley Health and Housing Coalition, Calexico, CA. $150,000, 2005. 3-year grant. For core operating support to continue to provide health education and information and referral services to farmworkers and other low-wage workers and their families in Calexico.

95. Instituto de Educacion Popular del Sur de California, Los Angeles, CA. $235,000, 2005. 3-year grant. For core operating support for Worker Health Program to provide health education and referrals to health care services for day laborers and domestic workers in Los Angeles region.

96. Swords to Plowshares, San Francisco, CA. $250,000, 2005. 3-year grant. For core operating support to continue to provide case management, health referrals and assistance to secure entitled health benefits to veterans in San Francisco.

The Capital Group Companies Charitable Foundation

Limitations: Giving on a national and internationl basis. No support for religious, political, or fraternal organizations or professional organizations. No grants to individuals.

97. Huntington Library, Art Collections and Botanical Gardens, San Marino, CA. $25,000, 2005.

98. Huntington Library, Art Collections and Botanical Gardens, San Marino, CA. $15,000, 2005.

99. Huntington Library, Art Collections and Botanical Gardens, San Marino, CA. $10,000, 2005.

100. Library Foundation of Los Angeles, Los Angeles, CA. $25,000, 2005.

101. Library Foundation of Los Angeles, Los Angeles, CA. $10,000, 2005.

102. Saint Paul Public Library, Friends of the, Saint Paul, MN. $10,000, 2005.

Chartwell Charitable Foundation

Limitations: Giving primarily in CA and NY.

103. Library Foundation of Los Angeles, Los Angeles, CA. $25,000, 2005.

104. National Coalition for Cancer Survivorship, Silver Spring, MD. $25,000, 2005.

105. Ronald Reagan Presidential Foundation, Simi Valley, CA. $100,000, 2005.

106. University of Southern California, Shoah Foundation Institute for Visual History and Education, Los Angeles, CA. $25,000, 2005.

Cisco Systems Foundation

Limitations: Giving primarily in CA. No support for religious or sectarian organizations. No grants to individuals, or for capital campaigns, start-up needs, research, athletic events, fundraising events, conferences, seminars, or field trips.

107. Community Voice Mail National Office, Seattle, WA. $499,379, 2005. For Unity Project.

108. Eden Information and Referral Service, Hayward, CA. $10,000, 2005. For Alameda County Housing Program.

109. One Economy Corporation, DC. $150,000, 2005. For Zip Road, providing online education resources.

Community Foundation for Monterey County

Limitations: Giving primarily in Monterey County, CA. No support for sectarian religious programs. No grants to individuals (except for scholarships), or for annual campaigns, deficit financing, operating costs, general endowments, fellowships, travel, research or publications.

110. Monterey County Free Libraries, Foundation for, Salinas, CA. $10,000, 2005. For staff salaries at homework centers.

Community Foundation Silicon Valley
(formerly Community Foundation of Santa Clara County)

Limitations: Giving primarily in Santa Clara and southern San Mateo counties, CA. No support for city or state government agencies or departments, academic or scientific research institutions, or private or parochial schools. No grants to individuals (except for scholarships), or for deficit financing, building funds, fundraising, endowment funds, capital campaigns, expenditures for equipment purchases, or fundamental or applied research projects.

111. Able Project, San Jose, CA. $10,000, 2005.

112. Charities Aid Foundation (CAF) America, Alexandria, VA. $100,000, 2005.

113. Council on Islamic Education, Fountain Valley, CA. $135,000, 2005.

114. Council on Islamic Education, Fountain Valley, CA. $15,000, 2005.

115. EdSource, Mountain View, CA. $700,000, 2005.

116. EdSource, Mountain View, CA. $210,000, 2005.

117. EdSource, Mountain View, CA. $75,000, 2005.

118. Foundation Center, New York, NY. $10,000, 2005.

119. Internet Archive, San Francisco, CA. $10,000, 2005.

120. Los Altos Library, Los Altos, CA. $15,000, 2005.

121. Nantucket Atheneum, Nantucket, MA. $100,000, 2005.

122. Philanthropic Research, Inc., Williamsburg, VA. $10,000, 2005.

123. San Jose Public Library Foundation, San Jose, CA. $50,000, 2005.

124. San Jose Public Library Foundation, San Jose, CA. $20,230, 2005.

125. San Jose Public Library Foundation, San Jose, CA. $10,000, 2005.

126. Santa Clara City Library Foundation, Santa Clara, CA. $12,500, 2005.

Compton Foundation, Inc.

Limitations: Giving on an international basis to U.S.-based organizations for projects in Mexico, Central America, and Sub-Saharan Africa and on a national basis for programs in peace and population and the environment. Other funding limited to areas where board members reside: primarily San Francisco, Marin, and Santa Clara counties, CA. No grants to individuals, or for capital or building funds, no loans (except for program-related investments).

127. National Security Archive Fund, DC. $35,000, 2004. For peace and security programs.

128. National Womens Health Network, DC. $45,000, 2004. For population and reproductive health programs.

129. Southwest Research and Information Center, Nuclear Watch of New Mexico, Albuquerque, NM. $25,000, 2004. For peace and security programs.

S. H. Cowell Foundation

Limitations: Giving limited to northern CA. No support for projects restricted to people with specific medical, physical, or health conditions, daycare centers, drug or alcohol abuse programs, environmental or conservation programs, health clinics or other medical service projects, political lobbying, population programs, post-secondary education, projects that are the responsibility of government agencies (except for school districts in the event of emergency funding and budget crises), or sectarian, politically partisan, or religious projects. No grants to individuals, or for general operating support, special events and conferences, books, films, videos, academic or medical research, or capital requests (when less than fifty percent of total funds have been raised).

130. Foundation Center, San Francisco, CA. $12,000, 2004.

D & DF Foundation

Limitations: Giving primarily in San Francisco, CA. No grants to individuals.

131. National First Ladies Library, Canton, OH. $25,000, 2005. For general support.

Carrie Estelle Doheny Foundation

Limitations: Giving primarily in the Los Angeles, CA, area. No support for tax-supported organizations, radio or television programs, or for political purposes. No grants to individuals, or for endowment funds, publications, travel, advertising, or scholarships.

132. Library Foundation of Los Angeles, Los Angeles, CA. $10,000, 2004. For Grandparents and Books program.

Joseph Drown Foundation

Limitations: Giving primarily in Los Angeles, CA. No support for religious purposes. No grants to individuals, or for endowments, capital campaigns, building funds, or seminars or conferences.

133. American Pain Foundation, Baltimore, MD. $10,000, 2005. For operating support.
134. BookEnds, West Hills, CA. $50,000, 2005. For operating support.
135. Boys and Girls Club of Annapolis, Bywater, Annapolis, MD. $10,000, 2005. For Library/Media Center.
136. Library Foundation of Los Angeles, Los Angeles, CA. $25,000, 2005. For Baldwin Hills Branch Library.
137. Wonder of Reading, Los Angeles, CA. $25,000, 2005. For 3R Program - Renovate, Restock and Read.

The Eisner Foundation, Inc.

Limitations: Giving limited to Los Angeles and Orange counties, CA. No support for sectarian purposes. Generally, no grants to individuals, annual campaigns, existing obligations, re-granting programs, sponsoring conferences or special events.

138. BookEnds, West Hills, CA. $15,000, 2004. For program support.

Energy Foundation

Limitations: Giving limited to the U.S. and China. No support for sectarian or religious purposes or political organizations. No grants to individuals, or for endowment funds, debt reduction, planning, renovation, maintenance, retrofit, or purchase of buildings, equipment purchases, land acquisition, general support grants, annual fundraising campaigns, research and development of technology, demonstration projects or capital construction.

139. Center for Resource Solutions, San Francisco, CA. $15,000, 2005. For creation of Western Renewable Energy Generation Information System.
140. China Certification Center for Energy Conservation Products, Beijing, China. $20,000, 2005. For China's efforts in developing set-top box energy efficiency standard and label.
141. China National Institute of Standardization, Beijing, China. $60,000, 2005. To design implementation guidelines for energy information labels for air conditioners.
142. Collaborative Labeling and Appliance Standards Program, DC. $10,000, 2005. To translate and publish guidebook for appliance standards and labels.
143. Midwest Energy Efficiency Alliance, Chicago, IL. $100,000, 2005. To educate utility regulators and key policymakers about benefits of energy efficiency standards and long-term resource planning, and to advocate for smart electric transmission growth.
144. Public Utility Law Project of New York, Albany, NY. $10,000, 2005. To continue support of Low Income Energy Project, which provides advocacy and informational services to advance energy efficiency and affordability programs for low-income households.

Flora Family Foundation

145. Global Footprint Network, Oakland, CA. $20,000, 2004. For general support.
146. Mills College, Oakland, CA. $40,000, 2004. For archival collection.
147. National Center for Family Philanthropy, DC. $10,000, 2004. For Generations Giving.

John Jewett & Helen Chandler Garland Foundation

Limitations: Giving primarily in CA, with emphasis on southern CA. No grants to individuals, or for seed money.

148. Huntington Library, Friends of the, San Marino, CA. $800,000, 2004. For general support and educational programs at Botanical Center.
149. Library Foundation of Los Angeles, Los Angeles, CA. $40,000, 2004. For general support and adult literacy program.
150. Pasadena Public Library Foundation, Pasadena, CA. $10,000, 2004. For general support and for adult and family literacy.

The Carl Gellert and Celia Berta Gellert Foundation

(formerly The Carl Gellert Foundation)
Limitations: Giving limited to the nine counties of the greater San Francisco Bay Area, CA, (Alameda, Contra Costa, Marin, Napa, San Francisco, San Mateo, Santa Clara, Solano and Sonoma). No grants to individuals, or

for seed money, emergency funds, land acquisition, matching gifts, conferences, sponsorships, fundraising events sponsorships, dinners, walk-a-thons, tournaments, or fashion shows; no loans.

151. Notre Dame de Namur University, Belmont, CA. $400,000, 2005. For Phase I of Master Plan Fundraising Campaign, naming current College library Carl Gellert and Celia Berta Gellert Library.
152. Saint Patricks Seminary, Menlo Park, CA. $200,000, 2005. For Carl Gellert and Celia Berta Gellert Library in Phase III capital improvements.
153. Santa Clara University, Santa Clara, CA. $250,000, 2005. For capital campaign for new library.

Wallace Alexander Gerbode Foundation

Limitations: Giving primarily to programs directly affecting residents of Alameda, Contra Costa, Marin, San Francisco, and San Mateo counties in CA, and HI. No support for religious purposes or private schools. No grants to individuals, or for direct services, deficit budgets, general operating funds, building or equipment funds, general fundraising campaigns, publications, or scholarships.

154. Friends and Foundation of the San Francisco Public Library, San Francisco, CA. $10,000, 2005. For One City, One Book: San Francisco Reads program.

The Ann and Gordon Getty Foundation

Limitations: Giving primarily in CA, with emphasis on the San Francisco Bay Area. No grants to individuals.

155. Library Foundation of San Francisco, San Francisco, CA. $10,000, 2004.

J. Paul Getty Trust

Limitations: Giving on an international basis. No grants for operating or endowment purposes, start-up, construction or maintenance of buildings, or acquisition of works of art.

156. Art Libraries Society of North America, Tucson, AZ. $28,500, 2005.
157. British Empire and Commonwealth Museum, Bristol, England. $87,000, 2005. For Archival Projects.
158. California Institute of the Arts, Valencia, CA. $86,900, 2005. For archival projects.
159. Huntington Library, Art Collections and Botanical Gardens, San Marino, CA. $120,000, 2005. For Senior Fellowship Program.
160. Library and Archives Canada, Ottawa, Canada. $24,000, 2005. For treatment and research.
161. Museum Associates, Los Angeles, CA. $122,000, 2005. For archival projects.
162. New School, New York, NY. $150,000, 2005. For archival projects.
163. Northeast Document Conservation Center, Andover, MA. $150,000, 2005. For conservation training.
164. Rochester Institute of Technology, Rochester, NY. $60,000, 2005. For archival projects.
165. Rutgers, The State University of New Jersey Foundation, New Brunswick, NJ. $149,000, 2005. For archival projects.
166. Trinity College, Dublin, Ireland. $100,000, 2005. For archival projects.
167. University of California, Los Angeles, CA. $190,000, 2005. For archival projects.
168. University of California, Los Angeles, CA. $180,000, 2005. For archival projects.
169. Visual Resources Association, Cambridge, MA. $137,000, 2005. For cataloging of collections.

Lisa and Douglas Goldman Fund

Limitations: Giving primarily in the San Francisco Bay Area, CA. No grants to individuals; no support for deficit budgets, endowments, conferences, events, documentaries, films, books, or research.

170. Foundation Center, San Francisco, CA. $10,000, 2005. For technology upgrade.
171. Jewish National and University Library, International Institute for Jewish Genealogy and Paul Jacobi Center, Jerusalem, Israel. $100,000, 2005. 2-year grant. For founding grant.

Richard and Rhoda Goldman Fund

Limitations: Giving primarily in the San Francisco Bay Area, CA, and Israel. Giving nationally and internationally in the areas of population and the environment. No grants to individuals, or for deficit budgets, endowment funds, documentary films, conferences, research, scholarships, fellowships, matching gifts, or general operating budgets of established organizations; no loans.

172. Bancroft Library, Friends of the, Berkeley, CA. $100,000, 2005. For Centennial Campaign for Renewal of Bancroft Library.

173. California Pacific Medical Center Foundation, San Francisco, CA. $10,000, 2005. For general support for Community Health Resource Center.

174. Foundation Center, San Francisco, CA. $10,000, 2005. For general operating support.

175. Friends of the Jewish Community Library, San Francisco, CA. $80,000, 2005. For Bringing It All Back Home Project, to expand Library's ability to serve public.

176. San Francisco Adult Day Services Network, San Francisco, CA. $10,000, 2005. For general operating support.

177. Sexuality Information and Education Council of the U.S. (SIECUS), New York, NY. $75,000, 2005. For Public Policy and Advocacy Programs, to ensure that young people have access to comprehensive information about sexual and reproductive health.

Henry L. Guenther Foundation

Limitations: Giving primarily in southern CA. Generally no support for government agencies, or religious organizations for religious purposes. No grants to individuals, including scholarships; or for operating deficits.

178. Library Foundation of Los Angeles, Los Angeles, CA. $25,000, 2005. For grandparents and books reading enrichment program.

Miriam and Peter Haas Fund

(formerly Miniam and Peter Haas Fund)
Limitations: Giving primarily in San Francisco, CA; early childhood, direct service component is limited to San Francisco. No grants to individuals.

179. Friends and Foundation of the San Francisco Public Library, San Francisco, CA. $10,000, 2004. For annual Literary Laureates Dinner.

180. University of California at Berkeley Foundation, Berkeley, CA. $100,000, 2004. For University Library Campaign Fund.

Walter and Elise Haas Fund

Limitations: Giving primarily in San Francisco and Alameda County, CA; Jewish Life grants are awarded throughout the Bay Area. No grants to individuals, or for general fundraising, endowment campaigns, scholarships, fellowships, or for video or film production (except through the Creative Work Fund).

181. Action Alliance for Children, Oakland, CA. $15,000, 2004. To inform low-income families and service agencies of programs to increase family incomes through series of articles in Childrens Advocate and summary report.

182. Bancroft Library, Friends of the, Berkeley, CA. $200,000, 2004. For capital campaign.

183. Eden Information and Referral Service, Hayward, CA. $50,000, 2004. For 2-1-1 telephone services.

184. Friends and Foundation of the San Francisco Public Library, San Francisco, CA. $10,000, 2004. For James C. Hormel Gay and Lesbian Center's Out at the Library anniversary exhibition.

185. Jewish Community Center, Berkeley/Richmond, Berkeley, CA. $18,000, 2004. For organizational and program development efforts at The Ritualist.

Evelyn and Walter Haas, Jr. Fund

Limitations: Giving primarily in San Francisco and Alameda counties, CA. No support for private foundations, consumer or professional groups, labor or trade associations, research centers, or religious organizations. No grants to individuals, or for deficit or emergency financing, workshops, major equipment, scholarships, direct mail campaigns, fundraising events, annual appeals, conferences, publications, capital or endowment campaigns, films or videos, or basic research.

186. California Child Care Resource and Referral Network, San Francisco, CA. $80,000, 2005. To study training needs of child care workforce in San Francisco and Alameda Counties.

187. California Child Care Resource and Referral Network, San Francisco, CA. $50,000, 2005. To protect and expand local and state funding for affordable, high-quality child care for low-income families.

188. Lavender Youth Recreation and Information Center, San Francisco, CA. $40,000, 2005. To provide supportive services to gay and lesbian teenagers and strengthen center's position as sustainable organization.

189. National Center for Family Philanthropy, DC. $100,000, 2005. For challenge grant to expand annual support and for FP Online.

190. Project Inform, San Francisco, CA. $35,000, 2005.

The Hamilton-White Foundation

Limitations: Giving primarily in San Diego, CA. No grants to individuals.

191. San Diego Public Library, San Diego, CA. $40,000, 2005.

The William and Flora Hewlett Foundation

Limitations: Giving limited to the San Francisco Bay Area, CA, for family and community development programs; performing arts primarily limited to the Bay Area. No support for medicine and health-related projects, law, criminal justice, and related fields, juvenile delinquency or drug and alcohol addiction, prevention or treatment programs, problems of the elderly and the handicapped, or television or radio projects. No grants to individuals, or for basic research, equipment, seminars, conferences, festivals, touring costs, fundraising drives, scholarships, or fellowships; no loans (except for program-related investments).

192. Association of Reproductive Health Professionals, DC. $400,000, 2005. 2-year grant. For Emergency Contraception Hotline and Website.

193. Cold Spring Harbor Laboratory, Cold Spring Harbor, NY. $470,000, 2005. 4-year grant. For project to develop, evaluate, and disseminate Genes to Cognition (G2C) Online, Internet site modeled on principles of neural networking, which examines current research to discover molecular and cellular basis of human thinking.

194. EdSource, Mountain View, CA. $1,200,000, 2005. 3-year grant. For general support.

195. Foothill-De Anza Community College District, Los Altos Hills, CA. $400,000, 2005. 1.50-year grant. For implementation of SAKAI open source software across California community colleges, and for contribution to development and enhancement of tools to support online learning.

196. Greatschools.net, Great Schools, San Francisco, CA. $580,000, 2005. 3-year grant. For general support, with goal of organization becoming self-sustaining after grant.

197. Institute for the Study of Knowledge Management in Education, Half Moon Bay, CA. $200,000, 2005. 1.50-year grant. For building website to increase awareness and understanding about open educational resources to help users find materials that meet their needs, and to provide tools for gathering user evaluations of materials.

198. Massachusetts Institute of Technology, Cambridge, MA. $3,000,000, 2005. 2-year grant. For continued support of MIT OpenCourseWare - free, open website offering high quality MIT teaching materials to educators, students and self-learners worldwide.

199. National Science Teachers Association, Arlington, VA. $800,000, 2005. 2-year grant. For development of open online science learning objects for K-12 science teachers.

200. National Security Archive Fund, DC. $620,000, 2005. 2-year grant. For FOIA Mexico Project.

201. Open University, Milton Keynes, England. $200,000, 2005. For preparatory phase of UK Open University's Open Content Initiative that will make its existing exemplary curriculum resources, wrapped with powerful tools to support learning, freely available on web.

202. Organisation for Economic Cooperation and Development, Paris, France. $270,000, 2005. 2-year grant. For international study of demand and supply side issues related to Open Educational Resources.

203. Organisation for Economic Cooperation and Development, Paris, France. $25,000, 2005. For international forum on e-learning.

204. San Francisco Performing Arts Library and Museum, San Francisco, CA. $150,000, 2005. 3-year grant. For general support.

205. San Mateo County Library Joint Powers Authority, San Mateo, CA. $200,000, 2005. 2-year grant. For Quest Learning Centers after school program for East Palo Alto children.

206. San Mateo County Library Joint Powers Authority, San Mateo, CA. $75,000, 2005. For Quest Learning Centers literacy after school program for East Palo Alto children.

207. Sexuality Information and Education Council of the U.S. (SIECUS), New York, NY. $30,000, 2005. For leadership and management skills development.

208. Stanford University, Center for the Study of Language and Information, Stanford, CA. $190,000, 2005. 2-year grant. For strategy to reach financial sustainability for online, open Stanford Encyclopedia of Philosophy.
209. Stanford University, Green Library, Stanford, CA. $125,000, 2005. For feasibility study on developing automated tools for determining copyright status of works published in U.S. between 1923 and 1964.
210. Stanford University, Green Library, Stanford, CA. $53,000, 2005. For organizing working group to plan for large-scale digitization of Arabic-language books.
211. Stanford University, School of Education, Stanford, CA. $25,000, 2005. For planning grant to create global education research and policy network.
212. University of California, Berkeley, CA. $1,250,000, 2005. For renovation and naming of Roger Heyns Reading Room at U.C. Berkeley Bancroft Library.
213. University of California, University Extension, Irvine, CA. $200,000, 2005. For development of open courses and support materials to prepare teachers in state of California for teaching credential in mathematics.
214. University of Colorado, Boulder, CO. $600,000, 2005. 3-year grant. For developing interactive simulations and supporting materials for teaching physics and chemistry to be freely available online.
215. University of Mauritius, Mauritius. $25,000, 2005. For 2005 edition of Second International Conference on Open and Online Learning (ICOOL) in South Africa.
216. University of Michigan, Ann Arbor, MI. $185,000, 2005. For University of Michigan and Foothill College to prototype conversion process that links Sakai and OpenCourseWare/EduCommons to rapidly and cost-efficiently generate open educational content.
217. Utah State University, Center for Open and Sustainable Learning, Logan, UT. $1,500,000, 2005. 1.50-year grant. For support for eduCommons, Open Learning Support, and Utah State University OpenCourseWare.
218. Western Interstate Commission for Higher Education (WICHE), Boulder, CO. $213,000, 2005. 2-year grant. For development of business plan and strategy to insure sustainability of EduTools and for support of WCET Director to serve as ambassador for Open Educational Resources at various meetings throughout world.

Jaquelin Hume Foundation
Limitations: Giving to organizations with a national impact. No support for organizations outside the U.S. No grants to individuals.
219. Charter School Resource Center of Texas, San Antonio, TX. $25,000, 2004. For unrestricted support.

The James Irvine Foundation
Limitations: Giving limited to CA. No support for agencies receiving substantial government support. No grants to individuals.
220. Crystal Stairs, Los Angeles, CA. $200,000, 2005. 2-year grant. To provide opportunities for low-income parents in Los Angeles to engage with public officials on issues related to quality child care.
221. Envision Schools, San Francisco, CA. $400,000, 2005. To expand innovative charter school model by supporting startup of campus in Oakland and open-source online instructional library.
222. Foundation Center, New York, NY. $25,000, 2005. To support technology upgrades in San Francisco library and learning center.
223. Fresno Historical Society, Fresno, CA. $35,000, 2005. 2-year grant. For Hmong of Central California: A Culture in Transition, traveling photographic exhibition and historical archive of Central Valley Hmong Refugee Community.
224. Library Foundation of Los Angeles, Los Angeles, CA. $75,000, 2005. To support weekly public radio show on current issues in Los Angeles civic life and to support cultural events in greater Los Angeles area.
225. Library Foundation of Los Angeles, Los Angeles, CA. $25,000, 2005. For ALOUD at Central Library, series of author talks, panel discussions, performances, and documentary screenings, to encourage dialogue and inquiry, inspire new ideas, and foster sense of community in Los Angeles.
226. Library Foundation of Los Angeles, Los Angeles, CA. $16,500, 2005. To support development of business plan for its monthly lecture series on civic and cultural affairs.
227. Philanthropic Research, Inc., Williamsburg, VA. $22,000, 2005. 2-year grant. To document philanthropic giving in California, drawing from publicly available data and itemizing geographic giving trends.

228. Social and Public Art Resource Center, Venice, CA. $100,000, 2005. 2-year grant. For preservation and restoration of the Great Wall of Los Angeles mural, depicting visual narrative history of California's ethnic populations.
229. Social and Public Art Resource Center, Venice, CA. $15,000, 2005. To support convening and consultant assistance around plans for new collaboration with Antioch University Los Angeles to develop new low-residency MFA program in Public Art and Community Development.

The Fletcher Jones Foundation
(formerly The Jones Foundation)
Limitations: Giving primarily in CA. No support for K-12 schools; political campaigns or organizations. No grants to individuals, or for operating funds, deficit financing, conferences, seminars, workshops, travel exhibits, surveys, or projects supported by government agencies; no loans.
230. Braille Institute of America, Los Angeles, CA. $50,000, 2005. Toward Library Services Improvement Project.
231. Library Foundation of Los Angeles, Los Angeles, CA. $100,000, 2005. To support and advance technology.

Kahle/Austin Foundation
Limitations: Giving primarily in San Francisco, CA. No grants to individuals.
232. Internet Archive, San Francisco, CA. $2,928,000, 2004. For general support.

Koret Foundation
Limitations: Giving limited to the Bay Area counties of San Francisco, Alameda, Contra Costa, Marin, Santa Clara, and San Mateo, CA; giving also in Israel. No support for private foundations, or veterans', fraternal, military, religious, or sectarian organizations whose principal activity is for the benefit of their own membership. No grants to individuals (except for the Koret Prize), or for general fundraising campaigns, scholarships, endowment funds, equipment funds, deficit financing, or emergency funds; no loans.
233. Stanford University, Stanford, CA. $100,000, 2004. For libraries.
234. University of California, Berkeley, CA. $15,000, 2004. For library.
235. University of California, Bancroft Library, Berkeley, CA. $50,000, 2004.

The John M. Lloyd Foundation
Limitations: Giving on a worldwide basis. No grants to individuals, or for annual campaigns; generally no grants for operating budgets of established organizations, capital expenditures, health care or service provision, or for indirect costs.
236. SATELLIFE, Watertown, MA. $15,000, 2005. For research and development of HIV/AIDS information tools.

The Thomas J. Long Foundation
Limitations: Giving primarily in northern CA and HI. No grants to individuals.
237. Oakland Public Library Foundation, Oakland, CA. $10,000, 2004. For main library children's room renovations.

Marin Community Foundation
Limitations: Giving from Buck Trust limited to Marin County, CA; other giving on a national and international basis with emphasis on the San Francisco Bay Area. No grants to individuals (except for scholarships), or for planning initiatives, or capital projects (except those meeting criteria specified in the funding guidelines). Other limitations specific to each program area are outlined in the funding guidelines.
238. Bancroft Library, Friends of the, Berkeley, CA. $10,500, 2005. For general operating support and Regional Oral History Project.
239. Marin County Library Foundation, Point Reyes Station, CA. $10,800, 2005. For general operating support, Mobile Van, and children's program.
240. Marin Link, San Rafael, CA. $10,500, 2005. For general operating support and Spirit Links Newsletter.
241. Sausalito Public Library, Friends of the, Sausalito, CA. $11,000, 2005. For general operating support and Centennial Fund.
242. University of California at Berkeley Foundation, Berkeley, CA. $254,600, 2005. For Bencroft library, annual fund, Men's Basketball Discretionary Fund, Cal performances, Cal Fund and Reunion Fund.

243. William J. Clinton Presidential Foundation, Little Rock, AR. $500,000, 2005. For general operating support.

The Marisla Foundation

Limitations: Giving primarily on the West Coast of the U.S. (including Baja, CA), HI, and the Western Pacific for the environment; funding for women limited to Los Angeles and Orange County, CA. No support for political campaigns. No grants to individuals, or for scholarships, fellowships, or film or video projects.

244. Earth Action Network, Norwalk, CT. $35,000, 2004. For Women's Health Issue of Environmental Magazine.
245. Huntington Library, Art Collections and Botanical Gardens, San Marino, CA. $15,000, 2004. For Junior Master Gardener Program.
246. Whittier Area First Day Coalition, Whittier, CA. $30,000, 2004. For social services.
247. Women at Work, Pasadena, CA. $30,000, 2004. For Solo Women's Program.

B. C. McCabe Foundation

Limitations: Giving primarily in CA.

248. Library Foundation of Los Angeles, Los Angeles, CA. $75,000, 2005. For improvements to Robert Louis Stevenson Branch and Cahuenga Branch.
249. Whittier Area First Day Coalition, Whittier, CA. $175,000, 2005. To address homelessness in Whittier community.
250. Whittier Public Library Foundation, Whittier, CA. $12,000, 2005. For Whittier Reads-One Book One Whittier program.

The McConnell Foundation

Limitations: Giving limited to Shasta, Trinity, Modoc, Tehema and Siskiyou counties, CA; and Nepal. No support for sectarian religious purposes. No grants to individuals, or for endowment funds, annual fund drives, budget deficits, or purchase or construction of buildings.

251. Mountain Resource Management Group, Nepal. $12,917, 2005. For Peacebuilding Resource Guide.

Gordon and Betty Moore Foundation

Limitations: Giving on a worldwide basis, with some focus on the San Francisco Bay Area, CA, for selected projects. No support for religious or political organizations. No grants to individuals, or for arts, building/renovation, endowments, capital campaigns, labor issues, or for sports programs.

252. Chemical Heritage Foundation, Philadelphia, PA. $294,850, 2004. To produce Moore Oral History and Historical Collection.
253. Duke University, Durham, NC. $1,062,140, 2004. For creation of global databases of incidental catch (bycatch) for seabirds, sea turtles, and marine mammals for key fisheries.
254. Foundation Center, New York, NY. $60,000, 2004. For Data Collection and Publication component, and San Francisco field office.
255. NatureServe, Arlington, VA. $1,522,000, 2004. For user needs assessment and market analysis, standards landscape assessment, technology framework and business process documentation, and to provide advisory service to IUCN Species Information Service.
256. NatureServe, Arlington, VA. $700,000, 2004. To produce integrated, comprehensive maps of ecological systems, protected areas, threats, and endemic species of Bolivia and Peru.
257. Philanthropic Research, Inc., Williamsburg, VA. $250,000, 2004. To participate in funding consortium and provide general operating support for capturing Forms 990 data, and displaying and distributing it via website while working toward revenue goals outlined in business plan.
258. Public Library of Science, San Francisco, CA. $4,150,000, 2004. To establish online scholarly publisher to make scientific and medical literature a public resource.
259. Royal Botanic Gardens, Kew, Richmond, England. $473,234, 2004. To prototype Global Plant Checklist.
260. University of California, Berkeley, CA. $772,906, 2004. For Legacy Nearby Supernova Catalog that will enable development of tools critical for greater understanding of Type la supernnovae as indicators of dark energy.
261. University of California, San Francisco, CA. $70,810, 2004. To study impact of Electronic Patient Records and Computerized Physician Order Entry on patient outcomes in VA hospital system.

262. University of California at San Diego, La Jolla, CA. $1,036,234, 2004. For project, Toward a Distributed Information System for Marine Biology and Limnology.
263. University of Guelph, Guelph, Canada. $996,338, 2004. For DNA bar-coding project, Bar Code of Life.

Dan Murphy Foundation

Limitations: Giving primarily in Los Angeles, CA.

264. Huntington Library, Art Collections and Botanical Gardens, San Marino, CA. $50,000, 2004. For general support.
265. Los Angeles Public Library, Central Library, Los Angeles, CA. $10,000, 2004. For general support.

The Kenneth T. and Eileen L. Norris Foundation

Limitations: Giving primarily in southern CA. No support for political organizations or campaigns. No grants to individuals, or for film or video projects; no loans.

266. BookEnds, West Hills, CA. $15,000, 2005. For general operating support.
267. Carnegie Institution of Washington, DC. $15,000, 2005. For Astronomical Glass Plate Archiving Project at Carnegie Observatories in Pasadena, CA.
268. Huntington Library, Art Collections and Botanical Gardens, San Marino, CA. $400,000, 2005. For Huntington Art Gallery renovation.
269. Library Foundation of Los Angeles, Los Angeles, CA. $25,000, 2005. For Grandparents and Books program.
270. Long Beach Public Library Foundation, Long Beach, CA. $10,000, 2005. For Raising a Reader Program.

Peter Norton Family Foundation

Limitations: Giving primarily in southern CA for human/social services; giving on a national basis for arts-related grants. No grants to individuals.

271. American Friends of the Royal Institution, DC. $50,000, 2004. For World Science Assembly.

PacifiCare Health Systems Foundation

Limitations: Giving limited to areas of company operations in AZ, CA, CO, NV, OK, OR, TX, and WA. No support for professional or technical associations or private foundations. No grants to individuals (except for scholarships), or for capital campaigns, annual campaigns, research, endowments, conferences or seminars, programs promoting religious doctrine, sponsorship of special events, or non-education arts and culture programs; no challenge or matching grants.

272. BookEnds, West Hills, CA. $10,000, 2004.
273. Info Link Orange County, Costa Mesa, CA. $10,000, 2004.
274. Library Foundation of Los Angeles, Los Angeles, CA. $10,000, 2004.

The David and Lucile Packard Foundation

Limitations: Giving for the arts and community development primarily in Los Altos and Santa Clara, San Mateo, Santa Cruz, and Monterey counties, CA; Pueblo, CO, and national giving for child health and development; national and international giving for population, conservation, and science. No support for religious purposes. No grants to individuals.

275. Americans for the Arts, DC. $85,000, 2005. For Creative Industries Reports.
276. California Child Care Resource and Referral Network, San Francisco, CA. $300,000, 2005. 1.25-year grant. For Core Support.
277. California Child Care Resource and Referral Network, San Francisco, CA. $50,000, 2005. For Assessment, Planning, and Training.
278. Center for Resource Economics, Island Press, DC. $49,652, 2005. For Ecosystem-based Management Stakeholders Database.
279. Forest Trends Association, DC. $150,000, 2005. For Ecosystem Marketplace: Information Building Block of New Green Markets.
280. George Washington University, DC. $249,099, 2005. For Education and Information for Policymakers on Children and Family Health Issues as part of National Health Policy Forum.
281. Health Action Information Network, Quezon City, Philippines. $300,000, 2005. 3-year grant. For Enhancing Communication Strategies of NGOs Working on Population Issues in Philippines.
282. Monterey County Free Libraries, Foundation for, Salinas, CA. $22,250, 2005. For Strategic Planning and Executive Search.

283. National Center for Family Philanthropy, DC. $25,000, 2005. For Foundation Assessment Tool.
284. NatureServe, Arlington, VA. $601,040, 2005. 2-year grant. For Development and Use of Ecosystem-based Management Tools for Coastal-Marine Systems.
285. NatureServe, Arlington, VA. $71,200, 2005. For Strategic Plan.
286. Philanthropic Research, Inc., Williamsburg, VA. $25,000, 2005. For TrueNorth Membership.
287. Public Library of Science, San Francisco, CA. $15,000, 2005. For Ecology Supplement.
288. Stanford University, School of Education, Stanford, CA. $250,000, 2005. For John W. Gardner Center for Youth and Their Communities Data Archive.

The Packard Humanities Institute
Limitations: Giving primarily in CA. No grants to individuals.
289. Bach-Archiv, Leipzig, Germany. $310,000, 2004. For library personnel costs and acquisitions; Klinkerfuss Collection and other historical books, computer equipment upgrades, and travel expenses; and restoration costs.
290. Sing-Akademie zu Berlin, Berlin, Germany. $605,000, 2004. For cataloguing, restoration, and preservation work on manuscripts in archive.
291. University of California, Pacific Film Archive, Los Angeles, CA. $321,345, 2004. For Film Preservation Laboratory, staff positions and operating costs.
292. University of California, Pacific Film Archive, Los Angeles, CA. $130,000, 2004. For Film Preservation Laboratory consultancy.
293. University of California, Pacific Film Archive, Berkeley, CA. $100,000, 2004. For Pacific Film Archive and for cataloguing and collection maintenance, database development, and exhibitions.

The Ralph M. Parsons Foundation
Limitations: Giving limited to Los Angeles County, CA, with the exception of some grants for higher education. No support for sectarian, religious, or fraternal purposes, or for political organizations. No grants to individuals, or for annual campaigns, fundraising events, dinners, mass mailings, workshops, federated fundraising appeals, seminars, conferences or generally for multi-year funding; no loans.
294. Huntington Library, Art Collections and Botanical Gardens, San Marino, CA. $25,000, 2004. For general support.
295. Library Foundation of Los Angeles, Los Angeles, CA. $100,000, 2004. For educational and cultural programs at Central Library.
296. Los Angeles County Public Library Foundation, Downey, CA. $25,000, 2004. For materials needed at homework centers in community libraries.
297. University of California, Los Angeles, CA. $100,000, 2004. For matching funds toward Conservation and Preservation Endowment for Library.

Peninsula Community Foundation
Limitations: Giving limited to San Mateo County and northern Santa Clara County, CA. No support for fraternal organizations, or religious organizations for religious purposes. No grants to individuals (except for scholarships and the awards program for artists), or for endowment funds, annual campaigns, building funds, deficit financing, land acquisition, research, fundraising events, or out of area travel.
298. Burlingame Public Library, Burlingame, CA. $36,100, 2005. To complete renovation of Easton Branch Library.
299. Homework Central, San Mateo, CA. $30,000, 2005. For staffing, tutor training and parent leadership training.
300. Library of Portola Valley, Friends of the, Portola Valley, CA. $20,000, 2005. For moving library to temporary location during construction of new Portola Valley library.
301. Long Beach Public Library Foundation, Long Beach, CA. $10,000, 2005. For Raising A Reader program to hire part-time bilingual homework and literacy helpers and also provide story time programs at libraries in Long Beach.
302. Long Now Foundation, San Francisco, CA. $4,500,000, 2005. For general operating support for Spring Valley Project.
303. Media Matters for America, DC. $25,000, 2005. For general support.
304. Pacifica Library Foundation, Pacifica, CA. $11,632, 2005. For Holiday Fund.

305. Palo Alto Medical Foundation for Health Care, Research and Education, Palo Alto, CA. $45,000, 2005. For Pediatric Endowment Fund, Carol Davis Children's Library, and Adolescent Health Projects.
306. Ravenswood City School District, East Palo Alto, CA. $25,000, 2005. For library activities.
307. Redwood City Library Foundation, Redwood City, CA. $50,000, 2005. Toward Traveling Storytime Program's Coordinator position.
308. Redwood City Library Foundation, Redwood City, CA. $10,000, 2005. For Traveling Storytime program.
309. Redwood City School District, Redwood City, CA. $25,000, 2005. For school library activities.
310. San Mateo Public Library Foundation, San Mateo, CA. $35,000, 2005. For Campaign for San Mateo Public Library.
311. San Mateo Public Library Foundation, San Mateo, CA. $15,000, 2005. For Capital Campaign.
312. University of California at Berkeley Foundation, Berkeley, CA. $22,650, 2005. For Rosston Family Achievement Award Alumni Scholarship Endowment, Doe Library, for UC Berkeley Library Associates Membership, Friends of Bancroft Library Membership, Regional Oral History Office, and Bear Backers Robert Kerley Scholarship Fund.
313. William J. Clinton Presidential Foundation, New York, NY. $1,000,000, 2005. For unrestricted support.

Pfaffinger Foundation
Limitations: Giving limited to Los Angeles and Orange counties, CA, for charitable institutions. No grants to individuals (except company employees); no scholarships.
314. Women at Work, Pasadena, CA. $10,000, 2004.

The San Diego Foundation
(formerly San Diego Community Foundation)
Limitations: Giving primarily in the greater San Diego, CA, region. No support for religious organizations. No grants to individuals (except for scholarships), or for annual or capital fund campaigns, endowment funds, conferences, travel, or to underwrite fundraising events and performances.
315. Athenaeum Music and Arts Library, La Jolla, CA. $79,119, 2006. For general support.
316. Athenaeum Music and Arts Library, La Jolla, CA. $50,000, 2006. For Campaign to Reclaim.
317. Californians Aware - The Center for Public Forum Rights, Carmichael, CA. $14,680, 2006. For educational seminar.
318. El Centro, City of, El Centro, CA. $55,610, 2006. For El Centro Public Library renovation.
319. Info Line of San Diego County, San Diego, CA. $50,000, 2006. For 211 Info Line for San Diego.
320. Lake Charles Boston High School, Lake Charles, LA. $10,000, 2006. For books, equipment, and furniture.
321. Law Library Justice Foundation, San Diego, CA. $70,000, 2006. To aid Law Library Justice Foundation in lessening burdens on government by aiding in maintenance of San Diego County Public Law Library.
322. San Diego Public Library, San Diego, CA. $82,000, 2006. For Development Team and for Point Loma Branch for Sunday hours.

The San Francisco Foundation
Limitations: Giving limited to the San Francisco Bay Area, CA, counties of Alameda, Contra Costa, Marin, San Francisco, and San Mateo. No support for religious purposes, or medical, academic, or scientific research. No grants to individuals (except scholarships and fellowships designated by a donor) or for conferences or one-time events.
323. Alameda County Library Foundation, Fremont, CA. $20,000, 2005. For library resources and programs to youth detained in Alameda County's juvenile detention system.
324. Bancroft Library, Friends of the, Berkeley, CA. $25,000, 2005. For Centennial Campaign.
325. Catholic Charities CYO, San Francisco, CA. $20,000, 2005. For information and referral services to low-income individuals and families throughout Bay Area.
326. Center for Community Benefit Organizations, Oakland, CA. $40,000, 2005. To provide core operating support.

327. Coalition to Preserve Oakland Cultural Venues, Oakland, CA. $10,000, 2005. To create resource guide for artists and organizations wanting to develop arts venues in Oakland.

328. EdSource, Mountain View, CA. $30,000, 2005. For Spring Forum.

329. EdSource, Mountain View, CA. $10,000, 2005. Toward Public Information Project to inform Californians about urgent need to improve state's high school performance and provide diverse student population with more support and options as they transition to post-secondary training, work, or college.

330. Foundation Center, San Francisco, CA. $15,000, 2005. For core operating support.

331. Friends and Foundation of the San Francisco Public Library, San Francisco, CA. $28,544, 2005. For general support.

332. Friends and Foundation of the San Francisco Public Library, San Francisco, CA. $10,000, 2005. For exhibitions, public programs, and catalog celebrating tenth anniversary of Hormel Center at Main Library.

333. Global Footprint Network, Oakland, CA. $20,000, 2005. To work with County of Marin to develop methods for measuring progress toward sustainability goals in general plan.

334. Greatschools.net, San Francisco, CA. $100,000, 2005. To build GreatSchools (GS) Network, grassroots constituency of parent-leaders advocating for policies and practices that will improve quality of parent involvement in San Francisco public schools.

335. Health-Interfaith Partnership, Martinez, CA. $20,000, 2005. To expand capacity of faith-based health ministries to provide information and referrals to health services for low-income and immigrant residents of Contra Costa County.

336. Lavender Youth Recreation and Information Center, San Francisco, CA. $15,000, 2005. For core operating support.

337. Life Frames, San Francisco, CA. $15,000, 2005. To continue community planning and design development of South Bernal Heights Living Library and Think Park Nature Walk, and Integrated Digital Gateways, and Multimedia Digital Archives.

338. Long Now Foundation, San Francisco, CA. $15,000, 2005. For general support.

339. Media Matters for America, DC. $10,000, 2005. For general support.

340. Mills College, Oakland, CA. $10,000, 2005. For Mills College Library Special Collection for rare books.

341. Multicultural Institute, Berkeley, CA. $25,000, 2005. To build capacity of organization to provide health information and referral services to youth, low-income families, and migrant day laborers in South and West Berkeley.

342. Oakland Public Library, Oakland, CA. $15,000, 2005. For expansion of literacy partnership between Oakland Public Library, Head Start centers, and childcare sites in Oakland.

343. Peninsula Library Foundation, Belvedere, CA. $10,000, 2005. For general support.

344. Project Inform, San Francisco, CA. $10,000, 2005. For general support.

345. University of California, Berkeley, CA. $50,000, 2005. For Class of '55 50th Reunion Campaign, Bancroft Library and for football stadium.

346. University of California, Berkeley, CA. $50,000, 2005. For Bancroft Centennial Fund designated for library from Class of '55.

347. University of California, Bancroft Library, Berkeley, CA. $10,000, 2005. For rare books.

348. University of California at Santa Cruz Foundation, Santa Cruz, CA. $10,000, 2005. For McEvoy Family Popular and World Music Endowment at UCSC Library.

349. Women of Color Resource Center, Oakland, CA. $10,000, 2005. For general support.

Santa Barbara Foundation

Limitations: Giving limited to Santa Barbara County, CA. No support for religious organizations for religious purposes. No grants to individuals (except for scholarships), or for deficit financing, general operating support, seed funding, endowment funds, fundraising drives, conferences, seminars, one-time events, fellowships, or for research.

350. Santa Barbara Public Library, Friends of the, Santa Barbara, CA. $42,563, 2004. For computers for Internet access at Main Library and branches.

351. Santa Barbara Public Library, Friends of the, Santa Barbara, CA. $12,500, 2004. For laptop computers and mobile cart for Internet access at Main library.

Charles and Helen Schwab Foundation

Limitations: Giving primarily in CA.

352. Community Technology Alliance, San Jose, CA. $50,000, 2005. For Regional Homeless Information Network Organization (RHINO) Regional Homeless Management Information System (HMIS) Project.

353. National Low Income Housing Coalition and Low Income Housing Information Service, DC. $50,000, 2005. For National Housing Trust Fund Project.

354. National Low Income Housing Coalition and Low Income Housing Information Service, DC. $50,000, 2005. For National Housing Trust Fund Campaign.

The Seaver Institute

Limitations: Giving on a national basis. No grants to individuals, or for operating budgets, continuing support, annual campaigns, emergency or endowment funds, scholarships, fellowships, deficit financing, capital or building funds, equipment, land acquisition, publications, or conferences; no loans.

355. Huntington Library, Art Collections and Botanical Gardens, San Marino, CA. $17,500, 2005.

356. Information for Families, New York, NY. $20,000, 2005.

Simpson PSB Fund

Limitations: Giving primarily in CA. No grants to individuals.

357. Oakland Public Library, Oakland, CA. $10,000, 2004.

358. University of California, Berkeley, CA. $500,000, 2004. For Library Fund.

The Skoll Foundation

Limitations: No support for organizations with less than a two-year track record, or public sector institutions. No grants to individuals, or for scholarships, endowments or land acquisition.

359. Action Without Borders, New York, NY. $100,000, 2005. For core support.

360. Philanthropic Research, Inc., Williamsburg, VA. $250,000, 2005. For core support.

361. Philanthropic Research, Inc., Williamsburg, VA. $25,000, 2005. For general operating support and tsunami relief.

Y & H Soda Foundation

Limitations: Giving limited to Alameda and Contra Costa counties, CA. No support for animal welfare, the arts, environmental causes, private foundations, national medical research organizations, or political organizations. No grants to individuals, or for annual fundraising campaigns, faculty chairs, or advocacy grants.

362. Delta 2000, Antioch, CA. $10,000, 2005. For part-time library coordinator for East County Library.

363. Eden Information and Referral Service, Hayward, CA. $15,000, 2005. To maintain and enhance current programs.

Levi Strauss Foundation

Limitations: Giving on a national and international basis, with emphasis on areas of company operations. No support for sports teams. No grants to individuals, or for capital campaigns or endowments, athletic competition, advertising, sponsorships, sectarian or religious activities, or political campaigns or causes.

364. Asian Migrant Centre, Hong Kong. $75,000, 2004.

365. Asian Migrant Centre, Hong Kong. $75,000, 2004.

366. Charities Aid Foundation (UK), West Malling, England. $430,000, 2004.

Stuart Foundation

(also known as Elbridge Stuart Foundation)

Limitations: Giving primarily in CA and WA. No support for political or lobbying activities. No grants to individuals, or generally for endowments, building funds, or annual campaigns, capital or operating support to sustain existing service capacity.

367. Charter Schools Development Center, Sacramento, CA. $250,000, 2005. For general support for statewide resource center for California's charter schools.

368. EdSource, Mountain View, CA. $50,000, 2005. For general support to continue work to address need in California for accurate and impartial data collection, research, and analysis that informs policy and practice relating to public education.

369. University of California, Center for Social Services Research, School of Social Welfare, Berkeley, CA. $200,000, 2005. For general support of California Children's Services Archive (The Children's Archive), longitudinal database that provides regularly updated indicators of key public child welfare program outcomes, processes, and receipt of critical services.

UniHealth Foundation

Limitations: Giving primarily in CA in the following areas: San Fernando and Santa Clarita Valley, Westside and Downtown Los Angeles, San Gabriel Valley, and Long Beach and Orange County. No support for propagandizing and/or influencing legislation, political campaigns, programs that promote religious doctrine, or biomedical/non-applied research. No grants to individuals, or for endowments, annual drives, or retirement of debt.

370. Library Foundation of Los Angeles, Los Angeles, CA. $100,000, 2005. For Health Information Resource Project.

371. OASIS Institute, Saint Louis, MO. $50,000, 2005. For Active Start.

The Valley Foundation

Limitations: Giving limited to Santa Clara County, CA. No support for religious purposes. No grants to individuals.

372. Able Project, San Jose, CA. $15,000, 2005.

373. Community Health Library of Los Gatos, Los Gatos, CA. $35,000, 2005.

Wayne & Gladys Valley Foundation

Limitations: Giving primarily in Alameda and Contra Costa counties, CA. No support for veterans, fraternal, labor, service club, military, or similar organizations. No grants to individuals, or for fundraising events, dinners, advertising, private operating foundations, or generally for endowments.

374. Black Pine Circle Day School, Berkeley, CA. $100,000, 2005. For construction of permanent facility for K-5 classrooms and library.

375. Diablo Valley College Foundation, Pleasant Hill, CA. $86,961, 2005. For library expansion and remodel, enhancements to Life Sciences Building remodel.

Waitt Family Foundation

Limitations: Giving primarily in the tri-state Siouxland region of IA, NE, and SD, and San Diego, CA.

376. William J. Clinton Presidential Foundation, New York, NY. $35,932, 2004.

Wallis Foundation

Limitations: Giving primarily in CA. No grants to individuals.

377. Carpinteria Library, Friends of the, Carpinteria, CA. $10,000, 2005.

378. Friends and Foundation of the San Francisco Public Library, San Francisco, CA. $10,000, 2005.

379. Survivors of the Shoah Visual History Foundation, Los Angeles, CA. $25,000, 2005.

Wasserman Foundation

Limitations: Giving primarily in CA. No grants to individuals.

380. Lyndon Baines Johnson Foundation, Austin, TX. $10,000, 2004.

381. Survivors of the Shoah Visual History Foundation, Los Angeles, CA. $200,000, 2004.

382. William J. Clinton Presidential Foundation, Little Rock, AR. $100,000, 2004.

Weingart Foundation

Limitations: Giving limited to 7 southern CA counties; Los Angeles, Kern, Orange, Santa Barbara, Riverside, San Bernadino, and Ventura. No support for environmental or religious programs, political refugee or international concerns, federated fundraising groups, or national organizations that do not have chapters operating in Southern California. No grants to individuals, or for endowment funds, normal operating expenses, annual campaigns, emergency funds, deficit financing, fellowships, seminars, conferences, publications, workshops, travel, surveys, films, medical research, or publishing activities.

383. BookEnds, West Hills, CA. $40,000, 2005. 2-year grant. For new position of Director of Operations.

384. California Western School of Law, San Diego, CA. $10,000, 2005. For annual fund, equal justice library and capital campaign.

385. Covina Library Fund, Covina, CA. $10,000, 2005. Toward implementation of Learning Differences Outreach program.

386. Crane Country Day School, Santa Barbara, CA. $100,000, 2005. For new library and art center and improvements in safety of traffic and parking.

387. Foundation Center, New York, NY. $27,500, 2005. To cover cost of staff, equipment and material to continue serving grantseekers and grantmakers.

388. Grandparents as Parents (GAP), Lakewood, CA. $35,000, 2005. To hire staff to formalize administration and operations.

389. Long Beach Public Library Foundation, Long Beach, CA. $75,000, 2005. For Raising-a-Reader 12-week bilingual reading development program.

390. UCLA Foundation, Los Angeles, CA. $10,000, 2005. For Clarke Library.

391. United Way, Inland Empire, Rancho Cucamonga, CA. $50,000, 2005. For 2-1-1 program development.

The Wells Fargo Foundation

(formerly Norwest Foundation)

Limitations: Giving primarily in areas of company operations; giving on a national basis for the Wells Fargo Housing Foundation. No support for religious organizations not of direct benefit to the entire community or fraternal organizations. No grants to individuals, or for conferences, tickets, or travel; no loans.

392. Contra Costa, County of, Martinez, CA. $10,000, 2004. For Public Library in Pleasant Hill.

393. Fort Worth Public Library Foundation, Fort Worth, TX. $10,000, 2004.

394. Francis House, Sacramento, CA. $10,000, 2004.

395. Friends and Foundation of the San Francisco Public Library, San Francisco, CA. $50,000, 2004.

396. George Bush Presidential Library Foundation, College Station, TX. $15,000, 2004.

397. Homer Public Library, Friends of the, Homer, AK. $18,000, 2004.

398. Huntington Library, Art Collections and Botanical Gardens, San Marino, CA. $65,000, 2004.

399. Minneapolis Neighborhood Employment Network, Minneapolis, MN. $20,000, 2004.

400. Minneapolis Public Library, Friends of the, Minneapolis, MN. $10,000, 2004.

401. Nonprofit Center of Milwaukee, Milwaukee, WI. $10,000, 2004.

402. Nonprofit Resource Center, Sacramento, CA. $15,000, 2004.

403. Project Inform, San Francisco, CA. $25,000, 2004.

404. Public Library of Des Moines Foundation, Des Moines, IA. $50,000, 2004.

405. Public Library of Des Moines Foundation, Des Moines, IA. $25,000, 2004.

406. Public Library of Des Moines Foundation, Des Moines, IA. $15,000, 2004.

407. Sacramento Public Library Foundation, Sacramento, CA. $10,000, 2004.

408. Twin Cities Community Voice Mail, Saint Paul, MN. $10,000, 2004.

The Winnick Family Foundation

(formerly The Gary and Karen Winnick Foundation)

Limitations: Giving in the U.S., with strong emphasis on CA and NY. No support for political organizations. No grants to individuals.

409. George Bush Presidential Library Center, College Station, TX. $200,000, 2004. For unrestricted operating support.

410. New York Public Library, New York, NY. $10,000, 2004. For unrestricted operating support.

411. William J. Clinton Presidential Center, Little Rock, AR. $250,000, 2004. For unrestricted operating support.

Wood-Claeyssens Foundation

Limitations: Giving limited to Santa Barbara and Ventura counties, CA. No support for tax-supported educational institutions, government-funded organizations, religious or political organizations, or for medical research. No grants to individuals.

412. Lompoc District Libraries Foundation, Lompoc, CA. $10,000, 2005. For learning center.

413. Santa Barbara County Genealogical Society, Goleta, CA. $125,000, 2005. For ongoing expenses at Pierre Claeyssens Military Museum and Library.
414. Santa Barbara Museum of Natural History, Santa Barbara, CA. $25,000, 2005. For nature collection lending library.

COLORADO

Avenir Foundation, Inc.

Limitations: Giving on a national basis with emphasis on CO, as well as in Vienna, Austria. No grants to individuals.
415. Schoenberg Institute, Vienna, Austria. $100,000, 2005. For general operating support.

Boettcher Foundation

Limitations: Giving limited to CO. No support for housing, open spaces/parks, organizations that primarily serve animals, large urban hospitals, gymnasiums, athletic fields, or religious groups or organizations for religious purposes. No grants to individuals (except from programs), or for endowment funds, pilot programs, operations, purchase of tables or tickets for dinners/events, media presentations, small business start-ups, conferences, seminars, workshops, debt reduction, or travel.
416. American Red Cross, Mile High Chapter, Denver, CO. $25,000, 2005. To construct Disaster Response Call Center.
417. Delta County Public Library District, Delta, CO. $25,000, 2005. To construct new Crawford Community Library.
418. Denver Public Schools, Denver, CO. $25,000, 2005. To rehabilitate historic library at Denver East High School.
419. La Veta Public Library District, La Veta, CO. $25,000, 2005. To expand library.

Temple Hoyne Buell Foundation

Limitations: Giving only in CO. No support for political organizations, sectarian programs, or promoting religion. Generally, no support for medical programs. No grants to individuals, or for past operating deficit, or retirement of debt. Generally, no grants for testimonial dinners, multi-year awards, events, annual campaigns, membership drives, conferences, or endowments; no loans.
420. Child Advocacy Resource and Education, Greeley, CO. $15,000, 2005. For children's and parenting education program.
421. Child Care Connections, Colorado Springs, CO. $30,000, 2005. For MERIT Program in new sites serving children 0-5.
422. Denver Public Library, Denver, CO. $20,000, 2005. For summer of reading program.
423. Denver Public Library Friends Foundation, Denver, CO. $20,000, 2005. For Read Aloud program.
424. Early Childhood Council of Larimer County, Fort Collins, CO. $16,000, 2005. For child care resource and referral program.
425. Summit County Child Care Resource and Referral Agency, Dillon, CO. $16,200, 2005. For Quality Improvement Project.

The Colorado Trust

Limitations: Giving limited to CO. No support for religious organizations for religious purposes, political organizations, private foundations, or direct subsidization of care to the medically indigent. No grants to individuals, or for endowments, deficit financing or debt retirement, building funds, real estate acquisition, fundraising drives and events, or testimonial dinners.
426. Colorado Health Institute, Denver, CO. $30,196, 2004.

Daniels Fund

(formerly Daniels Foundation)
Limitations: Giving primarily in CO, with emphasis on Denver; funding also in NM, WY and UT with a limited basis nationally. No support for arts and cultural programs. No grants to individuals (except for Daniels Fund Scholarship Program or Daniels Rapid Response Fund), or for academic, medical, or scientific research, or conferences, symposia, or workshops, or for debt elimination, endowments, fundraising or special events (purchase of tables or conferences), or for creation, publication or distribution of publications or for video productions.
427. Child Care Connections, Colorado Springs, CO. $30,000, 2005. For Improvement (MERIT) Program.
428. Embudo Valley Library and Community Center, Dixon, NM. $10,000, 2005. For Senior Read program.
429. Firstcall Service Net, Fort Collins, CO. $10,000, 2005. For program support.
430. HOME-New Mexico, Albuquerque, NM. $15,000, 2005. For general operating support.
431. Mapping Your Future, Round Rock, TX. $25,000, 2005. For National Financial Literacy Program.
432. School Choice Wisconsin, Milwaukee, WI. $50,000, 2005. For group educational visits.

The Denver Foundation

Limitations: Giving limited to Adams, Arapahoe, Boulder, Broomfield, Denver, Douglas, and Jefferson counties, CO. No support for government agencies, parochial or religious schools, or organizations that further religious doctrine. No grants to individuals (except for scholarships), or for sponsorships, debt liquidation, debt retirement, endowments or other reserve funds, membership or affiliation campaigns, dinners, or special events, research, publications, films, travel, or conferences, symposiums, workshops, or individual medical procedures, medical, scientific, or academic research, creation or installation of art objects, or multi-year funding requests.
433. Colorado Alliance for Environmental Education, Denver, CO. $15,000, 2005. For general operating support.
434. Denver Public Library Friends Foundation, Denver, CO. $10,000, 2005. For general operating support.
435. University of Colorado Foundation, Denver, CO. $10,000, 2005. For Library's computers and Mobile E-Learning Lab.
436. University of Colorado Foundation, Denver, CO. $10,000, 2005. For creating E-Learning Center at Auraria Library.

El Pomar Foundation

Limitations: Giving limited to CO. No support for organizations that distribute funds to other grantees, religious or political organizations, primary or secondary education, or for camps or seasonal facilities. No grants to individuals, or for travel, film or other media projects, conferences, seminars, deficit financing, endowment funds, research.
437. Delta County Public Library District, Delta, CO. $15,000, 2005. For new library in Crawford.
438. Grand County Library, Granby, CO. $25,000, 2005. For library construction.
439. Plains Medical Center, Limon, CO. $25,000, 2005. For new health information technology.

First Data Western Union Foundation

Limitations: Giving on a national and international basis in areas of company operations, with emphasis on the metropolitan Denver, CO, area, Coral Springs and Hollywood, FL, Hagerstown, MD, Omaha, NE, Melville, NY, Houston, TX, and in China, India, and Mexico. No support for pass-through organizations. No grants to individuals (except for scholarships), or for endowments, special events, capital campaigns, scholarship funds, early childhood education, or debt reduction.
440. Charities Aid Foundation (CAF) America, Alexandria, VA. $100,000, 2004. For operating support.
441. Charities Aid Foundation (CAF) America, Alexandria, VA. $20,000, 2004. For operating support.
442. Voluntary Organizations Initiative in Central and Eastern Europe and Eurasia (VOICE), Arlington, VA. $10,000, 2004. For operating support.

Gates Family Foundation

(formerly Gates Foundation)
Limitations: Giving limited to CO, with emphasis on the Denver area, except for foundation-initiated grants. No support for private foundations, medical facilities, or individual public schools or public school districts. No grants to individuals, or for operating budgets, medical research,

annual campaigns, emergency funds, deficit financing, purchase of tickets for fundraising dinners, parties, balls, or other social fundraising events, purchase of vehicles or office equipment, conferences, meetings, research, or scholarships; no loans.

443. Arapahoe Library Foundation, Englewood, CO. $15,000, 2005. To renovate interior of Sheridan Public Library.

444. La Veta Public Library District, La Veta, CO. $60,000, 2005. Toward new addition to library.

445. Red Feather Lakes Community Library, Red Feather Lakes, CO. $50,000, 2005. Toward library expansion.

The Gill Foundation

Limitations: Giving primarily to national and state-wide organizations. No support for clinical HIV/AIDS research, direct client services to community based HIV/AIDS organizations outside CO, or art programs for or about HIV. No support to individuals, endowments, scholarships, capital projects, direct care services, pride events, film or media production.

446. Center for Democratic Renewal and Education, Atlanta, GA. $15,000, 2004. For general operating support.

447. Human Rights Campaign Foundation, DC. $100,000, 2004. For general operating and program support for WorkNet, database of employers with non-discrimination policies, domestic partner benefits, and other beneficial policies for LGBT workers.

448. Pikes Peak Library District Foundation, Colorado Springs, CO. $18,000, 2004. For event sponsorship for World Music Series, program support for De Donde Eres and general operating support.

449. Pikes Peak Library District Foundation, Colorado Springs, CO. $10,000, 2004. For event sponsorship for Shivers Concert Series and fundraiser.

450. Pikes Peak Library District Foundation, Colorado Springs, CO. $10,000, 2004. For event sponsorship for All Pikes Peak Reads.

CONNECTICUT

Boehringer Ingelheim Cares Foundation, Inc.

Limitations: Giving primarily in northern Fairfield County, CT. No support for political or religious organizations.

451. Project Inform, San Francisco, CA. $20,000, 2004. For AIDS Treatment Advocacy.

The Louis Calder Foundation

Limitations: Giving primarily in the greater New York, NY, metropolitan area and surrounding areas. No support for political organizations, private foundations, or governmental organizations. No grants to individuals.

452. Foundation Center, New York, NY. $35,000, 2005. For programs and activities.

453. Friends of New Beginnings Family Academy, Bridgeport, CT. $50,000, 2005. For library and literacy initiatives.

454. Kingsbridge Heights Community Center, Bronx, NY. $75,000, 2005. For expanded computer lab and learning library.

455. New York Public Library, New York, NY. $80,000, 2005. For Classic Literature for Teens at the George Bruce Branch.

456. Notre Dame School, New York, NY. $100,000, 2005. For library renovations.

457. Patrons Program, New York, NY. $100,000, 2005. For Library Connections program.

458. Queens Library Foundation, Jamaica, NY. $50,000, 2005. For purchase of classic titles for the Young Adult Collections in ten branches.

The Dibner Fund, Inc.

Limitations: Giving primarily in CT, MA, and NY, some national and international giving. No support for religious sects or institutions, or political parties or programs. No grants to individuals, or generally for building or endowment funds, scholarships, fellowships (except through

universities, educational agencies and/or specific academic programs) capital expenditures, matching gifts or seed money; no loans.

459. Burndy Library, Cambridge, MA. $430,312, 2004. For unrestricted support.

460. National Yiddish Book Center, Amherst, MA. $15,000, 2004. For unrestricted support.

461. New York Public Library, New York, NY. $10,000, 2004. For unrestricted support.

462. Polytechnic University, Bern Dibner Library of Science and Technology, Brooklyn, NY. $125,000, 2004. For unrestricted support.

463. Smithsonian Institution, DC. $43,100, 2004. For unrestricted support of libraries.

464. YIVO Institute for Jewish Research, New York, NY. $25,000, 2004. For unrestricted support.

The Educational Foundation of America

Limitations: Giving limited to the U.S. No grants to individuals, annual fundraising campaigns, or for capital or endowment funds; no loans.

465. Environmental Protection Information Center (EPIC), Garberville, CA. $75,000, 2005. For Northern California Forest Protection Program.

466. Queens Library Foundation, Jamaica, NY. $25,000, 2005. For Professional Development for Latchkey Program Monitors.

GE Foundation

(formerly GE Fund)

Limitations: Giving on a national and international basis, with emphasis on areas of company operations. No support for religious or political organizations. No grants to individuals (except for employee-related scholarships and fellowships), or for capital campaigns, endowments, or other special purpose campaigns; no loans; no equipment donations.

467. Connecticut Library Consortium, Middletown, CT. $25,000, 2004.

468. Council for Basic Education, DC. $28,000, 2004.

469. Education Resources Institute, Boston, MA. $100,000, 2004.

470. Foundation Center, New York, NY. $25,000, 2004.

471. Mexican Center for Philanthropy, Mexico City, Mexico. $100,000, 2004.

472. New York Public Library, Astor, Lenox and Tilden Foundations, New York, NY. $25,000, 2004.

Hartford Foundation for Public Giving

Limitations: Giving limited to the Greater Hartford, CT, area. No support for sectarian purposes, private foundations, tax-supported agencies, or activities primarily national or international in perspective. No grants to individuals (except for scholarships), or for operating budgets, deficit financing, endowment funds, research, or conferences.

473. Connecticut State Library, Hartford, CT. $50,000, 2005. For program support.

474. Farmington Library, Farmington, CT. $20,000, 2005. For program support.

475. Farmington Library, Farmington, CT. $15,000, 2005.

476. Granby Public Library, Granby, CT. $14,010, 2005. For capital campaign.

477. Hartford Public Library, Hartford, CT. $50,000, 2005. For program support.

478. Hartford Public Library, Hartford, CT. $20,000, 2005. For program support.

479. Hartford Public Library, Hartford, CT. $15,000, 2005. For program support.

480. Hispanic Professional Network, Hartford, CT. $27,500, 2005. For general support.

481. West Hartford Public Library, West Hartford, CT. $170,000, 2005. For capital campaign.

482. West Hartford Public Library, West Hartford, CT. $18,000, 2005. For capital campaign.

483. Wethersfield Public Library, Wethersfield, CT. $20,000, 2005. For capital campaign.

Smith Richardson Foundation, Inc.

Limitations: Giving limited to U.S.-based organizations only. No support for programs in the arts and humanities, direct service programs, or historic restoration projects. No grants to individuals, or for deficit financing, building or construction projects, or research in the physical sciences; no loans.

484. Foundation Center, New York, NY. $12,000, 2004.

485. Jamestown Foundation, DC. $469,600, 2004.
486. Jamestown Foundation, DC. $139,796, 2004.
487. Jamestown Foundation, DC. $68,091, 2004.

The Smart Family Foundation
Limitations: Giving on a national basis. No grants to individuals.
488. Center for Jewish History, New York, NY. $50,000, 2004. For operating support.
489. Newberry Library, Chicago, IL. $110,000, 2004. For operating support.
490. Phillips-Morrison Institute of California, Tiburon, CA. $10,000, 2004. For operating support.
491. YIVO Institute for Jewish Research, New York, NY. $75,000, 2004. For operating support.

Malcolm Hewitt Wiener Foundation, Inc.
492. Pierpont Morgan Library, New York, NY. $10,000, 2004.

DELAWARE

Chichester duPont Foundation, Inc.
Limitations: Giving primarily in DE and MD. No grants to individuals.
493. Eleutherian Mills-Hagley Foundation, Wilmington, DE. $30,000, 2004. For renovation project.

Crystal Trust
Limitations: Giving primarily in DE, with emphasis on Wilmington. No grants to individuals, or for endowment funds, research, scholarships, fellowships, or matching gifts.
494. Hagley Museum and Library, Wilmington, DE. $500,000, 2005. For capital campaign.

Beatrice P. Delany Charitable Trust
Limitations: Giving primarily in the metropolitan Chicago, IL, area. No grants to individuals.
495. Library Foundation of Martin County, Stuart, FL. $10,000, 2004. For general support.

Longwood Foundation, Inc.
Limitations: Giving primarily in DE and southern Chester County, PA. No grants to individuals, or for special projects or events. Generally no grants for endowments or operating support.
496. Helpline of Delaware and Morrow Counties, Delaware, OH. $20,000, 2005.

The MBNA Foundation
Limitations: Giving primarily in areas of company operations, with emphasis on DE, ME, and OH. No support for religious organizations not of direct benefit to the entire community or political organizations or candidates. No grants for salaries or benefits, capital campaigns, large equipment purchases, school supplies customarily included in school budgets, private employer work programs, research, travel, or sponsorships or fundraising.
497. Camden Public Library, Camden, ME. $200,000, 2004. For general support.
498. Camden Public Library, Camden, ME. $12,500, 2004.
499. Camden Public Library, Camden, ME. $10,000, 2004. For general support.
500. Cushing Public Library, Cushing, ME. $10,952, 2004.
501. George Bush Presidential Library Center, College Station, TX. $500,000, 2004. For general support.
502. George Bush Presidential Library Center, College Station, TX. $400,000, 2004. For general support.

503. George Bush Presidential Library Center, College Station, TX. $300,000, 2004. For general support.
504. Stephen Phillips Memorial Library, Searsport, ME. $13,000, 2004.
505. William A. Farnsworth Library and Art Museum, Rockland, ME. $250,000, 2004. For general support.
506. William A. Farnsworth Library and Art Museum, Rockland, ME. $100,000, 2004. For general support.
507. William A. Farnsworth Library and Art Museum, Rockland, ME. $50,000, 2004. For general support.
508. William A. Farnsworth Library and Art Museum, Rockland, ME. $13,854, 2004. For general support.
509. Wilmington Public Library, Wilmington, DE. $25,000, 2004. For general support.

Raskob Foundation for Catholic Activities, Inc.
Limitations: Giving to domestic and international programs affiliated with the Roman Catholic church. No grants to individuals, or for continuing support, annual campaigns, deficit financing (except missions), endowment funds, tuition, scholarships, fellowships, individual research, capital campaigns, building projects prior to the start or after the completion of construction, continuing subsidies, or requests that are after-the-fact by the time of the spring and fall trustee meetings.
510. Diocese of Richmond, Richmond, VA. $15,000, 2004. For operating support (partial salaries/benefits, travel, telephone, postage, printing, training, supplies) of Wellness Work Program, initiative to support independence and health of elderly, disabled, and ill residents of Chesapeake and Portsmouth, Virginia by providing health education, home safety checks, medication reviews and community referrals.
511. Saint Augustine College of South Africa, Linden, South Africa. $10,000, 2004. To increase library holdings in non-religious fields by acquiring books in philosophy, education, social science, law, and politics.

Welfare Foundation, Inc.
Limitations: Giving limited to DE and southern Chester County, PA. No grants to individuals, endowments, or for operating support.
512. Laurel Public Library, Laurel, DE. $50,000, 2004. For facility expansion.
513. Woodlawn Library, Friends of, Wilmington, DE. $200,000, 2004. To acquire and renovate facility.

DISTRICT OF COLUMBIA

Bauman Family Foundation, Inc.
Limitations: Giving on a national basis. No grants to individuals.
514. Abraham Lincoln Brigade Archives, New York, NY. $10,000, 2005. For general support.
515. Media Matters for America, DC. $100,000, 2005. For general support.
516. Montefiore Medical Center, Bronx, NY. $200,000, 2005. For clinical information system.

The Morris and Gwendolyn Cafritz Foundation
Limitations: Giving limited to the Washington, DC, area and the immediate surrounding counties in MD and VA, specifically Prince George and Montgomery counties, MD, and Arlington and Fairfax counties, and the city of Alexandria, VA. No grants to individuals, or for emergency funds, deficit financing, capital, endowment, or building funds, demonstration projects, or conferences; no loans.
517. Catalogue for Philanthropy, DC. $20,000, 2005. For general support.
518. Folger Shakespeare Library, DC. $25,000, 2005. For general support.
519. Foundation Center, New York, NY. $15,000, 2005. For general support.

The Case Foundation
(formerly The Stephen Case Foundation)
Limitations: Giving in the U.S. and abroad. No grants to individuals.
520. Ronald Reagan Presidential Foundation, Simi Valley, CA. $50,000, 2004. For general support.

The Community Foundation for the National Capital Region
(formerly The Foundation for the National Capital Region)
Limitations: Giving limited to the Washington, DC, Prince George's and Montgomery counties, MD, and northern VA. No grants to individuals, or from discretionary funds for annual campaigns, endowment funds, equipment, land acquisition, renovation projects, operating budgets, or matching gifts.
521. Americans for the Arts, DC. $10,000, 2006.
522. Catalogue for Philanthropy, DC. $10,000, 2006. For general support.
523. Center for Information Therapy, DC. $25,000, 2006.
524. Cottonwood Community Library, Cottonwood, CA. $54,209, 2006.
525. Education Resources Institute, Boston, MA. $25,000, 2006.
526. Family Voices of DC, DC. $70,000, 2006. For general support.
527. Greater Washington Sports Alliance, DC. $15,000, 2006. For sponsorship of Redskins/Eagles Flag Football Game.
528. Laura Bush Foundation for Americas Libraries, DC. $1,000,000, 2006. For Gulf Coast Recovery.
529. Washington Child Development Council, DC. $20,097, 2006.

Fannie Mae Foundation
Limitations: Giving on a national basis, with emphasis on Washington, DC. No support for discriminatory organizations. No grants to individuals (except for fellowships); no mortgage loans.
530. National Low Income Housing Coalition and Low Income Housing Information Service, DC. $150,000, 2005. For general operating support to advance public education, research, and policy work to promote production and preservation of affordable housing and support of organization's move.
531. Women Work: The National Network for Womens Employment, DC. $10,000, 2005. For 2005 National Conference for organization that provides women in transition with necessary information and services to take control of their financial future.

The Gottesman Fund
Limitations: Giving primarily in NY. No grants to individuals.
532. American Jewish Historical Society, New York, NY. $50,000, 2005. For general support for The 350 Fund.
533. American Jewish Historical Society, New York, NY. $20,000, 2005. For general support.
534. Center for Jewish History, New York, NY. $12,500, 2005. For general support.

Philip L. Graham Fund
Limitations: Giving primarily in the metropolitan Washington, DC, area. No support for national or international organizations, membership organizations, lobbying or political activities, or for religious purposes. No grants to individuals, or for medical services, research, annual campaigns, fundraising events, endowments, seminars, conferences, publications, tickets, films, travel expenses, courtesy advertising, advocacy, or litigation.
535. National Archives, Foundation for the, DC. $100,000, 2004. For The Learning Center component of National Archives Experience.
536. Youth Organizations United to Rise (YOUR) Community Center, DC. $20,000, 2004. To renovate facility to provide library, counseling space and lavatory for teens.

Harman Family Foundation
Limitations: Giving primarily in Los Angeles, CA, Washington, DC, MD, and New York, NY. No grants to individuals.
537. Catalogue for Philanthropy, DC. $75,000, 2005.
538. William J. Clinton Presidential Foundation, Little Rock, AR. $50,000, 2005.

The J. Willard and Alice S. Marriott Foundation
(formerly The J. Willard Marriott Foundation)
Limitations: Giving primarily in Washington, DC. No grants to individuals.
539. Laura Bush Foundation for Americas Libraries, DC. $333,333, 2004. For capital campaign.

Eugene and Agnes E. Meyer Foundation
Limitations: Giving limited to the metropolitan Washington, DC, area, including Montgomery, Prince George's, Calvert, Charles, and St. Mary's counties in suburban MD and Arlington, Fairfax, Loudoun, Prince William and Stafford counties, and the cities of Alexandria, Falls Church, Manassas, and Manassas Park in northern VA. No support for sectarian purposes, or for programs that are national or international in scope. No grants to individuals, or for annual campaigns, deficit financing, endowment funds, equipment, scholarships, fellowships, scientific or medical research, publications, special events or conferences.
540. Catalogue for Philanthropy, DC. $25,000, 2005. To publish DC Catalogue for Philanthropy.
541. Foundation Center, DC. $18,500, 2005. For general operating support for DC office and to provide scholarships for Foundation Center programs.

Moriah Fund
Limitations: Giving nationally and internationally, including Israel and Latin America, specifically Guatemala; giving primarily in Washington, DC for poverty program. No support for lobbying or political campaigns, private foundations, or arts organizations. No grants to individuals, or for medical research.
542. Bank Information Center, DC. $25,000, 2005. For general support.
543. Bank Information Center, DC. $21,000, 2005. For SUNGI Development Foundation.
544. National Womens Health Network, DC. $30,000, 2005. For general support.
545. Sexuality Information and Education Council of the U.S. (SIECUS), New York, NY. $50,000, 2005. For general support.

Public Welfare Foundation, Inc.
Limitations: Giving is generally limited to the U.S. (more than 90 percent). No grants to individuals, or for building funds, capital improvements, endowments, government projects, scholarships, graduate work, foreign study, conferences, seminars, publications, research, workshops, or annual campaigns; no loans.
546. American University, Washington College of Law, National Equal Justice Library, DC. $50,000, 2005. 1.25-year grant. For general support.
547. DataCenter, Oakland, CA. $40,000, 2005. For Environmental Justice Project.
548. Foundation Center, New York, NY. $13,500, 2005.
549. Human Services Coalition of Dade County, Miami, FL. $50,000, 2005. For general support of Florida CHAIN (Community Health Action Information Network).
550. Kentucky Jobs with Justice, Louisville, KY. $25,000, 2005. For general support.
551. Miami Workers Center, Miami, FL. $40,000, 2005. For general support.
552. Southwest Research and Information Center, Albuquerque, NM. $100,000, 2005. For Uranium Impact Assessment Project.

Wallace Genetic Foundation, Inc.
553. American Public Information on the Environment, Northfield, MN. $10,000, 2004. For 800 Environmental Information Line.
554. Green Guide Institute, New York, NY. $35,000, 2004. For general support.
555. Institute for Local Self-Reliance, DC. $30,000, 2004. For archiving of photography and printed record of Hawaii Industrial Hemp Research Project.
556. Vetiver Network, Leesburg, VA. $20,000, 2004. For water quality activities.

Wallace Global Fund
Limitations: Giving on an international basis. No grants to individuals, or for scholarships, purchase of land, capital construction, profit-making businesses, debt reduction, endowment campaigns, fundraising drives/events, or tuition, assistance or other forms of personal financial aid.
557. Bank Information Center, DC. $70,000, 2004. To empower citizens in developing countries to influence multilateral bank-funded projects and policies by providing information and support to local communities affected by corporate abuses fueled by such public subsidies.
558. Research, Action and Information Network for the Bodily Integrity of Women (RAINBO), New York, NY. $75,000, 2004. For Integrated

Initiative Against Female Genital Mutilation: Technical Assistance and Information Exchange, disseminating lessons learned from FGM-eradication efforts to large bilateral and multilateral donors who can provide more funding than private donors.

559. Tides Center, San Francisco, CA. $25,000, 2004. For general support for National Voice, clearinghouse for technical and legal assistance for civic engagement groups and funders.

560. Womens International Network Foundation, Lexington, MA. $15,679, 2004. To print and distribute Childbirth Picture Books to affected communities in Africa in order to educate about harmful effects of female genital mutilation.

561. World Resources Institute, DC. $100,000, 2004. For Moving to a Hydrogen Economy, comparing fossil fuel- and nuclear-created hydrogen with renewable-created hydrogen, to determine correct path toward clean hydrogen future; and Climate Analysis Indicator Tool (CAIT), database of greenhouse gas emissions data from all sources for all countries, for use by governments regarding climate change policy, and by NGOs to formulate advocacy positions.

FLORIDA

The Chatlos Foundation, Inc.

Limitations: No support for individual church congregations, primary or secondary schools or for the arts, or for organizations in existence for less than two years. No grants to individuals, or for seed money, deficit financing, endowment funds, medical research, conferences, bricks and mortar, or multi-year grants; no loans.

562. Biblical Theological Seminary, Hatfield, PA. $25,000, 2005. To renovate Library of Congress Room.

563. Masters College, Santa Clarita, CA. $25,000, 2005. To assist in purchase of final reference segment of library acquisition project.

564. Ozark Christian College, Joplin, MO. $18,600, 2005. For library computer equipment/technology.

Community Foundation for Palm Beach and Martin Counties, Inc.

(formerly Palm Beach County Community Foundation)
Limitations: Giving primarily in Palm Beach and Martin counties, FL. No support for religious organizations for religious purposes. No grants to individuals (except for scholarships and the Dwight Allison Fellows Program), or for operating funds, building campaigns, computers, endowments, annual campaigns, fundraising events, fundraising feasibility studies, celebration functions, or deficit financing.

565. Nonprofit Resource Institute, West Palm Beach, FL. $95,306, 2005. For education, technical assistance, and consultation services designed to strengthen governance, organization, and fund development capacity of nonprofits.

566. Palm Beach County Youth Symphony Orchestras, Boca Raton, FL. $10,000, 2005. To expand Music Library.

The Community Foundation in Jacksonville

(also known as The Community Foundation)
Limitations: Giving primarily in northeastern FL, including Baker, Clay, Duval, Nassau and St. Johns counties. No support for food programs or religious instruction. No grants for general operating support, construction or renovation, equipment, or tickets for fundraising activities.

567. Kesler Mentoring Connection, Jacksonville, FL. $26,500, 2004. To formally assess program effectiveness and identity opportunities to enhance services.

568. Micahs Place, Yulee, FL. $25,000, 2004. For Community Services Project, designed to educate volunteers and staff about needs specific to rural victims of domestic violence, assist victims in overcoming barriers implicit in rural community, recruit staff and volunteers from minority community, and promote domestic violence awareness in that community.

The Community Foundation of Sarasota County, Inc.

(formerly The Sarasota County Community Foundation, Inc.)
Limitations: Giving primarily in Sarasota County, FL, and surrounding communities. No support for fraternal organizations, societies or orders, or religious organizations for sectarian purposes. No grants to individuals (except for selected scholarships), or for annual campaigns, building campaigns, endowment funds, deficit financing, debt retirement, publications, operating expenses, travel, fundraising events, scientific research, or conferences.

569. Sarasota, County of, Sarasota, FL. $25,500, 2005. For libraries.

Dade Community Foundation, Inc.

(formerly Dade Foundation)
Limitations: Giving limited to Miami-Dade County, FL. No grants to individuals (except through scholarship funds), or for memberships, fundraising, memorials, deficit financing, or conferences.

570. Miami Workers Center, Miami, FL. $35,000, 2005. To add Directors of Administration and Finance position in order to increase operational and administrative capacity and allow director to focus more time on growing organization, to provide salary support for staff organizers and to improve technology capacity through upgrades to computer network. Grant made through Fund for Community Organizing.

The Arthur Vining Davis Foundations

Limitations: Giving limited to the U.S. and its possessions and territories. No support for community chests, publicly governed colleges and universities, and institutions primarily supported by government funds (except in secondary education and health care programs), voter education, voter registration drives, or projects incurring obligations extending over many years. No grants to individuals; no loans.

571. Colgate University, Hamilton, NY. $200,000, 2005. For expansion and renovation of library.

572. Emory University, Candler School of Theology, Atlanta, GA. $150,000, 2005. For design phase of library building.

573. Phillips Theological Seminary, Tulsa, OK. $128,000, 2005. For integrated library management system.

574. Tuskegee University, Tuskegee, AL. $200,000, 2005. For construction of building for College of Business and Information Sciences.

Jessie Ball duPont Fund

(formerly Jessie Ball duPont Religious, Charitable and Educational Fund)
Limitations: Giving primarily in the South, especially DE, FL, and VA. No support for organizations other than those awarded gifts by the donor from 1960-1964. No grants to individuals, or generally for capital campaigns or endowments.

575. James Monroe Memorial Foundation, Richmond, VA. $10,000, 2005. For Executive Director's Discretionary Fund.

576. Lancaster Community Library, Kilmarnock, VA. $10,000, 2005. For Executive Director's Discretionary Fund.

577. Stephens College, Garment Research Library, Columbia, MO. $49,573, 2005. 3-year grant. To equip with teleconferencing equipment and digitize collection and train faculty and students in use.

Flight Attendant Medical Research Institute, Inc.

Limitations: Giving on a national basis. No grants to individuals who are currently receiving money from tobacco companies.

578. Roswell Park Alliance Foundation, Buffalo, NY. $227,873, 2005. For project, Tobacco Institute and Council for Tobacco Research Collection Development.

John S. and James L. Knight Foundation

(formerly Knight Foundation)
Limitations: Giving limited to projects serving the 26 communities where the Knight brothers published newspapers for Community Initiatives Program and local grants: Long Beach and San Jose, CA, Boulder, CO, Boca Raton, Bradenton, Miami, and Tallahassee, FL, Columbus, Macon, and Milledgeville, GA, Fort Wayne and Gary, IN, Wichita, KS, Lexington, KY, Detroit, MI, Duluth and St. Paul, MN, Biloxi, MS, Charlotte, NC, Grand Forks, ND, Akron, OH, Philadelphia and State College, PA, Columbia and Myrtle Beach, SC, and Aberdeen, SD; international for Journalism. No support for organizations whose mission is to prevent, eradicate and/or

alleviate the effects of a specific disease; hospitals, unless for community-wide capital campaigns; activities to propagate a religious faith or restricted to one religion or denomination; political candidates; international programs, except U.S.-based organizations supporting free press around the world; charities operated by service clubs; or activities that are the responsibility of government (the foundation will in selective cases, join with units of government in supporting special projects). No grants to individuals, or generally for fundraising events; second requests for previously funded capital campaigns; operating deficits; general operating support; films, videos, or television programs; honoraria for distinguished guests-except in initiatives of the foundation in all three cases; group travel; memorials; medical research; or conferences.

579. Harwood Institute for Public Innovation, Bethesda, MD. $200,000, 2005. 2-year grant. To place civic journalism archives at University of Kansas, and help develop tools to improve community journalism.

580. Philanthropic Research, Inc., Williamsburg, VA. $250,000, 2005. For consortium support of national database facilitating public access to information concerning operations and finances of nonprofit organizations.

581. United Way of the Big Bend, Tallahassee, FL. $50,000, 2005. For Whole Child Connection project, Web-based tool to link families with young children to resources in community, and for communications campaign to raise awareness about Whole Child Leon project.

582. University of Maryland Foundation, Adelphi, MD. $30,000, 2005. To identify and assess range of new state and local policies on community wealth building and asset development, and to make information available through the Web and other means, to increase knowledge of innovative economic development models and provide information and resources that can be applied to Knight Communities.

Forrest C. Lattner Foundation, Inc.

Limitations: Giving primarily in San Francisco, CA, Palm Beach County, FL, Atlanta, GA, Wichita, KS, Philadelphia, PA, Westerly, RI, and Dallas, TX.

583. Andover Public Library, Andover, ME. $200,000, 2004.
584. Delray Beach Public Library, Delray Beach, FL. $100,000, 2004.
585. Free Library of Philadelphia, Philadelphia, PA. $10,000, 2004.
586. Memorial and Library Association of Westerly, Westerly, RI. $13,300, 2004.

The Lennar Foundation, Inc.

Limitations: Giving primarily in Miami, FL. No grants to individuals.

587. Leap Learning Systems, Chicago, IL. $25,000, 2004.

Publix Super Markets Charities

(formerly George W. Jenkins Foundation, Inc.)
Limitations: Giving primarily in AL, FL, GA, SC, and TN. No grants to individuals.

588. Delray Beach Public Library, Delray Beach, FL. $16,667, 2004.

Scaife Family Foundation

Limitations: Giving on a national basis. No grants to individuals; no loans.

589. Institute for Research, Education, and Training in Addictions (IRETA), Pittsburgh, PA. $37,368, 2004. For Medical Student Program in Alcohol and Other Drug Dependencies.

GEORGIA

The Aflac Foundation, Inc.

Limitations: Giving primarily in areas of company operations, with emphasis on the greater Atlanta, GA, area. No support for religious or political organizations. No grants to individuals.

590. Chattahoochee Valley Regional Library System, Columbus, GA. $250,000, 2005. For capital campaign.

The Arthur M. Blank Family Foundation

Limitations: Giving primarily in Maricopa County, AZ, Atlanta, GA, and Beaufort County, SC. No support for government agencies, municipalities, parochial or private schools, or therapeutic programs. No grants to individuals, or for events.

591. Prevent Child Abuse, Bozeman, MT. $30,000, 2005. For Partner Project to Strengthen Families, home-visiting support program that provides parenting education, resource referral, and support of teen parents.

Bradley-Turner Foundation, Inc.

Limitations: Giving primarily in GA, with emphasis on Columbus. No grants to individuals.

592. Muscogee County Library Foundation, Columbus, GA. $125,000, 2004. For capital and operating support.

Community Foundation for Greater Atlanta, Inc.

(formerly Metropolitan Atlanta Community Foundation, Inc.)
Limitations: Giving limited to the 23-county metropolitan area of Atlanta, GA. No support for religious organizations (except through donor-advised funds). No grants to individuals (except for scholarships), or for endowment funds, continuing support, annual campaigns, special fundraising events, deficit financing, long-term research, films, equipment, vehicles, conferences, or fellowships; a limited number of grants for operating budgets.

593. Attachment Parenting International, Nashville, TN. $25,000, 2005.
594. Cherokee Garden Club Library, Atlanta, GA. $19,045, 2005.

Georgia-Pacific Foundation, Inc.

Limitations: Giving limited to areas of company operations. No support for discriminatory organizations, churches or religious denominations, religious or theological schools, social, labor, veterans', alumni, or fraternal organizations, athletic associations, national organizations with local chapters already supported by Georgia-Pacific, medical or nursing schools, pass-through organizations, or political candidates. No grants to individuals (except for scholarships), or for bail-out support, political causes or legislative lobbying or advocacy, advertising, general operating support for United Way member agencies, tickets or tables, academic chairs, fundraising events, trips or tours, or social sciences or health science programs.

595. Thompson Sawyer Public Library, Quanah, TX. $10,000, 2004.

Healthcare Georgia Foundation, Inc.

Limitations: Giving limited to GA. No support for sectarian programs (benefiting only one religious organization). No grants to individuals, or for capital campaigns, or major equipment.

596. Foundation Center, Atlanta, GA. $40,000, 2004. For grant writing workshops for nonprofit health organizations in LaGrange, Thomasville, and Gainesville.

597. PsychSource, Roswell, GA. $25,000, 2004. To expand database to include metropolitan areas of Columbus, Macon, Augusta, Rome, and Athens.

The Marcus Foundation, Inc.

Limitations: Giving primarily in Atlanta, GA. No grants to individuals.

598. Foundation Center, New York, NY. $25,000, 2004. For general operating support.

The UPS Foundation

Limitations: Giving on a national basis and in Canada and Mexico; giving also to statewide, regional, and national organizations. No support for religious organizations not of direct benefit to the entire community. No grants to individuals; generally, no grants for capital campaigns, endowments, or general operating support.

599. Foundation Center, New York, NY. $12,500, 2005.
600. HistoryMakers, The, Chicago, IL. $15,000, 2005.

Robert W. Woodruff Foundation, Inc.

(formerly Trebor Foundation, Inc.)
Limitations: Giving primarily in GA, with emphasis on the metropolitan Atlanta area. No support for churches, denominational programs, or youth

services outside Atlanta, GA. No grants to individuals, or for annual operating support, festivals or performances, films and documentaries, or seed money; no loans.

601. Atlanta University Center, Atlanta, GA. $300,000, 2005. For employment of new management team for Robert W. Woodruff Library.

602. Foundation Center, Atlanta, GA. $250,000, 2005. For continued support for programs.

HAWAII

The Earl & Doris Bakken Foundation
Limitations: Giving primarily in HI, with some emphasis on Kamuela. No grants to individuals.

603. Five Mountains Hawaii, Kamuela, HI. $100,000, 2004. For drug free coalition.

604. Five Mountains Hawaii, Kamuela, HI. $75,000, 2004. For general support.

Harold K. L. Castle Foundation
Limitations: Giving limited to HI with priority given to Windward Oahu. No grants to individuals, or for ongoing operating expenses, endowments, annual fund drives, vehicles, or sponsorships or special events.

605. Bishop Museum, Honolulu, HI. $150,000, 2005. For Hawaiian Newspaper Resource Project, Ho'olaupa'i.

606. Library of Hawaii, Friends of the, Kailua, HI. $70,000, 2005. For renovation and enhancement of patio area of library.

Hawaii Community Foundation
(formerly The Hawaiian Foundation)
Limitations: Giving limited to HI. No support for government agencies or large nonprofit organizations. No grants to individuals (except for scholarships), or for annual campaigns, emergency support, endowments, major capital projects, ongoing operating support, tuition aid programs, or deficit financing; no loans.

607. Five Mountains Hawaii, Kamuela, HI. $25,000, 2004.

HMSA Foundation
(also known as Hawaii Medical Service Association Foundation)
Limitations: Giving primarily in Honolulu, HI. No grants to individuals; or for scholarship funds, lobbying, voter registration, capital projects, endowments, development campaigns or multi-year commitments.

608. Hawaii Health Information Corporation, Honolulu, HI. $98,724, 2004. To develop a statewide patient safety data repository and reporting system.

609. Hawaii Health Information Corporation, Honolulu, HI. $79,423, 2004. For Health Trends in Hawaii, statistical information for health care planners.

IDAHO

CHC Foundation
Limitations: Giving limited to southeastern ID. No grants to individuals or for operating expenses.

610. Clark County District Library, Dubois, ID. $20,000, 2005.

ILLINOIS

Abbott Laboratories Fund
Limitations: Giving primarily in areas of company operations. No support for social, religious, or political organizations. No grants to individuals, or for symposia, conferences, or meetings, ticket purchases, memberships, business-related purposes, or marketing sponsorships.

611. Fundacion Luis Munoz Marin, San Juan, PR. $10,000, 2004.

Aon Foundation
(formerly Combined International Foundation)
Limitations: Giving on a national basis. No grants for secondary educational institution or vocational school operating support.

612. Abraham Lincoln Presidential Library Foundation, Springfield, IL. $50,000, 2004.

613. HistoryMakers, The, Chicago, IL. $25,000, 2004.

BP Foundation, Inc.
(formerly BP Amoco Foundation, Inc.)
Limitations: Giving on a national and international basis. No support for religious, fraternal, political, social, or athletic organizations; generally, no support for organizations already receiving general operating support through the United Way. No grants to individuals, or for endowments, medical research, publications, or conferences.

614. Charities Aid Foundation (UK), West Malling, England. $2,899,944, 2004. For unrestricted support.

615. Charities Aid Foundation (UK), West Malling, England. $250,000, 2004. For unrestricted support for Breslan.

616. Women at Work, Pasadena, CA. $12,500, 2004. For unrestricted support.

Burlington Northern Santa Fe Foundation
(formerly Santa Fe Pacific Foundation)
Limitations: Giving limited to areas of company operations in the Midwest, North, Northwest, Southeast, Southwest, and West. No support for religious organizations not of direct benefit to the entire community, public educational institutions or preschool, primary, or secondary educational institutions, political, fraternal, or veterans' organizations, national health or cultural organizations, or community and other grantmaking foundations. No grants to individuals (except for scholarships), or for conferences, seminars, travel, testimonial dinners, endowments, capital campaigns, salary wages, administrative expenses, computer-related projects, or television or film production.

617. Fort Worth Public Library Foundation, Fort Worth, TX. $10,000, 2004.

Caterpillar Foundation
Limitations: Giving primarily in areas of company operations. No support for fraternal organizations, religious organizations not of direct benefit to the entire community, or United Way-supported organizations. No grants to individuals, or for general operating support, tickets or advertising for fundraising benefits, or political activities.

618. Abraham Lincoln Presidential Library Foundation, Springfield, IL. $200,000, 2004.

619. Aurora Public Library Foundation, Aurora, IL. $10,000, 2004.

620. Everett McKinley Dirksen Endowment Fund, Pekin, IL. $26,000, 2004.

Chase Foundation
(formerly Bank One Foundation)
Limitations: Giving primarily in areas of company operations in AZ, DE, IL, MI, OH, and WI, with emphasis on the metropolitan Chicago, IL, area. No support for religious or fraternal organizations, preschool, elementary, or secondary schools, public agencies, or United Way/Crusade of Mercy-supported agencies (except for community/neighborhood organizations working in the areas of housing or commercial or industrial development). No grants to individuals, or for multi-year capital or operating pledges (except for program-related investments).

621. Abraham Lincoln Presidential Library Foundation, Springfield, IL. $33,334, 2004.

622. Columbus Metropolitan Library Foundation, Columbus, OH. $30,000, 2004.

623. Family and Workplace Connection, Wilmington, DE. $55,000, 2004.

624. Home Buyers Round Table of Dane County, Madison, WI. $10,000, 2004.

625. Indianapolis-Marion County Public Library Foundation, Indianapolis, IN. $74,900, 2004.

626. Milwaukee Public Library Foundation, Milwaukee, WI. $10,000, 2004.

The Chicago Community Trust

Limitations: Giving primarily in Cook County and the adjacent 5 counties of northeastern, IL. No support for religious purposes. No grants to individuals (except for limited fellowship programs), or for annual campaigns, deficit financing, endowment funds, publications, conferences, or scholarships; no support for the purchase of computer hardware; no general operating support for agencies or institutions whose program activities substantially duplicate those already undertaken by others.

627. Coordinated Advice and Referral Program for Legal Services, Chicago, IL. $12,000, 2005. For continued support for Domestic Relations Self-Help Desk.

628. Donors Forum of Chicago, Chicago, IL. $40,000, 2005. For evaluation of overall impact on programs, continued support of South Metropolitan Philanthropy Center and exploration of Philanthropy Center in Lake County.

629. Donors Forum of Chicago, Chicago, IL. $25,000, 2005. For general operating support.

630. Donors Forum of Chicago, Chicago, IL. $10,000, 2005. For Management/Organizational Development support to enable Donors Forum to be regional partner for national survey of nonprofit executives.

631. Leap Learning Systems, Chicago, IL. $200,000, 2005. To expand curriculum and professional development support in pre-school classrooms in Chicago Public Schools, and to conduct research.

632. Metropolitan Chicago Information Center, Chicago, IL. $70,000, 2005. For online public information resources and member services.

633. Metropolitan Chicago Information Center, Chicago, IL. $25,000, 2005. For Fellows Alumni Program.

634. Metropolitan Chicago Information Center, Chicago, IL. $24,990, 2005. To gather demographic and economic data to be used in strategic planning in Basic Human Needs and Community Development programs.

635. National Organization of Nurses with Disabilities, Morton Grove, IL. $35,000, 2005. For Regional Demonstration Project to establish Internet-based resource clearinghouse to address nursing and disability issues.

636. University of Illinois at Chicago, Library of Health Sciences, Chicago, IL. $17,000, 2005. For acquisition of books and journals in field of dermatology.

Arie and Ida Crown Memorial

Limitations: Giving primarily in metropolitan Chicago, IL. No support for government-sponsored programs. No grants to individuals, or for consulting services, conferences, or film or documentary projects; no loans.

637. Donors Forum of Chicago, Chicago, IL. $24,300, 2004.

638. Survivors of the Shoah Visual History Foundation, Los Angeles, CA. $50,000, 2004.

John Deere Foundation

Limitations: Giving primarily in areas of company operations in IL, IA, NC, and WI. No support for religious organizations, athletic organizations, political organizations, foundations, tax-supported organizations, or fraternal organizations or sororities. No grants to individuals, or for sports programs, political campaigns, advertising, or marketing; no loans.

639. Abraham Lincoln Presidential Library Foundation, Springfield, IL. $200,000, 2005.

Dillon Foundation

Limitations: Giving primarily in the Sterling, IL, area. No grants to individuals; no loans.

640. Sterling Public Library, Sterling, IL. $33,100, 2005.

Joseph and Bessie Feinberg Foundation

Limitations: Giving primarily in IL. No grants to individuals.

641. Donors Forum of Chicago, Chicago, IL. $15,300, 2005.

Lloyd A. Fry Foundation

Limitations: Giving generally limited to Chicago, IL. No support for medical research, religious purposes, governmental bodies, or tax-supported educational institutions for services that fall within their responsibilities. No grants to individuals, or for general operating support for new grantees, annual campaigns, emergency funds, deficit financing, building funds, fundraising benefits, land acquisition, renovation projects, or endowment funds; no loans.

642. Donors Forum of Chicago, Chicago, IL. $18,539, 2005. For unrestricted support.

643. Leap Learning Systems, Chicago, IL. $10,000, 2005. For Preschool Language and Literacy Curriculum Training at Saint Basil.

644. Newberry Library, Chicago, IL. $30,000, 2005. For Teachers as Scholars Program.

Grand Victoria Foundation

Limitations: Giving limited to IL, with emphasis on the Chicago metropolitan area, Elgin, and southern Cook, DeKalb, DuPage, Kane, Kendall, Lake, McHenry, Winnebago, and Will counties. No support for grantmaking organizations or federated funds. No grants to individuals, or for endowments, fundraising events, debt reduction, political campaigns, or religious programs; generally, no support for research or planning projects.

645. Child Care Resource and Referral, Chicago, IL. $35,000, 2005. For program support.

646. Child Care Resource and Referral, Chicago, IL. $32,800, 2005. For program support.

647. Donors Forum of Chicago, Chicago, IL. $10,483, 2005. For membership.

648. Illinois Network of Child Care Resource and Referral Agencies, Bloomington, IL. $75,000, 2005. For program support.

649. Prairie Rivers Network, Champaign, IL. $20,000, 2005. For program support.

The Irving Harris Foundation

(formerly The Harris Foundation)

650. Donors Forum of Chicago, Chicago, IL. $14,577, 2004. For institutional support.

Illinois Tool Works Foundation

Limitations: Giving primarily in areas of company operations, with emphasis on Chicago, IL. No grants to individuals (except for employee-related scholarships), or for endowments or research; no loans.

651. Newberry Library, Chicago, IL. $10,000, 2005. For general operating support.

The Joyce Foundation

Limitations: Giving primarily in the Great Lakes region, including IA, IL, IN, MI, MN, OH, and WI; limited number of environment grants made in Canada; culture grants restricted to the metropolitan Chicago, IL, area. No support for religious activities. No grants for endowment campaigns, scholarships, direct service programs, or capital proposals.

652. Center for Governmental Studies, Los Angeles, CA. $200,000, 2005. 2-year grant. To implement next phase of PolicyArchive.Net, Internet-based archive of public policy research which will initially collect and disseminate summaries and full texts of foundation-funded policy research through subject indexes, internal search engine, research abstracts, information on researchers and funders, email notifications of new research and user-generated research reviews.

653. Donors Forum of Chicago, Chicago, IL. $24,300, 2005. For membership.

654. Donors Forum of Chicago, Chicago, IL. $20,000, 2005. To expand geographic reach and ongoing public policy work.

655. Donors Forum of Chicago, Chicago, IL. $10,000, 2005. For public policy work.

656. Foundation Center, New York, NY. $20,000, 2005. For program support.

657. Global Philanthropy Partnership, Chicago, IL. $10,000, 2005. For workshop to bring together business, government, NGO, and union leaders to discuss short and long-term steps to address climate change from Midwest perspective.

658. HistoryMakers, The, Chicago, IL. $50,000, 2005. For salary of Director of Development to manage fundraising activities.

659. State and Territorial Injury Prevention Directors Association, Atlanta, GA. $20,000, 2005. To conduct educational forum regarding National Violent Death Reporting Systems (NVDRS) for all national partners of program.

Ann and Robert H. Lurie Foundation

(formerly Ann and Robert H. Lurie Family Foundation)
Limitations: Giving primarily in Chicago, IL, and MI. No grants to individuals.

660. Chicago Public Library Foundation, Chicago, IL. $50,000, 2004. For unrestricted support.

John D. and Catherine T. MacArthur Foundation

Limitations: Giving on a national and international basis, with emphasis on Chicago, IL. No support for religious programs, political activities or campaigns. No grants for capital or endowment funds, equipment purchases, plant construction, conferences, publications, debt retirement, development campaigns, fundraising appeals, tuition expenses, scholarships, or fellowships (other than those sponsored by the foundation).

661. American Library Association, Office for Information Technology Policy, DC. $630,000, 2005. 3-year grant. For research project on implications of digital copyright for libraries and their patrons.

662. Center for Information Research, Institute of the USA and Canada, Moscow, Russia. $70,000, 2005. 2-year grant. To develop and maintain publicly accessible electronic Web site with full collection of European Court for Human Rights documents, with Russian-language search tools.

663. Columbia University, Center for Human Rights Documentation and Research, New York, NY. $100,000, 2005. To establish Center to house archives of leading human rights organizations.

664. Duke University, School of Medicine, Services Effectiveness Research Program, Durham, NC. $450,000, 2005. 3-year grant. For research on virtual resource center for Psychiatric Advance Directives.

665. Foundation Center, New York, NY. $200,000, 2005. 3-year grant. For general operating support.

666. JSTOR, New York, NY. $122,000, 2005. 5-year grant. To extend access to scholarly resources in humanities and social sciences to Nigeria's research and higher education institutions.

667. Metropolitan Chicago Information Center, Chicago, IL. $900,000, 2005. 3-year grant. To assemble and analyze data about Chicago neighborhoods.

668. National Center for Victims of Crime, DC. $167,000, 2005. For national panel on ethical issues that may arise when using innovative technology to reduce crime and improve neighborhood safety.

669. National Low Income Housing Coalition and Low Income Housing Information Service, DC. $450,000, 2005. 3-year grant. For general operating support.

670. OMG Center for Collaborative Learning, Philadelphia, PA. $23,000, 2005. For final manuscript preparation of Anatomy of an Initiative that Worked, manual for comprehensive community developers.

671. Russia Donors Forum, Moscow, Russia. $120,000, 2005. 3-year grant. For communications and public relations activities aimed at enhancing strategy development and promoting positive public relations toward philanthropy in Russia.

672. Saratov Legal Reform Project, Saratov, Russia. $650,000, 2005. 3-year grant. For work on reform of legal science, practice, and education in Russia.

673. Shehu Musa Yaradua Foundation, Abuja, Nigeria. $50,000, 2005. For purchase of books and materials for Olusegun Obasanjo Research Library.

674. University of Illinois at Urbana-Champaign, Urbana, IL. $303,000, 2005. 3-year grant. To improve user access to research and information materials at university libraries in Illinois.

675. William K. Sullivan Elementary School, Chicago, IL. $10,000, 2005. For professional development programs for teachers, and to provide curriculum materials for Stock Market Game and books to augment classroom libraries.

The Offield Family Foundation

Limitations: Giving primarily in AZ, CA, the Chicago, IL, area and MI. No grants to individuals.

676. Harbor Springs Library, Harbor Springs, MI. $10,000, 2005.

Frank E. Payne and Seba B. Payne Foundation

Limitations: Giving primarily in Bethlehem, PA. No grants to individuals, or for fellowships; generally no support for endowments; no loans.

677. Bethlehem Area Public Library, Bethlehem, PA. $148,365, 2005.

Polk Bros. Foundation, Inc.

Limitations: Giving primarily in Chicago, IL. No support for political organizations or religious institutions seeking support for programs whose participants are restricted by religious affiliation, or for tax-generating entities (municipalities and school districts) for services within their normal responsibilities. No grants to individuals, or for medical, scientific or academic research, or purchase of dinner or raffle tickets.

678. Citizens Information Service of Illinois, Chicago, IL. $15,000, 2005.

679. Coordinated Advice and Referral Program for Legal Services, Chicago, IL. $40,000, 2005.

680. Donors Forum of Chicago, Chicago, IL. $24,300, 2005.

681. Donors Forum of Chicago, Chicago, IL. $20,000, 2005.

682. Newberry Library, Chicago, IL. $45,000, 2005.

Prince Charitable Trusts

Limitations: Giving limited to local groups in Washington, DC, Chicago, IL, and RI, with emphasis on Aquidneck Island. No support for national organizations. No grants to individuals.

683. Redwood Library and Athenaeum, Newport, RI. $50,000, 2004. For capital campaign.

684. Redwood Library and Athenaeum, Newport, RI. $50,000, 2004. For capital campaign.

685. Redwood Library and Athenaeum, Newport, RI. $15,000, 2004. For operating support.

Michael Reese Health Trust

(formerly Michael Reese Hospital Foundation)
Limitations: Giving limited to the metropolitan Chicago, IL, area with emphasis on the city of Chicago. No support for private foundations. No grants to individuals, or for capital campaigns, endowment funds, fundraising events, debt reduction, or scholarships.

686. Donors Forum of Chicago, Chicago, IL. $10,000, 2005. For Chicago's participation in Executive Leadership Survey, survey of local nonprofit leadership to determine future needs in nonprofit sector.

687. Gilead Outreach and Referral Center for the Medically Uninsured, Chicago, IL. $35,000, 2005. To connect uninsured individuals to health care benefits or resources for which they are eligible and to work with Logan Square Neighborhood Association to train health outreach workers to enroll people in neighborhoods.

688. Hektoen Institute for Medical Research, Chicago, IL. $30,000, 2005. To increase patient access to specialty care by expanding Cook County Bureau of Health Services' electronic referral system to Sengstacke Specialty Care Center at Provident Hospital on south side of Chicago.

689. Night Ministry, Chicago, IL. $25,000, 2005. For bus that cruises streets at night to provide services to homeless individuals, mostly youth; services include crisis intervention and linkages to community health care providers with goals to change risky behavior and increase number of youth receiving health services.

The Retirement Research Foundation

Limitations: Giving limited to the Midwest (IA, IL, IN, KY, MO, WI) and FL for direct service projects not having the potential of national impact. No support for governmental agencies (except area agencies on aging). No grants to individuals, or for computers, construction, general operating expenses of established organizations, endowment or developmental campaigns, emergency funds, deficit financing, land acquisition, publications, conferences, scholarships, media productions, dissertation research, annual campaigns, or biomedical research. Publications and conference support is generally limited to those which are components of larger foundation funded projects.

690. Benjamin Rose Institute, Cleveland, OH. $245,119, 2005. 2.50-year grant. For Enhancing the Role of Older Adults in Research and Care Planning.

691. Foundation Center, New York, NY. $10,000, 2005. For program support.

692. Generations on Line, Philadelphia, PA. $25,000, 2005. For program, Helping Older Adults in Milwaukee County Help Themselves to Access Services and Information Affecting Health and Wellbeing.

693. Gerontological Society of America, DC. $64,811, 2005. 2-year grant. For Online Clearinghouse for Internships in Aging.

694. Institute for Americas Future, DC. $25,000, 2005. For Social Security Information Project.

695. Institute for Womens Policy Research, DC. $30,000, 2005. For Social Security Education Project.

696. National Citizens Coalition for Nursing Home Reform, DC. $87,955, 2005. For Giving Voice to Quality: consumer education project to equip nursing home residents and their families.

697. Pension Rights Center, DC. $250,000, 2005. 2-year grant. For National Pension Assistance Resource Center.

Sara Lee Foundation
Limitations: Giving primarily in areas of company operations, with emphasis on the greater metropolitan Chicago, IL, area. No support for organizations with an accumulated deficit, organizations with a limited constituency, religious organizations not of direct benefit to the entire community, political or lobbying organizations, government units, disease-specific hospitals or health organizations, community development corporations, or discriminatory organizations. No grants for sports-related events or sponsorships.

698. Charities Aid Foundation (CAF) America, Alexandria, VA. $25,000, 2005. For general operating support.

699. Charities Aid Foundation (CAF) America, Alexandria, VA. $25,000, 2005. For general operating support.

700. Donors Forum of Chicago, Chicago, IL. $35,000, 2005. For Great Governance Series.

701. Illinois Arts Alliance Foundation, Chicago, IL. $20,000, 2005. For Mentor Connection Referral Service.

702. Newberry Library, Chicago, IL. $50,000, 2005. For Lewis and Clark and the Indian Country exhibit.

703. Newberry Library, Chicago, IL. $50,000, 2005. For Lewis and Clark and the Indian Country exhibit.

Dr. Scholl Foundation
Limitations: Giving primarily in the U.S., with some emphasis on the Chicago, IL area. No support for public education, political organizations, or political action committees. No grants to individuals, or for deficit financing, or unrestricted purposes, or to endowments, or capital campaigns, event sponsorship, liquidation of debt; no loans.

704. Newberry Library, Chicago, IL. $10,000, 2004. For Scholl Center for Family and Community History.

The Spencer Foundation
Limitations: Giving on a national and international basis. No grants to individuals (except those working under the auspices of an institution), or for capital funds, general purposes, operating or continuing support, sabbatical supplements, work in instructional or curriculum development, any kind of training or service program, scholarships, travel fellowships, endowment funds, or pre-doctoral research; no loans.

705. Donors Forum of Chicago, Chicago, IL. $25,000, 2005. For membership renewal.

706. Foundation Center, New York, NY. $27,500, 2005. For annual support.

707. Library of Congress, DC. $22,000, 2005. For conference, Stories of Our Nation, Footprints of Our Souls': What History Textbooks Convey to Middle School and High School Audiences.

State Farm Companies Foundation
Limitations: Giving on a national basis and in Canada. No support for teams or clubs, political organizations, or religious organizations. No grants to individuals (except for Doctoral Dissertation Awards and scholarships), or for one-time events, capital campaigns, or banquets, tours, or competitions.

708. Educational Information and Resource Center, Sewell, NJ. $10,000, 2005.

INDIANA

George and Frances Ball Foundation
Limitations: Giving primarily in Muncie and Delaware County, IN. No support for religious or political organizations. No grants to individuals.

709. Muncie Public Library, Muncie, IN. $50,000, 2005. For renovations at Kennedy branch.

710. Muncie Public Library, Muncie, IN. $40,000, 2005. For matching grant.

Allen Whitehill Clowes Charitable Foundation, Inc.
Limitations: Giving primarily in central IN. No grants for endowments.

711. Indianapolis-Marion County Public Library Foundation, Indianapolis, IN. $4,000,000, 2005. For library expansion.

Dekko Foundation, Inc.
Limitations: Giving primarily in Limestone County, AL; Clarke, Decatur, Lucas, Ringgold, and Union counties, IA; and DeKalb, Kosciousko, LaGrange, Noble, Steuben, and Whitley counties, IN. No grants to individuals.

712. Clearfield Public Library, Clearfield, IA. $20,000, 2005. For building improvements.

713. First Christian Academy, Kendallville, IN. $10,000, 2005. For library.

714. Gibson Memorial Library, Creston, IA. $30,000, 2005. For operating support.

715. Kendallville Public Library, Kendallville, IN. $846,111, 2005. For building project.

716. North Webster Tippecanoe Township Library, North Webster, IN. $75,000, 2005. For operating support.

717. Right Side Foundation, Columbia City, IN. $10,000, 2005. For Library Support.

718. Warsaw Christian School, Warsaw, IN. $10,000, 2005. For library.

719. Warsaw Community Public Library, Warsaw, IN. $25,000, 2005. For library.

English-Bonter-Mitchell Foundation
Limitations: Giving primarily in Fort Wayne, IN. No grants to individuals.

720. Taylor University, Fort Wayne, IN. $75,000, 2004. For library.

Richard M. Fairbanks Foundation, Inc.
(formerly Fairbanks Foundation, Inc.)
Limitations: Giving primarily in greater Indianapolis, IN. No support for political organizations. No grants to individuals.

721. Indiana Health Information Exchange, Indianapolis, IN. $2,000,000, 2005. For development of clinical quality support services.

Eugene and Marilyn Glick Foundation Corporation
Limitations: Giving primarily in Indianapolis, IN. No grants to individuals.

722. Indianapolis-Marion County Public Library Foundation, Indianapolis, IN. $33,334, 2005. For computer training lab.

Eli Lilly and Company Foundation
Limitations: Giving on a national and international basis, with emphasis on areas of company operations, including Indianapolis, IN. No support for religious or sectarian organizations not of direct benefit to the entire community, fraternal, labor, athletic, or veterans' organizations or bands, or non-accredited educational organizations. No grants to individuals, or for scholarships or travel, endowments, debt reduction, beauty or talent contests, fundraising activities related to individual sponsorship, conferences or media production, or memorials; no loans; no political contributions.

723. Indianapolis-Marion County Public Library Foundation, Indianapolis, IN. $200,000, 2004. For renovation and expansion of library.

724. Laura Bush Foundation for Americas Libraries, DC. $10,000, 2004.

725. National Coalition for Cancer Survivorship, Silver Spring, MD. $100,000, 2004. To increase distribution of Cancer Survivor Toolbox.

726. Sycamore School, Indianapolis, IN. $50,000, 2004. To expand school's library, add informal theater, and purchase portable planetarium to be used with Oaks Academy.

Lilly Endowment Inc.

Limitations: Giving limited to IN, with emphasis on Indianapolis, for community development projects (including the arts, preservation, capital building funds, operating funds, and social services). Education funding focused principally on Indiana under invitational grant programs. National giving in religion, philanthropic studies, leadership education, and selected higher education initiatives, principally to increase educational opportunities for minorities. Generally, no support for healthcare programs, or mass media projects; libraries, elementary/secondary schools or for human service projects. No grants to individuals (except for fellowships awarded under special programs) or endowments (except for community foundations in Indiana or in the context of special initiatives) or for building campaigns or operating funds.

727. Alban Institute, Bethesda, MD. $1,500,000, 2005. For organizational development efforts.

728. American Academy of Religion, Atlanta, GA. $150,000, 2005. For Religionsource, referral service that links journalists with experts on religion and public life issues.

729. American Theological Library Association, Chicago, IL. $257,700, 2005. To enhance ATLAS infrastructure.

730. Foundation Center, New York, NY. $125,000, 2005. For General operating support.

731. Fund for Theological Education, Atlanta, GA. $5,999,075, 2005. For strategic programs with congregations.

732. Indiana Grantmakers Alliance Foundation, Indianapolis, IN. $100,000, 2005. For development of website and collection and consolidation of data needed by Indiana nonprofit organizations.

733. Indiana University Foundation, Bloomington, IN. $500,000, 2005. For planning grant for statewide data management initiative.

734. Indianapolis Center for Congregations, Indianapolis, IN. $8,171,433, 2005. For operating support.

735. International Center of Indianapolis, Indianapolis, IN. $300,000, 2005. For general operating support.

736. Philanthropic Research, Inc., Williamsburg, VA. $50,000, 2005. For General operating support.

737. Philanthropy Roundtable, DC. $25,000, 2005. For general operating support.

Lincoln Financial Group Foundation

(formerly The Lincoln National Foundation, Inc.)

Limitations: Giving limited to areas of company operations, with emphasis on Hartford, CT, Schaumburg and the Chicago, IL, area, Fort Wayne, IN, Portland, ME, Omaha, NE, Concord, NH, Greensboro, NC, Philadelphia, PA, and London, United Kingdom. No support for religious or political organizations, public or private elementary or secondary schools or school foundations, hospitals, hospital foundations, or nursing homes, veterans' or fraternal organizations, or pass-through organizations. No grants to individuals, or for endowments, continuing support, general operating support, debt reduction, marketing programs, sporting events or tournaments, or fundraising for national organizations; generally, no grants for tickets, corporate tables, or testimonial events.

738. Free Library of Philadelphia Foundation, Philadelphia, PA. $20,000, 2005. For Reader Development Program Materials.

739. League for the Blind and Disabled, Fort Wayne, IN. $30,000, 2005. For information and referral program.

Lumina Foundation for Education, Inc.

Limitations: Giving on a national basis. No support for K-12 education reform, discipline-specific schools of study and training or religious activities (except for activities that promote educational access and success and that serve diverse recipients without regard to their religious background). No grants to individuals (except for employee matching gifts), or for scholarships, fundraisers, corporate sponsorships, meetings and conferences (except for those related to a strategic initiative of the foundation), capital campaigns, or endowment funds.

740. Education Resources Institute, Higher Education Information Center, Boston, MA. $500,000, 2005. 3-year grant. To support Pathways to College Network in developing and executing media campaign to improve college access and success.

741. INDEPENDENT SECTOR, DC. $75,000, 2005. To convene independent panel of experts to inform and advise the US Senate Finance Committee concerning nonprofit sector.

742. Indiana University, IUPUI Center on Philanthropy, Indianapolis, IN. $248,100, 2005. 3-year grant. To build scholarship and leadership in philanthropy.

743. Indianapolis Black Alumni Council, Indianapolis, IN. $10,000, 2005. For Black College Fair held during Circle City Classic.

Nina Mason Pulliam Charitable Trust

Limitations: Giving primarily in Phoenix, AZ, and Indianapolis, IN. No grants to individuals, or for academic research, non-operating private foundations, or international activities.

744. Body Positive, Phoenix, AZ. $150,000, 2005. To increase staff capacity and reduce waiting list for clinical services caused by increase in clients from closing of AIDS Project Arizona.

745. Information and Referral Network, Indianapolis, IN. $80,000, 2005. To extend statewide 211 system in Indiana from 12 to 24 hours.

IOWA

AEGON Transamerica Foundation

(formerly AEGON USA Charitable Foundation, Inc.)

Limitations: Giving on a national basis, with emphasis on areas of company operations. No grants to individuals.

746. Library Foundation, Louisville, KY. $10,000, 2005.

Martin Bucksbaum Family Foundation

(formerly Bucksbaum Foundation)

Limitations: Giving primarily in IA and NY. No grants to individuals.

747. Survivors of the Shoah Visual History Foundation, Los Angeles, CA. $25,000, 2004.

Roy J. Carver Charitable Trust

Limitations: Giving primarily in IA. No support for religious activities or political organizations. No grants to individuals, or for endowments, fundraising benefits, program advertising, annual operating support.

748. Columbus Community Civic Center Foundation, Columbus Junction, IA. $60,000, 2005. To construct and furnish combined library and civic center.

749. Coralville Public Library Foundation, Coralville, IA. $60,000, 2005. For renovation and expansion of library.

750. Cornell College, Mount Vernon, IA. $47,400, 2005. For development of academic counseling and library services.

751. Davenport Public Library, Davenport, IA. $60,000, 2005. To construct two new branch facilities.

752. Elberon Public Library, Elberon, IA. $18,760, 2005. To construct new library addition to community building.

753. Friends of Burlington Public Library Foundation, Burlington, IA. $60,000, 2005. For construction of new library.

754. Hull Public Library, Hull, IA. $60,000, 2005. To construct new library.

755. Humeston Public Library, Humeston, IA. $30,000, 2005. For construction of new library.

756. Malvern Public Library, Malvern, IA. $60,000, 2005. To construct addition to and remodel library.

757. Marengo Public Library, Friends of the, Marengo, IA. $60,000, 2005. For renovation and expansion of library.

758. Massena, Town of, Massena, IA. $32,000, 2005. To renovate building to house library.

759. Monroe Public Library, Friends of the, Monroe, IA. $60,000, 2005. For remodeling of building to house library.

760. Oelwein Public Library, Oelwein, IA. $60,000, 2005. To construct new library.

761. Rowan, City of, Rowan, IA. $20,000, 2005. To construct new library and community center.
762. Sigourney Public Library, Sigourney, IA. $60,000, 2005. To renovate building for relocation of library.
763. Springville Memorial Library, Springville, IA. $60,000, 2005. For construction of new library.
764. University of Iowa, Iowa City, IA. $118,977, 2005. To expand educational technology center within main library.
765. Waldorf College, Forest City, IA. $50,000, 2005. To expand business, biology and education collections at Luise V. Hanson Library.

V. O. Figge and Elizebeth Kahl Figge Charitable Foundation
Limitations: Giving primarily in IA.
766. Le Claire Community Library, Le Claire, IA. $10,000, 2004.

The Hall-Perrine Foundation, Inc.
(formerly The Hall Foundation, Inc.)
Limitations: Giving limited to Linn County, IA. No support for churches or their programs, or for elementary or secondary schools. No grants to individuals, or for deficit financing, endowment funds, continuing operating support, benefits, special events, conferences, or fellowships; no loans.
767. National Czech and Slovak Museum and Library, Cedar Rapids, IA. $16,000, 2005. For security system.

The John K. & Luise V. Hanson Foundation
(formerly The Hanson Foundation)
Limitations: Giving primarily in north central IA. No support for religious organizations, or political organizations. No grants to individuals.
768. Waldorf College, Forest City, IA. $575,000, 2005. For library.
769. Waldorf College, Forest City, IA. $400,000, 2005. For library project.

Iowa West Foundation
Limitations: Giving primarily in southwest IA and the Council Bluffs, Omaha, NE, area. No support for medical research or church-affiliated organizations for religious purposes. No grants to individuals, or for scholarships (except for foundation scholarship programs) fundraising, benefit, and social events, capital requests (for improvements to school property or for hospitals, medical facilities, assisted living projects, nursing homes, independent care, and extended care facilities), publications, films, books, seminars, symposia or for conferences.
770. Council Bluffs Public Library, Council Bluffs, IA. $25,000, 2004. To expand collection and authors visits.
771. Irwin, City of, Irwin, IA. $10,000, 2004. For construction of new library.
772. Massena, City of, Massena, NY. $31,000, 2004. For renovations to public library.
773. Nebraska Jewish Historical Society, Omaha, NE. $25,000, 2004. To archive Council Bluffs and Western Iowa collection.

Principal Financial Group Foundation, Inc.
Limitations: Giving limited to Des Moines, IA, and areas of company operations in Phoenix, AZ, Middletown, CT, Wilmington, DE, Cedar Falls, Mason City, Ottumwa, and Pella, IA, Indianapolis, IN, Grand Island, NE, Spokane, WA, and Appleton, WI. No support for political, sectarian, religious, or denominational organizations, athletic organizations, fraternal organizations, individual K-12 schools, libraries, pass-through organizations, private foundations, social organizations, tax-supported city, county, or state organizations, trade, industry, and/or professional associations, United Way organizations for United Way-funded programs, or veterans' groups. No grants to individuals, or for conference or seminar attendance, courtesy or goodwill advertising in benefit publications, endowments or memorials, fellowships, festival participation, or hospital or health care facility drives or capital campaigns.
774. Des Moines Public Library Foundation, Des Moines, IA. $300,000, 2004.

Rockwell Collins Charitable Corporation
Limitations: Giving on a national and international basis in areas of company operations, with emphasis on Pomona, San Jose, and Tustin, CA, Melbourne, FL, IA, Portland, OR, and Richardson, TX. No support for private foundations, religious organizations not of direct benefit to the entire community, or fraternal or social organizations. No grants to individuals, or for endowments, debt reduction, or federated campaigns.
775. Coralville Public Library, Coralville, IA. $35,000, 2005. For renovations and expansion.
776. National Czech and Slovak Museum and Library, Cedar Rapids, IA. $10,000, 2005. For Garnet Exhibit.

KANSAS

Israel Henry Beren Charitable Trust
Limitations: Giving primarily in NY; some giving also in Israel. No grants to individuals.
777. Chabad Lubavitch of North Broward and Palm Beach Counties, Coral Spring, FL. $18,000, 2004. For library and improvements.
778. Machon Chana Womens Institute, Brooklyn, NY. $50,000, 2004. For library and new building.

Capitol Federal Foundation
Limitations: Giving limited to major metropolitan areas of central and northeastern KS.
779. Kansas Association of Child Care Resources and Referral Agencies, Salina, KS. $10,000, 2004.

Kansas Health Foundation
(formerly Kansas Health Foundation/Kansas Health Trust)
Limitations: Giving limited to KS. No grants to individuals.
780. Foundation Center, New York, NY. $10,000, 2004. To analyze and disseminate information nationally about the field of philanthropy.
781. Kansas Association of Child Care Resources and Referral Agencies, Salina, KS. $25,000, 2004. To provide professional development training for child care staff on providing support to parents, developmental guidance and effective referrals for assistance when indicated.
782. Kansas Health Institute, Topeka, KS. $400,000, 2004. To increase collaboration and training in field of public health informatics to enhance availability of public health data.
783. Kansas Health Institute, Topeka, KS. $300,000, 2004. To assess current public health informatics systems and to recommend future needs.
784. Unified School District No. 259, Wichita, KS. $25,000, 2004. For Woodland Health and Wellness Magnet Elementary School for library books, tutor and parent-involvement materials, art supplies, and student computers.
785. United Way of the Plains, Wichita, KS. $300,000, 2004. To support development of statewide 211 Call Center to provide Kansans with information and services in times of crisis.

KENTUCKY

The C.E. and S. Foundation, Inc.
Limitations: Giving primarily in Louisville, KY. No support for medical research organizations, or for political organizations. No grants to individuals.
786. Louisville Free Public Library Foundation, Louisville, KY. $25,000, 2004. For phase II of Iroquois Library's programming with international populations.
787. Louisville Free Public Library Foundation, Louisville, KY. $10,000, 2004. For children's literacy programs.
788. Middlebury College, Middlebury, VT. $150,000, 2004. For new library.

E.ON U.S. Foundation

(formerly LG&E Energy Foundation, Inc.)

Limitations: Giving primarily in areas of company operations in KY. No support for political, fraternal, labor, or religious organizations or United Way or Fund for the Arts agencies. No grants to individuals, or for pageants or travel expenses, capital campaigns, medical research or disease campaigns/walks, or athletic sponsorships.

789. Trimble County Public Library, Bedford, KY. $13,500, 2004. For program support.

Mildred V. Horn Foundation

Limitations: Giving primarily in KY (for homeless shelters and education) and historic homes open to the public in KY, IL, IN, MO, OH, TN, VA, and WV. No grants to individuals.

790. Louisville Free Public Library Foundation, Louisville, KY. $66,035, 2005. For development software and director retention.

The Humana Foundation, Inc.

Limitations: Giving on a national and international basis in areas of company operations, with emphasis on Louisville, KY. No support for social, labor, political, veterans', or fraternal organizations. No grants for start up needs, lobbying efforts, or general operating support for religious organizations, construction or renovation of sanctuaries, or mission-focused activities.

791. Louisville Free Public Library Foundation, Louisville, KY. $15,000, 2005. For children's summer reading program.

792. Middlebury College, Middlebury, VT. $150,000, 2005. For capital campaign for new library.

793. University of Kentucky, Lexington, KY. $200,000, 2005. For W. T. Young Library.

The J & L Foundation

(formerly The Joan and Lee Thomas Foundation, Inc.)

Limitations: Giving primarily in Louisville, KY. No grants to individuals.

794. Louisville Free Public Library Foundation, Louisville, KY. $15,000, 2005.

Yum! Brands Foundation

(formerly Tricon Foundation, Inc.)

Limitations: Giving on a national basis, with some emphasis on Louisville, KY.

795. Library Foundation, Louisville, KY. $25,025, 2004.

LOUISIANA

Baptist Community Ministries

Limitations: Giving primarily in Jefferson, Orleans, Plaquemines, St. Bernard, and St. Tammany parishes, LA. No grants to individuals.

796. Greater New Orleans Knowledge Works, New Orleans, LA. $379,908, 2004.

Baton Rouge Area Foundation

Limitations: Giving limited to the Baton Rouge, LA, area, including East Baton Rouge, West Baton Rouge, Livingston, Ascension, Iberville, Pointe Coupee, East Feliciana, and West Feliciana parishes. No grants to individuals (except for scholarships), or for continuing support, annual campaigns, deficit financing, fellowships, or operating budgets.

797. Chamber of Commerce, Greater Baton Rouge, Baton Rouge, LA. $21,977, 2005. For displaced residents acclimate to Baton Rouge and return to stable and appropriate positions as quickly as possible by offering Welcome to Baton Rouge Kits that include area maps and listings of local attractions, schools and universities, intramural sports opportunities, churches, and employers seeking new employees.

798. East Baton Rouge Parish Public Library, Baton Rouge, LA. $16,122, 2005. For Hurricane Katrina for staffing the facility for six months with a library technician and library aide.

799. Family Service of Greater Baton Rouge, Baton Rouge, LA. $43,658, 2005. For Hurricane Katrina for coordinating appropriate referrals and linkages through the use of intake and assessment information, providing mental health counseling to displaced individuals at shelters and other venues, offering mental health training for working with children and families, and providing direct support and therapeutic services to other mental health professionals who may be suffering from stress and disaster fatigue..

800. Louisiana Family Recovery Corps, Baton Rouge, LA. $197,000, 2005. For Hurricane Katrina for case management support services to the residents of local shelters and to ensure that displaced residents have access to basic information, eligibility determination for benefits, family care planning, basic security, employment, healthcare, transportation and school registration.

The Ella West Freeman Foundation

Limitations: Giving primarily in the greater New Orleans, LA, area. No grants to individuals.

801. Keyes Foundation, New Orleans, LA. $10,000, 2005. To correct site drainage at Beauregard Memorial Library.

Irene W. & C. B. Pennington Foundation

Limitations: Giving limited to communities within or near Baton Rouge, LA. No grants to individuals.

802. Louisiana Library Foundation, Baton Rouge, LA. $10,000, 2004. For general support.

MAINE

Sam L. Cohen Foundation

Limitations: Giving primarily in southern ME. No grants to individuals, or for annual funds, endowments or multi-year commitments.

803. Jeremiah Cromwell Disabilities Center, Portland, ME. $32,500, 2005. For special needs library collection.

Stephen and Tabitha King Foundation, Inc.

Limitations: Giving limited to ME. No support for hospice programs or facilities, animal shelters/hospitals or rehabilitation centers. No grants to individuals, or for fellowships, scholarships, or for travel or sponsorships, student or athletic groups, graduation parties or events, renovations to churches or other religious properties or institutions, or renovations to historical society property unless connected to a library, or for film or video productions, transportation, book or publishing projects, conferences, meetings, exhibits, or workshops, construction of playgrounds; no loans.

804. Bangor Public Library, Bangor, ME. $31,000, 2004.

805. Brown Memorial Library, East Baldwin, ME. $25,000, 2004.

806. Brownfield Public Library, Brownfield, ME. $50,000, 2004.

807. Charlotte Hobbs Memorial Library, Lovell, ME. $52,000, 2004.

808. Hollis Center Library, Hollis, ME. $10,000, 2004.

809. John Curtis Free Library, Hanover, ME. $10,000, 2004.

810. New Portland Community Library, North New Portland, ME. $25,000, 2004.

811. Northeast Harbor Library, Northeast Harbor, ME. $25,000, 2004.

812. Old Town Library, Old Town, ME. $15,000, 2004.

813. Peabody Memorial Library, Jonesport, ME. $50,000, 2004.

814. Pittsfield Public Library, Pittsfield, ME. $25,000, 2004.

815. Porter Memorial Library, Machias, ME. $25,000, 2004.

816. Thompson Free Library, Dover Foxcroft, ME. $50,000, 2004.

817. Veterans Memorial Library, Patten, ME. $20,000, 2004.

818. Waldoboro Public Library, Waldoboro, ME. $25,000, 2004.

819. Wiscasset Public Library, Wiscasset, ME. $25,000, 2004.

Libra Foundation

Limitations: Giving limited to ME. No grants to individuals.

820. Bagaduce Music Lending Library, Blue Hill, ME. $80,000, 2004. To renovate facilities.

821. Berwick Library Association, Brunswick, ME. $10,000, 2004. To construct building.

822. Caswell Public Library Association, Harrison, ME. $10,000, 2004. For capital campaign.

823. Peabody Memorial Library, Jonesport, ME. $10,000, 2004. To build handicapped accessible entrance and bathroom facilities and additional technology space.

824. Pembroke Library Association, Pembroke, ME. $10,000, 2004. To renovate building to house Library.

825. Waldoboro Public Library, Waldoboro, ME. $10,000, 2004. For building.

826. William A. Farnsworth Library and Art Museum, Rockland, ME. $25,000, 2004. To upgrade collection storage areas.

The Maine Community Foundation, Inc.

Limitations: Giving limited to ME. No support for religious organizations for religious purposes. No grants to individuals (except for scholarship funds), or for equipment, annual campaigns for regular operations, or for capital campaigns.

827. Brown Memorial Library, East Baldwin, ME. $25,000, 2004. To expand existing library.

Maine Health Access Foundation

Limitations: Giving primarily in ME. No support for private foundations, political candidates, or lobbying. No grants to individuals, or for endowments, debt retirement, annual appeals or membership campaigns, fundraising or social events, or public relations campaigns.

828. CyberSeniors.org, Portland, ME. $10,000, 2005. To teach blind and visually impaired Maine seniors to use computers to access and use online health information and resources to enhance their health and well-being.

829. Maine Department of Corrections, Department of Health and Human Services, Augusta, ME. $99,891, 2005. To collect data and report on mental health status of Maine's children, in collaboration with Maine Children's Alliance (MCA) and national agencies, organizations and data experts.

830. Maine Health Information Center, Augusta, ME. $100,000, 2005. For Maine Health Information Network Technology (MHINT) Project Phase II, to plan and develop groundwork for statewide patient clinical information sharing network.

831. Maine Medical Center, Portland, ME. $77,390, 2005. For analysis of smokers seeking treatment, using data from Maine HelpLine, Adult Tobacco Survey, and Medicaid with aim to maximize use and outcomes of state-supported tobacco treatment services.

832. MaineGeneral Health, Augusta, ME. $100,000, 2005. For case management and intake services to provide referrals and individualized assistance in transitioning to Dingo, MaineCare, and other access programs.

The Sandy River Charitable Foundation

Limitations: Giving on an international and national basis, (particularly Board/staff areas), with a special emphasis on ME. No grants to individuals.

833. Middle Country Library Foundation, Centereach, NY. $40,000, 2005. For Family Place Long Island.

TD Banknorth Charitable Foundation

(formerly Banknorth Charitable Foundation)

Limitations: Giving limited to CT, MA, ME, NH, NY, and VT. No support for political, fraternal, religious, or labor organizations or teams. No grants to individuals, or for research projects, events not open to members of the general public, endowments, tournaments, fundraising events, or debt reduction.

834. Epsom Public Library, Epsom, NH. $10,000, 2004.

835. Homeworks, Augusta, ME. $10,000, 2004.

836. Springfield Library and Museums Association, Springfield, MA. $10,000, 2004.

MARYLAND

The Abell Foundation, Inc.

Limitations: Giving limited to MD, with emphasis on Baltimore. No support for educational programs at higher education institutions or medical facilities. No grants to individuals, or for scholarships, fellowships, endowments, travel, annual operating expenses, sponsorships, memberships, or deficit financing.

837. Chesapeake Center for Youth Development, Baltimore, MD. $29,000, 2005. For capital funding for Phase Two of Millennium Renovation Project to include library, private counseling offices, and additional classrooms.

838. Structured Employment Economic Development Corporation (SEEDCO), New York, NY. $75,000, 2005. For development of customized EarnBenefits Baltimore, Web-based initiative to help low-wage workers in Baltimore City determine what federal and state benefits they qualify for, and how to apply for them.

The Baltimore Community Foundation

Limitations: Giving primarily in Baltimore City and Baltimore County, MD. No support for religious or sectarian purposes. No grants to individuals (except for scholarships), or for capital campaigns, annual fund campaigns, or event sponsorships.

839. Citizens Planning and Housing Association, Baltimore, MD. $40,000, 2004. Toward Resource Center for Neighborhoods, which provides individualized assistance, resource library and volunteer bank.

840. Enoch Pratt Free Library, Baltimore, MD. $53,000, 2004.

841. Rachel Carson Council, Chevy Chase, MD. $10,000, 2004.

842. Village Learning Place, Baltimore, MD. $15,000, 2004. Toward Money WISE Financial Literacy Program.

The Jacob and Hilda Blaustein Foundation, Inc.

Limitations: Giving primarily in MD (no local projects outside Baltimore, MD); giving also in Israel. No support for unaffiliated schools or synagogues. No grants to individuals, or for fundraising events, or direct mail solicitations; no loans (except for program-related investments).

843. Jewish Womens Archive, Brookline, MA. $10,000, 2004. For unrestricted support.

The Annie E. Casey Foundation

Limitations: Giving on a national basis. No support for political committees-529s (PACs). No grants to individuals (except for Casey Children and Family Fellowship Program), or for capital projects or medical research.

844. Academy for Educational Development, DC. $15,000, 2005. To plan and design management information system for Mid-City Community Project and Horn of Africa, community organizations located in San Diego, California that work with recently arrived immigrants from Africa.

845. Center for Work-Life Policy, New York, NY. $100,000, 2005. To promote family-friendly policies in small business around country through creation of data banks and dissemination of best practices.

846. Cooper Foundation, Camden, NJ. $50,000, 2005. For baseline operating support for CAMConnect: Camden Data Warehouse. Purpose of CAMConnect is to expand and democratize access to information for residents and organizations that live and work in City of Camden.

847. Enoch Pratt Free Library, Baltimore, MD. $10,000, 2005. For Book Buggy, mobile library service that provides children in Head Start or large day care facilities with opportunities to develop pre-reading skills essential to success in formal education programs.

848. Foundation Center, New York, NY. $80,000, 2005. To provide facts and analysis to illuminate philanthropy's role in relief and recovery and reach out to nonprofits affected by the hurricanes with grantseeking training and tools.

849. Greater New Orleans Knowledge Works, New Orleans, LA. $25,000, 2005. To build strong communication infrastructure to help dispersed communities participate in rebuilding their towns and neighborhoods.

850. Greatschools.net, San Francisco, CA. $50,000, 2005. For pilot program that strengthens ability of families to be involved in education improvement efforts.

851. Hartford Public Library, Hartford, CT. $125,018, 2005. To further develop HarfordInfo (HI) so that will be respected and visible community information system and data warehouse.

852. New Inc./Fourth World Movement, Landover, MD. $10,000, 2005. Toward program publications.

853. Nonprofit Center of Milwaukee, Milwaukee, WI. $300,000, 2005. To continue to support work of Local Learning Partnership (LLP) in Milwaukee, Wisconsin, and to provide coordination and administrative services.

854. Nonprofit Center of Milwaukee, Milwaukee, WI. $106,500, 2005. Toward one position for local Technical Assistance Resource Center (TARC) for Making Connections Milwaukee site. Making Connections is Foundation initiative to improve outcomes for families and children in tough or isolated neighborhoods.

855. Rhode Island Parent Information Network, Pawtucket, RI. $50,000, 2005. For continued support for Rhode Island Father Coalition's efforts to increase capacity of non-custodial fathers who are interested in providing emotional and financial support for their children.

856. United Way, Metro, Louisville, KY. $300,000, 2005. To establish Community Data Center in Louisville which will serve as critical component for Local Learning Partnership (LLP).

857. United Way, Metro, Louisville, KY. $193,166, 2005. To establish Community Data Center in Louisville which will serve as critical component for Local Learning Partnership (LLP).

858. University of Chicago, Chicago, IL. $125,000, 2005. To develop State Center for Adoption and Foster Care Data.

859. University of Hawaii, Honolulu, HI. $40,000, 2005. To conduct in-depth analysis of Hawaii's Homeless Management Information System (HMIS) data and to prepare and disseminate more accurate and detailed profiles of Hawaii's homeless children and families at state and county levels.

860. University of South Dakota, Vermillion, SD. $36,413, 2005. To develop model for working with Native American Tribal governments to develop system for collecting and compiling data about children and youth and to document strengths and weaknesses of various sources of data on Native American children and youth.

861. Village Learning Place, Baltimore, MD. $10,000, 2005. For Family Adventures with Literature, which focuses on literacy, educational enrichment, and opportunities for social interaction among participants.

862. West Virginia Kids Count Fund, Charleston, WV. $75,000, 2005. For continued KIDS COUNT activities.

Naomi and Nehemiah Cohen Foundation

Limitations: Giving primarily in Washington, DC, and Israel. No grants to individuals.

863. NatureServe, Arlington, VA. $25,000, 2004.

The Shelby Cullom Davis Foundation

Limitations: Giving on a national basis. No grants to individuals.

864. Huntington Library, Friends of the, San Marino, CA. $100,000, 2005. For general operating support.

865. Jamestown Foundation, DC. $10,000, 2005. For publication Terrorism Weekly.

866. Microfinance Information Exchange, DC. $40,000, 2005. For growth and expansion in Peru.

The Sherman Fairchild Foundation, Inc.

Limitations: Giving on a national basis.

867. Huntington Library, Art Collections and Botanical Gardens, San Marino, CA. $857,956, 2004. For construction of conservation laboratory.

The James M. Johnston Trust for Charitable and Educational Purposes

Limitations: Giving primarily in Washington, DC, and NC. No support for private foundations. No grants to individuals.

868. George C. Marshall Research Foundation, Lexington, VA. $30,000, 2004. For scholarships.

The John W. Kluge Foundation

869. Library of Congress, DC. $500,000, 2005. For National Digital Library.

870. Library of Congress, DC. $500,000, 2005. For Leadership Development Trust Fund.

871. Library of Congress, DC. $396,635, 2005. For Creative Space: Fifty Years of Robert Blackburn's Printmaking Workshop.

872. Library of Congress, DC. $350,000, 2005. For Song of America Project.

873. Library of Congress, DC. $250,000, 2005. For Librarian's Discretionary Fund.

874. Library of Congress, DC. $78,000, 2005. For general support.

Lockheed Martin Corporation Foundation

(formerly Martin Marietta Corporation Foundation)

Limitations: Giving primarily in areas of company operations. No support for religious organizations not of direct benefit to the entire community, professional associations, labor or fraternal organizations, social clubs, or athletic organizations. No grants to individuals (except for employee-related scholarships), or for booklet, yearbook, or journal advertising, or home-based child care or educational services.

875. William J. Clinton Presidential Foundation, Little Rock, AR. $20,000, 2004.

876. Women Work: The National Network for Womens Employment, DC. $10,000, 2004.

The Harry and Jeanette Weinberg Foundation, Inc.

Limitations: Giving on a national basis. No support for political organizations, colleges, universities, think tanks, or for arts organizations. No grants to individuals, or for deficit financing, annual giving, publications or for scholarships.

877. Enoch Pratt Free Library, Baltimore, MD. $170,000, 2005.

878. Maryland Regional Practitioners Network for Fathers and Families, Baltimore, MD. $25,000, 2005.

MASSACHUSETTS

The George I. Alden Trust

Limitations: Giving limited to NY, NJ, PA and the six New England states. No grants to individuals; no loans.

879. Higher Education Resource Center, Boston, MA. $15,000, 2004. For operating support.

880. Worcester Public Library, Worcester, MA. $15,000, 2004. For operating support.

L. G. Balfour Foundation

Limitations: Giving primarily in New England, with emphasis on Attleboro, MA. No grants to individuals.

881. Balfour Gold Dusters, Mansfield, MA. $56,000, 2005. For general operating support and for prescription and emergency medical fund.

Barr Foundation

(formerly The Hostetter Foundation)

Limitations: Giving primarily in the greater Boston, MA, area. No grants to individuals.

882. Boston Athenaeum, Boston, MA. $10,000, 2004.

883. Education Resources Institute, Boston, MA. $40,000, 2004.

Berkshire Taconic Community Foundation

(formerly Berkshire-Taconic Foundation)

Limitations: Giving limited to northwest Litchfield County, CT, Berkshire County, MA, and Columbia County and northeast Dutchess County, NY.

884. American Jewish Historical Society, New York, NY. $10,000, 2005. For general operating support.

885. Scoville Memorial Library Association, Salisbury, CT. $60,000, 2005. For building renovations.

Boston Foundation, Inc.

Limitations: Giving from discretionary funds limited to the greater Boston, MA, area. No support for religious purposes, city or state government agencies or departments, private schools, municipalities, or national or international programs. No grants to individuals, or for scientific or academic research, books or articles, films, radio, or television programs, equipment, travel, endowments, scholarships, fellowships, conferences, or symposia or capital campaigns; no loans.

886. Charities Aid Foundation (CAF) America, Alexandria, VA. $43,750, 2005. For general operating support.

887. Charities Aid Foundation (CAF) America, Alexandria, VA. $32,250, 2005. For general operating support.

888. Ipswich Public Library, Ipswich, MA. $10,000, 2005. For general operating support.

889. John F. Kennedy Library Foundation, Boston, MA. $25,000, 2005. For co-presentation of public forums on immigration and companion executive sessions at John F. Kennedy Library.

890. Massachusetts Affordable Housing Alliance, Dorchester, MA. $40,000, 2005. For Greater Boston Homebuyers Union.

891. Safe Harbor Retreat, Los Angeles, CA. $10,000, 2005. For general operating support.

892. Social Law Library, Boston, MA. $100,000, 2005. For general operating support.

Community Foundation of Western Massachusetts

Limitations: Giving limited to western MA, including Franklin County, Hampden County, and Hampshire County. No support for religious purposes, or private education. No grants to individuals directly, or for operating budgets, endowments, fundraising events, tickets for benefits, courtesy advertising, academic or medical research or multi-year funding.

893. Western Massachusetts Regional Library System, Hatfield, MA. $10,000, 2005. For materials for bookmobiles.

The William F. Connell Charitable Trust

Limitations: Giving primarily in MA. No grants to individuals.

894. John F. Kennedy Library Foundation, Boston, MA. $50,000, 2005.

The Ellison Foundation

Limitations: Giving primarily in MA. No grants to individuals.

895. Elkland Area Community Library, Elkland, PA. $20,000, 2004.

Fidelity Foundation

Limitations: Giving on a national basis and in Canada, with emphasis on areas of company operations, including Northern KY, Boston and Marlborough, MA, Merrimack, NH, Jersey City, NJ, lower Manhattan, NY, NC, Cincinnati, OH, Smithfield, RI, Dallas, Fort Worth, and northern TX, Salt Lake City, UT, and Toronto, Canada. No support for start-up, sectarian, or civic organizations, public school systems, or disease-specific organizations. No grants to individuals, or for general operating support, sponsorships, scholarships, benefits, corporate memberships, or video or film projects.

896. Fort Worth Public Library Foundation, Fort Worth, TX. $50,000, 2004. For information technology equipment.

The Highland Street Connection

(also known as The Highland Street Foundation)

Limitations: Giving primarily in MA. No grants to individuals.

897. Morse Institute Library, Natick, MA. $10,000, 2004. For general operating support.

898. Ronald Reagan Presidential Foundation, Simi Valley, CA. $50,000, 2004. For capital support.

The Hyams Foundation, Inc.

(formerly Sarah A. Hyams Fund)

Limitations: Giving primarily in Boston and Chelsea, MA. No support for municipal, state, or federal agencies; institutions of higher learning for standard educational programs; religious organizations for sectarian religious purposes; or national or regional health organizations; support for medical research is being phased out. No grants to individuals, or for endowment funds, hospitals and health centers, capital campaigns,

fellowships, publications, conferences, films or videos or curriculum development.

899. Massachusetts Affordable Housing Alliance, Dorchester, MA. $40,000, 2004.

The Melville Charitable Trust

Limitations: Giving primarily in CT. No support for religious organizations for religious purposes. No grants to individuals, for scholarships, budget deficits, or general fundraising drives or events.

900. Legal Assistance Resource Center of Connecticut, Hartford, CT. $42,200, 2005. To computerize Legal Services Housing Index, housing law research tool.

901. National Low Income Housing Coalition and Low Income Housing Information Service, DC. $240,000, 2005. To establish National Housing Trust Fund.

902. National Low Income Housing Coalition and Low Income Housing Information Service, DC. $100,000, 2005. Toward National Housing Voucher Summit.

The John Merck Fund

Limitations: Giving on a national basis in the areas of reproductive health, the environment, and job opportunities; giving in Latin America in the area of human rights. Generally, no support for large organizations with well-established funding sources. No grants to individuals, or for endowment or capital fund projects, generally no general support grants.

903. Commonweal, Bolinas, CA. $175,000, 2004. To develop state and national alliances of constituencies with health problems linked to chemical exposures and health professionals who support them and alliances within learning and developmental disability communities nationally, and to create centralized source of information about biomonitoring projects, data, collection protocols, and communications strategies for organizations interested in chemical body burden and environmental testing.

904. National Security Archive Fund, DC. $55,000, 2004. To provide expertise in freedom of information requests and documentation of human rights violations to Latin American organizations.

905. Sexuality Information and Education Council of the U.S. (SIECUS), New York, NY. $50,000, 2004. To protect and expand national and state policies that support comprehensive sexuality education, access to reproductive health care, and teen pregnancy prevention.

V. Kann Rasmussen Foundation

906. Earth Action Network, Norwalk, CT. $107,000, 2005. For E The Environmental Magazine.

State Street Foundation

Limitations: Giving on a national and international basis, with emphasis on the greater Boston, MA, area. No support for political organizations or religious organizations not of direct benefit to the entire community. No grants to individuals, or for general operating support, endowments or capital campaigns, equipment, hospital programs, medical research, or disease-specific initiatives, travel, or television or film projects; no multi-year grants.

907. Boston University, Boston, MA. $25,000, 2004. For program support in African Presidential Archives and Research Center.

908. Education Resources Institute, Boston, MA. $15,000, 2004. For TERI College Access satellite center program serving low to moderate income (LMI) youth.

909. Massachusetts Affordable Housing Alliance, Dorchester, MA. $50,000, 2004. For financial literacy programs serving low to moderate income (LMI) individuals and their families.

Yawkey Foundation II

(also known as The Jean R. Yawkey Foundation)

Limitations: Giving primarily in MA, with emphasis on the greater metropolitan Boston area. Generally, no support for private foundations, political, fraternal, trade, civic or labor organizations, religious organizations for sectarian purposes, public schools or districts, charter schools, community or economic development corporations or programs, advocacy groups, pass-through or intermediary organizations, or workforce development programs. No grants to individuals. Generally, no grants for operating deficits, retirement of debt, endowments, capital campaigns, events, conferences, seminars, group travel, awards, prizes, monuments, music, video, or film production, feasibility or research studies.

910. Boston Public Library Foundation, Boston, MA. $30,000, 2005. For education programs for children and youth.

911. Jeremiah Cromwell Disabilities Center, Portland, ME. $25,000, 2005. For special needs library collections program in Massachusetts.

MICHIGAN

The Eugene Applebaum Family Foundation

Limitations: Giving primarily in MI, and New York, NY; some funding nationally.

912. National Yiddish Book Center, Amherst, MA. $87,500, 2005.

Arcus Foundation

(formerly Jon L. Stryker Foundation)

Limitations: Giving on a national basis, with emphasis on Kalamazoo, MI for some programs. No grants to individuals, of for religious or political activities, medical research or film/video production.

913. Sexuality Information and Education Council of the U.S. (SIECUS), New York, NY. $65,000, 2004. For general support.

The Carls Foundation

Limitations: Giving primarily in MI. No grants to individuals, or for publications, film, research, endowments, fellowships, travel, conferences, special event sponsorships, playground or athletic facilities, or seminars; no educational loans.

914. Communities in Schools of Detroit, Detroit, MI. $30,000, 2005. For Readetroit Corps Program for recreation or to augment libraries in Detroit Public Schools.

Comerica Foundation

Limitations: Giving in areas of company operations, with emphasis on MI.

915. Survivors of the Shoah Visual History Foundation, Los Angeles, CA. $12,500, 2004.

Community Foundation for Muskegon County

(formerly Muskegon County Community Foundation, Inc.)

Limitations: Giving limited to Muskegon County, MI. No support for sectarian religious programs, or individual schools or districts. No grants to individuals (except for scholarships), or for deficit financing, routine operating expenses, capital equipment, endowment campaigns, special fundraising events, conferences, camps, publications, videos, films, television or radio programs, or for advertising.

916. Hackley Public Library, Friends of, Muskegon, MI. $20,000, 2004. For Stained Glass Window Repair.

917. Senior Resources of West Michigan, Muskegon Heights, MI. $30,000, 2004. For development of Mukegon County 2-1-1.

Community Foundation for Southeast Michigan

(formerly Community Foundation for Southeastern Michigan)

Limitations: Giving limited to southeast MI. No support for sectarian religious programs. No grants to individuals (from unrestricted funds), or for capital projects, endowments, annual campaigns, general operating support, conferences, computers and computer systems, fundraising, annual meetings, buildings, or equipment.

918. National Bone Marrow Transplant Link, Southfield, MI. $75,000, 2004. For program support.

919. Oakland Livingston Human Service Agency, Pontiac, MI. $20,000, 2004. To implement information and referral call center in Livingston County.

DaimlerChrysler Corporation Fund

(formerly Chrysler Corporation Fund)

Limitations: Giving primarily in areas of company operations in Wittman, AZ, Irvine, CA, Englewood, CO, Newark, DE, Washington, DC, Orlando, FL, Belvidere and Lisle, IL, Indianapolis and Kokomo, IN, Elkridge, MD, Detroit, MI, Fenton, MO, Syracuse and Tappan, NY, Perrysburg, Toledo, and Twinsburg, OH, and Addison, TX, Kenosha, WI; giving also to regional and national organizations. No support for discriminatory organizations or private or corporate foundations. No grants to individuals (except for employee-related scholarships), or for endowments, general operating support for local United Way agencies, direct health care delivery programs, additions or renovations to real estate, fundraising activities related to individual sponsorship, debt reduction, religious or sectarian programs, athletic programs involving individual teams; no loans; no vehicle donations.

920. Detroit Public Library, Friends of the, Detroit, MI. $20,000, 2004. For reading programs.

921. District of Columbia Public Library Foundation, DC. $10,000, 2004. For African American History and Culture Book Donation.

922. National Center for Policy Analysis, Dallas, TX. $15,000, 2004. For E-Team, which corrects misinformation and seeks solutions to environmental problems.

The Richard and Helen DeVos Foundation

Limitations: Giving primarily in central FL and western MI. No grants to individuals.

923. Christian Foundation Center of America, Olathe, KS. $10,000, 2004. For general support.

924. Grandville Avenue Arts and Humanities, Grand Rapids, MI. $20,000, 2004. For general support.

The Dow Chemical Company Foundation

Limitations: Giving primarily in areas of company operations. No support for political or religious organizations. No grants to individuals (except through special relief funds), or for travel or administrative costs.

925. Garfield Memorial Library, Clare, MI. $10,000, 2005.

The Herbert H. and Grace A. Dow Foundation

Limitations: Giving limited to MI, with emphasis on Midland County. No support for political organizations or sectarian religious organizations or programs, other than churches in Midland County. No grants to individuals, or for travel or conferences; no loans.

926. Alma Public Library, Alma, MI. $50,000, 2004.

927. Farwell Area Schools, Farwell, MI. $77,094, 2004. For library renovation.

928. Rauchholz Memorial Library, Hemlock, MI. $100,000, 2004. For library renovation.

Earhart Foundation

929. Jamestown Foundation, DC. $55,100, 2004. For publication of Terrorism Focus.

930. Jamestown Foundation, DC. $50,000, 2004. For general operating support.

931. University of Michigan, Bentley Historical Library, Ann Arbor, MI. $25,000, 2004. For general operating support.

Ford Motor Company Fund

Limitations: Giving primarily in areas of company operations, with emphasis on southeastern MI. No support for religious organizations not of direct benefit to the entire community, political or fraternal organizations, animal rights organizations, labor groups, private schools, or species-specific organizations. No grants to individuals (except for employee-related scholarships), or for fellowships, endowments, debt reduction, general operating support, or beauty or talent contests; no loans or program-related investments; no vehicle donations.

932. BBB Wise Giving Alliance, Arlington, VA. $10,000, 2004.

933. Library Foundation of Los Angeles, Los Angeles, CA. $50,000, 2004.

Fremont Area Community Foundation

(formerly The Fremont Area Foundation)

Limitations: Giving primarily in Newaygo County, MI. No support for religious organizations for specific religions. No grants to individuals (except for scholarships), or for contingencies, reserves, services which are considered general government or school obligations, or deficit financing.

934. Fremont Area District Library, Fremont, MI. $20,000, 2005. For circulating materials.

935. Grant Area District Library, Grant, MI. $30,000, 2005. For circulating materials.

936. Hesperia Public Library, Hesperia, MI. $11,000, 2005. For circulating materials.

937. Land Information Access Association, Traverse City, MI. $24,315, 2005. For Partnerships for Change multi jurisdictional collaboration.

938. Newaygo Carnegie Library, Newaygo, MI. $27,700, 2005. For consultant fees for district library and building.

939. Newaygo Carnegie Library, Newaygo, MI. $17,000, 2005. For circulating materials.

940. Newaygo Carnegie Library, Newaygo, MI. $10,750, 2005. For library materials for people with disabilities. Grant made through Amazing X Charitable Trust.

941. White Cloud Public Library, White Cloud, MI. $75,000, 2005. For building expansion project.

942. White Cloud Public Library, White Cloud, MI. $20,000, 2005. For circulating materials.

943. Womens Information Service, Fremont, MI. $60,000, 2005. For Newaygo County Domestic Violence Outreach program.

Frey Foundation

Limitations: Giving primarily in Emmet, Charlevoix, and Kent counties, MI. No support for sectarian charitable activity. No grants to individuals, or for endowment funds, debt retirement, general operating expenses, scholarships, conferences, speakers, travel, or to cover routine, current, or emergency expenses.

944. Charlevoix Public Library, Charlevoix, MI. $50,000, 2004. For renovations and expansions to former Charlevoix Middle School as new public library.

945. Grandville Avenue Arts and Humanities, Grand Rapids, MI. $33,000, 2004. To stabilize the Academy through fund development initiative.

946. HIV-AIDS Network and Direct Services (HANDS), Petoskey, MI. $10,000, 2004. For general operating support.

The Rollin M. Gerstacker Foundation

Limitations: Giving primarily in MI; giving also in OH. No grants to individuals, or for scholarships or fellowships; no loans.

947. Braille Circulating Library, Richmond, VA. $10,000, 2005.

948. Pere Marquette District Library, Clare, MI. $50,000, 2005.

Grand Rapids Community Foundation

(formerly The Grand Rapids Foundation)

Limitations: Giving limited to Kent County, MI. No support for religious programs, hospitals, child care centers, or nursing homes/retirement facilities. No grants to individuals (except for scholarships), or for continued operating support, annual campaigns, travel expenses, medical or scholarly research, deficit financing, endowment funds, computers, vehicles, films, videos, or conferences; no student loans; no venture capital for competitive profit-making activities.

949. Grand Rapids Student Advancement Foundation, Grand Rapids, MI. $40,000, 2005. To fully equip and name Fountain Street Elementary, Grand Rapids Public School library on behalf of DA Peterson Memorial Fund.

950. Grand Rapids Student Advancement Foundation, Grand Rapids, MI. $25,000, 2005. For annual support to Fountain Street Elementary, Grand Rapids Public School library for ongoing purchase of books.

Heritage Mark Foundation

Limitations: Giving on a national basis. No grants to individuals.

951. Jewish Womens Archive, Brookline, MA. $25,000, 2005.

Herrick Foundation

Limitations: Giving primarily in MI; giving also in the New York Metropolitan area, Washington, DC, IN, MS, OH, OK, TN, and WI. No support for international organizations, or for domestic organizations for international programs. No grants to individuals.

952. Tecumseh District Library, Tecumseh, MI. $50,000, 2005. For permanent endowment fund for purchase of library books.

Hudson-Webber Foundation

Limitations: Giving primarily in the city of Detroit, and the tri-county Wayne, Oakland, and Macomb area of southeastern MI. No support for educational institutions or neighborhood organizations (except for projects that fall within current program missions). No grants to individuals (except for J.L. Hudson Co. employees and their families), or for emergency funds, deficit financing, endowment funds, scholarships, fellowships, publications, conferences, fundraising, social events, or exhibits; no loans.

953. Detroit Public Library, Friends of the, Detroit, MI. $10,000, 2005. For general program support.

954. United Way for Southeastern Michigan, Detroit, MI. $300,000, 2005. For 2-1-1 Call Center.

Kalamazoo Community Foundation

(formerly Kalamazoo Foundation)

Limitations: Giving generally limited to Kalamazoo County, MI. No grants to individuals (except for scholarships), or for endowment funds.

955. Child Care Resource and Referral, Kalamazoo, MI. $116,000, 2005. To increase literacy opportunities and quality of care for children in home child care programs.

956. Child Care Resource and Referral, Kalamazoo, MI. $37,729, 2005. For Keeping Little Ones in Care project, working to improve overall quality of child care in Kalamazoo County and prevent challenging children from being expelled.

W. K. Kellogg Foundation

Limitations: Giving primarily in the U.S., Latin America and the Caribbean, and the South African countries of Botswana, Lesotho, Malawi, South Africa, Swaziland, Zimbabwe and Mozambique. No support for religious purposes or for capital facilities. No grants to individuals (except through fellowship programs), or for endowment funds, development campaigns, films, equipment, publications, conferences, or radio and television programs unless they are an integral part of a project already being funded; no grants for operating budgets.

957. Foundation Center, New York, NY. $175,000, 2005. To provide annual program subsidies.

958. Mexican Center for Philanthropy, Centro Mexicano para la Filantropia, Mexico City, Mexico. $185,000, 2005. 3-year grant. To promote creation of community, family, corporate, and independent grantmaking foundations in Mexico.

959. Mexican Center for Philanthropy, Centro Mexicano para la Filantropia, Mexico City, Mexico. $155,000, 2005. 3-year grant. To foster transparency and credibility of nonprofit organizations affiliated with Registry of Philanthropic Institutions to become reliable source of information for donors and general public.

960. Mexican Center for Philanthropy, Centro Mexicano para la Filantropia, Mexico City, Mexico. $55,000, 2005. To promote voluntarism and civic participation in Mexico.

961. National Center for Black Philanthropy, DC. $50,000, 2005. Toward Fifth National Conference on Black Philanthropy.

962. National Resource Center for the Healing of Racism, Albion, MI. $684,598, 2005. 4.25-year grant. To develop and implement strategies to address structural racism in Battle Creek.

963. Washington Sustainable Food and Farming Network, Bellingham, WA. $40,000, 2005. To expand institutional change work in state of Washington, particularly with Washington State University, by supporting family farms and local sustainable food and farming systems.

964. Willard Library, Battle Creek, MI. $195,000, 2005. 1.50-year grant. To provide support to NonProfit Alliance to plan and design comprehensive capacity-building network to improve performance and impact of local nonprofit organizations and institutions in Calhoun County.

965. Willard Library, Battle Creek, MI. $125,174, 2005. To support Nonprofit Alliance in delivering services to nonprofit organizations in Calhoun County.

Kellogg's Corporate Citizenship Fund

Limitations: Giving primarily in areas of company operations.

966. National Resource Center for the Healing of Racism, Albion, MI. $25,000, 2004. For general support.

The Kresge Foundation

Limitations: No support for religious organizations, (unless applicant is operated by a religious organization and it serves secular needs and has financial and governing autonomy separate from the parent organization with space formally dedicated to its programs) community colleges, private foundations, or elementary or secondary schools (unless they predominantly serve individuals with physical and/or developmental disabilities). No grants to individuals, or for debt retirement or minor equipment, furnishings, operating/program support, or endowment funds by themselves; no loans.

967. Otis Library, Norwich, CT. $300,000, 2005. For challenge grant toward construction of replacement library.

968. Redwood Library and Athenaeum, Newport, RI. $500,000, 2005. For challenge grant toward purchase of property and to restore, renovate and expand facilities.

969. University of Waterloo, Waterloo, Canada. $600,000, 2005. For challenge grant toward renovation of libraries.

McGregor Fund

Limitations: Giving primarily in the metropolitan Detroit, MI, area, including Wayne, Oakland, and Macomb counties. No support for disease-specific organizations (or their local affiliates). No grants to individuals, or for scholarships directly, fellowships, travel, workshops, seminars, special events, film or video projects, or conferences; no loans.

970. United Way for Southeastern Michigan, Detroit, MI. $600,000, 2005. 3-year grant. For implementation of a 2-1-1 telephone referral system in metropolitan Detroit, providing callers with access to health and human service providers 24 hours a day seven days per week.

Charles Stewart Mott Foundation

Limitations: Giving nationally and to emerging countries in Central and Eastern Europe, Russia, and South Africa. No support for religious organizations for religious purposes. No grants to individuals, or for building or endowment funds in general or for research, film or video projects, books, scholarships, or fellowships.

971. Agency for Social Information, Moscow, Russia. $100,000, 2005. 3-year grant. For general support.

972. Bank Information Center, DC. $440,000, 2005. 2-year grant. For general support.

973. Bank Information Center, DC. $70,000, 2005. 2-year grant. For general support.

974. Bertelsmann Stiftung, Gutersloh, Germany. $450,000, 2005. 3-year grant. For Transatlantic Community Foundations Network, initiative to focus on shared learning, mutual skills building, and development of information products for network and broader community foundation field.

975. BlueLink Foundation, Sofia, Bulgaria. $60,000, 2005. 3-year grant. For technical assistance work to strengthen NGO networking and communication in Bulgaria through the Internet.

976. Charities Aid Foundation (UK), West Malling, England. $135,000, 2005. For staff person and travel support for New Philanthropists: Development of Giving, initiative to design approaches that encourage high net worth individuals from middle-income countries (including Russia, Central and Eastern Europe and Brazil with expansion planned for South Africa and China) to become effective philanthropists.

977. Charities Aid Foundation-Southern Africa, Johannesburg, South Africa. $100,000, 2005. 2-year grant. For general support.

978. Collaborative Communications Group, DC. $1,225,000, 2005. 2-year grant. For Statewide After-School Network Meetings, initiative to promote learning and development for elementary school-age children through quality programs that provide safety and enrichment outside the traditional classroom.

979. Czech Donors Forum, Prague, Czech Republic. $113,000, 2005. 2-year grant. For Central and Eastern European Network for Responsible Giving (CEENERGI), initiative to increase level and effectiveness of corporate giving in Central and Eastern Europe.

980. Documenta, Zagreb, Croatia. $60,000, 2005. 2-year grant. For general support.

981. Ecopravo-Lviv, Lviv, Ukraine. $30,000, 2005. 3-year grant. For general support.

982. European Foundation Centre, Brussels, Belgium. $125,000, 2005. 1.25-year grant. To purchase new hardware and software and toward salary of intern and systems administrator.

983. European Foundation Centre, Brussels, Belgium. $100,000, 2005. 3-year grant. For Community Philanthropy Initiative.

984. European Foundation Centre, Brussels, Belgium. $83,000, 2005. Toward Coordinator position for Orpheus Programme, knowledge base which provides public record and information services on foundations and corporate funders and programs throughout Europe gathering, analyzing, processing and disseminating information through decentralized network.

985. European Foundation Centre, Brussels, Belgium. $75,000, 2005. For operating support for Good Neighbours Programme, projects to grow ethical, effective, accountable, and transparent giving in six countries/regions that neighbor European Union, Russia, Ukraine, Belarus, and Moldova, Southeastern Europe and Turkey.

986. European Foundation Centre, Brussels, Belgium. $61,000, 2005. For general support.

987. European Foundation Centre, Brussels, Belgium. $60,000, 2005. For Europe in the World Initiative, campaign to mobilize leadership, collaboration, and partnership and to leverage knowledge and networking among European foundations for global development.

988. European Foundation Centre, Brussels, Belgium. $25,000, 2005. 2-year grant. For symposium on community foundations' activities of Worldwide Initiatives for Grantmaker Support (WINGS), global network of membership associations and support organizations serving grantmakers, which have joined together to create opportunities to learn from and support one another, develop modes of communication and collaboration, and contribute to strengthening of philanthropy worldwide.

989. European Foundation Centre, Brussels, Belgium. $22,600, 2005. 1.75-year grant. For symposium on community foundations' activities of Worldwide Initiatives for Grantmaker Support (WINGS), global network of membership associations and support organizations serving grantmakers, which have joined together to create opportunities to learn from and support one another, develop modes of communication and collaboration, and contribute to strengthening of philanthropy worldwide.

990. Mexican Center for Philanthropy, Mexico City, Mexico. $120,000, 2005. For coordination of Mexico's Community Foundations Group.

991. National Center for Black Philanthropy, DC. $40,000, 2005. 1.25-year grant. For National Conference on Black Philanthropy.

992. National Center for Family Philanthropy, DC. $50,000, 2005. To develop and test strategies that help community foundations attract and develop relationships with donor families.

993. Natural Resources Defense Council, New York, NY. $200,000, 2005. 2-year grant. For continued support for Clean Water Network.

994. Romanian Donors Forum, Bucharest, Romania. $25,000, 2005. For general support.

995. Slovak Donors Forum, Bratislava, Slovakia. $60,000, 2005. 3-year grant. For general support.

996. Tip of the Mitt Watershed Council, Petoskey, MI. $652,000, 2005. 2-year grant. For Great Lakes Aquatic Habitat Network and Fund, organization providing information and financial support to grassroots citizen initiatives working to protect and restore Great Lakes shorelines, inland lakes, rivers, wetlands, and other aquatic habitats in the Great Lakes Basin.

997. Twenty-First Century Foundation, New York, NY. $72,000, 2005. 2-year grant. Toward New York Black Communities in Philanthropy Initiative, program that connects African-American assets with black-led charities.

998. William J. Clinton Presidential Foundation, New York, NY. $65,579, 2005. To provide technical assistance to Ukrainian Presidential Office to help it become more effective in implementing democratic reforms and more responsive to concerns of its citizens.

Ruth Mott Foundation

Limitations: Giving primarily in Genesee County and Flint, MI. No support for religious programs for religious purposes. No grants to individuals.

999. Flint Public Library, Flint, MI. $24,500, 2004. For Dr. Bernice Reagon Residency.

1000. Flint Public Library, Flint, MI. $20,790, 2004. For One Book - One Community Project.

1001. Flint Public Library, Flint, MI. $18,050, 2004. For Black Heritage Month Author Series.

1002. Flint Public Library, Flint, MI. $16,750, 2004. For Black Heritage Month Author Series.

1003. Ready Set Grow Passport Initiative, Flint, MI. $64,005, 2004.

The Skillman Foundation

Limitations: Giving primarily in southeastern MI, with emphasis on metropolitan Detroit, and Macomb, Oakland, and Wayne counties. No support for long-term projects not being aided by other sources, sectarian religious activities, political lobbying or legislative activities, or new organizations which do not have an operational and financial history. The foundation does not make grants to organizations that had public support and revenues of less than $100,000 for the preceding year. No grants to individuals, or for endowment funds, annual campaigns, purchase, construct or renovate facilities, basic research or deficit financing; no loans.

1004. Chandler Park Academy - Greenfield, Detroit, MI. $15,000, 2005. To assist in development of digital library media center.

1005. Foundation Center, New York, NY. $10,000, 2005. For general operating support.

1006. Laurence A. McKenny Elementary School, Detroit, MI. $15,000, 2005. To increase library and media center resources, and provide summer and after-school programs.

1007. Mann Elementary School, Detroit, MI. $15,000, 2005. To assist in implementation of library/media center.

1008. Michigan League for Human Services, Lansing, MI. $85,000, 2005. For Kids Count in Michigan Data Book, which provides credible information on well-being of children in Michigan.

1009. Peter G. Monnier Elementary School, Detroit, MI. $15,000, 2005. To assist in implementation of library/media center.

Steelcase Foundation

Limitations: Giving limited to areas of company operations, with emphasis on Athens, AL, City of Industry, CA, Grand Rapids, MI, and Markham, Canada. No support for churches or religious organizations not of direct benefit to the entire community or discriminatory organizations. No grants to individuals (except for employee-related scholarships), or for endowments or conferences or seminars.

1010. Gerald R. Ford Foundation, Grand Rapids, MI. $25,000, 2005.

Jay and Betty Van Andel Foundation

Limitations: Giving primarily in MI, with some emphasis on Grand Rapids. No grants to individuals.

1011. Jamestown Foundation, DC. $25,000, 2004.

Wege Foundation

Limitations: Giving primarily in greater Kent County, MI, with emphasis on the Grand Rapids area. No grants to individuals, or for operating budgets.

1012. Chase Township Library, Chase, MI. $13,800, 2005.

MINNESOTA

3M Foundation

(also known as Minnesota Mining and Manufacturing Foundation)

Limitations: Giving on a national and international basis in areas of company operations. No support for religious organizations, conduit agencies, political, fraternal, social, or veterans' organizations, hospitals, K-12 schools, or military organizations, animal-related organizations, or disease-specific organizations. No grants to individuals, or for endowments, emergency operating support, advocacy and lobbying efforts, fundraising events and associated advertising, travel, publications, start-up needs, non-3M equipment, debt reduction, conferences, athletic events, film or video production, or scholarship funds; no loans or investments.

1013. Saint Paul Public Library, Friends of the, Saint Paul, MN. $10,000, 2004.

Fred C. and Katherine B. Andersen Foundation

(formerly Andersen Foundation)

Limitations: Giving on a national basis for higher education, locally for all other areas. No support for federally funded colleges, universities, or endowment programs. No grants to individuals.

1014. Bayport Public Library, Bayport, MN. $56,000, 2004.

1015. Bayport Public Library Foundation, Bayport, MN. $70,000, 2004.

Best Buy Children's Foundation

Limitations: Giving on a national basis. No support for labor organizations, fraternal organizations or social clubs, religious organizations, or local affiliates of national organizations. No grants to individuals (except for scholarships), or for travel, general operating support, or treatment or residential programs; no in-kind gifts.

1016. Saint Paul Public Library, Friends of the, Saint Paul, MN. $20,000, 2005. For Twin City Metro Hometown grant.

F. R. Bigelow Foundation

Limitations: Giving limited to the Greater St. Paul, MN, metropolitan area, which includes; Ramsey, Washington, and Dakota counties, with a particular emphasis on serving people who live and work in the city of St. Paul. No support for sectarian religious programs. No grants to individuals, or for annual operating expenses, medical research, or ongoing, open-ended needs.

1017. Saint Paul Public Library, Friends of the, Saint Paul, MN. $30,000, 2005. Toward operating support for Homework Center at Rondo Library.

The Blandin Foundation

(formerly Charles K. Blandin Foundation)

Limitations: Giving limited to rural areas of MN; scholarships limited to graduates of an Itasca County, Hill City, or Remer, Blackduck, or Northome, MN, high school. No support for religious activities or camping programs. No grants to individuals (except for Blandin Educational Awards), for operating budgets, annual campaigns, deficit financing, government services, capital funds (outside home community), endowments, publications, travel, medical research, films or videos, conferences, or seminars (outside of those sponsored by the foundation and related to its grantmaking).

1018. Bemidji State University, Bemidji, MN. $39,000, 2005. 2-year grant. For continued support of Northern Tier Technology Corridor project throughout rural Minnesota, website providing information resources for business, entrepreneurs, and nonprofits.

1019. First Call for Help of Itasca County, Grand Rapids, MN. $45,000, 2005. For sustaining contribution for emergency, information and referral services in Itasca County.

Otto Bremer Foundation

Limitations: Giving limited to organizations whose beneficiaries are residents of MN, MT, ND and WI with preference given to those in regions served by Bremer Banks. No support for economic development, or historic preservation, museums and interpretive centers, sporting activities. No grants to individuals, or for endowment funds, medical research, professorships, annual fund drives, benefit events, camps, or artistic or media projects.

1020. Bridges of Hope, Brainerd, MN. $25,000, 2005. To connect low-income families with community resources.

1021. Center for Cross-Cultural Health, Minneapolis, MN. $50,000, 2005. For general operating support and development of fundraising plan.

1022. Community Referral Agency, Milltown, WI. $25,000, 2005. For general operating support.

1023. Early Childhood Resource Center, Minneapolis, MN. $70,000, 2005. For general operating support.

1024. Early Childhood Resource Center, Minneapolis, MN. $12,195, 2005. For strategic planning.

1025. Firstlink, Fargo, ND. $25,000, 2005. For relocation and referral service.

1026. Firstlink, Fargo, ND. $11,500, 2005. To conduct strategic planning.

1027. Frederic Public Library, Frederic, WI. $20,000, 2005. To renovate library.

1028. Milaca Area Community Library, Milaca, MN. $50,000, 2005. For construction of library.

1029. Minneapolis Community and Technical College, Minneapolis, MN. $25,000, 2005. To upgrade library and technology resources.

1030. New Pathways, Cambridge, MN. $15,000, 2005. For Interfaith Hospitality Network, transitional shelter and skills development program for people who are homeless.

1031. North Central Region Health Ministries Network, Brooklyn Center, MN. $10,000, 2005. For general support.

1032. Twin Cities Community Voice Mail, Saint Paul, MN. $25,000, 2005. For New Visibility, leadership program to empower low-income residents.

Bush Foundation

Limitations: Giving primarily in MN, ND, and SD. No support for private foundations or for organizations lacking 501c(3) status. No grants to individuals (except for fellowships), or for research in biomedical and health sciences. Generally, no grants for continuing operating support; construction of hospitals or medical facilities, church sanctuaries, individual day care centers, municipal buildings, or buildings in public colleges and universities; or for covering operating deficits or to retire mortgages or other debts; no loans.

1033. Center for Cross-Cultural Health, Minneapolis, MN. $35,000, 2005. To implement market research study to inform development of business and marketing plan.

1034. Early Childhood Resource Center, Minneapolis, MN. $136,000, 2005. To expand home visiting early literacy program.

1035. Mental Health Association in North Dakota, Bismarck, ND. $50,000, 2005. 1.25-year grant. Toward cost of operating statewide, 24-hour telephone crisis counseling 2-1-1 help line.

1036. New Pathways, Cambridge, MN. $35,000, 2005. 2-year grant. For staff to expand transitional services for homeless families to Morrison County.

The Cargill Foundation

Limitations: Giving primarily in Minneapolis, MN, and its western suburbs. No support for political, fraternal, veterans', or professional organizations or religious organizations not of direct benefit to the entire community. No grants to individuals, or for endowments, recognition or testimonial events, benefit fundraisers, travel, conferences, athletic scholarships, or projects at K-12 schools.

1037. Minneapolis Public Library, Friends of the, Minneapolis, MN. $250,000, 2005. For capital support.

General Mills Foundation

Limitations: Giving primarily in areas of major company operations. No support for religious, political, social, labor, veterans', alumni, or fraternal organizations, disease-specific organizations, or athletic associations. No grants to individuals (except for scholarships), or for endowments, research, publications, films, advertising, athletic events, testimonial dinners, workshops, symposia, travel, fundraising events, debt reduction, or recreation; no loans.

1038. American Indian Treaty Council Information Center, Minneapolis, MN. $10,000, 2005. For operating support.

1039. Minneapolis Neighborhood Employment Network, Minneapolis, MN. $20,000, 2005. For operating support.

1040. Southern Maryland Child Care Resource Center, Charlotte Hall, MD. $10,000, 2005. For Kids Under Construction.

Jerome Foundation

Limitations: Giving limited to MN and New York, NY. No support for educational programs in the arts and humanities. No grants to individuals (except for Film and Video program, and Travel and Study Grant program) or for undergraduate or graduate student research projects, capital or endowment funds, equipment, scholarships, or matching gifts.

1041. Franklin Furnace Archive, New York, NY. $77,000, 2005. For Fund for Performance Art and The Future of the Present.

The McKnight Foundation

Limitations: Giving limited to organizations in MN, especially the seven-county Twin Cities, MN, area, except for programs in the environment, international aid, and research. No support for religious organizations for religious purposes. No grants to individuals (except for the Virginia McKnight Binger Awards in Human Service), or for basic research in academic disciplines (except for defined programs in crop research and neuroscience) endowment funds, scholarships, fellowships, national fundraising campaigns, or ticket sales.

1042. Housing Link, Minneapolis, MN. $25,000, 2005. To create and launch special statewide Katrina Housing Relocation version of online directory of affordable housing, and use ramp up for ongoing statewide expansion.

1043. Minneapolis Public Library, Friends of the, Minneapolis, MN. $1,000,000, 2005. For New Central Library Capital Campaign.

1044. Prairie Rivers Network, Champaign, IL. $420,000, 2005. 3-year grant. To strengthen efforts to improve water quality in Mississippi River.

1045. Twin Cities Community Voice Mail, Saint Paul, MN. $55,000, 2005. 2-year grant. For voicemail program to serve parents.

The Medtronic Foundation

Limitations: Giving primarily in areas of company operations, with emphasis on Phoenix and Tempe, AZ, Goleta, Northridge, Santa Ana, and Santa Rosa, CA, Louisville and Parker, CO, Warsaw, IN, Danvers and the Twin Cities-Seven County metro, MN, area, Humacao and Villalba, PR, Memphis, TN, and Redmond, WA; giving also to national and international organizations active in areas of company operations. Generally, no support for social organizations, religious, political, or fraternal organizations, or United Way-supported organizations located in Minneapolis, Minnesota. No grants to individuals, or for debt reduction, capital campaigns, scientific research, travel, fundraising, general operating support, advertising, conferences, continuing support, reimbursable health treatment, or substance abuse programs.

1046. American Pain Foundation, Baltimore, MD. $75,000, 2005. For Pain Information Center Expansion and Online Searchable Database.

1047. American Pain Foundation, Baltimore, MD. $25,000, 2005. For general support.

1048. National Pain Foundation, Denver, CO. $60,000, 2005. For Caregiver Directory.

1049. PACER Center, Minneapolis, MN. $15,000, 2005. For Health Information and Advocacy Center.

1050. Parent Trust for Washington Children, Seattle, WA. $10,000, 2005. For Family Help Line, Support Network, Youth and Leadership, and Conscious Fathering.

1051. World Internet Resources for Education and Development (WiRED), Montara, CA. $35,000, 2005. For Medical Information Centers in Kosovo, Belgrade and Serbia.

The Minneapolis Foundation

Limitations: Giving limited to MN, with emphasis on organizations in the Twin Cities metropolitan region. No support for national campaigns, direct religious activities, veterans' or fraternal organizations, or organizations within umbrella organizations. No grants to individuals, or for annual campaigns, deficit financing, building or endowment funds, scholarships, fellowships, conferences, courtesy advertising, direct fundraising efforts, benefit tickets, telephone solicitations, or memberships.

1052. Lewis and Clark College, Portland, OR. $10,000, 2006. For History Library Endowment Fund.

1053. Minneapolis Public Library, Minneapolis, MN. $200,000, 2006. 2-year grant. For capital support.

1054. Minneapolis Public Library, Minneapolis, MN. $25,000, 2006. For general support.

1055. Minneapolis Public Library, Minneapolis, MN. $10,000, 2006. For New Building Fund.

1056. Minnesota State Law Library, Saint Paul, MN. $10,000, 2006. For Juvenile Court Committee.

Northwest Area Foundation

Limitations: Giving limited to IA, ID, MN, MT, ND, OR, SD, and WA. No support for lobbying activities. No grants to individuals.

1057. Foundation Center, New York, NY. $12,500, 2005.

I. A. O'Shaughnessy Foundation, Inc.

Limitations: Giving limited to the U.S., with emphasis on areas where foundation directors live. No support for religious missions or individual parishes, or for national fundraising organizations, or political organizations. No grants to individuals, or for operational dependence, lobbying, or capital campaign gifts exceeding twenty percent of the campaign goal; no loans.

1058. Johnson County Library Foundation, Overland Park, KS. $50,000, 2004. For endowment and capital campaign for programming and books.

The Jay and Rose Phillips Family Foundation

(formerly The Phillips Foundation)

Limitations: Giving primarily in the Twin Cities metropolitan, MN, area. No support for political campaigns or lobbying efforts to influence legislation. No grants to individuals.

1059. Face to Face Health and Counseling Service, Saint Paul, MN. $20,000, 2004. For transitional operating support for SafeZone program.

1060. Minneapolis Public Library, Friends of the, Minneapolis, MN. $250,000, 2004. For capital support for new Minneapolis Central Library, targeted to the New Citizens Center.

1061. Minnesota Child Care Resource and Referral Network, Saint Paul, MN. $40,000, 2004. For TEACH (Teacher Education And Compensation Helps) and REETAIN (Retaining Early Educators Through Attaining Incentives Now) programs.

1062. Survivors of the Shoah Visual History Foundation, Los Angeles, CA. $80,000, 2004. For plan to place Holocaust visual histories in the classrooms of Polish schools.

Carl and Eloise Pohlad Family Foundation

Limitations: Giving primarily in Minneapolis and St. Paul, MN. No grants to individuals.

1063. Minneapolis Public Library, Friends of the, Minneapolis, MN. $250,000, 2004. For capital support.

The Saint Paul Foundation, Inc.

Limitations: Giving limited to Dakota, Ramsey, and Washington counties in the metropolitan Saint Paul, MN, area. No support for sectarian religious programs (except from designated funds). No grants to individuals (except from designated funds), or for ongoing annual operating budgets, agency endowment funds, and capital projects located outside the East Metro area.

1064. Metropolitan State University Foundation, Saint Paul, MN. $274,387, 2004. Toward completion of capital campaign for new library.

1065. Minneapolis Public Library, Friends of the, Minneapolis, MN. $30,000, 2004. For general support.

1066. Minnesota Child Care Resource and Referral Network, Saint Paul, MN. $20,000, 2004. Toward Early Childhood Training Education, Compensation and Retention Project.

1067. Saint Johns University, Collegeville, MN. $11,000, 2004. For Hill Monastic Manuscript Library, new Saint John's Bible and Richard Bresnahan's Pottery.

1068. Saint Paul Jaycees Charitable Foundation, Saint Paul, MN. $12,256, 2004. For Library Project in honor of Anniversary.

1069. Saint Paul Public Library, Friends of the, Saint Paul, MN. $75,000, 2004. Toward start-up of Dayton's Bluff Branch Library.

1070. Stillwater, City of, Stillwater, MN. $100,000, 2004. For Stillwater Public Library Centennial Capital Campaign.

1071. Stillwater, City of, Stillwater, MN. $100,000, 2004. For Stillwater Public Library Centennial Capital Campaign.

1072. Stillwater, City of, Stillwater, MN. $12,500, 2004. For Stillwater Public Library Centennial Capital Campaign.

1073. Third Way Network, Minneapolis, MN. $25,000, 2004. For Organizational Expansion.

St. Paul Travelers Foundation

(formerly The St. Paul Companies, Inc. Foundation)

Limitations: Giving primarily in areas of significant company operations, with emphasis on the Twin Cities, MN; giving also to national organizations. No support for discriminatory organizations, sectarian religious

organizations, political, lobbying, veterans', or fraternal organizations, health or disease-specific organizations, or hospitals or other health services organizations generally supported by third-party reimbursement mechanisms. No grants to individuals, or for benefits, fundraisers, walk-a-thons, telethons, galas, or other revenue-generating events, advertising, health care or other health-related emergency assistance for individuals, direct delivery of health or medical services, medical research, medical equipment, or hospital capital campaigns or general operating support, replacement of government funding, start-up needs, capital campaigns, or general operating support for public or charter schools, human services such as counseling, chemical abuse services, or family programs, environmental programs, or special events not a key strategy in a continuum of efforts to achieve community goals in the foundation's priority areas.

1074. Charities Review Council of Minnesota, Saint Paul, MN. $10,000, 2004. For operating support for education and information services that strengthen and enhance the nonprofit sector and those who support it.

1075. Enoch Pratt Free Library, Baltimore, MD. $15,000, 2004. For project support for Teen Summer Reading program, which encourages teens to read during summer months and increases their chances for academic success.

1076. Housing Link, Minneapolis, MN. $15,000, 2004. For operating support to provide information and access for low-income families seeking affordable housing throughout the Twin Cities.

1077. Minnesota Child Care Resource and Referral Network, Saint Paul, MN. $55,000, 2004. For project support for pilot program to identify and demonstrate community-based strategies for helping family, friend and neighbor child caregivers to improve early literacy skills of children.

1078. Saint Paul Public Library, Friends of the, Saint Paul, MN. $20,000, 2004. For project support for Homework Help Center program, which empowers at-risk, low-income students to take responsibility for their academic achievement in East Side, West Side and Frogtown libraries.

1079. Vietnam Center, Saint Paul, MN. $10,000, 2004. For project support to establish Vietnamese library that would include teaching Vietnamese as a second language.

U.S. Bancorp Foundation, Inc.

(formerly First Bank System Foundation)

Limitations: Giving primarily in AR, AZ, CA, CO, ID, IA, IL, IN, KS, KY, MN, MO, MT, ND, NE, NV, OH, OR, SD, TN, UT, WA, WI, and WY. No support for fraternal organizations, merchant associations, or 501(c)(4) or (6) organizations, pass-through organizations or private foundations, religious organizations, political organizations or lobbying organizations, United Way-supported organizations, or child care providers. No grants to individuals, or for fundraising events or sponsorships, travel, endowments, debt reduction, or chamber memberships or programs.

1080. Alameda County Library Foundation, Fremont, CA. $13,000, 2004. For project support.

1081. Sacramento Public Library Foundation, Sacramento, CA. $10,000, 2004. For program support.

1082. Seattle Public Library Foundation, Seattle, WA. $10,000, 2004. For capital support.

WEM Foundation

Limitations: Giving primarily in MN. No grants to individuals.

1083. Carnegie Public Library, Big Timber, MT. $25,000, 2005. For campaign.

Xcel Energy Foundation

Limitations: Giving on a national basis, with emphasis on areas of company operations. No support for religious, political, veterans', or fraternal organizations not of direct benefit to the entire community or disease-specific organizations; generally, no support for national organizations. No grants for endowments, athletic or scholarship competitions, benefits or fundraising activities, sports or athletic programs, or capital campaigns; generally, no grants for research programs.

1084. Providers Resource Clearinghouse, Denver, CO. $10,000, 2004.

MISSISSIPPI

Oakwood Foundation Charitable Trust
Limitations: Giving primarily in MS.
1085. Eudora Welty Foundation, Jackson, MS. $10,000, 2004.

The Riley Foundation
Limitations: Giving limited to Meridian, and Lauderdale County, MS.
1086. Mississippi State University, Mississippi State, MS. $20,000, 2005. For Book Collection Enhancement.

MISSOURI

Anheuser-Busch Foundation
Limitations: Giving primarily in areas of company operations. No support for political candidates or organizations, religious organizations, fraternal, social, or similar organizations, or athletic organizations. No grants to individuals, or for general operating support for hospitals.
1087. OASIS Institute, Saint Louis, MO. $30,000, 2005. For general support.

The Danforth Foundation
Limitations: Giving limited to the metropolitan St. Louis, MO, area. No grants to individuals.
1088. Saint Louis University, Saint Louis, MO. $1,200,000, 2005. To carry out process in which region's progress in meeting important community goals is measured, evaluated, and shared with public through RegionWise Initiative.
1089. United Way of Greater Saint Louis, Saint Louis, MO. $33,000, 2005. To carry out process in which region's progress in meeting important community goals is measured, evaluated, and shared with public through RegionWise Initiative.

Emerson Charitable Trust
Limitations: Giving primarily in areas of company operations.
1090. Lebanon-Laclede Public Library Foundation, Lebanon, MO. $10,000, 2004. For general support.
1091. Lebanon-Laclede Public Library Foundation, Lebanon, MO. $10,000, 2004. For general support.
1092. Saint Louis County Library Foundation, Saint Louis, MO. $10,000, 2004. For general support.

Enterprise Rent-A-Car Foundation
(formerly Enterprise Leasing Foundation)
Limitations: Giving on a national and international basis in areas of company operations, including in Canada and the United Kingdom. No support for schools, churches, or sports teams. No vehicle or rental donations.
1093. Ronald Reagan Presidential Foundation, Simi Valley, CA. $10,000, 2005.

Hall Family Foundation
Limitations: Giving limited to greater Kansas City, MO. No support for international or religious organizations or for political purposes. No grants to individuals (except for employee-related scholarships), or for travel, operating deficits, conferences, scholarly or medical research, or fundraising campaigns or event promotion such as telethons, or for endowments.
1094. Harry S. Truman Library Institute for National and International Affairs, Independence, MO. $40,000, 2005. For Churchill and the Great Republic exhibition.

1095. Library of Congress, DC. $10,000, 2005. For Song of America tour and educational outreach.
1096. United Way, Heart of America, Kansas City, MO. $300,000, 2005. 3-year grant. For 2-1-1 program.

Ewing Marion Kauffman Foundation
Limitations: Giving limited to the U.S., with emphasis on the bi-state metropolitan Kansas City area (KS/MO) for K-12 education initiatives focused on math and science. No support for international programs, political, social, fraternal, or arts organizations, and capital campaigns or construction projects. No grants for fund endowments, or for special events.
1097. Foundation Center, New York, NY. $60,000, 2005. For core operating support.
1098. James Jerome Hill Reference Library, Saint Paul, MN. $105,000, 2005. For HillSearch access and training for FastTrac participants.
1099. James Jerome Hill Reference Library, Saint Paul, MN. $19,000, 2005. To provide premium business information and services online for FastTrac participants.
1100. James Jerome Hill Reference Library, Saint Paul, MN. $15,900, 2005. For discovery phase of online Entrepreneur Library.
1101. University of Missouri, Columbia, MO. $191,007, 2005. To develop digital library and database of contract forms and related data on investments made by angel groups in entrepreneurial firms.

Muriel McBrien Kauffman Foundation
Limitations: Giving primarily in Kansas City, MO, and New York, NY. No support for religious or political organizations. No loans or program-related investments.
1102. New York Public Library, Library for the Performing Arts, New York, NY. $10,000, 2004. For general operating support.

William T. Kemper Foundation
Limitations: Giving primarily in the Midwest with emphasis on MO and surrounding areas. No support for private foundations. No grants to individuals, or for tickets for dinners, benefits, exhibits, sports and other event activities, advertisements, endowment funds, or fundraising activities.
1103. Kansas City Public Library, Kansas City, MO. $50,000, 2005. For grant made through Greater Kansas City Community Foundation.
1104. Kansas City Public Library, Kansas City, MO. $10,047, 2005.
1105. Library of Congress Millennium Foundation, DC. $10,000, 2005.

The May Department Stores Foundation
(formerly The May Department Stores Company Foundation, Inc.)
Limitations: Giving on a national basis in areas of company operations; giving also to national organizations. No grants to individuals.
1106. American Library Association, Chicago, IL. $10,000, 2005. For general support.
1107. Dallas Public Library, Friends of the, Dallas, TX. $10,000, 2005. For general support.
1108. OASIS Institute, Saint Louis, MO. $252,628, 2005. For general support.
1109. OASIS Institute, Saint Louis, MO. $252,625, 2005. For general support.
1110. OASIS Institute, Saint Louis, MO. $252,624, 2005. For general support.
1111. OASIS Institute, Saint Louis, MO. $252,624, 2005. For general support.
1112. OASIS Institute, Saint Louis, MO. $115,502, 2005. For general support.
1113. OASIS Institute, Saint Louis, MO. $115,500, 2005. For general support.
1114. OASIS Institute, Saint Louis, MO. $115,500, 2005. For general support.
1115. OASIS Institute, Saint Louis, MO. $115,499, 2005. For general support.
1116. OASIS Institute, Saint Louis, MO. $15,000, 2005. For general support.
1117. OASIS Institute, Saint Louis, MO. $10,000, 2005. For general support.
1118. OASIS Institute, Saint Louis, MO. $10,000, 2005. For general support.

MONTANA

The Cinnabar Foundation
Limitations: Giving limited to MT and the Yellowstone area.
1119. Montana Environmental Information Center, Helena, MT. $15,000, 2005. To promote environmental protection and conservation.

First Interstate BancSystem Foundation, Inc.
Limitations: Giving primarily in areas of company operations in MT and WY. No support for sectarian or religious organizations not of direct benefit to the entire community. No grants for general operating support for established organizations or discriminatory programs.
1120. Livingston-Park County Library, Friends of the, Livingston, MT. $16,500, 2004. For Library Expansion Campaign.

Gilhousen Family Foundation
Limitations: Giving primarily in Gallatin County, MT. No grants to individuals.
1121. Bozeman Public Library Foundation, Bozeman, MT. $25,000, 2005. For building.

NEBRASKA

The Susan Thompson Buffett Foundation
(formerly The Buffett Foundation)
Limitations: Giving on a national basis; scholarships awarded only to residents in NE. No grant to individuals (except for Teacher Awards).
1122. Sexuality Information and Education Council of the U.S. (SIECUS), New York, NY. $50,000, 2005. For general support.

ConAgra Foods Foundation
(formerly The ConAgra Foundation, Inc.)
Limitations: Giving on a national basis in areas of company operations, with emphasis on NE. No support for religious organizations not of direct benefit to the entire community, clubs, fraternal or social organizations, grantmaking organizations, public or private K-12 schools, or athletic teams. No grants to individuals (except for scholarships), or for fundraising or testimonial events or dinners, travel or tours, advertising, endowments, conferences, seminars, workshops, symposia, or publication of proceedings, radio or television programming underwriting, emergency needs, or athletic events; no product donations or in-kind gifts; no grants totaling more than 10 percent of an organization's campaign goal or budget.
1123. Carthage Public Library, Friends of the, Carthage, MO. $10,000, 2005.

Peter Kiewit Foundation
Limitations: Giving limited to Rancho Mirage, CA, western IA, NE, and Sheridan, WY; college scholarships available to graduating seniors in NE. No support for elementary or secondary schools, churches, or religious groups. No grants to individuals (except for scholarships), or for endowment funds or annual campaigns.
1124. Imperial, City of, Imperial, NE. $75,000, 2005. For Imperial Library Foundation.
1125. Lexington, City of, Lexington, NE. $75,000, 2005. For Lexington Community Foundation and construction of new public library facility.
1126. Missouri Valley, City of, Missouri Valley, IA. $80,000, 2005. For Missouri Valley Public Library.
1127. Omaha Public Library, Omaha, NE. $13,800, 2005. For Omaha Reads program.
1128. Saint Edward, City of, Saint Edward, NE. $50,000, 2005. For construction of new library facility.

1129. South Sioux City, City of, South Sioux City, NE. $200,000, 2005. Toward construction and furnishing of new library facility.

Union Pacific Foundation
Limitations: Giving on a national basis in areas of company operations. No support for specialized national health and welfare organizations, religious or labor organizations, social clubs, or fraternal or veterans' organizations. No grants to individuals, or for sponsorship of dinners, benefits, seminars, or other special events or non-capital support for United Way-supported organizations.
1130. Friends of the Library Smithville Texas, Smithville, TX. $10,000, 2004.
1131. University of Missouri, John W. Barriger III National Railroad Library/Saint Louis Mercantile Library, Saint Louis, MO. $12,500, 2004.

NEVADA

Bing Fund Corporation
Limitations: Giving on a national basis. No grants to individuals.
1132. Huntington Library, Art Collections and Botanical Gardens, San Marino, CA. $10,000, 2005. For general support.
1133. Library Foundation of Los Angeles, Los Angeles, CA. $50,000, 2005. For David Macaulay exhibition.

Conrad N. Hilton Foundation
Limitations: No support for political organizations. No grants to individuals, or for fundraising events.
1134. Ronald Reagan Presidential Foundation, Simi Valley, CA. $275,000, 2005. For education programs.

Lied Foundation Trust
Limitations: Giving primarily in NE and Las Vegas, NV.
1135. Avera Saint Anthonys Hospital, ONeill, NE. $300,000, 2004. For picture archives communication system.
1136. Imperial Library Foundation, Imperial, NE. $58,191, 2004. For construction of library.

Wayne L. Prim Foundation
Limitations: Giving primarily in CA and NV. No grants to individuals.
1137. Sierra Nevada College, Incline Village, NV. $1,097,550, 2005. For student library.

Nell J. Redfield Foundation
Limitations: Giving primarily in northern NV.
1138. Oneida Library, Oneida, NY. $10,000, 2004. To purchase books for teen center.
1139. Washoe Library Foundation, Reno, NV. $100,833, 2004. For Young People's Library.

Donald W. Reynolds Foundation
Limitations: Giving primarily in AR, NV, and OK for capital and planning grants. Giving nationally for cardiovascular clinic research and geriatrics training of physicians, and business journalism. No support for elementary or secondary education, or religious institutions or hospitals. No grants to individuals, or for continuing support, program or operating support, or endowment funds.
1140. Baxter County Public Library Foundation, Mountain Home, AR. $49,800, 2005. For planning and technical assistance.
1141. Choctaw County Library, Hugo, OK. $104,913, 2005. For art for new library.

E. L. Wiegand Foundation
Limitations: Giving primarily in NV and adjoining western states, including AZ, ID, OR, UT and WA; public affairs grants given primarily in Washington,

DC, and New York, NY. No support for organizations receiving significant support from the United Way or public tax funds; organizations with beneficiaries of their own choosing; or federal, state, or local government agencies or institutions. No grants to individuals, or for endowment funds, fundraising campaigns, debt reductions, emergency funding, film or media presentations, or operating funds; no loans.

1142. Our Lady of Lourdes School, Great Falls, MT. $57,444, 2004. For library/computer resource center.

1143. Sage Ridge School, Reno, NV. $20,000, 2004. For library materials.

1144. Sisters of Our Lady of Mount Carmel, Reno, NV. $208,199, 2004. For library.

NEW HAMPSHIRE

Norwin S. and Elizabeth N. Bean Foundation
Limitations: Giving limited to Amherst and Manchester, NH. No grants to individuals, or for scholarships, fellowships, operating budgets, deficit financing, or endowment funds.

1145. Manchester City Library, Manchester, NH. $10,000, 2004. For Learn to Read program for adults.

1146. Parent Information Center, Concord, NH. $24,450, 2004. To sustain parents involved in education program.

The Byrne Foundation, Inc.
Limitations: Giving primarily in NH, NY, and VT. No grants to individuals.

1147. Dartmouth College, Tucker Foundation, Hanover, NH. $20,000, 2004. For general/operating support.

1148. Howe Library, Hanover, NH. $25,050, 2004. For general/operating support.

Cogswell Benevolent Trust
Limitations: Giving primarily in NH (90 percent of funding limited to NH). No grants to individuals, or for endowment funds, operating budgets, or deficit financing.

1149. Manchester City Library, Manchester, NH. $25,000, 2005. To purchase books and audio books.

The New Hampshire Charitable Foundation
Limitations: Giving in the Lakes, Manchester, Monadnock, Nashua, North Country, Piscataqua, and Upper Valley regions in NH. No support for sectarian or religious purposes. No grants to individuals (except for student aid and special awards); generally no grants for building funds, endowments, deficit financing, capital campaigns for acquisition of land or renovations to facilities, purchase of major equipment, academic research, travel, or to replace public funding or for purposes which are a public responsibility.

1150. Organic Center, Foster, RI. $25,000, 2005.

1151. Organic Center for Education and Promotion, Greenfield, MA. $25,000, 2005.

1152. Organic Center for Education and Promotion, Greenfield, MA. $25,000, 2005.

1153. Park Street Foundation, Concord, NH. $10,000, 2005.

NEW JERSEY

Geraldine R. Dodge Foundation, Inc.
Limitations: Giving primarily in NJ, with support for the arts and local humane groups limited to NJ, and support for other local projects limited to the Morristown-Madison area; some giving to national organizations. No support for religious, higher education, health, or conduit organizations. No grants for capital projects, equipment purchases, indirect costs, endowment funds, deficit financing, or scholarships.

1154. Educational Information and Resource Center, Sewell, NJ. $120,000, 2005. For activities of Earth Education and New Jersey Teachers for Biodiversity programs.

1155. Urban Libraries Council, Evanston, IL. $20,000, 2005. For general operating support.

The Hyde and Watson Foundation
Limitations: Giving is focused in the five boroughs of New York, NY, and Essex, Union and Morris counties in NJ. No giving outside the U.S. No grants for endowments, operating support, benefit fundraisers, annual fund appears, or scholarships or from fiscal agents.

1156. Morristown and Morris Township Library Foundation, Morristown, NJ. $15,000, 2005. For facility renovations and expansion.

1157. Nonprofit Connection, Brooklyn, NY. $10,000, 2005. For leasehold improvements, computer equipment and office furnishings.

1158. Plainfield Public Library, Friends of the, Plainfield, NJ. $15,000, 2005. For facility renovations and improvements.

Johnson & Johnson Family of Companies Contribution Fund
Limitations: No support for fraternal, political, religious, or athletic organizations. No grants to individuals, or for debt reduction, trips, tours, capital campaigns or endowments, or publications; no loans.

1159. Foundation for American Communications, Pasadena, CA. $50,000, 2004. For operating support for educational programs and resources for media that focus on science, engineering, economics, and risk.

1160. Foundation of the ARC of the United States, Silver Spring, MD. $25,000, 2004. For Web site where families can access information and resources and cost-efficient ways of providing resources.

1161. Fundacion Luis Munoz Marin, San Juan, PR. $20,000, 2004. For permanent exhibit on life and work of Luis Munoz Marin.

1162. Info Line of Middlesex County, Milltown, NJ. $15,000, 2004. For operating support.

1163. National Coalition for Cancer Survivorship, Silver Spring, MD. $10,000, 2004. For Ribbon of Hope Awards Gala.

1164. National Womens Health Resource Center, DC. $25,000, 2004.

1165. New Jersey Symphony Orchestra, Newark, NJ. $100,000, 2004. For outreach efforts to young children, nursing homes, and libraries, and for Family Concert event in New Brunswick.

1166. University of the Sacred Heart, San Juan, PR. $25,000, 2004. For Virtual Center to Train Leaders of Third Sector.

1167. Wisconsin Womens Health Foundation, Madison, WI. $10,000, 2004. For Women's Health grant.

The Robert Wood Johnson Foundation
Limitations: Giving limited to the U.S. No support for political organizations, international activities, programs or institutions concerned solely with a specific disease or basic biomedical research. No grants to individuals, or for ongoing general operating expenses, endowment funds, capital costs, including construction, renovation, or equipment, or research on unapproved drug therapies or devices.

1168. Austin Health and Human Service Department, Austin, TX. $75,000, 2005. For new initiative, InformationLinks: Connecting Public Health with Health Information Exchanges.

1169. Colorado Department of Public Health and Environment, Denver, CO. $92,030, 2005. For new initiative, InformationLinks: Connecting Public Health with Health Information Exchanges.

1170. Council of State Governments, Southern Governors Association, Lexington, KY. $735,060, 2005. To develop Gulf Coast Health Information Technology Task Force.

1171. Denver Health and Hospital Authority, Denver, CO. $74,257, 2005. For new initiative, InformationLinks: Connecting Public Health with Health Information Exchanges.

1172. General Hospital Corporation, Massachusetts General Hospital, Boston, MA. $50,000, 2005. To sponsor meeting to formulate guidelines for monitoring diffusion of health information technology.

1173. Greenlights for Nonprofit Success, Austin, TX. $45,460, 2005. For Reducing Underage Drinking Through Coalitions: Youth and Adults United for Change, initiative which seeks policy solutions that significantly reduce underage drinking and creates healthier, safer communities for everyone.

1174. Hamilton County General Health District, Cincinnati, OH. $74,408, 2005. For new initiative, InformationLinks: Connecting Public Health with Health Information Exchanges.

1175. Health Level Seven, Ann Arbor, MI. $381,600, 2005. For technical assistance to develop optimal organizational structure and process redesign for electronic health information technical standards organization.

1176. Health-Equity.Org, Arlington, VA. $66,599, 2005. To convene diverse set of health professionals to review and provide guidance to Refugee Health Information Network.

1177. Imperial, County of, County Administration Center, El Centro, CA. $75,000, 2005. For new initiative, InformationLinks: Connecting Public Health with Health Information Exchanges.

1178. Indiana State Department of Health, Indianapolis, IN. $100,000, 2005. For new initiative, InformationLinks: Connecting Public Health with Health Information Exchanges.

1179. Info Line of Middlesex County, Milltown, NJ. $85,482, 2005. 2-year grant. For county-wide information and referral service for health and social services.

1180. Ingham, County of, Mason, MI. $74,518, 2005. For new initiative, InformationLinks: Connecting Public Health with Health Information Exchanges.

1181. Kansas Department of Health and Environment, Topeka, KS. $96,037, 2005. For new initiative, InformationLinks: Connecting Public Health with Health Information Exchanges.

1182. Louisiana Public Health Institute, New Orleans, LA. $74,980, 2005. For new initiative, InformationLinks: Connecting Public Health with Health Information Exchanges.

1183. Maine Center for Public Health, Augusta, ME. $100,000, 2005. For new initiative, InformationLinks: Connecting Public Health with Health Information Exchanges.

1184. Mendocino County Public Health Department, Ukiah, CA. $74,800, 2005. For new initiative, InformationLinks: Connecting Public Health with Health Information Exchanges.

1185. Mesa County Health Department, Grand Junction, CO. $75,000, 2005. For new initiative, InformationLinks: Connecting Public Health with Health Information Exchanges.

1186. Minnesota Department of Health, Department of Health, Saint Paul, MN. $100,000, 2005. For new initiative, InformationLinks: Connecting Public Health with Health Information Exchanges.

1187. National Center for Learning Disabilities, New York, NY. $50,000, 2005. To develop online national resource center for parents of children (ages 5-14) with learning disabilities.

1188. National Conference of State Legislatures, DC. $959,965, 2005. 3-year grant. For forum and information resources for state legislator health policy leadership.

1189. National Network of Public Health Institutes, New Orleans, LA. $447,663, 2005. 1.25-year grant. For technical assistance and direction for Multistate Learning Collaborative for Public Health.

1190. National Network of Public Health Institutes, New Orleans, LA. $170,141, 2005. To assess, through evaluation, local emergency preparedness using common assessment tool.

1191. National Network of Public Health Institutes, New Orleans, LA. $25,629, 2005. For temporary infrastructure needs due to displacement by Hurricane Katrina.

1192. National Opinion Research Center (NORC), Chicago, IL. $170,874, 2005. 1.75-year grant. To assess InformationLinks: Connecting Public Health with Health Information Exchanges.

1193. New York Academy of Medicine, New York, NY. $400,000, 2005. 2-year grant. For research to evaluate pharmacy-based drug treatment links through New York State Expanded Syringe Access Demonstration Program.

1194. New York City Department of Health and Mental Hygiene, New York, NY. $75,000, 2005. For new initiative, InformationLinks: Connecting Public Health with Health Information Exchanges.

1195. Puerto Rico Department of Health, San Juan, PR. $96,780, 2005. For new initiative, InformationLinks: Connecting Public Health with Health Information Exchanges.

1196. Research Foundation of the State University of New York, Albany, NY. $74,949, 2005. For new initiative, InformationLinks: Connecting Public Health with Health Information Exchanges.

1197. Rhode Island Department of Health, Providence, RI. $96,317, 2005. For new initiative, InformationLinks: Connecting Public Health with Health Information Exchanges.

1198. Santa Cruz, City of, County Administrative Office, Santa Cruz, CA. $74,839, 2005. For new initiative, InformationLinks: Connecting Public Health with Health Information Exchanges.

1199. Tennessee Department of Finance and Administration, Nashville, TN. $100,000, 2005. For new initiative, InformationLinks: Connecting Public Health with Health Information Exchanges.

1200. University of Kentucky Research Foundation, Lexington, KY. $163,999, 2005. 1.50-year grant. For efforts to increase availability and promote use of National Library of Medicine's datasets for public health systems research.

1201. University of Michigan, Institute for Social Research, Ann Arbor, MI. $355,057, 2005. 2-year grant. To provide data preparation and archiving services to Foundation.

1202. University of Pennsylvania, School of Medicine, Philadelphia, PA. $200,000, 2005. For research to plan expansion and sustainability of African-American Collaborative Obesity Research Network.

1203. Utah Department of Health, Salt Lake City, UT. $99,780, 2005. For new initiative, InformationLinks: Connecting Public Health with Health Information Exchanges.

1204. Wisconsin Department of Health and Family Services, Department of Health and Family Services, Madison, WI. $100,000, 2005. For new initiative, InformationLinks: Connecting Public Health with Health Information Exchanges.

The Kaplen Foundation

Limitations: Giving primarily in NJ, with some emphasis on Englewood. Some giving also in NY. No grants to individuals.

1205. Healing the Children Midlantic, Butler, NJ. $10,000, 2005. For general support.

1206. National Yiddish Book Center, Amherst, MA. $475,000, 2005. For general support.

F. M. Kirby Foundation, Inc.

Limitations: Giving primarily in Raleigh-Durham, NC, Morris County, NJ, and eastern PA. Generally no support for churches, hospitals, schools and colleges, other than ones attended by or used by members of the family. No grants to individuals, or for fundraising benefits, dinners, theater, or sporting events; no loans or pledges.

1207. First Call for Help, Parsippany, NJ. $10,000, 2005. Toward public education campaign.

1208. Foundation Center, New York, NY. $12,500, 2005. For general operating support.

1209. Jamestown Foundation, DC. $10,000, 2005. For general operating support.

1210. Morristown and Morris Township Library Foundation, Morristown, NJ. $85,000, 2005. Toward New Edition capital campaign to name F.M. Kirby Exhibition Gallery.

1211. New Jersey Coalition for Battered Women, Trenton, NJ. $20,000, 2005. For matching support for Legal Services Project.

1212. Sexuality Information and Education Council of the U.S. (SIECUS), New York, NY. $30,000, 2005. For education programs.

1213. Wyoming Seminary, Kingston, PA. $35,000, 2005. For Kirby Library.

Lucent Technologies Foundation

Limitations: Giving on a national and international basis, with emphasis on areas of company operations. No support for political candidates. No grants to individuals (except for Graduate Research Fellowships and Conqueror of the Hill), or for political causes, sectarian religious activities, capital campaigns, chairs or endowments, or conferences or fundraising events; no product donations.

1214. Charities Aid Foundation (CAF) America, Alexandria, VA. $49,800, 2004. For Global Days of Caring employee volunteer program.

The MCJ Foundation

1215. Morristown and Morris Township Library Foundation, Morristown, NJ. $10,000, 2004. For general operating support.

The Merck Company Foundation

Limitations: Giving on a national and international basis in areas of company operations. No support for political organizations, fraternal, labor, or veterans' organizations, religious organizations not of direct benefit to the entire community, or discriminatory organizations. No grants to individuals, or for political campaigns or activities, fundraising, capital campaigns, non-public broadcasting media productions, basic or clinical research projects, direct medical care or the purchase of medications, devices, or biologics, meetings, conferences, symposia, or workshops, fellowships or scholarships for training purposes intended for a specific individual or institution, debt reduction, beauty or talent contests, or programs directly supporting marketing or sales objectives of Merck.

1216. Philanthropic Research, Inc., Williamsburg, VA. $10,000, 2004.

Merrill Lynch & Co. Foundation, Inc.

Limitations: Giving to national and international organizations. No support for private foundations, political or lobbying organizations, religious, fraternal, social, or other membership organizations, or United Way-supported organizations (except for emergency needs). No grants to individuals (except for employee-related scholarships), or for fundraising activities related to individual sponsorships, start-up needs, athletic events or sports tournaments (except for the Special Olympics), fundraising events, endowments, construction or renovation, special purpose campaigns, chairs, or equipment, conferences, workshops, or seminars, research, or film or video production; no loans.

1217. Charities Aid Foundation (CAF) America, Alexandria, VA. $380,000, 2004. For general support.

1218. Foundation Center, New York, NY. $10,000, 2004. For general support.

1219. New York Public Library, New York, NY. $25,000, 2004. For general support.

The Prudential Foundation

Limitations: Giving primarily in areas of company operations, with emphasis on Phoenix, AZ, Los Angeles, CA, Jacksonville, FL, Atlanta, GA, Minneapolis, MN, Newark, NJ, Philadelphia, PA, and Houston, TX. No support for veterans', labor, religious, fraternal, or athletic organizations. No grants to individuals (except for employee-related scholarships), or for advertising, fundraising , or disease-specific general operating support.

1220. Jersey City Connections, Jersey City, NJ. $40,000, 2004. For Girls Living in the Trans Zone (GLITZ).

The Schumann Center for Media and Democracy, Inc.

(formerly The Florence and John Schumann Foundation)

Limitations: Giving on a national basis. No grants to individuals, or for annual campaigns, capital campaigns, deficit financing, equipment and materials, land acquisition, or endowment funds; no loans.

1221. Media Matters for America, DC. $500,000, 2005. For general support for work to monitor and analyze U.S. media.

1222. National Security Archive Fund, DC. $420,000, 2005. Toward Iraq War Media Project.

Turrell Fund

Limitations: Giving limited to Essex, Union, Hudson and Passaic counties, NJ, and VT. No support for advocacy work, most hospital work, or health delivery services; generally no support for cultural activities. No grants to individuals, or for endowment funds, conferences, or research; no loans.

1223. Goodrich Memorial Library, Newport, VT. $10,000, 2005. For Big Read Wagon Bookmobile.

1224. Kellogg-Hubbard Library, Montpelier, VT. $20,000, 2005. For Van Go bookmobile.

1225. Lanpher Memorial Library, Hyde Park, VT. $15,000, 2005. For children's area.

1226. Newark Family Resource Network, Newark, NJ. $25,000, 2005. For child abuse prevention services.

1227. Vershare, Vershire, VT. $12,000, 2005. For summer camp and library.

UBS Foundation U.S.A.

(formerly PaineWebber Foundation)

Limitations: Giving primarily in NY. No grants to individuals.

1228. Smith County Champions for Children, Tyler, TX. $14,500, 2004.

Unilever United States Foundation

Limitations: Giving primarily in areas of company operations. No support for religious, labor, political, or veterans' organizations. No grants to individuals (except for employee-related scholarships), or for goodwill advertising, fundraising events or testimonial dinners, or capital campaigns; no loans.

1229. International Food Information Council, DC. $93,800, 2004.

Verizon Foundation

(formerly Bell Atlantic Foundation)

Limitations: Giving on a national basis and in PR, the Dominican Republic, and Venezuela. No support for religious organizations not of direct benefit to the entire community, religious organizations duplicating the work of other organizations in the same community, political organizations or candidates, discriminatory organizations, lobbying organizations, or organizations that duplicate or significantly overlap the work of public agencies on the local, state, or federal level. No grants to individuals (except for scholarships), or for political causes or campaigns, endowments or capital campaigns, film, music, television, video, or media production or broadcast underwriting, research studies not related to projects already being supported by the Verizon Foundation, sports sponsorships, performing arts tours, or association memberships.

1230. 211 Tampa Bay Cares, Largo, FL. $12,000, 2004. For unrestricted support.

1231. Atlanta University Center, Atlanta, GA. $14,000, 2004. For unrestricted support.

1232. Beaumont District Library, Friends of, Beaumont, CA. $25,000, 2004. For unrestricted support.

1233. BookEnds, West Hills, CA. $20,000, 2004. For unrestricted support.

1234. Boston Public Library Foundation, Boston, MA. $20,050, 2004. For unrestricted support.

1235. Cedar Creek Library, Seven Points, TX. $19,613, 2004. For unrestricted support.

1236. Cedar Mill Community Library Association of Washington County, Portland, OR. $15,000, 2004. For unrestricted support.

1237. Central Library, Friends of the, Syracuse, NY. $23,250, 2004. For unrestricted support.

1238. Citizens Advice Bureau, Bronx, NY. $15,000, 2004. For unrestricted support.

1239. Clearwater Library Foundation, Clearwater, FL. $10,000, 2004. For unrestricted support.

1240. Community Library, Friends of the, Salem, WI. $14,813, 2004. For unrestricted support.

1241. Covina Library Fund, Covina, CA. $10,000, 2004. For unrestricted support.

1242. Downey City Library, Friends of the, Downey, CA. $25,000, 2004. For unrestricted support.

1243. Elder Wisdom Circle, Walnut Creek, CA. $24,800, 2004. For unrestricted support.

1244. Fairfax County Public Library Foundation, Fairfax, VA. $10,000, 2004. For unrestricted support.

1245. Library of Hawaii, Friends of the, Waimanalo, HI. $10,000, 2004. For unrestricted support.

1246. Marathon County Public Library Foundation, Wausau, WI. $12,000, 2004. For unrestricted support.

1247. National Institute for Literacy, DC. $50,000, 2004. For unrestricted support.

1248. Oakland Public Library Foundation, Oakland, CA. $20,000, 2004. For unrestricted support.

1249. Park Street Foundation, Concord, NH. $10,000, 2004. For unrestricted support.

1250. Port Hueneme Library, Friends of, Port Hueneme, CA. $25,000, 2004. For unrestricted support.

1251. Providence Public Library, Providence, RI. $26,000, 2004. For unrestricted support.

1252. Queens Library Foundation, Jamaica, NY. $15,300, 2004. For unrestricted support.

1253. SeniorNavigator.com, Richmond, VA. $25,000, 2004. For unrestricted support.

1254. Sterling Municipal Library, Friends of, Baytown, TX. $12,000, 2004. For unrestricted support.

1255. Talbot County Free Library, Easton, MD. $20,000, 2004. For unrestricted support.

1256. Washington Information Network 2-1-1, Seattle, WA. $35,000, 2004. For unrestricted support.

1257. Wilmington Institute Free Library, Wilmington, DE. $12,500, 2004. For unrestricted support.

1258. Women Work: The National Network for Womens Employment, DC. $30,000, 2004. For unrestricted support.

Victoria Foundation, Inc.

Limitations: Giving limited to greater Newark, NJ; environmental grants limited to NJ. No support for organizations dealing with specific diseases or afflictions, geriatric needs, or day care. No grants to individuals, or for publications or conferences.

1259. Newark Family Resource Network, Newark, NJ. $25,000, 2005. For services to clients referred to organization who are not currently involved in Division of Youth and Family Services (DYFS), but who require assistance.

1260. Saint Mary School, Newark, NJ. $20,000, 2005. To hire media specialist and upgrade computers and library materials.

Charles B. Wang Foundation

Limitations: Giving primarily in NY. No grants to individuals.

1261. Queens Library Foundation, Jamaica, NY. $100,000, 2004. For program support.

NEW MEXICO

The R. D. & Joan Dale Hubbard Foundation

Limitations: Giving primarily in CA, KS, NM, OK, and TX. No grants to individuals (except from designated scholarship funds).

1262. University of Kentucky, Lexington, KY. $25,000, 2004. For library endowment fund.

Lannan Foundation

Limitations: Giving on a national basis. No grants to individuals (except for Lannan Literary Awards and certain fellowships in the Literary and Cultural Freedom program areas).

1263. Dalkey Archive Press, Normal, IL. $150,000, 2005. For salaries and publication.

1264. Dalkey Archive Press, Normal, IL. $25,000, 2005. For marketing support for The Tunnel.

1265. Folger Shakespeare Library, DC. $25,000, 2005. For grant made through Amherst College Trustees.

1266. Newberry Library, Chicago, IL. $50,000, 2005. For Native American scholars summer institute.

1267. Santa Fe Indian School, Santa Fe, NM. $35,000, 2005. For library.

1268. Sinte Gleska University, Mission, SD. $35,000, 2005. For library.

1269. Southwest Research and Information Center, Albuquerque, NM. $50,000, 2005.

McCune Charitable Foundation

(formerly Marshall L. & Perrine D. McCune Charitable Foundation)

Limitations: Giving limited to NM. No grants to individuals, or for endowments, research, operating or capital expenses, voter registration drives, or to cover deficits.

1270. Southwest Research and Information Center, Albuquerque, NM. $25,000, 2004. To continue environmental education outreach and to continue to provide technical assistance to dozens of community groups in New Mexico on environmental and health issues.

1271. Southwest Research and Information Center, Albuquerque, NM. $10,000, 2004. To bring together native and non-native environmental organizations to address environmental, social and cultural issues facing Navajo communities and to train grassroots Navajo leaders to be more effective.

1272. Southwest Research and Information Center, Albuquerque, NM. $10,000, 2004. For general operating support for Nuclear Watch New Mexico.

Messengers of Healing Winds Foundation

Limitations: Giving primarily in the lake region of northwest IA, FL, SD, Santa Fe, NM, and the Southwest. Giving on a national basis for environmental concerns. No grants to individuals.

1273. Phoebe Apperson Hearst Library, Lead, SD. $10,000, 2004.

The New Mexico Community Foundation

Limitations: Giving limited to NM, with emphasis on rural communities. No support for religious purposes or the United Way or other federated giving organizations. No grants for endowment funds.

1274. Embudo Library Fund, Dixon, NM. $15,000, 2004.

Stockman Family Foundation Trust

Limitations: Giving primarily in NM. No grants to individuals.

1275. Canajoharie Library and Art Gallery, Canajoharie, NY. $12,000, 2005. For conservation of paintings, prints and drawings.

Eugene V. & Clare E. Thaw Charitable Trust

Limitations: Giving on a national basis. No grants to individuals or for operating support.

1276. Josef Albers Foundation, Bethany, CT. $12,500, 2004. For challenge grant toward archives organization project.

1277. Pierpont Morgan Library, New York, NY. $500,000, 2004. Toward capital campaign.

1278. Pierpont Morgan Library, New York, NY. $20,000, 2004. For annual support of Director's Roundtable.

NEW YORK

Louis and Anne Abrons Foundation, Inc.

Limitations: Giving primarily in the metropolitan New York, NY, area. No grants to individuals.

1279. New York Public Library, New York, NY. $25,000, 2005.

Altman Foundation

Limitations: Giving limited to NY, with emphasis on the boroughs of New York City. No grants to individuals, or for building funds, or capital equipment.

1280. Archdiocese of New York, Patron's Program, New York, NY. $132,000, 2005. To renew support for Acrete Corporation's evaluation plan for Library Connections.

1281. Brooklyn Public Library, Brooklyn, NY. $100,000, 2005. To renew support for First Five Years initiative to enhance environment, collections, and program offerings for young children and families.

1282. Child Care, Inc., New York, NY. $50,000, 2005. To improve access to early learning opportunities for children in New York City.

1283. Citizens Advice Bureau, Bronx, NY. $40,000, 2005. To provide support for Center for Achieving Future Education, high school and college access program.

1284. Literacy Assistance Center, New York, NY. $200,000, 2005. To renew support for Health Literacy Resource Center.

1285. New York Academy of Medicine, New York, NY. $169,000, 2005. To support Medication Information for Immigrant New Yorkers: Research and Intervention for New York City Pharmacies.

1286. Queens Borough Public Library, Jamaica, NY. $600,000, 2005. 3-year grant. To provide support for immigrant, family literacy and youth programming.

1287. Queens Museum of Art, Flushing, NY. $150,000, 2005. To help support Sharing Cultures: An Art Museum and Library Partnership on English Literacy and Visual Literacy Programming for Newest New Yorkers.

American Express Foundation

Limitations: Giving on a national and international basis, including in Asia, Canada, the Caribbean, Europe, and Latin America, with emphasis on Phoenix, AZ, South FL, New York, NY, Greensboro, NC, and Salt Lake City, UT. No support for discriminatory organizations, religious organizations not of direct benefit to the entire community, or political organizations. No grants to individuals (except for employee-related scholarships), or for fundraising, goodwill advertising, souvenir journals, or dinner programs, travel, books, magazines, or articles in professional journals, endowments or capital campaigns, traveling exhibitions, or sports sponsorships.

1288. Americans for the Arts, DC. $25,000, 2004.

1289. BBB Wise Giving Alliance, Arlington, VA. $10,000, 2004.

1290. Body Positive, Phoenix, AZ. $10,000, 2004.

1291. Charities Aid Foundation (UK), West Malling, England. $82,550, 2004.

1292. Charities Aid Foundation (UK), West Malling, England. $71,175, 2004.

1293. Child Care, Inc., New York, NY. $10,000, 2004.

1294. European Foundation Centre, Brussels, Belgium. $15,000, 2004.

1295. Foundation Center, New York, NY. $10,000, 2004.

1296. New York Public Library, Astor, Lenox and Tilden Foundations, New York, NY. $25,000, 2004.

The AVI CHAI Foundation

(formerly AVI CHAI - A Philanthropic Foundation)

Limitations: Giving primarily in North America and Israel. No grants for building projects or deficits.

1297. Association of Jewish Libraries, New York, NY. $35,198, 2004. For general support.

Beldon Fund

(also known as Beldon II Fund)

Limitations: Giving on a national basis. No support for forest, wildlife habitat/ refuges, land, marine, river, lake, wilderness preservation, protection or restoration, arts and culture, international programs, service delivery programs, academic or university projects, school- or classroom-based environmental education. No grants to individuals, or for land acquisition, endowment or capital campaigns, scholarships, research, film, video and radio projects, publications, deficit reduction, or museums or collections acquisitions.

1298. Working Group on Community Right-To-Know, DC. $50,000, 2004. To promote public awareness of toxic exposure and health, and work to protect and strengthen state and federal right-to-know policies. Grant made through U.S. Public Interest Research Group Education Fund.

The Bodman Foundation

Limitations: Giving primarily in northern NJ and New York, NY. Generally, no support for colleges or universities, international projects, government agencies, public schools, (except charter schools), nonprofit programs and services mostly funded or wholly reimbursed by government, small performing arts groups, or national health or mental health organizations. No grants to individuals; generally no grants for travel, endowments, capital campaigns, housing, annual appeals, dinner functions, fundraising events, deficit financing, or films; no loans.

1299. Resources for Children with Special Needs, New York, NY. $15,000, 2005. For Database on Web.

Booth Ferris Foundation

Limitations: Giving limited to the New York, NY, metropolitan area for the arts, K-12 education, and civic and urban affairs; a broader geographic scope for higher education. No support for federated campaigns, community chests, social services and cultural institutions from outside the New York metropolitan area, or for work with specific diseases or disabilities. No grants to individuals, or for research; generally no grants to educational institutions for scholarships, fellowships, or unrestricted endowments; no loans.

1300. Foundation Center, New York, NY. $30,000, 2005. For general operating support.

1301. Graduate Theological Union, Berkeley, CA. $150,000, 2005. For repairs to Flora Lamson Hewlett library.

1302. Nonprofit Connection, Brooklyn, NY. $100,000, 2005. To expand its training program.

1303. Trinity College, Hartford, CT. $150,000, 2005. For renovation of Watkinson Library.

The Bristol-Myers Squibb Foundation, Inc.

(formerly The Bristol-Myers Fund, Inc.)

Limitations: Giving on a national and international basis, including in Africa, with emphasis on Wallingford, CT, Evansville, IN, New Brunswick, Princeton, and Skillman, NJ, and Buffalo and Syracuse, NY. No support for political, fraternal, social, or veterans' organizations, religious or sectarian organizations not of direct benefit to the entire community, or federated campaign-supported organizations. No grants to individuals (except for Distinguished Achievement Awards and employee-related scholarships), or for endowments, conferences, sponsorships or independent medical research, or specific public broadcasting or films; no loans.

1304. New York Academy of Medicine, New York, NY. $50,000, 2004. For Being Healthy program.

1305. New York Public Library, Science, Industry and Business Library (SIBL), New York, NY. $50,000, 2004.

J. E. & Z. B. Butler Foundation, Inc.

Limitations: Giving primarily in New York, NY. No grants to individuals.

1306. Girls Coalition of Boston, Boston, MA. $35,000, 2005.

Carnegie Corporation of New York

Limitations: Giving primarily for U.S. projects, although some grants are made to selected countries in Sub-Saharan Africa through the International Development Program. No support for libraries, cultural institutions, programs or facilities of community-based educational or human services institutions. No grants for scholarships, fellowships (except the Carnegie Scholars Program), travel, capital campaigns, endowments or program-related investments.

1307. American Forum for Global Education, New York, NY. $25,000, 2005. Toward strategic planning to revitalize programming in field of global education.

1308. American Jewish Historical Society, New York, NY. $10,000, 2005. For general support.

1309. Anthology Film Archives, New York, NY. $25,000, 2005. For general support.

1310. BBB Wise Giving Alliance, Arlington, VA. $50,000, 2005.

1311. Center for Jewish History, New York, NY. $25,000, 2005. For general support.

1312. Centre for Higher Education Transformation Trust, Pretoria, South Africa. $49,000, 2005. For distributing higher education publications to libraries at African universities.

1313. City University of New York, Louis Armstrong House and Archives, Flushing, NY. $25,000, 2005. For general support.

1314. Foundation Center, New York, NY. $33,000, 2005. Toward membership support.

1315. Foundation for Library and Information Service Development, Pretoria, South Africa. $2,000,000, 2005. 3-year grant. For model national library in South Africa.

1316. Fund for Constitutional Government, DC. $50,000, 2005. Toward coalition to ensure access to government information.

1317. Fund for Public Schools, New York, NY. $100,000, 2005. 2-year grant. For collection development for two school libraries in Lower Manhattan.

1318. Hoboken Board of Education, Hoboken, NJ. $100,000, 2005. Toward web-based integrated library system for Hoboken Public Schools district.

1319. Johannesburg, City of, Johannesburg, South Africa. $1,996,500, 2005. 3-year grant. Toward development of model city library in Johannesburg.

1320. Learning Matters, New York, NY. $50,000, 2005. Toward education coverage for NewsHour with Jim Lehrer.

1321. New York Academy of Medicine, New York, NY. $35,000, 2005. Toward conference on transatlantic immigrant health issues.

1322. Poets House, New York, NY. $50,000, 2005. For general support.

1323. probono.net, New York, NY. $40,000, 2005. Toward planning web-based information portal on immigrant legal issues.

1324. University of Arizona, Tucson, AZ. $50,000, 2005. Toward data retrieval system linking student achievement data to individual teachers.

1325. University of Illinois at Urbana-Champaign, Urbana, IL. $499,900, 2005. 3-year grant. For strategic planning and automation of African grantee university libraries.

The Carson Family Charitable Trust

Limitations: Giving primarily in New York, NY. No grants to individuals.

1326. New York Public Library, New York, NY. $50,000, 2004. For emergency campaign for branch libraries.

Central New York Community Foundation, Inc.

Limitations: Giving limited to Onondaga and Madison counties, NY, for general grants; giving in a wider area for Donor-Advised funds. No support for religious purposes. No grants to individuals (except for scholarships), or for conferences and seminars, deficit financing, consulting services, endowment funds, fellowships, operating budgets, medical or academic research (except where directed by a donor), or travel expenses; no loans.

1327. Manlius Library, Manlius, NY. $25,000, 2005. For renovation and expansion of library.

1328. Sullivan Free Library, Chittenango, NY. $25,000, 2005. To renovate newly acquired library building.

1329. Tully Free Library, Tully, NY. $25,000, 2005. For roofing and siding for building.

Citigroup Foundation

(formerly Citicorp Foundation)

Limitations: Giving on a national and international basis, with emphasis on areas of company operations. No support for political candidates or religious, veterans', or fraternal organizations not of direct benefit to the entire community. No grants to individuals, or for political causes, fundraising events, telethons, marathons, races, or benefits, advertising, sponsorships, dinners or luncheons, or membership fees.

1330. Alliance for the Arts, New York, NY. $50,000, 2005. For NYCkidsARTS: Culture Calendar.

1331. Brooklyn Public Library, Brooklyn, NY. $100,000, 2005. For Power Up: Business Plan Competition.

1332. Charities Aid Foundation (CAF) America, Alexandria, VA. $600,000, 2005. For Leopold Kronenberg Foundation in Poland.

1333. Charities Aid Foundation (CAF) America, Alexandria, VA. $200,000, 2005. For Partners in Change: Global Microentrepreneurship Awards in India.

1334. Charities Aid Foundation (CAF) America, Alexandria, VA. $160,000, 2005. For Specialist Schools Trust: TeachNet United Kingdom Program in United Kingdom.

1335. Charities Aid Foundation (CAF) America, Alexandria, VA. $150,000, 2005. For Leopold Kronenberg Foundation: My Finances National Economic Education Program in Poland.

1336. Charities Aid Foundation (CAF) America, Alexandria, VA. $90,000, 2005. For Teach First U.K. Program in United Kingdom.

1337. Charities Aid Foundation (CAF) America, Alexandria, VA. $90,000, 2005. For London Bombing Relief Charitable Fund in United Kingdom.

1338. Charities Aid Foundation (CAF) America, Alexandria, VA. $78,000, 2005. For Tongji University: Case Competition in China.

1339. Charities Aid Foundation (CAF) America, Alexandria, VA. $75,000, 2005. For Center for Innovation in Voluntary Action: SpeakersBank Financially Speaking Program in United Kingdom.

1340. Charities Aid Foundation (CAF) America, Alexandria, VA. $70,000, 2005. For Working Women's Forum: Employment Training and Financial Education Programs in India.

1341. Charities Aid Foundation (CAF) America, Alexandria, VA. $66,000, 2005. For Aldeburgh Productions: Sound Moves Music Education Project in United Kingdom.

1342. Charities Aid Foundation (CAF) America, Alexandria, VA. $50,000, 2005. For Working Women's Forum: Entrepreneurship and Capacity Building Program in India.

1343. Charities Aid Foundation (CAF) America, Alexandria, VA. $43,000, 2005. For Renmin University: Corporate Governance Education Center in China.

1344. Charities Aid Foundation (CAF) America, Alexandria, VA. $41,000, 2005. For Business in the Community: ENGAGE Program in Europe.

1345. Charities Aid Foundation (CAF) America, Alexandria, VA. $40,000, 2005. For Create: Count the Beat Music Education Program in United Kingdom.

1346. Charities Aid Foundation (CAF) America, Alexandria, VA. $35,000, 2005. For Tower Hamlets Education Business Partnership, Langdon Park School's New Horizon Project in United Kingdom.

1347. Charities Aid Foundation (CAF) America, Alexandria, VA. $30,000, 2005. For African-Caribbean Diversity Mentoring and Enrichment Program in United Kingdom.

1348. Charities Aid Foundation (CAF) America, Alexandria, VA. $30,000, 2005. For Saahasee: Thrift and Credit-Based Cooperation Groups Strengthening Program in India.

1349. Charities Aid Foundation (CAF) America, Alexandria, VA. $30,000, 2005. For Sarba Shanti Ayog, Sasha: Spice Business Project in India.

1350. Charities Aid Foundation (CAF) America, Alexandria, VA. $25,000, 2005. For United Kingdom Career Academy Foundation: Development of the Academy of Finance Program in Ireland.

1351. Charities Aid Foundation (CAF) America, Alexandria, VA. $25,000, 2005. For Beijing University: Insurance Initiatives in China.

1352. Charities Aid Foundation (CAF) America, Alexandria, VA. $25,000, 2005. For Fudan University: Science Faculty Fellowships in China.

1353. Charities Aid Foundation (CAF) America, Alexandria, VA. $25,000, 2005. For Shantou University: Citigroup Negotiation and Dispute Resolution Program in China.

1354. Charities Aid Foundation (CAF) America, Alexandria, VA. $25,000, 2005. For Charities Aid Foundation Russia: Life Line Program.

1355. Charities Aid Foundation (CAF) America, Alexandria, VA. $25,000, 2005. For Foundation for Supporting Women's Work: Solidarity Funds and Savings Group Programs in Turkey.

1356. Charities Aid Foundation (CAF) America, Alexandria, VA. $25,000, 2005. For Shakti Foundation for Disadvantaged Women: Entrepreneurship Program in Bangladesh.

1357. Charities Aid Foundation (CAF) America, Alexandria, VA. $15,000, 2005. For Beijing University Information Technology (IT) Course in China.

1358. Charities Aid Foundation (CAF) America, Alexandria, VA. $15,000, 2005. For Fudan University Information Technology (IT) Course in China.

1359. Charities Aid Foundation (CAF) America, Alexandria, VA. $15,000, 2005. For Huazhong University Information Technology (IT) Course in China.

1360. Child Care, Inc., New York, NY. $150,000, 2005. For Talk, Reach, Read Program.

1361. Microfinance Information Exchange, DC. $150,000, 2005. For general operating support.

1362. National Association of Child Care Resource and Referral Agencies (NACCRA), Arlington, VA. $55,000, 2005. For Daily Parent Newsletter.

1363. New York Public Library, New York, NY. $25,000, 2005. For Preschool Family Literacy Programs.

1364. Newark Public Schools, Newark, NJ. $46,000, 2005. For New Teacher Resource Program.

1365. Nonprofit Connection, Brooklyn, NY. $67,500, 2005. For Retainer Program, Nonprofit Days, and General Operating Support.

1366. Nonprofit Resource Center, Sacramento, CA. $25,000, 2005. For CEO-Link Program.

1367. Queens Library Foundation, Jamaica, NY. $50,000, 2005. For Toddler Learning Center and Family Literacy Programs.

1368. Santa Barbara County Education Office, Santa Barbara, CA. $144,900, 2005. For California New Teacher Resource Program.

1369. Teachers Network, New York, NY. $150,000, 2005. For New York New Teacher Resource Program.

1370. Teachers Network, New York, NY. $54,000, 2005. For California New Teacher Resource Program.

1371. United Way International, Alexandria, VA. $231,500, 2005. For Fundacion Educacional y Cultural: Financial Education in Community and School Libraries in Chile.

1372. United Way International, Alexandria, VA. $200,000, 2005. For Foundation for Development Cooperation: Banking with the Poor Network and Online Asia Resource Center for Microfinance in Asia Pacific.

1373. United Way International, Alexandria, VA. $113,000, 2005. For Schuldnerhilfe Koln: Debt First Aid Phone and Internet Helpline Project in Germany.

The Edna McConnell Clark Foundation

Limitations: Giving on a national basis. No grants to individuals, or for capital funds, construction and equipment, endowments, scholarships, fellowships, annual appeals, deficit financing, or matching gifts; no loans to individuals.

1374. Foundation Center, New York, NY. $40,000, 2005. For membership dues.

1375. Philanthropic Research, Inc., Williamsburg, VA. $25,000, 2005. For operation of GuideStar, national database containing information for public about operations and finances of charities in U.S. and for new fundraising arm for GuideStar, called True North.

Robert Sterling Clark Foundation, Inc.

Limitations: Giving primarily in New York State for the Public Institutions Program and in New York City for the Cultural Program; giving nationally for reproductive freedom and arts advocacy projects. No grants to individuals, or for annual campaigns, seed money, emergency funds, deficit financing, capital or endowment funds, scholarships, fellowships, conferences, or films.

1376. Americans for the Arts, DC. $65,000, 2005. For overall arts advocacy efforts that include coordinating Arts Advocacy Day, educating the nation's elected and appointed officials about the value of the arts; and the building of the state-level arts advocacy infra-structure.

1377. Child Care, Inc., New York, NY. $60,000, 2005. To promote improvement in administration and regulation of child care, publicize the economic value of child care sector, and advocate for increased public support.

1378. Sexuality Information and Education Council of the U.S. (SIECUS), New York, NY. $60,000, 2005. To educate policy makers, the press, and public about importance of comprehensive sex education and risks associated with abstinence-only programs.

1379. Sterling and Francine Clark Art Institute, Williamstown, MA. $50,000, 2005. For Institute's 50th Anniversary festivities and special events.

The Clark Foundation

Limitations: Giving primarily in Cooperstown, NY and New York City; scholarships restricted to students residing in the Cooperstown, NY, area. No grants to individuals (except as specified in restricted funds), or for deficit financing or matching gifts.

1380. Foundation Center, New York, NY. $80,000, 2006.

The Commonwealth Fund

Limitations: Giving on a national basis. No support for religious organizations for religious purposes, or basic biomedical research. No grants to individuals (except through the Commonwealth Fund's fellowship programs), or for scholarships, general planning or ongoing activities, existing deficits, endowment or capital costs, construction, renovation, equipment, conferences, symposia, major media projects, or documentaries (unless they are an out growth of one of the fund's programs).

1381. Foundation Center, New York, NY. $15,000, 2005. For general support.

1382. Health Systems Research, DC. $11,518, 2005. For Mapping Referral Resources to Support Children's Development.

1383. Rockefeller University, New York, NY. $90,000, 2005. For transfer and maintenance of Commonwealth Fund's archives at Archive Center in Sleepy Hollow.

The Jon S. Corzine Foundation

Limitations: Giving primarily in NJ. No grants to individuals.

1384. William J. Clinton Presidential Foundation, Little Rock, AR. $250,000, 2004. For general support.

Credit Suisse Americas Foundation

(formerly Credit Suisse First Boston Foundation Trust)

Limitations: Giving primarily in areas of company operations, with emphasis on New York, NY. No support for religious organizations not of direct benefit to the entire community, veterans', fraternal, or political organizations, or public or private schools. No grants to individuals, or for scholarships, capital campaigns, endowments, dinners or events, or medical research; no matching gifts.

1385. Resources for Children with Special Needs, New York, NY. $25,000, 2004.

Lewis B. & Dorothy Cullman Foundation, Inc.

Limitations: Giving primarily in NY. No grants to individuals.

1386. New York Public Library, New York, NY. $1,751,000, 2005. For general support.

1387. New York Public Library, New York, NY. $48,000, 2005. For general support.

1388. New York Public Library, New York, NY. $40,000, 2005. For general support.

1389. New York Public Library, New York, NY. $24,670, 2005. For general support.

1390. Pierpont Morgan Library, New York, NY. $19,150, 2005. For general support.

The Nathan Cummings Foundation

Limitations: Giving primarily in the U.S. and Israel. No support for specific diseases, general support for Jewish education, Holocaust-related projects, foreign-based organizations, or local synagogues or institutions with local projects. No grants to individuals, scholarships, sponsorships, projects with no plans for replication, endowments or capital campaigns.

1391. Center for Jewish History, New York, NY. $19,500, 2004.

1392. Franklin Furnace Archive, New York, NY. $25,000, 2004.

1393. National Security Archive Fund, DC. $10,000, 2004.

1394. Princeton Public Library, Princeton, NJ. $50,000, 2004.

The Dana Foundation

(formerly The Charles A. Dana Foundation, Inc.)

Limitations: Giving on a national basis. No support for professional organizations, or for organizations outside the U.S. No grants to individuals, or for annual operating costs, deficit reduction, capital campaigns, or individual sabbaticals.

1395. Folger Shakespeare Library, DC. $50,000, 2004. For restoration of Dana Wing.

1396. Foundation Center, New York, NY. $13,000, 2004. For general support.

1397. Live Oak Public Libraries Foundation, Nassau, Bahamas. $10,000, 2004. For general support.

1398. Ronald Reagan Presidential Foundation, Simi Valley, CA. $10,000, 2004. For general support.

The Ira W. DeCamp Foundation

Limitations: Giving primarily in the New York City metropolitan area. No support for private foundations. No grants to individuals, or for general support, land acquisition, matching gifts, publications, conferences, endowment funds, operating budgets, continuing support, annual campaigns, emergency funds, scholarships, fellowships, or deficit financing; no loans.

1399. City Futures, New York, NY. $65,000, 2005. For child welfare coverage by City Limits and reports by Center for an Urban Future's Child Welfare Watch.

Deutsche Bank Americas Foundation

(formerly BT Foundation)

Limitations: Giving on a national basis in areas of company operations and in Canada and Latin America. No support for political parties or candidates, or for legal advocacy, religious purposes, veterans', military, or fraternal organizations, United Way agencies (except for those providing a fundraising waiver), or professional or trade associations. No grants to individuals, or for endowments, or capital campaigns.

1400. Charities Aid Foundation (CAF) America, Alexandria, VA. $250,000, 2004. For Donor Advised Fund.

1401. Charities Aid Foundation (CAF) America, Alexandria, VA. $116,795, 2004. For Donor Advised Fund - Initiative Plus International.

1402. Charities Aid Foundation (CAF) America, Alexandria, VA. $110,000, 2004. For Donor Advised Fund.

1403. Charities Aid Foundation (CAF) America, Alexandria, VA. $100,000, 2004. For Donor Advised Fund.

1404. Charities Aid Foundation (CAF) America, Alexandria, VA. $100,000, 2004. For Donor Advised Fund.

1405. Charities Aid Foundation (CAF) America, Alexandria, VA. $83,205, 2004. For Donor Advised Fund.

1406. New York Public Library, New York, NY. $50,000, 2004. To support Computer Page Program.

1407. Robin Hood Foundation, New York, NY. $25,000, 2004. For Stack the Shelves, Holiday fundraiser.

1408. Robin Hood Foundation, New York, NY. $13,500, 2004. To support Library Initiative.

Irene Diamond Fund
Limitations: Giving primarily in NY. No grants to individuals; no loans.
1409. New York Public Library, New York, NY. $50,000, 2004. For supplemental general support.

The William H. Donner Foundation
Limitations: Giving on a national basis.
1410. Foundation Center, New York, NY. $10,000, 2005. For general support.

Doris Duke Charitable Foundation
Limitations: Giving on a national basis. No support for water or aquatic issues, air or climate change issues, toxic issues, litigation, the visual arts, museums or galleries, or arts programs for rehabilitative or therapeutic purposes. No grants to individuals (except through special foundation programs), or for conferences or publications.
1411. American Medical Informatics Association, Bethesda, MD. $50,000, 2005. For planning phase of Global Trial Bank, public register of computable peer-reviewed results from clinical trials conducted worldwide.
1412. Foundation Center, New York, NY. $25,000, 2005. For general operating support.
1413. NatureServe, Arlington, VA. $1,209,440, 2005. To strengthen long-term capacity to maintain Natural Heritage Network by providing endowment support, raising matching endowment funds, and expanding development capacity.

Dyson Foundation
Limitations: Giving primarily in Dutchess County, NY, and organizations providing services in Dutchess County; limited grants to other Mid-Hudson Valley counties. National and other grants on a solicited basis. No support for international organizations. No grants to individuals, or for debt reduction, direct mail campaign or fundraising events.
1414. Marietta College, Marietta, OH. $5,000,000, 2005. 5-year grant. For Dyson Foundation 50th Anniversary Grant toward construction of new college library, to be known as Learning and Library Resource Center.
1415. Media Matters for America, DC. $100,000, 2005. Toward update and redesign of website.
1416. New York State Archives Partnership Trust, Cultural Education Center, Albany, NY. $10,000, 2005. Toward preserving and restoring New York State's documents from Revolutionary War.
1417. Philanthropic Research, Inc., GuideStar, Williamsburg, VA. $25,000, 2005. For general operating support.
1418. William J. Clinton Presidential Foundation, Little Rock, AR. $50,000, 2005. For general operating support.

The Charles Engelhard Foundation
Limitations: Giving primarily on a national basis. No grants to individuals.
1419. Charities Aid Foundation (CAF) America, Alexandria, VA. $18,000, 2004.
1420. Charities Aid Foundation (CAF) America, Alexandria, VA. $18,000, 2004.
1421. Concord Free Public Library, Concord, MA. $20,000, 2004.
1422. New York Public Library, New York, NY. $100,000, 2004.
1423. Pierpont Morgan Library, New York, NY. $20,000, 2004.
1424. Pierpont Morgan Library, New York, NY. $15,000, 2004.
1425. Teton County Library Foundation, Jackson, WY. $20,000, 2004.

Englander Foundation, Inc.
Limitations: Giving primarily in the metropolitan New York, NY, area. No grants to individuals.
1426. Charities Aid Foundation (CAF) America, Teenage Cancer Trust, Alexandria, VA. $18,000, 2005.

The Ford Foundation
Limitations: Giving on an international basis, including the U.S., Africa and the Middle East, Asia, Russia, Latin America and the Caribbean. No support for programs for which substantial support from government or other sources is readily available, or for religious sectarian activities. No grants for routine operating costs, construction or maintenance of buildings, or

undergraduate scholarships; graduate fellowships generally channeled through grants to universities or other organizations; no grants for purely personal or local needs.
1427. African Women and Child Information Network, Nairobi, Kenya. $229,943, 2005. For exploratory activities feeding into organization of series of events to mark 20th anniversary of United Nation's Third World Conference on Women, held in Nairobi in July 1985.
1428. African Women and Child Information Network, Nairobi, Kenya. $125,286, 2005. For media activities with respect to Beijing Plus 10 conference at United Nations.
1429. American Library Association, Chicago, IL. $380,000, 2005. 2-year grant. For surveys, workshops and training institutes to educate librarians, lawyers and library users about process of compliance with USA PATRIOT Act and consequent dangers to privacy.
1430. Americans for the Arts, New York, NY. $1,500,000, 2005. For grant-making activities of Animating Democracy and Working Capital Reserve programs for small- to medium-sized arts programs and for meetings, documentation and publications.
1431. Arab Network of NGOs for Development, Beirut, Lebanon. $250,000, 2005. 2-year grant. For networking, educational and awareness activities to advance regional civil society voices in global debates on trade and sustainable development.
1432. Assabil Association, Beirut, Lebanon. $25,000, 2005. 1.50-year grant. To develop strategic plan, communications tools and fundraising plan to coordinate and maintain Lebanon's network of public libraries.
1433. Bank Information Center, DC. $450,000, 2005. 2-year grant. For general support to empower community voices within international financial institutions and to advocate for policies that include public.
1434. BBB Wise Giving Alliance, Arlington, VA. $150,000, 2005. 2-year grant. For general support to enhance and publicize accountability mechanisms for nonprofit sector.
1435. Center for National Independence in Politics (CNIP), Philipsburg, MT. $300,000, 2005. 2-year grant. For general support for Project Vote Smart, multimedia source of information about local, state and federal elected officials and candidates.
1436. Charities Aid Foundation (UK), West Malling, England. $2,000,000, 2005. 5-year grant. For contribution to CAF-Russia's Endowment for Sustainable Future.
1437. Charities Aid Foundation (UK), West Malling, England. $260,000, 2005. 2-year grant. For small grants competitions and technical assistance to build capacity of self-help groups of people living with HIV-AIDS across Russia.
1438. Charities Aid Foundation-Southern Africa, Johannesburg, South Africa. $150,000, 2005. For research, policy analysis, and related activities to improve legal, regulatory and financial environment for South African nonprofit sector.
1439. China NPO Network, Beijing, China. $199,900, 2005. 2-year grant. For training, publication and human resources development related to civil society organizations' capacity building.
1440. Combine Resource Institution, Bandung, Indonesia. $131,000, 2005. 1.50-year grant. For general support to coordinate community-based information network for development planning and provide technical assistance to civil society organizations and local governments in community radio.
1441. Coptic Evangelical Organization for Social Services, Cairo, Egypt. $100,000, 2005. To develop skills and educational capacities of field practitioners involved in reproductive health education for women and girls by improving their access to diverse sources of information.
1442. Cunningham Dance Foundation, New York, NY. $100,000, 2005. 1.25-year grant. For archival elements of campaign to preserve artistic accomplishments of Merce Cunningham and his dance company.
1443. Education Development Center, Newton, MA. $57,510, 2005. 1.25-year grant. For Dancing Forward for Change, book and digital archive documenting experience, history and impact of gender equity movement.
1444. Environment Support Group, Bangalore, India. $24,465, 2005. For workshop and public launch of Access Initiative to strengthen civil society's capacity to promote access to information, participation and justice in decision making around the environment.
1445. Euro-Mediterranean Human Rights Network, Copenhagen, Denmark. $45,000, 2005. 2-year grant. To translate reports, news bulletins and meeting documents into Arabic for dissemination in Middle East and North Africa.

1446. European Foundation Centre, Brussels, Belgium. $600,000, 2005. 2-year grant. For core support for Worldwide Initiatives for Grantmaker Support (WINGS) to promote and strengthen philanthropy globally.

1447. European Foundation Centre, Brussels, Belgium. $200,000, 2005. For emergency general support to sustain core programs during leadership transition and anticipated restructuring.

1448. European Foundation Centre, Brussels, Belgium. $150,000, 2005. 3-year grant. For Community Philanthropy Initiative to build capacity of organizations in Europe by providing information services, networking activities and technical assistance.

1449. European Foundation Centre, Brussels, Belgium. $37,800, 2005. For symposium examining current and future roles of community foundations around world.

1450. European Foundation Centre, Brussels, Belgium. $11,000, 2005. For annual membership dues.

1451. Fideicomiso Fondo para la Biodiversidad (Trust Fund for Biodiversity), Mexico City, Mexico. $320,000, 2005. 3-year grant. To generate innovative models for in situ conservation of biological diversity and collective and sustainable management, harvesting and marketing of derived natural products.

1452. Foundation Center, New York, NY. $700,000, 2005. 2-year grant. For general support to collect, organize, analyze and disseminate information on foundation and corporate giving and for expansion of online activities.

1453. Foundation Center, New York, NY. $200,000, 2005. To compile and analyze expense and compensation patterns of largest U.S. foundations.

1454. Galileo Foundation, San Jose, Costa Rica. $100,000, 2005. 1.50-year grant. For Web-based information clearinghouse on microenterprise, microfinance, remittances and development in Latin America.

1455. Habitat International Coalition, Housing and Land Rights Network, Geneva, Switzerland. $140,000, 2005. 2-year grant. For networking, training and advocacy on protection of housing and land rights in Arab region.

1456. Indigenous Information Network, Nairobi, Kenya. $100,000, 2005. To strengthen environmental conservation, sustainable development and income generation skills of nomadic pastoralists and hunter gatherers in Eastern Africa.

1457. La Mama Experimental Theater Club, New York, NY. $250,000, 2005. 2-year grant. For general support for Preserving the Legacy, project to make archive documenting birth of experimental theater in America and cultural movement that ensued available to public.

1458. Media Tank, Philadelphia, PA. $70,000, 2005. 1.50-year grant. To plan national Media Justice Network of grassroots groups working on social justice issues in historically marginalized communities.

1459. Mexican Commission for the Defense and Promotion of Human Rights, Mexico City, Mexico. $60,000, 2005. To produce accurate and meaningful information regarding feminicide in Mexico and Guatemala and disseminate it at international forums.

1460. Mexican Council for Popular Savings and Credit (COMACREP), Cuauhtemoc, Mexico. $50,000, 2005. For coalition of popular finance networks to develop training programs, information services and management practices that respond to new regulatory environment.

1461. Miami Workers Center, Miami, FL. $200,000, 2005. 2-year grant. For media and communications capacity building to develop grassroots organizations and leadership in low-income communities in Florida.

1462. National Center for Black Philanthropy, DC. $200,000, 2005. For general support to expand and solidify philanthropy within black community.

1463. National Center for Higher Education Management Systems, Boulder, CO. $15,000, 2005. To develop appropriate technical and organizational infrastructure to enable efficient, equitable and professionally responsible access to student records for academic and policy research.

1464. National Womens Health Network, DC. $150,000, 2005. 2-year grant. For general support to advance women's self-determination in all aspects of their sexual and reproductive health.

1465. Nelson Mandela Foundation, Johannesburg, South Africa. $200,000, 2005. 3-year grant. For start-up support for Nelson Mandela Centre of Memory, which will honor and document life of Nelson Mandela.

1466. Network of Entrepreneurship and Economic Development (NEED), Lucknow, India. $125,000, 2005. 3-year grant. To expand outreach and professionalize microfinance services for low-income women in Uttar Pradesh.

1467. New York Foundation for the Arts, New York, NY. $100,000, 2005. For NYFA Source, extensive online resource for opportunities for artists in all disciplines.

1468. Objective Reality Foundation, Moscow, Russia. $164,000, 2005. 2.25-year grant. For general support to promote documentary and art and maintain photographer.ru, its online information resource.

1469. Open Memory Civil Association-Human Rights Organizations Coordinated Action, Buenos Aires, Argentina. $400,000, 2005. 3-year grant. For general support to preserve and disseminate historical documents on state terrorism in Argentina.

1470. Orient Foundation, Bath, England. $200,000, 2005. 2-year grant. For tie-off support for creation of multimedia library network of classical Tibetan literature, arts and philosophy.

1471. Paul Robeson Foundation, New York, NY. $100,000, 2005. To digitize archives of performance artist and human rights activist Paul Robeson.

1472. Romare Bearden Foundation, New York, NY. $176,235, 2005. 2-year grant. To restructure programmatic and administrative infrastructure, including expansion of arts-in-education programming and implementation of scholarship and internship programs.

1473. Sexuality Information and Education Council of the U.S. (SIECUS), New York, NY. $150,000, 2005. For general support to promote comprehensive sexuality education and expand outreach activities.

1474. Stiftelsen Studio Emad Eddin, Stockholm, Sweden. $70,000, 2005. For general support for rehearsal studios and resource center in Cairo for Independent Theater Movement.

1475. Syracuse University, Syracuse, NY. $150,000, 2005. 2-year grant. For Transactional Records Access Clearinghouse to make data on administrative enforcement of U.S. immigration laws available to public.

1476. Thibitisha Trust, Nairobi, Kenya. $130,000, 2005. 1.50-year grant. To complete development of Internet-based index of newspaper and journal articles on Kenyan cultural affairs and pilot publication and distribution of these materials on CD-ROM.

1477. Transatlantic Futures, The Globalist, DC. $100,000, 2005. To create and publish Globalist Bookshelf and Globalist PhotoGallery, two major online projects providing news and features about process and impact of globalization.

1478. Triangle Arts Trust, London, England. $190,000, 2005. For digital networking and practical exchanges between visual artist communities in North, South, East and West Africa.

1479. University of Mysore, Mysore, India. $400,000, 2005. 3-year grant. For core support for Vidyanidhi digital library to expand its archive of Indian doctoral dissertations, offer masters degree in information management and advance digitally enabled scholarship.

1480. University of the Americas Foundation, Puebla, Puebla, Mexico. $60,000, 2005. 1.25-year grant. For Center for Quality of Life to offer training & technical assistance on computer-enhanced learning to network of TV secondary schools & establish teachers' virtual learning community.

1481. University of the Philippines, Los Banos, Philippines. $100,000, 2005. 2-year grant. To strengthen Asia Regional Sexuality Resource Center through enhancing sexuality research in South East Asia.

1482. University of the Western Cape, Bellville, South Africa. $35,000, 2005. For Centre for Study of Higher Education to expand its collection of resource materials, build digital library, enhance its Web site and transform into state-of-the-art knowledge hub.

1483. Vietnam Cinema Association, Vietnam. $350,200, 2005. 2-year grant. To establish film library and conduct short film courses and master classes for film students and young professionals.

1484. Women of Color Resource Center, Oakland, CA. $200,000, 2005. For general support for activities to educate public on and build coalitions around impact of foreign policy, economic inequity, racial bias and gender-based discrimination on women of color.

Foundation for Child Development

Limitations: Giving limited to research and policy grants related to foundation focus and restricted to the U.S. No support for the direct provision of pre-kindergarten education, child care, or health care. No grants for capital campaigns, endowments, or for the purchase, construction, or renovation of buildings.

1485. Grantmakers Concerned with Immigrants and Refugees, Sebastopol, CA. $10,000, 2006. For program and information resources activities to educate foundations about issues facing immigrant children, youth, and families.

Freeman Foundation

Limitations: Giving primarily in VT for conservation and environment grants; Asian studies grants are awarded nationally. No grants to individuals, or for endowments or capital campaigns.

1486. American Forum for Global Education, New York, NY. $350,000, 2005. For Asia Project for students in grades K-12 and China Student Exchange Program.

1487. Asia Society, New York, NY. $1,000,000, 2005. For Asia in Schools, nationwide education program for students in grades K-12 and for Asian Educational Resource Center.

1488. Cambodian Family, Santa Ana, CA. $100,000, 2005. For Asian immigrant and refugee economic education and opportunity programs.

1489. Columbia University, C.V. Starr East Asian Library, New York, NY. $126,000, 2005. To digitize Barbara C. Adachi's Bunraku Collection. Bunraku is a type of traditional Japanese puppet theater.

1490. Five College Center for East Asian Studies, Northampton, MA. $70,000, 2005. For newsletter, resource library and related activities for students in grades K-12.

1491. Foundation Center, New York, NY. $10,000, 2005. For general support.

1492. University of Colorado, Boulder, CO. $10,000, 2005. For Japanese/Oriental Language School Archival Project.

Gilder Foundation, Inc.

Limitations: Giving primarily in NY. No grants to individuals.

1493. New York Public Library, New York, NY. $130,000, 2004.

1494. Pierpont Morgan Library, New York, NY. $1,088,290, 2004.

Gleason Foundation

(formerly Gleason Memorial Fund, Inc.)

Limitations: Giving primarily in Monroe County, NY. No support for United Way-supported agencies. No grants to individuals.

1495. Rundel Library Foundation, Rochester, NY. $170,000, 2004.

1496. School Choice Wisconsin, Milwaukee, WI. $50,000, 2004.

1497. University of Rochester, River Campus Library, Rochester, NY. $1,000,000, 2004.

Horace W. Goldsmith Foundation

Limitations: Giving primarily in AZ, MA, and New York, NY. No grants to individuals.

1498. American Trust for the British Library, New York, NY. $100,000, 2004.

1499. Archives of American Art of the Smithsonian Institution, DC. $25,000, 2004.

1500. Center for Jewish History, New York, NY. $250,000, 2004.

1501. Free Library of Philadelphia Foundation, Philadelphia, PA. $100,000, 2004.

1502. Philanthropic Research, Inc., Williamsburg, VA. $250,000, 2004.

1503. Philanthropic Research, Inc., Williamsburg, VA. $35,000, 2004.

1504. William J. Clinton Presidential Center, Little Rock, AR. $100,000, 2004.

The Florence Gould Foundation

Limitations: Giving primarily in the U.S. and France. No grants to individuals.

1505. Athenaeum of Philadelphia, Philadelphia, PA. $153,270, 2004. To exhibit architectural drawings of Paul Phillippe Cret.

1506. Athenaeum of Philadelphia, Philadelphia, PA. $47,495, 2004. To exhibit architectural drawings of Paul Philippe Cret.

1507. Dalkey Archive Press, Normal, IL. $11,000, 2004. For French Language and Literature Fellowship.

1508. Grolier Club of the City of New York, New York, NY. $15,000, 2004. For French Book Sale Catalogues in the Library of the Grolier Club 1643-1830.

1509. Harvard University, Cambridge, MA. $50,000, 2004. To replace missing volumes at Villa I Tatti in Florence, Italy.

1510. Medici Archive Project, New York, NY. $50,000, 2004. For general support.

1511. New York Public Library, New York, NY. $114,000, 2004. For exhibition, Rose Adler and Pierre Legrain: Bindings for Jacques Doucet.

1512. Pierpont Morgan Library, New York, NY. $100,000, 2004. To assist in acquisition of Babar manuscripts and drawings.

1513. Princeton University, Princeton, NJ. $75,000, 2004. To categorize and publish Papers of Thomas Jefferson.

1514. University of Toronto, Toronto, Canada. $10,000, 2004. For Correspondence de Madame de Gaffigny.

1515. University of Virginia, Charlottesville, VA. $54,000, 2004. For on-line access to Gordon Collection.

1516. Yale University, New Haven, CT. $75,000, 2004. For renewed support for Papers of Benjamin Franklin.

William T. Grant Foundation

Limitations: Giving on a national basis; giving limited to NY, NJ, and CT for youth service grants. No grants to individuals (except for W.T. Grant Scholars Program), or for annual fundraising campaigns, equipment and materials, land acquisition, building or renovation projects, operating budgets, endowments, or scholarships; no loans.

1517. Health and Education Research Operative Services (HEROS), Lebanon, TN. $149,115, 2005. 2-year grant. For research project entitled, A Data Archive for Project STAR and Beyond. Project will create Project STAR public use data file. Project STAR was experimental study of effects of reducing class size on student outcomes. File will include 13 years of data on students followed from kindergarten though high school. STAR-and-beyond database will be publicly available, along with user guide and documentation, to researchers and policymakers for continued analysis.

The Greenwall Foundation

Limitations: Giving primarily in New York, NY, for arts and humanities; giving nationally for bioethics. No grants for building or endowment funds, operating budgets, annual campaigns, deficit financing, or conferences; no loans.

1518. Brooklyn Public Library, Brooklyn, NY. $10,000, 2004. For renewed support for contemporary art program at Central Library.

1519. Poets House, New York, NY. $20,000, 2004. For Poetry Publication Showcase.

The Gruss-Lipper Family Foundation

(formerly The Kenneth & Evelyn Lipper Foundation)

Limitations: Giving on a national basis and in Israel.

1520. Center for Jewish History, New York, NY. $652,622, 2005. For general support.

1521. New York Public Library, New York, NY. $25,000, 2005. For general support.

Gladys and Roland Harriman Foundation

Limitations: Giving on a national basis. No grants to individuals.

1522. New York Public Library, New York, NY. $45,000, 2004. For general support.

1523. Patten Free Library, Bath, ME. $20,000, 2004. For general support.

The John A. Hartford Foundation, Inc.

Limitations: Giving primarily on a national basis. No grants to individuals, or for annual or capital campaigns, building renovations, equipment, general operating support, technical assistance, seed money, emergency or endowment funds, or deficit financing.

1524. Foundation Center, New York, NY. $10,000, 2005. For annual support.

1525. New York Academy of Medicine, New York, NY. $5,119,908, 2005. For Partnership Practicum Program and Adoption Initiative for MSW degrees in aging-rich fields.

1526. Project HOPE - People-to-People Health Foundation, Millwood, VA. $150,000, 2005. For Health Affairs Journal: Thematic Issues on Aging and Health.

Charles Hayden Foundation

Limitations: Giving limited to the metropolitan Boston, MA, and the metropolitan New York, NY areas (including the cities of Newark, Jersey City, and Paterson, NJ). No support for fraternal groups, religious organizations other than community youth-related projects, arts exposure programs, institutions of higher education except to support work on precollegiate programs (other than recruitment programs for a particular college), hospitals, hospices, or projects essentially medical in nature. No grants to individuals, or for endowment funds, operating budgets, fellowships, annual campaigns, emergency funds, deficit financing, publications, or conferences; no loans.

1527. Higher Education Resource Center, Boston, MA. $100,000, 2005. Toward renovations.

1528. Saint Athanasius School, Bronx, NY. $78,000, 2005. Toward construction of library/media center.

The Hearst Foundation, Inc.

Limitations: Giving limited to the U.S. and its territories. No support for public policy, or public policy research, advocacy, or foreign countries. No grants to individuals, or for media or publishing projects, conferences, workshops, seminars, seed funding, multi-year grants, special events, tables, or advertising for fundraising events; no loans or program-related investments.

1529. Foundation Center, New York, NY. $50,000, 2005. For general support.

1530. Heritage Foundation, DC. $75,000, 2005. For operations of Center for Data Analysis (CDA).

The F. B. Heron Foundation

Limitations: Giving primarily in Appalachia; CA; Chicago, IL; Kansas City, MO; Twin Cities, MN; the Mississippi Delta; NC; NJ; New York, NY; and TX. No grants to individuals, or for endowments or capital campaigns.

1531. Child Care Resources, Seattle, WA. $40,000, 2005. For general support.

1532. Philanthropic Research, Inc., Williamsburg, VA. $10,000, 2005. For general support.

Independence Community Foundation

Limitations: Giving primarily in Nassau, New York, Suffolk, and Westchester counties, NY, and Bergen, Essex, Hudson, Middlesex, Monmouth, Ocean, and Union counties, NJ. No support for political or religious organizations. No grants to individuals, or for tickets for dinners, golf outings, or fundraising events.

1533. Brooklyn Public Library Foundation, Brooklyn, NY. $25,000, 2004.

1534. Newark Public Library, Newark, NJ. $25,000, 2004.

1535. Poets House, New York, NY. $20,000, 2004.

1536. Queens Library Foundation, Jamaica, NY. $100,000, 2004.

1537. Queens Library Foundation, Jamaica, NY. $25,000, 2004.

1538. Resources for Children with Special Needs, New York, NY. $10,000, 2004.

Christian A. Johnson Endeavor Foundation

Limitations: No support for government agencies, or for community or neighborhood projects, religious institutions, or for health care. No grants to individuals, or for annual campaigns, emergency funds, deficit financing, land acquisitions, building projects, medical research, demonstration projects, publications, or conferences; no loans (except for program-related investments).

1539. Bloomfield College, Bloomfield, NJ. $20,000, 2005. For library campaign.

The JPMorgan Chase Foundation

(formerly The Chase Manhattan Foundation)

Limitations: Giving on a national basis in areas of company operations; giving also to U.S.-based international organizations active in areas of company operations abroad. No support for religious, fraternal, social, or other membership organizations not of direct benefit to the entire community. No grants for capital campaigns or endowments, scholarships, fundraising, or special events or other short-term projects.

1540. Brooklyn Public Library, Brooklyn, NY. $20,000, 2004.

1541. Centro Peruano de Audicion Lenguaje y Aprendizaje, Peru. $10,000, 2004. To buy supplies for workshop, hospital, library, school and school for parents.

1542. Changshou Duzhou Middle School of Chongqing, Chongqing, China. $15,000, 2004. Toward multi-function school library.

1543. Charities Aid Foundation (CAF) America, Alexandria, VA. $13,779, 2004. For employee programs.

1544. Child Care, Inc., New York, NY. $90,000, 2004.

1545. Citizens Advice Bureau, Bronx, NY. $25,000, 2004.

1546. Fundacion de Educacion Nocedal, Providencia, Chile. $15,000, 2004. Toward books and reading material for school's library.

1547. Fundacion Educacional y de Beneficlenca Alto las Condes, Santiago, Chile. $23,000, 2004. To fully equip modern library for students.

1548. Initiative for Children Foundation, DC. $15,000, 2004.

1549. Nonprofit Connection, Brooklyn, NY. $10,000, 2004.

1550. Pro Mujer, New York, NY. $50,000, 2004. For new Management Information System (MIS) for Pro Mujer Peru.

1551. Women Work: The National Network for Womens Employment, DC. $25,000, 2004.

Max Kade Foundation, Inc.

Limitations: Giving primarily in the U.S. and Europe. No grants to individuals, or for operating budgets, capital funds, development campaigns, or endowment funds; no loans.

1552. Stiftung Weimarer Klassik und Kunstsammlungen, Weimar, Germany. $300,000, 2005. For restoration of historic library in Weimar.

The J. M. Kaplan Fund, Inc.

Limitations: Giving primarily in New York City, NY; cross-borders of North America; and worldwide. No grants to individuals, including scholarships and fellowships, or for construction or building programs, endowment funds, operating budgets of educational or medical institutions, film or video, or sponsorship of books, dances, plays, or other works of art.

1553. Poets House, New York, NY. $30,000, 2004. For general support.

1554. Westminster College, Winston Churchill Memorial and Library, Fulton, MO. $10,000, 2004.

Anna Maria & Stephen Kellen Foundation, Inc.

Limitations: Giving primarily in New York, NY. No grants to individuals.

1555. Leo Baeck Institute, New York, NY. $10,000, 2005.

1556. Pierpont Morgan Library, New York, NY. $20,000, 2005.

The Esther A. & Joseph Klingenstein Fund, Inc.

1557. New York Public Library, New York, NY. $50,000, 2005.

The Kohlberg Foundation, Inc.

Limitations: Giving primarily in the U.S., with emphasis on CA and MA; giving also in Baja CA, Mexico. No grants to individuals.

1558. National Center for Family Philanthropy, DC. $27,000, 2004. For research on administrative costs in Family Foundations.

1559. National Center for Family Philanthropy, DC. $27,000, 2004. For research on administrative costs.

Henry R. Kravis Foundation, Inc.

1560. Americans for the Arts, DC. $10,000, 2004.

1561. Laura Bush Foundation for Americas Libraries, DC. $83,333, 2004.

1562. New York Public Library, New York, NY. $48,350, 2004.

1563. Pierpont Morgan Library, New York, NY. $19,150, 2004.

Samuel H. Kress Foundation

Limitations: Giving primarily in the U.S. and Europe. No support for art history programs below the pre-doctoral level, or the purchase of works of art. No grants for living artists, or for operating budgets, continuing support, annual campaigns, endowments, deficit financing, capital funds exhibitions, or films; no loans.

1564. American Antiquarian Society, Worcester, MA. $10,000, 2005. For general operating support.

1565. New York Preservation Archive Project, New York, NY. $10,000, 2005. For research.

1566. New York Public Library, New York, NY. $20,000, 2005. For publication.

1567. Northeast Document Conservation Center, Andover, MA. $30,000, 2005. For fellowships.

1568. Northeast Document Conservation Center, Andover, MA. $12,500, 2005. For conferences and seminars.

1569. Northeast Document Conservation Center, Andover, MA. $12,500, 2005. For conferences and seminars.

1570. Northeast Document Conservation Center, Andover, MA. $10,000, 2005. For conferences and seminars.

1571. Sterling and Francine Clark Art Institute, Williamstown, MA. $12,500, 2005. For general operating support.

Lavelle Fund for the Blind, Inc.

Limitations: Giving primarily in the New York City metropolitan area. No grants to individuals, or for deficit reduction, emergency funds, medical research programs, conferences or media events (unless an integral part of a broader program of direct service), or advocacy programs; no loans.

1572. Visions Services for the Blind and Visually Impaired, New York, NY. $105,000, 2005. 2-year grant. To provide continued support for Blind Line, telephone-based information and referral service for blind people in New York State.

Leon Lowenstein Foundation, Inc.

Limitations: Giving primarily in the metropolitan New York, NY, area. No support for international organizations. No grants to individuals.

1573. New York Public Library, New York, NY. $10,000, 2005. For general operating support.

1574. Wilton Library Association, Wilton, CT. $32,300, 2005. For capital campaign.

LSR Fund

Limitations: Giving on a national basis. No grants to individuals.

1575. Calvin Coolidge Memorial Foundation, Plymouth, VT. $10,000, 2004.

The Henry Luce Foundation, Inc.

Limitations: Giving on a national and international basis; international activities limited to East and Southeast Asia. No support for journalism, medical or media projects. No grants to individuals (except for specially designated programs), or for endowments, domestic building campaigns, general operating support, annual fund drives; no loans.

1576. Americans for the Arts, DC. $75,000, 2005. To plan and implement Benchmark National Public Opinion Arts Survey.

1577. Art 21, New York, NY. $75,000, 2005. To develop Art21 Archive.

1578. Foundation Center, New York, NY. $30,000, 2005. For annual support.

1579. Museum of Modern Art, New York, NY. $300,000, 2005. 2-year grant. For Museum Archives Collection.

1580. Orange County Museum of Art, Newport Beach, CA. $100,000, 2005. 2-year grant. For Archives of California Artists.

1581. University of California, Riverside, CA. $150,000, 2005. 3-year grant. For Southeast Asian Studies Library collection.

The M & T Charitable Foundation

Limitations: Giving on a national basis, with emphasis on Washington, DC, DE, MD, NY, PA, and WV. No support for political, fraternal, or veterans' organizations. No grants to individuals.

1582. Buffalo Niagara Enterprise, Buffalo, NY. $162,951, 2004.

Josiah Macy, Jr. Foundation

1583. Association of Academic Health Centers, DC. $421,578, 2005. 2-year grant. To maintain and further develop ExploreHealthCareers.org website.

1584. Association of Teachers of Preventive Medicine, DC. $497,218, 2005. 3-year grant. For development of common curriculum framework for education about prevention among seven health professions and to establish web-based Prevention Education Resource Center for faculty in health profession disciplines.

1585. Cold Spring Harbor Laboratory, Cold Spring Harbor, NY. $500,000, 2005. 2-year grant. For project, Preserving the Past and the Present, Looking to the Future: Preserving and Digitizing the Cold Spring Harbor Laboratory Archives Collections.

1586. New York Academy of Medicine, New York, NY. $25,000, 2005. For conference to help faculty and students maximize effectiveness of mentoring programs.

The G. Harold & Leila Y. Mathers Charitable Foundation

Limitations: Giving on a national basis. No grants to individuals.

1587. Montecito Library, Friends of, Santa Barbara, CA. $20,000, 2004. For general support.

The Andrew W. Mellon Foundation

Limitations: Giving on a national basis. No support for primarily local organizations. No grants to individuals (including scholarships); no loans.

1588. American Antiquarian Society, Worcester, MA. $1,210,000, 2005. 4-year grant. For Postdoctoral Fellowships in Humanities.

1589. American University of Paris, Paris, France. $23,500, 2005. For American International Consortium of Academic Libraries (AMICAL).

1590. Appalachian College Association, Berea, KY. $740,000, 2005. 3-year grant. For JSTOR (Journal Storage Project) in Appalachia.

1591. ARTstor, New York, NY. $6,500,000, 2005. 2.75-year grant. For general support.

1592. ARTstor, New York, NY. $2,300,000, 2005. 3-year grant. For collection development.

1593. Association Tela Botanica, Montpellier, France. $110,000, 2005. 2-year grant. For African Plant Initiative as part of Aluka Initiative.

1594. Association Tela Botanica, Montpellier, France. $55,000, 2005. For African Plant Initiative as part of Aluka Initiative.

1595. Atlanta University Center, Robert W. Woodruff Library, Atlanta, GA. $120,000, 2005. For JSTOR and ARTstor.

1596. Atlanta University Center, Robert W. Woodruff Library, Atlanta, GA. $90,000, 2005. For Information Literacy Program.

1597. Boston University, Boston, MA. $787,000, 2005. 3-year grant. For phase II of Bibliographic Database for East Asian Archaeology.

1598. Botanische Staatssammlung Munchen, Munich, Germany. $100,000, 2005. 2-year grant. For African Plants Initiative as part of Aluka Initiative.

1599. British Library, London, England. $695,000, 2005. 3.50-year grant. For Conservation Research Agenda for Libraries and Archives.

1600. Cambridge University, Cambridge, England. $1,421,000, 2005. 1.50-year grant. For Phase II of database, Matthew Parker on the Web.

1601. Cambridge University, Cambridge, England. $231,000, 2005. 2.75-year grant. For conservation and cataloging of archival collection at Churchill Archives Centre.

1602. Carleton College, Northfield, MN. $265,000, 2005. 2-year grant. For Library Consortium (in collaboration with Saint Olaf College).

1603. Center for Research Libraries, Chicago, IL. $433,000, 2005. 1.50-year grant. For Auditing and Certification of Digital Archives.

1604. Center for Research Libraries, Chicago, IL. $16,100, 2005. For Developing Resources for International Studies.

1605. Centro Studi Erbario Tropicale, Florence, Italy. $55,000, 2005. 2-year grant. For African Plants Initiative as part of Aluka Initiative.

1606. Conservatoire et Jardin Botaniques, Geneva, Switzerland. $75,000, 2005. 2-year grant. For African Plant Initiative as part of Aluka Initiative.

1607. Council of Independent Colleges, DC. $500,000, 2005. 2-year grant. For Libraries Workshops (in collaboration with Ithaka Harbors).

1608. Council on Library and Information Resources, DC. $750,000, 2005. 1.25-year grant. For general support.

1609. Die Deutsche Bibliothek, Frankfurt, Germany. $50,000, 2005. For Library Catalog Transition.

1610. Ecological Society of America, DC. $300,000, 2005. 2-year grant. For Digitization of JSTOR (Journal Storage Project).

1611. Foundation Center, New York, NY. $30,000, 2005. For general support.

1612. Foundation for Library and Information Service Development, Pretoria, South Africa. $25,000, 2005. For Cape Town Clippings.

1613. Gallaudet University, DC. $500,000, 2005. 1.50-year grant. For Digital Video Archive.

1614. Grantmakers in the Arts, Seattle, WA. $10,000, 2005. For Information Services.

1615. Harvard University, Villa I Tatti, Cambridge, MA. $50,000, 2005. 2-year grant. For I Tatti Renaissance Library.

1616. Indiana University, Bloomington, IN. $438,000, 2005. 1.50-year grant. For Library Systems Development.

1617. Ithaka Harbors, New York, NY. $6,000,000, 2005. 1.50-year grant. For NITLE (National Institute for Technology and Liberal Education) Funding.

1618. Ithaka Harbors, New York, NY. $3,700,000, 2005. 4-year grant. For capital support.

1619. Ithaka Harbors, New York, NY. $2,500,000, 2005. 2.25-year grant. For Phase II of Content Development for Aluka, online database of scholarly resources from developing countries, with initial focus on Africa.

1620. Ithaka Harbors, New York, NY. $1,500,000, 2005. For Portico (E-Archive).

1621. Ithaka Harbors, New York, NY. $500,000, 2005. For NITLE (National Institute for Technology and Liberal Education) Funding.

1622. Ithaka Harbors, New York, NY. $48,000, 2005. For Samora Machel Documentation Center.

1623. Ithaka Harbors, New York, NY. $44,000, 2005. For International Botanical Congress and African Plant Initiative as part of Aluka Initiative.

1624. Ithaka Harbors, New York, NY. $40,100, 2005. For BiblioVault.

1625. Ithaka Harbors, New York, NY. $35,000, 2005. For Organization for Open Source Software (OOSS).

1626. Johnson C. Smith University, Charlotte, NC. $300,000, 2005. 2-year grant. For Information Literacy Program.

1627. Judisches Museum Berlin, Berlin, Germany. $75,000, 2005. For Library Systems Development for ArteFact collection management system.

1628. Library of Congress, DC. $40,000, 2005. 1.25-year grant. For Photographic Conservation Assessment.

1629. Medici Archive Project, New York, NY. $50,000, 2005. For Web Interface.

1630. Middlebury College, Middlebury, VT. $1,475,000, 2005. 5-year grant. For College Sports Project: Northwestern Center for Data Collection.

1631. Missouri Botanical Garden, Saint Louis, MO. $75,000, 2005. For African Plant Initiative as part of Aluka Initiative.

1632. Musee National dHistoire Naturelle, Paris, France. $72,000, 2005. For Digitization of African Plant Initiative as part of Aluka Initiative.

1633. Musee National dHistoire Naturelle, Paris, France. $60,000, 2005. For African Plant Initiative as part of Aluka Initiative.

1634. National Botanic Garden of Belgium, Meise, Belgium. $220,000, 2005. 2-year grant. For African Plant Initiative as part of Aluka Initiative.

1635. National Botanical Research Institute, Windhoek, Namibia. $80,000, 2005. 2-year grant. For Digitization of African Plant Initiative as part of Aluka Initiative.

1636. National Herbarium and Botanic Garden, Harare, Zimbabwe. $84,000, 2005. 2-year grant. For Digitization of African Plant Initiative as part of Aluka Initiative.

1637. Natural History Museum, London, England. $126,000, 2005. 2-year grant. For African Plants Initiative as part of Aluka Initiative.

1638. Natural History Museum, London, England. $120,000, 2005. For African Plants Initiative as part of Aluka Initiative.

1639. New York University, New York, NY. $744,000, 2005. 2-year grant. For Digital Video Archive (Hemispheric Institute).

1640. New York University, New York, NY. $639,000, 2005. 3-year grant. For Audio Preservation in Research Libraries as part of Moving Image Archiving and Preservation Program for Special Collections.

1641. New York University, New York, NY. $48,300, 2005. 1.25-year grant. For Scholar Librarians Training.

1642. Research Libraries Group, Mountain View, CA. $750,000, 2005. 2-year grant. For Strengthening Library Systems.

1643. Royal Botanic Gardens, Kew, Richmond, England. $520,000, 2005. 2-year grant. For African Plant Initiative as part of Aluka Initiative.

1644. Royal Botanic Gardens, Kew, Richmond, England. $337,000, 2005. For African Plant Initiative as part of Aluka Initiative.

1645. Royal Botanic Gardens, Kew, Richmond, England. $260,000, 2005. 2-year grant. For Digitization of African Plant Initiative as part of Aluka Initiative.

1646. Saint Lawrence University, Canton, NY. $10,000, 2005. For ConnectNY Library Consortium.

1647. South African National Biodiversity Institute, Cape Town, South Africa. $480,000, 2005. 2-year grant. For African Plant Initiative as part of Aluka Initiative.

1648. Southeastern Library Network, Atlanta, GA. $29,000, 2005. For academic libraries in southern U.S. affected by hurricanes in late summer and fall.

1649. Swedish Museum of Natural History, Stockholm, Sweden. $110,000, 2005. 2-year grant. For African Plant Initiative as part of Aluka Initiative.

1650. Tropical Pesticides Research Institute, Arusha, Tanzania. $50,000, 2005. 2-year grant. For Digitization of African Plant Initiative as part of Aluka Initiative.

1651. University of California, Oakland, CA. $294,000, 2005. 1.25-year grant. For Strengthening Library Systems.

1652. University of Cape Town, Cape Town, South Africa. $70,000, 2005. 3-year grant. For African Plant Initiative as part of Aluka Initiative.

1653. University of Cape Town, Cape Town, South Africa. $10,000, 2005. For efforts to create comprehensive catalog of archived materials of Black Sash organization.

1654. University of Chicago, Chicago, IL. $473,000, 2005. For BiblioVault.

1655. University of Connecticut, Storrs, CT. $250,000, 2005. 2-year grant. For African National Congress Archives.

1656. University of Dublin, Trinity College, Dublin, Ireland. $80,000, 2005. 2-year grant. For African Plant Initiative as part of Aluka Initiative.

1657. University of KwaZulu-Natal, Durban, South Africa. $48,000, 2005. 2-year grant. For Digitization of African Plant Initiative for Aluka Initiative.

1658. University of Montpellier II, Montpellier, France. $77,000, 2005. 2-year grant. For Digitization of African Plant Initiative as part of Aluka Initiative.

1659. University of Montpellier II, Montpellier, France. $36,000, 2005. 2-year grant. For African Plant Initiative as part of Aluka Initiative.

1660. University of the Witwatersrand, Johannesburg, South Africa. $25,000, 2005. For South African Rock Art Digital Archive.

1661. Wageningen University, Department of Plant Sciences, Wageningen, Netherlands. $134,000, 2005. 2-year grant. For African Plant Initiative as part of Aluka Initiative.

1662. Yale University, New Haven, CT. $789,000, 2005. 3.50-year grant. For Cataloging Historical Audio Collections, collaborative project with New York Public Library and Stanford University - Special Collections.

Mertz Gilmore Foundation

(formerly Joyce Mertz-Gilmore Foundation)
Limitations: Giving on a national basis with some emphasis on the New York City Program. No support for sectarian religious concerns. No grants to individuals, or for endowments, annual fund appeals, fundraising events, conferences, workshops, publications, film or media projects, scholarships, research, fellowships, or travel.

1663. Kav LaOved-Workers Hotline for the Protection of Workers Rights, Tel Aviv, Israel. $40,000, 2004. To improve outreach and institutional capacity.

MetLife Foundation

(formerly Metropolitan Life Foundation)
Limitations: Giving on a national basis. No support for private foundations, religious, fraternal, athletic, political, social, or veterans' organizations, hospitals, United Way-supported organizations, local chapters of national organizations, disease-specific organizations, labor groups, international organizations, organizations primarily engaged in patient care or direct treatment, drug treatment centers or community health clinics, or elementary or secondary schools. No grants to individuals (except for Medical Research Awards and employee-related scholarships), or for endowments, courtesy advertising, or festival participation.

1664. Education Trust, DC. $18,200, 2005. For Community Data Guide.

1665. New York Academy of Medicine, New York, NY. $50,000, 2005. For National Medical School Clinical Training Program.

1666. New York Academy of Medicine, New York, NY. $45,000, 2005. For Partnering with Parents Project, promoting healthy development of young children enrolled in Medicaid.

1667. New York Academy of Medicine, New York, NY. $35,000, 2005. For Partnering with Parents Project, promoting healthy development of young children enrolled in Medicaid.

1668. New York Public Library, New York, NY. $20,000, 2005. For public education programs.

Paul and Irma Milstein Foundation

Limitations: Giving primarily in New York, NY. No grants to individuals.
1669. New York Public Library, New York, NY. $50,000, 2004.

The Ambrose Monell Foundation

1670. Brooklyn Public Library Foundation, Brooklyn, NY. $25,000, 2004. For general operating support.

1671. Brooklyn Public Library Foundation, Brooklyn, NY. $10,000, 2004. For Plaza and Auditorium Campaign.

1672. George C. Marshall Research Foundation, Lexington, VA. $10,000, 2004. For general operating support.

1673. MDRC, New York, NY. $50,000, 2004. For dissemination of information generated.

1674. New York Academy of Medicine, New York, NY. $25,000, 2004. For general operating support.

1675. New York Public Library, New York, NY. $100,000, 2004. For general operating support.

1676. Pierpont Morgan Library, New York, NY. $100,000, 2004. For general operating support.

Monterey Fund, Inc.

1677. Charities Aid Foundation (CAF) America, Alexandria, VA. $12,000, 2005.

1678. William J. Clinton Presidential Foundation, New York, NY. $17,800, 2005.

Morgan Stanley Foundation
(formerly Morgan Stanley Dean Witter Foundation)

Limitations: Giving primarily in areas of company operations, with emphasis on the Phoenix, AZ, Los Angeles and San Francisco, CA, Wilmington, DE, Chicago, IL, Baltimore, MD, New York, NY, Columbus, OH, Philadelphia, PA, Dallas and Houston, TX, and Salt Lake City, UT, metropolitan areas; giving also to national organizations. No support for local organizations with which Morgan Stanley employees are not involved, political candidates or lobbying organizations, religious, fraternal, or professional sports organizations, or individual performing arts organizations. No grants to individuals (except for the Morgan Stanley Scholars Program), or for capital campaigns or endowments, construction or renovation, political causes or campaigns, or documentaries or productions.

1679. Resources for Children with Special Needs, New York, NY. $12,500, 2004.

The Nash Family Foundation, Inc.
Limitations: Giving primarily in New York, NY and Israel. No support for political organizations. No grants to individuals or for conferences.

1680. New York Public Library, New York, NY. $205,000, 2005.
1681. New York Public Library, New York, NY. $45,000, 2005.
1682. New York Public Library, New York, NY. $24,585, 2005.
1683. YIVO Institute for Jewish Research, New York, NY. $33,000, 2005.
1684. YIVO Institute for Jewish Research, New York, NY. $25,000, 2005.
1685. YIVO Institute for Jewish Research, New York, NY. $15,000, 2005.
1686. YIVO Institute for Jewish Research, New York, NY. $15,000, 2005.
1687. YIVO Institute for Jewish Research, New York, NY. $12,500, 2005.
1688. YIVO Institute for Jewish Research, New York, NY. $12,500, 2005.

The New York Community Trust
Limitations: Giving limited to the metropolitan New York, NY, area. No support for religious purposes. No grants to individuals (except for scholarships), or for deficit financing, emergency funds, building campaigns, films, endowment funds, capital projects or general operating support.

1689. Andrews School, Willoughby, OH. $50,000, 2005. To remodel and modernize school library and assist in furnishing new volumes and reference materials.
1690. Arcadia University, Glenside, PA. $25,000, 2005. For Library construction.
1691. Athenaeum Music and Arts Library, La Jolla, CA. $25,000, 2005. For Barbara and William Karatz Fund for Endowment of Annual Classical Concert Series.
1692. Athenaeum Music and Arts Library, La Jolla, CA. $25,000, 2005. For Barbara and William Karatz Fund for Endowment of Annual Classical Concert Services.
1693. Brooklyn Academy of Music, Brooklyn, NY. $10,000, 2005. To help catalog, preserve, and make accessible archive collection.
1694. Brooklyn College Foundation, Brooklyn, NY. $200,000, 2005. For Library.
1695. Brooklyn Public Library Foundation, Brooklyn, NY. $60,000, 2005. To expand storytelling and reading program for disabled children in Brooklyn.
1696. Brown University, Providence, RI. $10,000, 2005. For establishment of undergraduate teaching and research assistantship, and for annual support of library.
1697. Charities Aid Foundation (CAF) America, Alexandria, VA. $50,000, 2005. For general support of Tiger Kloof School.
1698. Citizens Advice Bureau, Bronx, NY. $139,000, 2005. To expand work with elementary schools.
1699. Cornell University, Ithaca, NY. $25,000, 2005. For Library and for Cornell Scholarship Fund.
1700. Foundation Center, New York, NY. $10,000, 2005. For general support.
1701. Greenwich Library, Greenwich, CT. $50,000, 2005. For general support.
1702. Historic Districts Council, New York, NY. $10,000, 2005. For outreach programs to inform neighborhood residents about preservation.
1703. Keene Valley Library Association, Keene Valley, NY. $12,000, 2005. For publication of Recollections of Adirondacker.
1704. Metropolitan Museum of Art, New York, NY. $62,500, 2005. For Friends of Watson Library, Department of Objects Conservation, work of Maryan Ainsworth, and for Friends of European Painting.

1705. Middle Country Library Foundation, Centereach, NY. $25,000, 2005. For general support.
1706. Middle Country Library Foundation, Centereach, NY. $10,000, 2005.
1707. Morris Public Library, Morris, CT. $17,468, 2005. For staff support.
1708. New York Academy of Medicine, New York, NY. $110,000, 2005. For research program in hip fractures.
1709. New York Public Library, Astor, Lenox and Tilden Foundations, New York, NY. $100,000, 2005. For New York Public Library matching challenge grant from Andrew W. Mellon Foundation for Schomburg Center.
1710. New York Public Library, Astor, Lenox and Tilden Foundations, New York, NY. $68,000, 2005. For planned exhibition celebrating Joseph Papp and Anniversary of New York Shakespeare Festival.
1711. New York Public Library, Astor, Lenox and Tilden Foundations, New York, NY. $50,000, 2005. For general support.
1712. New York Public Library, Astor, Lenox and Tilden Foundations, New York, NY. $50,000, 2005. To be added to emergency fund for branch libraries.
1713. New York Public Library, Astor, Lenox and Tilden Foundations, New York, NY. $30,000, 2005. To be added to emergency fund for branch libraries.
1714. New York Public Library, Astor, Lenox and Tilden Foundations, New York, NY. $25,000, 2005. For general support.
1715. New York Public Library, Astor, Lenox and Tilden Foundations, New York, NY. $25,000, 2005. For President's Council.
1716. New York Public Library, Astor, Lenox and Tilden Foundations, New York, NY. $25,000, 2005. For President's Council.
1717. New York Public Library, Astor, Lenox and Tilden Foundations, New York, NY. $25,000, 2005. For Audio Project.
1718. New York Public Library, Astor, Lenox and Tilden Foundations, New York, NY. $25,000, 2005. For general support.
1719. New York Public Library, Astor, Lenox and Tilden Foundations, New York, NY. $25,000, 2005. For general support.
1720. New York Public Library, Astor, Lenox and Tilden Foundations, New York, NY. $25,000, 2005. For Barbara and William Karatz Fund for Center for Scholar and Writers.
1721. New York Public Library, Astor, Lenox and Tilden Foundations, New York, NY. $24,000, 2005. For recorded sound collections at New York Public Library for Performing Arts.
1722. New York Public Library, Astor, Lenox and Tilden Foundations, New York, NY. $23,350, 2005. For Literary Lions Event.
1723. New York Public Library, Astor, Lenox and Tilden Foundations, New York, NY. $20,000, 2005. For general support.
1724. New York Public Library, Astor, Lenox and Tilden Foundations, New York, NY. $20,000, 2005. For general support.
1725. New York Public Library, Astor, Lenox and Tilden Foundations, New York, NY. $20,000, 2005. For President's Council.
1726. New York Public Library, Astor, Lenox and Tilden Foundations, New York, NY. $10,000, 2005. For general support.
1727. New York Public Library, Astor, Lenox and Tilden Foundations, New York, NY. $10,000, 2005. For general support.
1728. New York Public Library, Astor, Lenox and Tilden Foundations, New York, NY. $10,000, 2005. For general support.
1729. New York Public Library, Astor, Lenox and Tilden Foundations, New York, NY. $10,000, 2005. For President's New Initiatives Fund.
1730. New-York Historical Society, New York, NY. $10,000, 2005. For Library Collection.
1731. Northeast Harbor Library, Northeast Harbor, ME. $10,000, 2005. For general support.
1732. Operation Truth, New York, NY. $50,000, 2005. For general support.
1733. Pierpont Morgan Library, New York, NY. $120,000, 2005. For Director's Purchasing Fund, earmarked for Sunny Crawford von Bulow Fund.
1734. Pierpont Morgan Library, New York, NY. $100,000, 2005. For campaign.
1735. Pierpont Morgan Library, New York, NY. $25,000, 2005. For campaign.
1736. Port Washington Public Library, Port Washington, NY. $25,000, 2005.
1737. Providence Public Library, Providence, RI. $10,000, 2005. For Capital Funding.
1738. Queens Council on the Arts, Woodhaven, NY. $10,000, 2005. To implement tracking and reporting database for Queens Arts Council.
1739. Quogue Free Library, Quogue, NY. $20,000, 2005. For technological improvements for card catalogue, and to add to endowment for future construction and expansion of library.
1740. Resources for Children with Special Needs, New York, NY. $65,000, 2005. To educate parents and school staff about how to get services for disabled children in public schools.

1741. Resources for Children with Special Needs, New York, NY. $10,000, 2005. For programs dealing with needs of immigrant families.

1742. Richard Nixon Library and Birthplace Foundation, Yorba Linda, CA. $25,000, 2005. For general support.

1743. State University of New York at Albany, Regents Research Fund, Albany, NY. $100,000, 2005. For work of States Impact on Federal Education Policy Archival Project.

1744. Westchester Childrens Association, White Plains, NY. $75,000, 2005. For development of proposed Westchester Children's Data Book.

1745. White Plains Library Foundation, White Plains, NY. $10,000, 2005. For Teacher in Library Program and new children's wing.

New York Foundation

Limitations: Giving limited to local programs in the New York, NY, metropolitan area. No grants to individuals, or for capital campaigns, research studies, films, conferences, or publications (except for those initiated by the foundation).

1746. Chardon Press, Oakland, CA. $14,885, 2005. For Klein and Roth Consulting's workshop series, Raise Money You Need: Building Individual Donor Program.

1747. New York City Tibetan Outreach Center, New York, NY. $47,500, 2005. For general support to link Tibetan refugees and immigrants residing in New York City with information and services they need.

1748. Nonprofit Connection, Brooklyn, NY. $30,000, 2005. To provide individual technical assistance to New York Foundation grantees.

1749. Nonprofit Connection, Brooklyn, NY. $15,000, 2005. To provide individual technical assistance to New York Foundation grantees.

New York Life Foundation

Limitations: Giving primarily in New York and Westchester County, NY; giving also to national organizations serving two or more of the following cities and regions: Tampa, FL, Atlanta, GA, Minneapolis, MN, Clinton/Hunterdon counties and Morris/Parsippany counties, NJ, Cleveland, OH, Dallas, TX, and the Gulf Coast region. No support for religious or sectarian organizations not of direct benefit to the entire community, fraternal, social, professional, veterans', or athletic organizations, or discriminatory organizations. No grants for seminars, conferences, or trips, endowments, memorials, or capital campaigns, fundraising events, telethons, races, or other benefits, goodwill advertising, or basic or applied research.

1750. National Archives, Foundation for the, DC. $400,000, 2005.

1751. New York Public Library, New York, NY. $300,000, 2005.

The New York Times Company Foundation, Inc.

Limitations: Giving primarily in areas of company operations, with emphasis on the New York, NY, metropolitan area. No support for religious organizations not of direct benefit to the entire community. No grants to individuals (except for scholarships), or for capital campaigns or health, drug, or alcohol therapy purposes; no loans.

1752. American Antiquarian Society, Worcester, MA. $10,000, 2005. For general operating support for newspaper preservation.

1753. Horticultural Society of New York, New York, NY. $10,000, 2005. For gardens at community libraries.

1754. New York Public Library, New York, NY. $65,000, 2005. For operations of research libraries.

1755. Student Press Law Center, Arlington, VA. $10,000, 2005. For legal advice and information for college and high school journalists.

1756. Syracuse University, Syracuse, NY. $10,000, 2005. For database for journalists on crime, justice, and Department of Homeland Security.

Samuel I. Newhouse Foundation, Inc.

1757. Dauphin County Library System, Harrisburg, PA. $10,000, 2005.

1758. Library of Congress, Center for the Book, DC. $25,000, 2005.

Jessie Smith Noyes Foundation, Inc.

Limitations: Giving limited to the U.S. No grants to individuals, or for scholarships, fellowships, endowment funds, deficit financing, capital construction funds, or general fundraising drives; generally no support for conferences, research, college and university based programs, or media; no loans.

1759. Interfaith Center on Corporate Responsibility, New York, NY. $100,000, 2005. For Jessie Smith Noyes Award.

1760. Interfaith Center on Corporate Responsibility, New York, NY. $20,000, 2005. For program support for shareholder actions and organizing on issues of global warming, environmental justice, and water and food.

1761. Southwest Research and Information Center, Albuquerque, NM. $30,000, 2005. For project support for Uranium Impact Assessment Program, assisting Navajo Nation and communities in mitigating and preventing environmental impacts of uranium mining.

Open Society Institute

Limitations: Giving on a national and international basis.

1762. American Library Association, DC. $13,500, 2004. For amicus brief in Cheney v. U.S. District Court case.

1763. Baku Education and Information Center, Baku, Azerbaijan. $20,500, 2004. To pass on Department of State funds supporting continued operations.

1764. DataCenter, Oakland, CA. $75,000, 2004. For customized research and analysis, campaign strategy assistance, training and consultation, and online resources for organizations working in criminal justice policy reform.

1765. Foundation Center, New York, NY. $20,000, 2004. For general support.

1766. Maryland Regional Practitioners Network for Fathers and Families, Baltimore, MD. $50,000, 2004. For general support.

1767. Microfinance Information Exchange, DC. $26,000, 2004. To conduct feasibility study supporting standardized commercial investment vehicle for MFIs.

1768. National Security Archive Fund, DC. $100,000, 2004. For Center for National Security Studies Emergency Project to Defend Civil Liberties and Protect Security.

1769. Pain Relief Network, New York, NY. $60,000, 2004. For Clinical Litigation Project.

1770. W G B H Educational Foundation, Boston, MA. $100,000, 2004. For digital library collection focused on U.S. civil rights movement.

The Overbrook Foundation

Limitations: Giving primarily in New York, NY. No grants to individuals.

1771. New York Academy of Medicine, New York, NY. $25,000, 2004. For Doctors Against Handgun Injury (DAHI).

1772. William A. Farnsworth Library and Art Museum, Rockland, ME. $35,000, 2004. For general operating support.

Park Foundation, Inc.

Limitations: Giving limited to the eastern U.S., primarily in central NY, Washington, DC, and North Carolina. No grants to individuals.

1773. Beyond Pesticides/NCAMP, DC. $25,000, 2004. For Center for Community Pesticide and Alternatives Information.

1774. Earth Action Network, Norwalk, CT. $25,000, 2004. For weekly column entitled, Earth Talk: Questions and Answers About Our Environment.

1775. Green Guide Institute, New York, NY. $25,000, 2004. For general operating support.

The PepsiCo Foundation, Inc.

Limitations: Giving on a national basis. No support for religious, fraternal, or political organizations. No grants to individuals (except for employee-related and Diamond scholarships), or for fundraising or sponsorship events.

1776. Charities Aid Foundation (CAF) America, Alexandria, VA. $665,500, 2004.

1777. Duke University, Durham, NC. $200,000, 2004. For library.

Perelman Family Foundation

Limitations: Giving on a national basis. No grants to individuals.

1778. New York Public Library, New York, NY. $25,000, 2004.

1779. YIVO Institute for Jewish Research, New York, NY. $25,000, 2004.

1780. YIVO Institute for Jewish Research, New York, NY. $18,000, 2004.

The Pfizer Foundation, Inc.

Limitations: No support for political organizations. No grants to individuals, or for capital campaigns or scholarships; no loans to individuals.

1781. New York Public Library, New York, NY. $100,000, 2004.

The Carl and Lily Pforzheimer Foundation, Inc.

Limitations: No support for religious or political organizations. No grants to individuals, or for building funds; no loans.

1782. Cambodian Association of Illinois, Chicago, IL. $25,000, 2005. For library and literacy projects.

1783. Frick Collection, New York, NY. $25,000, 2005. For creation of digital archives for art reference library.

1784. Harvard University, Radcliffe Institute for Advanced Study, Cambridge, MA. $400,000, 2005. For fellowships program and Schlesinger Library endowment fund.

1785. New York Public Library, New York, NY. $200,000, 2005. Toward Emergency Fund.

1786. Resources for Children with Special Needs, New York, NY. $10,000, 2005. For general support.

1787. White Plains Library Foundation, White Plains, NY. $15,000, 2005. For programs in new children's room.

The Picower Foundation

(formerly The Jeffry M. & Barbara Picower Foundation)

Limitations: Giving on a national basis, primarily in southeast FL and the Northeast. No grants to individuals.

1788. New York Public Library, New York, NY. $1,023,500, 2004. To install PC Management System.

The Pincus Family Fund

Limitations: Giving primarily in NY. No loans or grants to individuals, or for capital funds, construction and equipment, scholarships, or fellowships.

1789. New York Public Library, New York, NY. $1,000,000, 2005.

1790. New York Public Library, New York, NY. $98,350, 2005.

1791. New York Public Library, New York, NY. $13,350, 2005.

1792. New York Public Library, New York, NY. $10,000, 2005.

The Pinkerton Foundation

Limitations: Giving primarily in New York, NY. No support for medical research, the media, the direct provision of health care, or religious education. Generally no grants to individuals, or for emergency assistance, conferences, publications, media, building renovations, or other capital projects, unless they are integrally related to foundation's program objectives or an outgrowth of grantee's programs; no loans.

1793. Citizens Advice Bureau, Bronx, NY. $35,000, 2005. For operating support.

1794. Foundation Center, New York, NY. $10,000, 2005. For operating support.

1795. Queens Library Foundation, Jamaica, NY. $25,000, 2005. For operating support.

Charles H. Revson Foundation, Inc.

Limitations: Giving primarily in New York, NY. No support for local or national health appeals or direct service programs. No grants to individuals, or for endowment funds, building, renovation, or construction funds, book projects, charity events, travel expenses, or budgetary support.

1796. Center for National Independence in Politics (CNIP), Project Vote Smart, Philipsburg, MT. $100,000, 2004. For database, web site, and national 800 number.

1797. Jewish Womens Archive, Brookline, MA. $25,000, 2004. To join with Dorot Foundation to create virtual exhibition on Feminism, Jewish Women, and the Transformation of the American Jewish Community, in conjunction with upcoming 350th anniversary of Jewish life in North America.

1798. P.E.F. Israel Endowment Funds, New York, NY. $50,000, 2004. For interim support of Jerusalem Virtual Library, joint project of Al-Quds University and Hebrew University of Jerusalem.

1799. United States Holocaust Memorial Museum, DC. $450,000, 2004. For continued support of Charles H. Revson Fellowships for Archival Research at Museum's Center for Advanced Holocaust Studies.

Rochester Area Community Foundation

(formerly Rochester Area Foundation)

Limitations: Giving limited to Genesee, Livingston, Monroe, Ontario, Orleans, and Wayne counties, NY, except for donor-designated funds. No support for religious projects. No grants to individuals (except from restricted

funds), or for capital or annual campaigns, debt reduction, special events, land acquisition, or endowment or emergency funds.

1800. Candy Apple Preschool Center, Newark, NY. $20,000, 2005. To hire health coordinator to assist with telemedicine project and coordinate health and early intervention resources at child care center.

1801. Richmond Memorial Library, Batavia, NY. $30,000, 2005. For grant made through Muriel H. Marshall Fund for the Aging in Genesee County.

1802. Rundel Library Foundation, Rochester, NY. $21,500, 2005. To enhance quality of after-school programs.

Rockefeller Brothers Fund, Inc.

Limitations: Giving on a national basis, and in Central and Eastern Europe, East and Southeast Asia, and South Africa. No grants to individuals (including research, graduate study, or the writing of books or dissertations by individuals, with 3 exceptions: the RBF Fellowships under the education program, which are limited to those students nominated by the colleges that have been selected to participate in this program, the Ramon Magsaysay Awards through the Program for Asian Projects, and the Culpeper Medical Scholarships), or land acquisitions or building funds.

1803. American Forum for Global Education, New York, NY. $25,000, 2005. For organization of Global Youth Leadership Summit at UN.

1804. BBB Wise Giving Alliance, Arlington, VA. $50,000, 2005. 2-year grant. For general support.

1805. Ramon Magsaysay Award Foundation, Manila, Philippines. $43,543, 2005. For documentation and dissemination of information about recipients of Ramon Magsaysay Awards.

1806. Transatlantic Futures, The Globalist, DC. $25,000, 2005. For electronic newsletter, Globalist, in development of information services on global issues.

The Rockefeller Foundation

Limitations: Giving primarily in Africa, North America, and Southeast Asia. No grants to individuals for personal aid, or except in rare cases, for endowment funds or building or operating funds.

1807. AfriAfya, Nairobi, Kenya. $250,000, 2005. Toward strengthening health management information systems by ensuring links to community-based information to improve health care provision in Kenya.

1808. African Medical and Research Foundation, Nairobi, Kenya. $258,310, 2005. For project to develop functional model for improved and sustainable community-based health management information system in Kitui and Makueni districts of Kenya.

1809. Aga Khan Foundation USA, DC. $502,565, 2005. Toward Phase II of project to replicate, in three districts of Coast Province, Kenya, reliable, efficient and standardized health management information system, already in use in four districts of Coast Province, which will strengthen potential of being adopted as prototype for the entire country.

1810. Cornell University, Ithaca, NY. $34,400, 2005. Toward dissemination of Essential Electronic Agricultural Library to sub-Saharan universities and agricultural research institutions.

1811. Feminist Press, New York, NY. $132,500, 2005. Toward distributing Women Writing Africa to university libraries, teacher education and women's studies programs in Africa.

1812. Leveraging Investments in Creativity, Boston, MA. $100,000, 2005. Toward development of National Information Network for Arts.

1813. National Low Income Housing Coalition and Low Income Housing Information Service, DC. $300,000, 2005. For general support.

1814. Rockefeller University, Archive Center, New York, NY. $900,099, 2005. Toward operating support associated with preservation and continuing use of Foundation records.

1815. Teachers College Columbia University, Gottesman Libraries, New York, NY. $100,000, 2005. To complete and field-test comprehensive digital archive of documents related to school finance reform activities in New York State.

1816. Texas Low Income Housing Information Service, Austin, TX. $200,000, 2005. For general support.

1817. William J. Clinton Presidential Foundation, New York, NY. $250,000, 2005. Toward inaugural meeting of Clinton Global Initiative, nonpartisan conference dedicated to identifying immediate and pragmatic solutions to some of world's most pressing problems.

Frederick P. & Sandra P. Rose Foundation

Limitations: Giving primarily in New York, NY. No grants to individuals.

1818. Center for Jewish History, New York, NY. $20,000, 2004.
1819. New York Public Library, New York, NY. $100,000, 2004.
1820. New York Public Library, New York, NY. $50,000, 2004.
1821. Rye Free Reading Room, Rye, NY. $25,000, 2004.

Murray & Sydell Rosenberg Foundation

(formerly Murray M. Rosenberg Foundation)
Limitations: Giving primarily in NY, NJ, and Israel.
1822. YIVO Institute for Jewish Research, New York, NY. $11,500, 2005.

Arthur Ross Foundation, Inc.

Limitations: Giving primarily in NY.
1823. Century Association Archives Foundation, New York, NY. $60,000, 2005.

Helena Rubinstein Foundation, Inc.

Limitations: Giving primarily in New York, NY. No grants to individuals, or for emergency funds or film or video projects; no loans.
1824. Child Care, Inc., New York, NY. $20,000, 2006. For general support of child care referral, research, training, and advocacy initiatives.

The Fan Fox and Leslie R. Samuels Foundation, Inc.

Limitations: Giving limited to New York, NY. No support for education. No grants to individuals, or for scholarships, fellowships, or film or video projects.
1825. Encore Community Center, New York, NY. $29,700, 2005. To expand Encore's case management program for seniors.
1826. New York Public Library, New York, NY. $50,000, 2005. For Theater on Film and Tape Archive (TOFT).

The Scherman Foundation, Inc.

Limitations: Giving in NY and nationally in all areas, except for the arts and social welfare, which are primarily in New York City. No support for colleges, universities, or other higher educational institutions. No grants to individuals, or for building or endowment funds, capital campaigns scholarships, fellowships, conferences or symposia, specific media or arts production, medical, science or engineering research.
1827. New York Public Library, New York, NY. $135,000, 2005. To support Research Libraries.
1828. Sexuality Information and Education Council of the U.S. (SIECUS), New York, NY. $25,000, 2005. For general support.

The Peter Jay Sharp Foundation

(formerly Sharp Foundation)
Limitations: Giving primarily in New York, NY. No grants to individuals.
1829. Amagansett Free Library, Amagansett, NY. $25,000, 2004. For Capital Improvement Campaign.
1830. Graduate Center, City University of New York, New York, NY. $50,000, 2004. To preserve 20 years of presentations by Works and Process, discussion series which explores the creative process by providing behind-the-scenes insight into music, dance, opera, literary, and theatrical performances.
1831. Jamestown Foundation, DC. $100,000, 2004. For Study of International Terrorism.
1832. Manhattan School of Music, New York, NY. $500,000, 2004. For Peter Jay Sharp Library.
1833. Metropolitan Museum of Art, New York, NY. $825,000, 2004. For Fund for Ruth and Harold D. Uris Center for Education.
1834. New York Public Library, New York, NY. $50,000, 2004. For Computer Page Program, which trains young people of high school and college age to help others use computers at the public library.

The Shubert Foundation, Inc.

Limitations: Giving limited to the U.S. No grants to individuals, or for capital or endowment funds, conduit organizations, renovation projects, audience development, direct subsidy of reduced-price admissions, no loans.
1835. Foundation Center, New York, NY. $10,000, 2005. For general support.
1836. New York Public Library, New York, NY. $30,000, 2005. For general operating support for Library for the Performing Arts.

SI Bank & Trust Foundation

(formerly SISB Community Foundation)
Limitations: Giving only in Staten Island, NY. No support for political causes, candidates, or lobbying efforts, fraternal or veterans organizations, business, professional, or civic associations or clubs, animal welfare groups, cemetery associations, or private foundations. No grants to individuals, or for renovations/repairs to places of worship, yearbook advertisements, research including medical research, memorial fundraising events, or tickets to fundraising events.
1837. Poets House, New York, NY. $20,000, 2005. For Poetry in the Branches, initiative at Staten Island branches of New York Public Library.

Marty and Dorothy Silverman Foundation

Limitations: Giving primarily in NY. No grants to individuals.
1838. Citizens Advice Bureau, Bronx, NY. $15,000, 2005.
1839. New York Academy of Medicine, New York, NY. $20,000, 2005.

William E. Simon Foundation, Inc.

(formerly William E. & Carol G. Simon Foundation, Inc.)
Limitations: Giving on a national basis, with emphasis on New York, NY, and Los Angeles and the San Francisco Bay Area, CA. No support for foreign charities. No grants to individuals.
1840. Gerald R. Ford Foundation, Grand Rapids, MI. $100,000, 2004.
1841. Morristown and Morris Township Library Foundation, Morristown, NJ. $10,000, 2004.
1842. Richard Nixon Library and Birthplace Foundation, Yorba Linda, CA. $25,000, 2004.

The Simons Foundation

1843. New York Public Library, New York, NY. $10,000, 2005.

Skirball Foundation

Limitations: Giving primarily in CA. No grants to individuals.
1844. Center for Jewish History, New York, NY. $25,000, 2004. For operating support.

Alan B. Slifka Foundation, Inc.

Limitations: Giving primarily in NY. No support for political organizations, environmental, medical, or health-related fields. No grants to individuals, or for endowments, for-profit organizations or acquisitions of land. Generally no grants for major equipment purchases, individual research or media projects.
1845. Charities Aid Foundation (CAF) America, Alexandria, VA. $11,000, 2004. For unrestricted support.

Alfred P. Sloan Foundation

Limitations: No support for the creative or performing arts, humanities, religion, or primary or secondary education. No grants to individuals (except for research and publication), or for endowment or building funds, medical research, or equipment not related directly to foundation-supported projects; no loans.
1846. Boston College, Chestnut Hill, MA. $44,000, 2005. To construct database of Sloan-sponsored studies and projects.
1847. Congressional Quarterly, DC. $129,280, 2005. To enable Governing Magazine to execute multi-media publishing program on performance measurement in government.
1848. Consortium for Oceanographic Research and Education, DC. $400,000, 2005. 2-year grant. To operate US National Committee for Census of Marine Life.
1849. Council of State Governments, Lexington, KY. $45,000, 2005. 1.75-year grant. To improve terrorism preparedness by outlining content for public education and information standards.
1850. Dalhousie University, Halifax, Canada. $900,000, 2005. 3-year grant. To lead data synthesis and prediction of future marine populations for Census of Marine Life.
1851. Foundation Center, DC. $195,000, 2005. 2.75-year grant. For renewed operating support.
1852. Fulbright Academy of Science and Technology, Cape Elizabeth, ME. $35,000, 2005. 1.50-year grant. To develop internet memory board as

way to collect current and historical information on role of Fulbright scholarships in history of science and engineering.

1853. George Mason University Foundation, Fairfax, VA. $45,000, 2005. To develop digital memory bank for residents of Gulf Coast in wake of Hurricanes Katrina and Rita.

1854. Internet Archive, San Francisco, CA. $2,000,000, 2005. 2-year grant. To launch building of open access archive of millions of books.

1855. Louisiana State University and A & M College, Baton Rouge, LA. $400,000, 2005. 1.75-year grant. To develop, manage, and integrate global census of continental margins for Census of Marine Life.

1856. Society for Womens Health Research, DC. $45,000, 2005. To launch national award clearinghouse to facilitate nomination of women for scientific and medical achievement awards.

1857. Universidad Simon Bolivar, Caracas, Venezuela. $45,000, 2005. 1.50-year grant. To strengthen implementation of Census of Marine Life in Caribbean.

1858. University of California at San Diego, La Jolla, CA. $500,000, 2005. 4-year grant. For final support for Information Storage Industry Center.

1859. University of Colorado, Boulder, CO. $1,152,033, 2005. 3-year grant. To begin cataloging indoor microbial world.

1860. University of Connecticut, Storrs, CT. $350,000, 2005. For transfer grant to initiate and manage Census of Marine Zooplankton for Census of Marine Life, from University of New Hampshire.

1861. University of Connecticut, Storrs, CT. $45,000, 2005. For workshop to advance use of DNA barcoding in Census of Marine Life.

1862. University of Wisconsin System, Madison, WI. $28,500, 2005. 1.25-year grant. Toward weekly Academic Advanced Distributed Learning (ADL) Co-Lab Newsletter.

George D. Smith Fund, Inc.

Limitations: Giving primarily in CA and UT.

1863. University of Utah, Salt Lake City, UT. $600,000, 2005. For special collections.

The Speyer Family Foundation, Inc.

(formerly Tishman Speyer Properties Foundation, Inc.)
Limitations: Giving primarily in New York, NY. No grants to individuals.

1864. New York Public Library, New York, NY. $33,000, 2004.

The Starr Foundation

Limitations: Giving primarily on a national and international basis, with emphasis on New York City, NY nationally and emphasis on Asia internationally.

1865. Americans for the Arts, DC. $50,000, 2005. For general support.

1866. Brewster Public Library, Brewster, NY. $10,000, 2005. 2-year grant. For general support.

1867. Foundation Center, New York, NY. $300,000, 2005. 2-year grant. For Foundation Center Online.

1868. Foundation Center, New York, NY. $100,000, 2005. 2-year grant. For general support.

1869. George Bush Presidential Library Foundation, College Station, TX. $50,000, 2005. For U.S.-China Relations Conference in Beijing.

1870. Loyola Jesuit College, Abuja, Nigeria. $25,000, 2005. For financial aid and books for library. Grant made through Jesuit Seminary and Mission Bureau.

1871. Queens Library Foundation, Jamaica, NY. $300,000, 2005. 2-year grant. For general support.

1872. Richard Nixon Library and Birthplace Foundation, Yorba Linda, CA. $1,500,000, 2005. 2-year grant. For general support and support for National Interest magazine.

Surdna Foundation, Inc.

Limitations: Giving on a national basis. No support for international projects, or programs addressing toxics, hazardous waste, environmental education, sustainable agriculture, food production and distribution. No grants for endowments or land acquisition. Generally, no grants to individuals, or for capital campaigns or building construction.

1873. Foundation Center, New York, NY. $25,000, 2005. To expand information resources and educational services on philanthropy and nonprofit management and promote discussion and better understanding of issues critical to nonprofit sector.

1874. H. John Heinz III Center for Science, Economics and the Environment, DC. $75,000, 2005. To summarize state of science of thresholds for ecosystem response to climate change and engage decision makers and managers in policy dialogue on what they might do about such behavior.

1875. National Center for Victims of Crime, DC. $85,000, 2005. For Teen Action Partnership, where teen leaders will mobilize in four communities to help teen victims in their neighborhoods find assistance to recover from their experiences and reduce risk they will be victimized again.

1876. National Low Income Housing Coalition and Low Income Housing Information Service, DC. $80,000, 2005. For organizing and communication activities of National Housing Trust Fund Campaign to support production, preservation, and rehabilitation of rental housing affordable for lowest income people.

1877. Nonprofit Technology Enterprise Network (N-TEN), San Francisco, CA. $75,000, 2005. For TechFinder, searchable online directory of nonprofit technology service providers that launched in partnership with TechSoup and is free to nonprofits and to providers.

1878. OMG Center for Collaborative Learning, Philadelphia, PA. $15,000, 2005. For final editing and publication of handbook examining Comprehensive Community Revitalization Program.

1879. Pace University Law School, Land Use Law Center, White Plains, NY. $15,000, 2005. For national land use library database and to help with efforts to get substantial grant to complete library and ensure that it is used by those involved in place-based initiatives.

1880. Social Venture Partners International, Seattle, WA. $100,000, 2005. 2-year grant. For learning cluster of SVP Affiliates to develop and implement evaluation and outcomes measurement tools to build unique value propositions in order to provide Affiliates with resources to demonstrate their impact in their communities.

1881. Wesleyan University, Middletown, CT. $75,000, 2005. For continued support for service-learning initiative that will help faculty develop new courses, develop library resources and continue to build strong community relations both in Middletowne and with other colleges engaged in similar work.

The Teagle Foundation

Limitations: Giving limited to the U.S. No grants to community organizations outside New York City. No grants to U.S. organizations for foreign programmatic activities. No grants to individuals; no loans.

1882. Citizens Advice Bureau, Bronx, NY. $40,000, 2006. For college preparatory programming.

1883. Social Science Research Council, New York, NY. $40,000, 2006. For pamphlet, What College Teachers Should Know About the Religious Engagement of Today's Undergraduates.

1884. Teachers College Columbia University, Hechinger Institute on Education and the Media, New York, NY. $40,000, 2006. For primer on importance of value-added assessment for higher education.

Tiger Foundation

Limitations: Giving primarily in New York, NY. No support for political organizations or public policy. No grants to individuals, or for endowments, annual or capital campaigns, benefits, legal aid, obligations or debt.

1885. Child Care, Inc., New York, NY. $150,000, 2005. For Quality of Care Initiative.

Tisch Foundation, Inc.

Limitations: Giving primarily in NY. No grants to individuals, or for endowment funds, scholarships, fellowships, or matching gifts; no loans.

1886. Center for Jewish History, New York, NY. $50,000, 2005.

Triad Foundation, Inc.

Limitations: Giving primarily in FL, NC, and NY. No grants to individuals, or for endowments or capital campaigns.

1887. Childrens Theater of Charlotte, Charlotte, NC. $150,000, 2004. For ImaginOn The Joe and Joan Martin Center.

The Trust for Mutual Understanding

Limitations: Giving for exchanges between the U.S. and the countries of Central and Eastern Europe, primarily the Czech Republic, Hungary, Poland, Russia, and Slovakia. Support is also provided, to a lesser extent, for exchanges involving Albania, Belarus, Bosnia and Herzegovina, Bulgaria, Croatia, Georgia, Macedonia, Moldova, Mongolia, Romania, Serbia and Montenegro, Slovenia, and Ukraine. No support for large-scale institutional programs lacking an individual exchange component, youth or undergraduate exchanges, economic development, medicine, public health, agricultural issues, or activities pertaining to nuclear weapons and arms control. No grants to individuals, or for fellowships, capital campaigns, deficit financing, endowments, general program and operating costs, salaries, honoraria, publications, library and equipment purchases, film, media, or one-person exhibitions or performance tours.

1888. Bank Information Center, DC. $20,000, 2005. For international travel for American and Central European participants in Europe and Central Asia Program.

1889. Internews Interactive, San Anselmo, CA. $20,000, 2005. For international travel expenses in connection with research in Russia on cultural and environmental components of US-USSR Citizen Diplomacy Archive Project.

1890. Northeast Document Conservation Center, Andover, MA. $40,000, 2005. For international travel of conservators from Central and Eastern Europe participating in photographic conservation training program, and of conservators from NEDCC conducting follow-up workshops at Academy of Fine Arts and Design in Bratislava.

van Ameringen Foundation, Inc.

Limitations: Giving primarily in metropolitan New York, NY, and Philadelphia, PA. No support for international activities and institutions, or for programs for the mentally retarded, the physically handicapped, drug abuse, or alcoholism. No grants to individuals, or for endowments, annual campaigns, deficit financing, emergency funds, capital campaigns, scholarships, or fellowships; no loans.

1891. Child and Adolescent Bipolar Foundation, Wilmette, IL. $36,000, 2005. For reference guide summarizing agency's material on Internet.

Sue and Edgar Wachenheim Foundation

Limitations: Giving primarily in NY. No grants to individuals.

1892. New York Public Library, New York, NY. $1,400,000, 2005. For general support.

1893. New York Public Library, New York, NY. $850,000, 2005. For general support.

1894. New York Public Library, New York, NY. $50,000, 2005. For general support.

1895. New York Public Library, New York, NY. $50,000, 2005. For general support.

1896. New York Public Library, New York, NY. $25,000, 2005. For general support.

The Wallace Foundation

(formerly Wallace-Reader's Digest Funds)

Limitations: Giving on a national basis. No support for religious or fraternal organizations; environmental or conservation programs, health, medical or social service programs, international programs, or for private foundations. No grants to individuals, or for annual campaigns, emergency funds, conferences, historical restoration, capital campaigns, or for deficit financing.

1897. Foundation Center, New York, NY. $115,000, 2005. For services to the field.

The Andy Warhol Foundation for the Visual Arts

1898. Anthology Film Archives, New York, NY. $10,000, 2005. For exhibition of Jonas Mekas' films and materials at Venice Biennale.

The Margaret L. Wendt Foundation

Limitations: Giving primarily in Buffalo and western NY. No grants to individuals, or for scholarships.

1899. Christ the King Seminary, East Aurora, NY. $40,000, 2005. For computerization of library.

1900. Medaille College, Buffalo, NY. $150,000, 2005. For challenge grant in support of library expansion project.

The Robert W. Wilson Charitable Trust

Limitations: Giving primarily in NY. No grants to individuals.

1901. New York Public Library, New York, NY. $1,000,000, 2004. For acquisitions and preservation.

1902. New York Public Library, New York, NY. $1,000,000, 2004. For general support.

1903. New York Public Library, New York, NY. $1,000,000, 2004. For matching grant for acquisitions and preservation.

The Norman and Rosita Winston Foundation, Inc.

Limitations: Giving in the U.S., with emphasis on national and local organizations in NY. No grants to individuals.

1904. Harvard College Library, Cambridge, MA. $10,000, 2005. For general support.

1905. New York Academy of Medicine, New York, NY. $35,000, 2005. For general support.

1906. New York Public Library, New York, NY. $25,000, 2005. For general support.

NORTH CAROLINA

The Bank of America Charitable Foundation, Inc.

Limitations: Giving limited to areas of major company operations. No support for political, labor, or fraternal organizations, civic clubs, religious organizations not of direct benefit to the entire community, public or private pre-K-12 schools, United Way- or arts council-supported organizations, or disease advocacy organizations. No grants to individuals (except for Joe Martin Scholarships), or for fellowships, advertising, sports, athletic events, or athletic programs, travel-related events, student trips, or tours, development or production of books, films, videos, or television programs, endowments, or memorial campaigns.

1907. Child Care Resources, Charlotte, NC. $100,000, 2004. For general support.

1908. Enoch Pratt Free Library, Baltimore, MD. $10,000, 2004.

1909. Fort Worth Public Library Foundation, Fort Worth, TX. $10,000, 2004.

1910. George Bush Presidential Library Foundation, College Station, TX. $15,000, 2004.

1911. Home Buyer Assistance and Information Center (HBAIC), Oakland, CA. $20,000, 2004. For general support.

1912. King County Library System Foundation, Issaquah, WA. $10,000, 2004. For general support.

1913. Nashville Public Library Foundation, Nashville, TN. $100,000, 2004. For general support.

1914. National Low Income Housing Coalition and Low Income Housing Information Service, DC. $75,000, 2004.

1915. New York Public Library, Astor, Lenox and Tilden Foundations, New York, NY. $50,000, 2004.

1916. Public Library of Charlotte and Mecklenburg County, Friends of the, Charlotte, NC. $12,500, 2004.

1917. San Antonio Public Library Foundation, San Antonio, TX. $30,000, 2004.

BB&T Charitable Foundation

Limitations: Giving primarily in areas of company operations. No grants to individuals.

1918. Richmond Public Library Foundation, Richmond, VA. $10,000, 2004.

Burroughs Wellcome Fund

Limitations: Giving limited to the U.S. and Canada. No grants to individuals, or for building or endowment funds, equipment, operating budgets, continuing support, annual campaigns, deficit financing, publications, conferences, or matching gifts; no loans.

1919. Foundation Center, New York, NY. $10,000, 2005. For Online Project.

The Cannon Foundation, Inc.

Limitations: Giving primarily in NC, with emphasis on the Cabarrus County area. No grants to individuals, or for operating budgets, seed money, emergency funds, deficit financing, land acquisition, endowment funds, demonstration projects, research, publications, conferences, seminars, scholarships, or fellowships; no loans.

1920. Macon County Public Library, Friends of, Franklin, NC. $25,000, 2005. For New Library Construction.

1921. MemoryCare, Inc., Asheville, NC. $15,000, 2005. For equipment and furnishings.

The Community Foundation of Western North Carolina, Inc.

Limitations: Giving limited to Avery, Buncombe, Burke, Cherokee, Clay, Graham, Haywood, Henderson, Jackson, Macon, Madison, McDowell, Mitchell, Polk, Rutherford, Swain, Transylvania, and Yancey counties, NC. No support for religious organizations or sectarian purposes (except from designated funds). No grants to individuals (except for undergraduate student scholarships), or for capital campaigns, endowment funds, start-up funds, or debt retirement.

1922. MemoryCare, Inc., Asheville, NC. $50,000, 2005. To develop staff and board capacity to provide expanded medical care for adults suffering from progressive memory disorders, in-depth education and support for caregivers, and improved access to support services and education for community.

The Duke Endowment

Limitations: Giving limited to NC and SC. No grants to individuals or for deficit financing; no loans.

1923. Bertie Memorial Hospital, Windsor, NC. $242,725, 2005. To assist in third year of three-year period to develop electronic medical record system to improve community-based care for chronic disease management.

1924. Duke University Health System, Durham, NC. $407,850, 2005. To assist in first year of two-year period to implement computerized physician order entry system at Durham Regional Hospital.

1925. FirstHealth of the Carolinas, Pinehurst, NC. $141,840, 2005. To assist in first year of two-year period to establish electronic medical record and case management program at Moore Free Care Clinic.

1926. Foundation Center, New York, NY. $25,000, 2005. For general operating support.

1927. Georgetown County Memorial Hospital, Georgetown, SC. $84,125, 2005. To assist in implementation of community medication safety tracking program.

1928. Hot Springs Health Program, Mars Hill, NC. $210,000, 2005. To assist in implementing electronic medical record system.

1929. Rex Healthcare, Raleigh, NC. $250,000, 2005. To assist in implementing electronic medical records system.

1930. Sampson Regional Medical Center, Clinton, NC. $150,000, 2005. To assist in implementing picture archiving communications system.

1931. Stanly Health Services, Albemarle, NC. $193,248, 2005. To assist in implementing electronic medical record system.

1932. Transylvania Community Hospital, Brevard, NC. $150,000, 2005. To assist in purchasing picture archiving and communications system.

1933. University of South Carolina Research Foundation, Office of Research and Health Sciences, Columbia, SC. $117,588, 2005. To assist in first year of two-year period to integrate health information technology into primary care education and training.

1934. University of South Carolina Research Foundation, Office of Research and Health Sciences, Columbia, SC. $70,000, 2005. To assist in first year of two-year period to develop statewide seniors healthcare database.

1935. WESTCARE Health System, Sylva, NC. $300,000, 2005. To assist in implementation of comprehensive hospital information system.

Foundation for the Carolinas

Limitations: Giving primarily to organizations serving the citizens of NC and SC, with emphasis on the greater Charlotte, NC, region. No grants to individuals (except for scholarships), or for deficit financing, capital campaigns, ongoing operating budgets, publications, conferences, videos, travel, equipment, small businesses, business start-up, or advertising.

1936. Richmond County Community Support Center, Rockingham, NC. $46,000, 2004. For Indigent Prescription Drug Program, which provides counseling and serves as information and referral source to residents. Grant made through the Cole Foundation.

Janirve Foundation

Limitations: Giving primarily in western NC. No support for public and private elementary schools, or churches and religious programs. No grants to individuals (except for scholarships), or generally for operating budgets, endowments or for research programs, publication of books or printed material, theatrical productions, videos, radio or television programs; no loans.

1937. Avery-Mitchell-Yancey Regional Library, Spruce Pine, NC. $300,000, 2005.

1938. Macon County Public Library, Friends of, Franklin, NC. $100,000, 2005. To purchase furnishings, fixtures and equipment for new facility.

1939. Polk County Library, Friends of, Columbus, NC. $200,000, 2005.

Kate B. Reynolds Charitable Trust

Limitations: Giving limited to NC; social welfare grants limited to Winston-Salem and Forsyth County; health care giving, statewide. No support for political organizations. No grants to individuals, or for endowment funds or medical research; grants on a highly selective basis for construction of facilities or purchase of equipment.

1940. MemoryCare, Inc., Asheville, NC. $207,258, 2005. 2-year grant. For expansion of clinical assessment, monitoring, and long-term treatment for low-income, memory-impaired older adults and integrated support services for family caregivers.

1941. Positive Wellness Alliance, Lexington, NC. $47,000, 2005. 2-year grant. For operating support to increase services to financially needy individuals living with HIV/AIDS in Davidson County.

1942. WESTCARE Health System, Sylva, NC. $200,000, 2005. For capital support for purchase and installation of comprehensive hospital information system for rural hospital serving significant number of low-income individuals.

Z. Smith Reynolds Foundation, Inc.

Limitations: Giving limited to NC. No support for athletic teams, civic clubs, day care centers, fraternal groups, parent/teachers associations, private K-12 schools, single site public schools, volunteer fire departments, or emergency medical service organizations, art organizations, historic preservation organizations, homeless shelters, or health care (physical and mental health). No grants to individuals (except for Nancy Susan Reynolds Awards and Sabbatical Program), or for endowment funds, equipment purchases, research, athletic events, building projects or renovations (including construction materials and labor costs), capital campaigns, computer hardware or software purchases (where it is the principal purpose of the grant), conferences, seminars, symposiums, fundraising events, initiatives promoting religious education or doctrine, land purchases, payment of debts, salaries for personnel or other general operating expenses in public schools, or after-school programs. Additionally, no grants for adoption and foster care, annual species preservation or rehabilitation, crisis intervention, greenways, senior citizen services, social/human direct services, substance abuse treatment, transitional housing, or treatment or rehabilitation.

1943. Agricultural Resources Center and Pesticide Education Project, Raleigh, NC. $55,000, 2005. For general operating support to promote alternatives to toxic pesticides.

1944. Mountain Area Information Network (MAIN), Asheville, NC. $25,000, 2005. For general operating support to continue to provide local radio programming and technology assistance to western NC.

C. D. Spangler Foundation, Inc.

Limitations: Giving primarily in NC. No grants to individuals.

1945. Cleveland County Memorial Library, Shelby, NC. $125,000, 2004. For program support.

The Sunshine Lady Foundation, Inc.

Limitations: Giving on a national basis. No grants for endowments or deficit funding.

1946. James Monroe Memorial Foundation, Richmond, VA. $12,000, 2004. For pianoforte for museum.

1947. John A. Stahl Library, Leila Stahl Buffett Genealogy Center, West Point, NE. $20,000, 2004.

Triangle Community Foundation

Limitations: Giving limited to Chatham, Durham, Orange, and Wake counties, NC. No grants for operating budgets.

1948. Charities Aid Foundation-India, New Delhi, India. $48,000, 2005.

1949. University of North Carolina, Library Development, Chapel Hill, NC. $20,000, 2005.

NORTH DAKOTA

Tom and Frances Leach Foundation, Inc.

(also known as Leach Foundation)

Limitations: Giving primarily in ND, particularly in Bismarck and Mandan, and the upper Midwest. No grants for travel, or for fellowships or conferences; generally, limited grants for capital expenditures or endowments.

1950. International Music Camp, Minot, ND. $43,750, 2005. For International Arts Music Center and for Frances Leach library.

MDU Resources Foundation

Limitations: Giving primarily in areas of company operations. No support for athletic, labor, fraternal, veterans', political, lobbying, social, or religious organizations or regional or national organizations without local affiliation. No grants to individuals (except for employee-related scholarships); generally, no endowments.

1951. Library Foundation, Bismarck, ND. $10,000, 2005. For endowment.

OHIO

Akron Community Foundation

Limitations: Giving primarily in Summit County, OH. No support for religious organizations for religious purposes. No grants to individuals, or for endowment funds, capital campaigns, or fellowships; no loans.

1952. ARC of Summit and Portage Counties, Akron, OH. $10,000, 2005. For People Together disability-awareness program.

Eva L. and Joseph M. Bruening Foundation

Limitations: Giving limited to the Cuyahoga, OH. No support for international funding. No grants to individuals, or for endowment funds, general operating budgets, research, symposia or seminars, mass mailings, or annual campaigns.

1953. East Cleveland Public Library, East Cleveland, OH. $20,000, 2005. For renovations and expansion.

1954. Fairhill Center for Aging, Cleveland, OH. $45,000, 2005. For Greater Cleveland Access to Benefits Coalition, collaborative initiative enrolling people in Low Income Subsidy Program of Medicare Part D.

1955. Saint Mary-Collinwood School, Cleveland, OH. $25,000, 2005. For renovation of stage area into multimedia computer library center.

The Greater Cincinnati Foundation

Limitations: Giving limited to southeastern IN, northern KY, and the greater Cincinnati, OH area. No support for private or parochial religious purposes, units of government or government agencies, schools, hospitals, nursing homes, or retirement centers. No grants to individuals (except for scholarships), or for operating budgets, fundraising drives, event sponsorship, or underwriting, equipment, stand-alone publications or videos, annual campaigns, deficit financing, endowments, travel, fellowships, internships, exchange programs, or scholarly or medical research; no loans.

1956. Applied Information Resources, Cincinnati, OH. $10,000, 2005. For Study of Racial Attitudes in Cincinnati.

1957. Health Improvement Collaborative of Greater Cincinnati, Cincinnati, OH. $50,000, 2005. For Cincinnati MD Resource Center.

1958. Ohio Grantmakers Forum, Columbus, OH. $25,000, 2005. For Organized Philanthropy in SW Ohio.

The Cleveland Foundation

Limitations: Giving limited to the greater Cleveland, OH, area, with primary emphasis on Cleveland, Cuyahoga, Lake, and Geauga counties, unless specified by donor. No support for sectarian or religious activities, community services such as fire and police protection, government staff positions, or library and welfare services. No grants to individuals (except for scholarships), or for endowment funds, operating costs, debt reduction, fundraising campaigns, publications, films and audiovisual materials (unless they are an integral part of a program already being supported), memberships, travel for bands, sports teams, classes and similar groups; no capital support for planning, construction, renovation, or purchase of buildings, equipment and materials, land acquisition, or renovation of public space unless there is strong evidence that the program is of priority to the foundation.

1959. Case Western Reserve University, Cleveland, OH. $25,000, 2005. For renovation of Hatch Reading Room, Smith Library.

1960. Child Care Resource Center of Cuyahoga County, Cleveland, OH. $200,000, 2005. For core support for resource and referral services.

1961. Citizens Academy, Cleveland, OH. $10,000, 2005. For Hugh Calkins Library Fund.

1962. Cleveland Grays, Cleveland, OH. $139,200, 2005. For restructuring financing for Museum property.

1963. Cleveland Grays, Cleveland, OH. $50,450, 2005. For income distribution from Gerber Trust.

1964. Community Vision Council, Cleveland, OH. $30,000, 2005. For clinical data-sharing network for local health care providers.

1965. Cuyahoga County Public Library, Cleveland, OH. $25,000, 2005. For distribution from Cuyahoga County Public Library Endowment Fund.

1966. East Cleveland Public Library, East Cleveland, OH. $25,000, 2005. For presentation of local artists in new building.

1967. Foundation Center, Cleveland, OH. $175,959, 2005. For program and operating support for library and learning center.

1968. Friends of the New Netherland Project, Albany, NY. $10,000, 2005. For general support.

1969. Morley Library, Painesville, OH. $50,000, 2005. For Children's Room.

1970. Ohio Grantmakers Forum, Columbus, OH. $200,000, 2005. For operations and membership dues.

1971. Older Adult Service and Information Systems (OASIS), Parma, OH. $60,000, 2005. For Lifelong Learning and Development Center.

1972. United Way Services of Geauga County, Chardon, OH. $30,000, 2005. For technology and capacity building for 211 information and referral line.

1973. Westminster School, Simsbury, CT. $1,000,000, 2005. 2-year grant. For new academic center and library.

The Columbus Foundation and Affiliated Organizations

(formerly The Columbus Foundation)

Limitations: Giving limited to central OH. No support for religious purposes, or for projects normally the responsibility of a public agency. No grants to individuals, or generally for budget deficits, conferences, scholarly research, or endowment funds.

1974. Association of Fundraising Professionals, Central Ohio Chapter, Columbus, OH. $10,000, 2005. For educational conference to be held on Philanthropy Day.

1975. Central Community House, Columbus, OH. $25,800, 2005. To increase community access to health care and related services and programs and to increase community knowledge of health care issues and resources.

1976. Columbus Metropolitan Library, Columbus, OH. $30,000, 2005. To sponsor Summer Reading Program designed to encourage children to love reading and to become good readers.

1977. Columbus Metropolitan Library, Columbus, OH. $25,000, 2005.

1978. Community Research Partners, Columbus, OH. $80,000, 2005. To enhance Community Indicators Database and DataSource, web-based data system to make accessible social and demographic indicator data to understand and address community conditions, trends, needs and issues.

1979. National Association for the Education of African American Children with Learning Disabilities, Columbus, OH. $20,000, 2005. To provide train-the-trainer event for parent leaders.

1980. Nelsonville Public Library, Nelsonville, OH. $25,000, 2005. For Capital Improvement Project.

1981. Ohio Grantmakers Forum, Columbus, OH. $15,000, 2005. To provide general operating support.

1982. Ohio Grantmakers Forum, Columbus, OH. $10,000, 2005. For new staff person whose responsibilities will include directing programs and services for member community foundations throughout state.

1983. Ohio Grantmakers Forum, Columbus, OH. $10,000, 2005.

The Community Foundation of Greater Lorain County

Limitations: Giving limited to Huron County and Lorain County, OH, and immediate vicinity. No support for religious purposes, street repair, government services, public or non-public school services required by law, or self-help clubs that meet the needs of a small population. No grants to individuals (except for scholarships), or for annual campaigns, medical research, deficit financing, membership fees, tickets for benefits, tours, equipment, group travel, or capital campaigns; no loans.

1984. Child Care Resource Center of Lorain County, Elyria, OH. $22,512, 2005. For Food Pantry.

1985. Lorain Public Library, Lorain, OH. $13,288, 2005. For Project Lite.

The Eaton Charitable Fund

Limitations: Giving on a national and international basis in areas of company operations. No support for religious organizations, fraternal or labor organizations, or organizations that could be members of a United Fund or federated community fund but choose not to participate. No grants to individuals, or for endowments, medical research, general operating support for United Way agencies or hospitals, or debt reduction; no loans.

1986. Cumberland County Schools, Fayetteville, NC. $25,000, 2005. For science inquiry libraries.

1987. Downtown Cleveland Partnership, Cleveland, OH. $11,000, 2005. For downtown housing guide.

The Fifth Third Foundation

Limitations: Giving primarily in areas of company operations, with emphasis on the Cincinnati, OH, area. No support for public schools or elementary schools. No grants to individuals, or for capital campaigns for individual churches, endowments, or fellowships; no loans.

1988. Athenaeum of Ohio, Cincinnati, OH. $100,000, 2005. For capital support.

1989. Athenaeum of Ohio, Cincinnati, OH. $100,000, 2005. For capital support.

FirstEnergy Foundation

(formerly Centerior Energy Foundation)

Limitations: Giving primarily in areas of company operations in NJ, OH, and PA. No support for largely tax-supported organizations, fraternal, religious, labor, athletic, social, or veterans' organizations not of direct benefit to the entire community, national or international organizations, United Way-supported organizations, public or private schools, or foundations. No grants to individuals, or for political or legislative activities, research, equipment, endowments, or debt reduction; no loans.

1990. Ohio Grantmakers Forum, Columbus, OH. $10,000, 2005.

Forest City Enterprises Charitable Foundation, Inc.

Limitations: Giving primarily in OH. No grants to individuals.

1991. National First Ladies Library, Canton, OH. $25,000, 2005.

The GAR Foundation

Limitations: Giving primarily in the Akron-Summit County area and secondarily in Cuyahoga, Stark, Medina, Portage and Wayne counties, OH. No support for private non-operating foundations, health care institutions,

or national organizations. No grants to individuals, or for medical research, capital funding for churches or synagogues, or computers for schools.

1992. Info Line, Akron, OH. $130,000, 2004. For general operating support of Project Connect and for business plan development.

1993. Ohio Grantmakers Forum, Columbus, OH. $25,000, 2004. For regionalism conference and operating support.

The George Gund Foundation

Limitations: Giving primarily in northeastern OH and the greater Cleveland, OH, area. No support for political groups, services for the physically, mentally or developmentally disabled, or the elderly. Generally, no grants to individuals, or for building or endowment funds, political campaigns, debt reduction, equipment, renovation projects, or to fund benefit events.

1994. Americans for the Arts, DC. $15,000, 2005. For arts education activities.

1995. Educational Fund to Stop Gun Violence, DC. $25,000, 2005. For Firearms Litigation Clearinghouse.

1996. Foundation Center, Cleveland, OH. $25,000, 2005. For operating support.

Key Foundation

(formerly Society Foundation)

Limitations: Giving primarily in areas of company operations in AK, CO, FL, ID, IN, ME, MI, NY, OH, OR, UT, VT, and WA. No support for political, sensitive, or controversial organizations, churches or religious organizations, preschool or primary educational institutions, fraternal, social, labor, or veterans' organizations, private foundations, international or foreign organizations, trade or professional associations, athletic organizations, or lobbying organizations. No grants to individuals, or for start-up needs, endowments, matching support, scholarships or fellowships, special projects, research, publications, conferences, memberships, or journal advertisements.

1997. Roswell P. Flower Memorial Library, Watertown, NY. $15,000, 2004. For capital campaign.

The Fred A. Lennon Charitable Trust

Limitations: Giving primarily in OH, with emphasis on Cleveland. No grants to individuals; no loans.

1998. Cleveland Public Library, Friends of the, Cleveland, OH. $100,000, 2004.

Mathile Family Foundation

Limitations: Giving primarily in the Dayton and Montgomery County, OH, areas. No support for political organizations. No grants to individuals, or for sponsorships, endowment funds, or mass appeals for funding.

1999. Athenaeum of Ohio, Cincinnati, OH. $1,000,000, 2005. For operating support.

2000. Child Care Choices, Tipp City, OH. $10,000, 2005. For operating support.

2001. Child Care Works, Dayton, OH. $175,000, 2005. For operating support.

2002. Ohio Grantmakers Forum, Columbus, OH. $15,000, 2005. For operating support.

Nationwide Foundation

(formerly Nationwide Insurance Enterprise Foundation)

Limitations: Giving primarily in areas of company operations, with emphasis on OH, including Columbus. No support for athletic teams, public or private primary or secondary schools, pass-through organizations (except the United Way), veterans', labor, religious, or fraternal organizations not of direct benefit to the entire community, or lobbying or political organizations; generally, no support for hospitals or hospital foundations or national organizations (except local branches or chapters). No grants to individuals, or for fundraising events, sponsorships, athletic events, debt reduction, research, travel, endowments, or bands or choirs.

2003. Ohio Grantmakers Forum, Columbus, OH. $10,000, 2004.

2004. Public Library of Des Moines Foundation, Des Moines, IA. $120,000, 2004.

NCC Charitable Foundation

(formerly NCC Charitable Foundation II)
Limitations: Giving primarily in IL, IN, KY, MI, OH, and PA, with emphasis on OH. No grants to individuals.
2005. Columbus Metropolitan Library, Columbus, OH. $15,000, 2005. For general support.
2006. Indianapolis-Marion County Public Library, Indianapolis, IN. $10,000, 2005. For general support.
2007. Library Foundation, Louisville, KY. $25,000, 2005. For general support.
2008. Ohio Grantmakers Forum, Columbus, OH. $25,000, 2005. For general support.
2009. Saint Louis County Library Foundation, Saint Louis, MO. $12,000, 2005. For general support.

Osteopathic Heritage Foundations

Limitations: Giving primarily in the following OH counties: Athens, Delaware, Fairfield, Fayette, Franklin, Hocking, Jackson, Knox, Licking, Madison, Meigs, Morgan, Perry, Pickaway, Ross, Union, Vinton, and Washington.
2010. Firstlink, Columbus, OH. $94,997, 2004. To provide education, resources, and referrals to affordable services and on-going support for older adults, persons with limiting illness and caregivers.

The Procter & Gamble Fund

Limitations: Giving on a national basis, with emphasis on areas of company operations.
2011. Athenaeum of Ohio, Cincinnati, OH. $21,388, 2005.
2012. National Archives, Foundation for the, DC. $20,000, 2005.
2013. Ohio Grantmakers Forum, Columbus, OH. $10,000, 2005.

The Reinberger Foundation

Limitations: Giving primarily in Columbus and northeast OH. No grants to individuals, or for seed money, emergency funds, land acquisition, demonstration projects, or conferences; no loans.
2014. East Cleveland Public Library, East Cleveland, OH. $75,000, 2005. For Capital Campaign.

Saint Luke's Foundation of Cleveland, Ohio

Limitations: Giving primarily in Cleveland and Cuyahoga counties, OH. No support for for-profit organizations or for religious purposes. No grants to individuals or for capital campaigns, fundraising events, endowments, or debt retirement.
2015. Hunger Task Force of Greater Cleveland, Hunger Network of Greater Cleveland, Cleveland, OH. $20,000, 2004. For community liaison project linking hungry with other vital services.

Scripps Howard Foundation

Limitations: Giving on a national basis, with emphasis on areas of company operations. No support for religious organizations not of direct benefit to the entire community, political candidates, anti-business organizations, discriminatory organizations, private foundations, or veterans', fraternal, or labor organizations. No grants to individuals (except for fellowships, scholarships, internship grants, and National Journalism Awards), or for tables, walks, runs, golf outings, or neighborhood special events (except for employee team sponsorships), disease-related events, research-related events, political causes, advertising, or continuing support.
2016. Knox County Public Library, Friends of the, Knoxville, TN. $10,000, 2004. For Imagination Library.
2017. Thomas More College, Crestview Hills, KY. $25,000, 2004. For library renovation.

Stark Community Foundation

(formerly The Stark County Foundation, Inc.)
Limitations: Giving limited to Stark County, OH. No support for religious organizations for religious purposes. No grants for endowment funds, operating budgets, continuing support, annual campaigns, publications, conferences or deficit financing; no grants or loans to individuals (except to college students who are permanent residents of Stark County, OH).

2018. Military Aviation Preservation Society (MAPS), North Canton, OH. $20,000, 2004. For Library relocation and expansion. Grant made through Henry and Louise Timken Foundation.

Timken Foundation of Canton

Limitations: Giving primarily in local areas of Timken Co. domestic operations in Torrington, and Watertown, CT; Cairo, Dahlonega, and Sylvania, GA; Bucyrus, Canton, Eaton, New Philadelphia, and Wooster, OH; Ashboro, Columbus, and Lincolnton, NC; Keene, and Lebanon, NH; Latrobe, PA; Honea Path, Walhalla, Clinton, Union, and Gaffney, SC; Altavista, VA; and Mascot and Pulaski, TN. Giving also in local areas in Brazil, Canada, China, Czech Republic, France, Germany, Great Britain, India, Italy, Poland, Romania, and South Africa where Timken Co. has manufacturing facilities. No support for projects for religious or political purposes. No grants to individuals. Generally, no grants for operating budgets, endowments, or program development.
2019. Stark County District Library, Canton, OH. $150,000, 2005. For new Perry Branch Library.

The Turner Foundation

(formerly Harry and Violet Turner 95 Charitable Trust)
Limitations: Giving primarily in Springfield and Clark County, Ohio. No support for religious or political organizations. No grants to individuals.
2020. New Carlisle Public Library, Friends of, New Carlisle, OH. $12,000, 2004.

The Raymond John Wean Foundation

Limitations: Giving primarily in Allegheny County, PA, and northeast OH, with emphasis on Cuyahoga, Mahoning, and Trumbull counties. No support for sectarian religious activities, veterans' or fraternal organizations, or local or national offices of organizations combating a particular disease or family of diseases. No grants to individuals; or for endowment funds, debt reduction, foreign operations, national fundraising campaigns or film or video production.
2021. Bristol Public Library, Bristolville, OH. $14,656, 2005. For notebook computers and digital projector.
2022. Help Hotline Crisis Center, Youngstown, OH. $15,000, 2005. For 211 Crisis Worker.
2023. Info Line, Akron, OH. $113,500, 2005. For Child Care Connection Program's Quality Enhancement Grants.
2024. Info Line, Akron, OH. $30,000, 2005. For Child Care Connection's Quality Enhancement Project: Phase 3.
2025. Ohio Grantmakers Forum, Columbus, OH. $15,000, 2005. For general operating support.

OKLAHOMA

Inasmuch Foundation

Limitations: Giving primarily in Colorado Springs, CO, and OK. No grants to individuals, or for regular operating expenses or endowments.
2026. Pioneer Multi-County Library System, Norman, OK. $15,000, 2005. For Family Literacy Kits.

The Samuel Roberts Noble Foundation, Inc.

Limitations: Giving primarily in the Southwest, with emphasis on OK. No grants to individuals (except through Noble Educational Fund and Sam Noble Scholarship Program); no loans (except for program-related investments).
2027. Arbuckle Life Solutions, Ardmore, OK. $35,000, 2005. For renewed operating support.
2028. Foundation Center, New York, NY. $10,000, 2005. For renewed operating support.
2029. Oklahoma Garden Clubs, Ardmore, OK. $21,000, 2005. For Carnegie Library building improvements.

Southern Oklahoma Memorial Foundation

Limitations: Giving limited to OK organizations within a 50-mile radius of Ardmore. No support for churches or political organizations. No grants to individuals.

2030. Arbuckle Drug and Alcohol Information Center, Ardmore, OK. $135,000, 2005. For intensive outpatient program.

2031. Library Endowment Trust, Madill, OK. $15,000, 2005. For Madill Marshall County Library Furnishings.

2032. National Heritage Foundation, Falls Church, VA. $25,000, 2005. For library multimedia equipment for Ardmore Christian School.

Tulsa Community Foundation

Limitations: Giving limited to northeastern OK through discretionary funds; donor-advised giving is nationwide.

2033. Tulsa Library Trust, Tulsa, OK. $25,435, 2004.

The Anne and Henry Zarrow Foundation

Limitations: Giving primarily in the Tulsa, OK, area.

2034. Survivors of the Shoah Visual History Foundation, Los Angeles, CA. $15,655, 2005. For operating support.

2035. Tulsa Library Trust, Tulsa, OK. $40,000, 2005. For operating support.

2036. Tulsa Library Trust, Tulsa, OK. $18,520, 2005. For operating support.

OREGON

The Collins Foundation

Limitations: Giving limited to OR, with emphasis on Portland. No support for individual religious congregations, elementary, secondary or public higher educational institutions. No grants to individuals, or for endowments, operational deficits, financial emergencies, debt retirement, or annual fundraising activities.

2037. Birth to Three, Eugene, OR. $100,000, 2005. 3-year grant. For Parent HelpLine Call Center, child abuse prevention program offering support and service referrals to at-risk families.

2038. Creswell Public Library Foundation, Creswell, OR. $20,000, 2005. For relocation and expansion of Creswell Library.

2039. Elgin Public Library, Elgin, OR. $25,000, 2005. For new library facility.

2040. Estacada Public Library Foundation, Estacada, OR. $50,000, 2005. For construction of new Estacada Public Library.

2041. Port Orford Public Library Foundation, Port Orford, OR. $40,000, 2005. For construction of new Port Orford Library.

2042. Siletz Valley Friends of the Library, Siletz, OR. $40,000, 2005. For construction of new Siletz Library.

2043. Stayton Public Library Foundation, Stayton, OR. $75,000, 2005. 2-year grant. For expansion of Stayton Public Library.

2044. Sutherlin, City of, Sutherlin, OR. $50,000, 2005. For expansion and renovation of Sutherlin Public Library.

2045. Winston Area Community Partnership, Winston, OR. $50,000, 2005. For construction of Winston Area Community Center and Library.

The Ford Family Foundation

Limitations: Giving primarily in rural OR, with special interest in Douglas and Coos counties; giving also in Siskiyou County, CA. No grants to individuals (except for scholarships), endowment funds, general fund drives, indirect or overhead expenses, debt retirement or operating expenses, fundraising events, or purchase of art.

2046. Banks Community Library, Friends of, Banks, OR. $10,000, 2005. To establish Banks Community Foundation.

2047. Forest Grove Library Foundation, Forest Grove, OR. $100,000, 2005. For capital expansion.

2048. Harney County Library Foundation, Burns, OR. $125,000, 2005. For Northern Expansion Project.

2049. La Grande Community Library Foundation, La Grande, OR. $350,000, 2005. For new La Grande Library construction.

2050. North Plains Public Library, Friends of the, North Plains, OR. $100,000, 2005. For new library facility.

2051. Oregon Partnership, Portland, OR. $100,000, 2005. For Champions for Healthy Kids and Communities in Southern Oregon.

2052. Port Orford Public Library Foundation, Port Orford, OR. $150,000, 2005. For new library construction.

2053. Siletz Valley Friends of the Library, Siletz, OR. $100,000, 2005. For construction of new library.

2054. Stayton Public Library Foundation, Stayton, OR. $100,000, 2005. For expansion.

2055. Talent Library, Friends of the, Talent, OR. $70,000, 2005. For larger community room for new Talent Library.

2056. Tillamook County Library Foundation, Tillamook, OR. $150,000, 2005. For new main library.

2057. Tulelake Community Partnership, Tulelake, CA. $10,000, 2005. For Tri-Unity Community directory and Web site.

2058. Winston Area Community Partnership, Winston, OR. $150,000, 2005. For community center and library.

Intel Foundation

Limitations: Giving primarily in Phoenix, AZ, Folsom and Santa Clara, CA, Colorado Springs, CO, Hudson, MA, Albuquerque, NM, Portland, OR, Austin, TX, Riverton, UT, and Dupont, WA; giving also to national organizations. No support for religious, sectarian, fraternal, or political organizations, arts or health care organizations, private schools, or sports teams. No grants to individuals (except for fellowships), or for endowments, capital campaigns, general fund drives, annual campaigns, fundraising events, sporting events, travel or tours, or equipment.

2059. MentorNet, San Jose, CA. $25,000, 2004.

2060. OCCUR Community Information Service, Oakland, CA. $30,000, 2004.

The Jeld-Wen Foundation

(formerly Jeld-Wen, Wenco Foundation)

Limitations: Giving primarily in areas of company operations in AZ, FL, IA, KY, NC, OR, SD, and WA. No grants to individuals, or for religious activities or programs that duplicate services provided by other government or private agencies; no loans.

2061. Hawkins Area Library, Hawkins, WI. $121,500, 2004.

Meyer Memorial Trust

(formerly Fred Meyer Charitable Trust)

Limitations: Giving primarily in OR and Clark County, WA. No support for sectarian or religious organizations for religious purposes. No grants to individuals or for endowment funds, annual campaigns, deficit financing, scholarships, fellowships, or indirect or overhead costs, except as specifically and essentially related to the grant project.

2062. Creswell Public Library Foundation, Creswell, OR. $60,000, 2006. For tenant improvements to convert leased commercial space to new, expanded public library.

2063. Curry Public Library District, Gold Beach, OR. $150,000, 2006. 2-year grant. To help build new library in Gold Beach.

2064. Disability Navigators, Portland, OR. $95,000, 2006. 3.75-year grant. To expand program that provides access to information about disability resources.

2065. Dora Sitkum Rural Fire Protection District, Myrtle Point, OR. $85,000, 2006. To expand and renovate facility that serves as fire department, library, and community center.

2066. Elgin, City of, Elgin Public Library, Elgin, OR. $25,000, 2006. To help purchase new building for library.

2067. Estacada Public Library Foundation, Estacada, OR. $155,000, 2006. 1.25-year grant. To build new public library.

2068. Foundation Center, New York, NY. $17,500, 2006. For general support for collection and dissemination of information about private philanthropy.

2069. Jackson County Library Services, Medford, OR. $30,000, 2006. To fund collaborative planning process for Jackson and Josephine County library systems.

2070. Jefferson County Library District, Madras, OR. $90,000, 2006. 2-year grant. To establish inter-library network in central Oregon.

2071. Klamath County Library Foundation, Klamath Falls, OR. $120,000, 2006. 3-year grant. For improvements to main branch library's children's area and other facility upgrades.

2072. Library Foundation, Portland, OR. $750,000, 2006. 4-year grant. To expand children's literacy programs and launch donor challenge for Multnomah County Library.

2073. Phoenix Library, Friends of the, Phoenix, OR. $60,000, 2006. 2-year grant. For construction of new library.

2074. Stayton Public Library Foundation, Stayton, OR. $150,000, 2006. 2-year grant. To renovate and expand library.

2075. Sutherlin, City of, C. Giles Hunt Memorial Library, Sutherlin, OR. $125,000, 2006. 3-year grant. To construct new wing and upgrade C. Giles Hunt Memorial Library.

2076. Talent Library, Friends of the, Talent, OR. $68,796, 2006. 1.75-year grant. Toward construction of new public library.

2077. Trappist Abbey of Our Lady of Guadalupe, Lafayette, OR. $300,000, 2006. For construction of library and learning center open to community.

2078. Union County Library District, La Grande, OR. $69,200, 2006. 2-year grant. For Friendly Visitors program to deliver library materials to frail elderly and housebound residents of Union County.

2079. Washington County Cooperative Library Services, Hillsboro, OR. $30,456, 2006. 2-year grant. For intergenerational literacy program targeting low-income and Latino families.

NIKE Foundation

(formerly NIKE P.L.A.Y. Foundation)

Limitations: Giving on an international basis, with emphasis on Bangladesh, Brazil, China, Ethiopia, and Zambia; giving also to national organizations. No support for discriminatory organizations. No grants to individuals, or for general operating support for established programs, research or travel, films, television, or radio programs not an integral part of a project, religious programs, endowments or fundraising campaigns, lobbying or political activities, or depreciation or debt reduction.

2080. Charities Aid Foundation (CAF) America, Alexandria, VA. $1,000,000, 2005. For donor-advised fund.

The Oregon Community Foundation

Limitations: Giving limited to OR. No support for religious organizations for religious purposes or projects in individual schools. No grants to individuals (except for scholarships), or for annual fund appeals, sponsorship of one-time events or performances, emergency funding, endowments, annual campaigns, deficit financing, scientific research, publications, films, or conferences, unless so designated by a donor; no loans.

2081. 211 Info, Portland, OR. $19,000, 2005. For development of program.

2082. Douglas County Library Foundation, Roseburg, OR. $10,000, 2005. For Community Campaign.

2083. Estacada Public Library Foundation, Estacada, OR. $30,000, 2005. Toward construction of community room of new Estacada Public Library.

2084. Independence Public Library, Friends of the, Independence, OR. $10,600, 2005. To increase online resources available to public.

2085. North Plains Public Library, Friends of the, North Plains, OR. $25,000, 2005. For construction of new building for library.

2086. Oregon Child Care Resource and Referral Network, Salem, OR. $15,000, 2005. For early childhood literacy education and development through regularly scheduled literacy presentations to children at provider sites, distribution of early literacy materials, and training of child care providers and parents.

2087. Oregon Health Access Project, Salem, OR. $15,000, 2005. For implementation of health helpline to facilitate enrollment of eligible, uninsured children and adults into publicly funded health programs.

2088. Oregon Partnership, Portland, OR. $15,000, 2005. For substance abuse prevention initiative targeting youth, parents and broader community in Coos, Curry and Douglas counties.

2089. SMG Foundation, Portland, OR. $15,000, 2005. For Portland Ninos, project to reduce health disparities by providing child development and health education and referral assistance to Latino families with children ages 0-8.

2090. Stayton Public Library Foundation, Stayton, OR. $30,000, 2005. For design and construction of additions to Stayton Public Library, including children's library area.

2091. Tillamook County Library Foundation, Tillamook, OR. $25,000, 2005. For construction of new library to replace old facility.

2092. Winston Area Community Partnership, Winston, OR. $30,000, 2005. For construction of new facility to house Winston Community Center and Library.

Ann and Bill Swindells Charitable Trust

Limitations: Giving primarily in OR. No support for religious organizations or their capital fund drives or for activist organizations. No grants to individuals, or for annual operating budgets, development office personnel, annual fund raising activities, endowments, operational deficits, financial emergencies or for debt retirements.

2093. Estacada Public Library, Estacada, OR. $15,000, 2005. For capital campaign.

2094. Libraries of Eastern Oregon, Cove, OR. $58,253, 2005. To purchase equipment.

2095. Library Foundation, Portland, OR. $25,000, 2005. For capital campaign.

2096. Winston Area Community Partnership, Winston, OR. $25,000, 2005. For community center and library.

PENNSYLVANIA

Alcoa Foundation

Limitations: Giving on a national and international basis in areas of company operations; giving also to national and international organizations. No support for political or lobbying organizations, sectarian or religious organizations not of direct benefit to the entire community, private foundations, or trust funds. No grants to individuals (except for fellowships and employee-related scholarships), or for endowments, capital campaigns, debt reduction, or general operating support, fundraising events or sponsorships, trips, conferences, seminars, festivals, one-day events, documentaries, videos, or research projects/programs, or indirect or overhead costs.

2097. Biblioteca Argentina para Ciegos, Buenos Aires, Argentina. $15,000, 2005. For reading program for blind.

2098. Carnegie Library of Pittsburgh, Pittsburgh, PA. $20,000, 2005. 2-year grant. For Economic Impact Study.

2099. Charities Aid Foundation (UK), West Malling, England. $153,600, 2005. For ambulance in Belaya Kalitva, Rostov oblast, Russia, and renovation of apartments of WWII veterans.

2100. Charities Aid Foundation Australia, Sydney, Australia. $23,000, 2005. For Timehelp Program in Geelong and Yennora.

2101. Charities Aid Foundation-Russia, Moscow, Russia. $15,000, 2005. For community development grant program in Chekhov region.

2102. Collingwood and District Information Centre, Collingwood, Canada. $20,000, 2005. For implementation of 211 telephone number to access community information and referral services.

2103. Connecticut Childrens Medical Center Foundation, Hartford, CT. $25,000, 2005. For Connecticut Violent Injury Statistics System.

2104. Denbigh High School, May Pen, Jamaica. $25,000, 2005. For high school library and computer-aided learning center.

2105. Glenmuir High School, May Pen, Jamaica. $35,000, 2005. 2-year grant. For high schools library, research, and career guidance programs.

2106. Help Office of Hancock County, Hawesville, KY. $15,000, 2005. For Help Office of Hancock County.

2107. Hetvezer Altalanos Iskola, Szekesfehervar, Hungary. $42,000, 2005. 2-year grant. For school library program.

2108. Instituto Educacion Secundaria Antonio Jose Cavanilles, Alicante, Spain. $29,200, 2005. For school library also serving local community.

2109. MentorNet, San Jose, CA. $50,000, 2005. For development of NGO partnerships to increase participation in MentorNet program.

2110. SickKids Foundation, Toronto, Canada. $15,000, 2005. For B.r.a.i.n. Child, Pediatrics Information Day and b.r.a.i.n.source newsletter.

2111. United States Catholic Conference, Greensburg, PA. $55,400, 2005. For assistance and relief for individuals/families who are still trying to recover from damages sustained in flooding of September 2004 through Information and Referral Program.

2112. Visalia-Tulare County Library Foundation, Visalia, CA. $25,000, 2005. For Tulare County Library Early Literacy Program.

The Annenberg Foundation

Limitations: Giving nationally with preference for southern CA, greater Philadelphia, PA, and New York, NY; some unsolicited grants to the United Kingdom, France, Africa and Asia. No support for political activities or individual K-12 schools. No grants to individuals, or for scholarships or basic research.

2113. American Library in Paris USA Foundation, Marion, MA. $12,922, 2005. For general support.

2114. American Trust for the British Library, New York, NY. $95,885, 2005. For general support.

2115. Bosque Preparatory School, Albuquerque, NM. $500,000, 2005. To complete Gerald and Betty Ford Library.

2116. Churchill Center, DC. $25,000, 2005. To distribute copies of Celia Sandy's biography of Sir Winston Churchill to high school libraries across the U.S..

2117. Crisler Biblical Institute, Cincinnati, OH. $10,000, 2005. For Crisler Library in Ephesus, Turkey.

2118. Episcopal Academy, Merion, PA. $1,000,000, 2005. For Roger Annenberg Library on new campus in Newtown Square.

2119. Free Library of Philadelphia, Philadelphia, PA. $1,666,000, 2005. For expansion and renovation of Central Library.

2120. George Bush Presidential Library Foundation, College Station, TX. $600,000, 2005. For George Bush Presidential Library.

2121. Huntington Library, Art Collections and Botanical Gardens, San Marino, CA. $333,000, 2005. For general support.

2122. Lompoc District Libraries Foundation, Lompoc, CA. $100,000, 2005. For Charlotte's Web Children's Library Learning Center.

2123. Los Angeles County Public Library Foundation, Downey, CA. $150,000, 2005. To purchase books and audiovisual materials to enhance collections of libraries in areas with substantial Spanish-speaking communities.

2124. New York Academy of Medicine, New York, NY. $10,000, 2005. For general support.

2125. PUENTE Learning Center: People United to Enrich the Neighborhood Through Education, Los Angeles, CA. $250,000, 2005. To support English language and educational programs, and to create lending libraries.

2126. Ronald Reagan Presidential Foundation, Simi Valley, CA. $250,000, 2005. For construction of hangar to display Air Force One.

2127. Ronald Reagan Presidential Foundation, Simi Valley, CA. $50,000, 2005. For Ambassadors' Sky View Terrace Project.

2128. Ronald Reagan Presidential Foundation, Simi Valley, CA. $25,000, 2005.

2129. White House Historical Association, DC. $16,500, 2005. For acquisition of books for White House Library.

2130. Wild Dolphin Project, Jupiter, FL. $50,000, 2005. For underwater video and sound library of Three Generations of Wild Spotted Dolphins.

2131. Wildscreen Trust, Bristol, England. $25,000, 2005. For ARKive project, a digital archive of films, photographs and audio recordings of the world's species.

2132. Wonder of Reading, Los Angeles, CA. $105,000, 2005. To implement 3R Program (Renovate, Restock, and Read) at public elementary schools in Los Angeles.

The Arcadia Foundation

Limitations: Giving limited to eastern PA organizations whose addresses have zip codes beginning with 18 and 19. Generally, low support for cultural programs. No grants to individuals, or for deficit financing, land acquisition, fellowships, demonstration projects, publications, or conferences; no loans.

2133. Exeter Community Library, Reading, PA. $10,000, 2005.

2134. Phoenixville Public Library, Phoenixville, PA. $11,200, 2005.

2135. Rosenbach Museum and Library, Philadelphia, PA. $25,000, 2005.

Claude Worthington Benedum Foundation

Limitations: Giving limited to southwestern PA and WV. No support for biomedical research, religious activities, national organizations, or individual elementary or secondary schools. No grants to individuals, or for student aid, fellowships, travel, ongoing operating expenses, annual appeals, membership drives, conferences, films, books, or audio-visual productions, unless an integral part of a foundation supported program.

2136. West Virginia Kids Count Fund, Charleston, WV. $120,000, 2004. For second-year support for Birth-to-Three Early Literacy and Learning Community Partnerships Project.

2137. West Virginia Kids Count Fund, Charleston, WV. $60,000, 2004. For Birth-to-Three Early Literacy and Learning Community Partnerships Project, community-focused public awareness campaign about importance of early literacy.

E. Rhodes & Leona B. Carpenter Foundation

Limitations: Giving primarily in areas east of the Mississippi River. No support for private secondary education, or large public charities. No grants to individuals.

2138. Chicago Theological Seminary, Chicago, IL. $30,000, 2004. For lesbian, gay, bisexual and transgender religious archive network project.

2139. Duke University, Perkins Library, Durham, NC. $310,000, 2004. Toward construction of new library space.

2140. Duke University, Perkins Library, Durham, NC. $300,000, 2004. Toward construction of new library space.

2141. Saint Paul University, Ottawa, Canada. $50,000, 2004. For library expansion project.

The Comcast Foundation

Limitations: Giving primarily in areas of company operations. No support for discriminatory organizations, private foundations, or political organizations. No grants to individuals (except for scholarships), or for marketing sponsorships, sporting events, trips or tours, or capital campaigns.

2142. Allegheny County Library Association, Pittsburgh, PA. $10,000, 2004. For One Book, One Community program, in partnership with Comcast Reading Network, countywide literacy initiative which incorporates community volunteers and partners, conducting educational activities and reading forums around book, Flowers for Algernon.

2143. Arlington Public Library Foundation, Arlington, TX. $15,000, 2004. To recognize Teens Connect in partnership with Comcast Reading Network, providing access to resources and information that enhance educational advancement for local youth through workshops, technology training, and computer assistance programs.

2144. Boston Public Library Foundation, Boston, MA. $50,000, 2004. For Homework Assistance Program in partnership with Comcast Reading Network.

2145. Carnegie Library of Pittsburgh Foundation, Pittsburgh, PA. $10,000, 2004. For Summer Reading Program for children and teens, in partnership with Comcast Reading Network, providing educational material and supplemental program materials.

2146. Dallas Public Library, Friends of the, Dallas, TX. $15,000, 2004. For Mayors Summer Reading Program, designed to promote literacy and strengthen reading skills.

2147. DeLay Foundation, Houston, TX. $25,000, 2004. For central library and library materials for each home within facility for abused and foster children.

2148. Free Library of Philadelphia Foundation, Philadelphia, PA. $10,000, 2004. For One Book, One Philadelphia community literacy initiative, in partnership with Comcast Reading Network.

2149. Friends of the Library Montgomery County, Rockville, MD. $15,000, 2004. For Linkages to Learning Summer Reading Program assisting families with reading and internet skills to enrich life-long learning.

2150. Oaks at Rio Bend, Richmond, TX. $25,000, 2004. For central library and library materials for each home within facility for abused and foster children.

2151. Public Library of Nashville and Davidson County, Friends of the, Nashville, TN. $20,000, 2004. For Summer Reading Program in partnership with The Comcast Reading Network, providing materials to children and young adults participating at all branches of library city-wide to improve reading skills.

Connelly Foundation

Limitations: Giving primarily in Philadelphia, and surrounding counties of Bucks, Chester, Delaware and Montgomery, PA and Camden, NJ. No support for political or national organizations. No grants to individuals, or for research or annual appeals.

2152. Chester County Cares, West Chester, PA. $25,000, 2004. For general operating support.

2153. Friends Academy of Westampton, Westampton, NJ. $10,000, 2004. To purchase books, multimedia materials and equipment, encyclopedias and other relevant reference materials for establishment of Friends Academy Library and Resource Center.

2154. Politz Hebrew Academy of Northeast Philadelphia, Philadelphia, PA. $20,000, 2004. For capital support to transform existing classrooms into library, computer room, and science lab.

2155. Saint Charles Borromeo Seminary, Wynnewood, PA. $75,000, 2004. For renovation of Ryan Memorial Library into state-of-the-art facility for seminarians, students, faculty, and community, including equipment for computer lab and audiovisual area.

2156. Unemployment Information Center, Philadelphia, PA. $10,000, 2004. For Benefits Counseling Hotline, Mortgage Foreclosure Prevention Clinic, Jobs Club, Unemployment Compensation Project, and HealthCare Hotline.

The 1994 Charles B. Degenstein Foundation

Limitations: Giving within a 75-mile radius of Sunbury, PA.

2157. Degenstein Community Library, Sunbury, PA. $35,000, 2005. Toward renovations.

2158. Degenstein Community Library, Sunbury, PA. $10,000, 2005. For summer jobs program.

2159. Hughesville Public Library, Hughesville, PA. $20,000, 2005. For building renovation.

2160. Northumberland, Borough of, Northumberland, PA. $10,000, 2005. For law library.

2161. Union County Library System, Lewisburg, PA. $10,000, 2005. For general support.

2162. West End Library, Laurelton, PA. $150,000, 2005. For building campaign.

Dominion Foundation

(formerly Consolidated Natural Gas Company Foundation)

Limitations: Giving on a national basis in areas of company operations. No support for churches or other sectarian organizations, fraternal, political, advocacy, or labor organizations, or discriminatory organizations. No grants to individuals, or for religious programs, general operating support for individual United Way agencies, fundraising events, golf tournaments or other sporting events, benefit or courtesy advertising, travel or student trips or tours, or memorial campaigns.

2163. Carnegie Library of Pittsburgh, Pittsburgh, PA. $10,000, 2005. For reading extravaganza.

2164. George C. Marshall Research Foundation, Lexington, VA. $10,000, 2005. For outreach and educational programs.

2165. Hampden-Sydney College, Hampden Sydney, VA. $25,000, 2005. For capital campaign for construction of new library.

2166. James Monroe Memorial Foundation, Richmond, VA. $25,000, 2005. For capital campaign for farmhouse reconstruction.

2167. OASIS Institute, Pittsburgh, PA. $10,000, 2005. For intergenerational tutoring program.

2168. Richmond Public Library Foundation, Richmond, VA. $37,500, 2005.

2169. SeniorNavigator.com, Richmond, VA. $50,000, 2005. For pilot program for senior services.

Eden Hall Foundation

Limitations: Giving limited to southwestern PA. No support for private foundations, sectarian or denominational religious organizations (except those providing direct educational or health care services to the public), or political or fraternal organizations. No grants to individuals, or generally for operating budgets, endowments, or deficit financing.

2170. Carnegie Library of Pittsburgh, Pittsburgh, PA. $334,000, 2005. For Library Capital Improvements Program.

2171. Carnegie Library of Pittsburgh, Pittsburgh, PA. $125,000, 2005. For capacity building for Carnegie Library of Pittsburgh Foundation office.

2172. Ligonier Valley Library, Ligonier, PA. $50,000, 2005. For children and young adult collections and programs.

2173. Rostraver Public Library, Belle Vernon, PA. $50,000, 2005. For construction and furnishing new building.

2174. Westminster College, New Wilmington, PA. $22,000, 2005. For Susan Shifler Library Memorial Fund and Foster and Shifler Discretionary Fund.

The Grable Foundation

Limitations: Giving primarily in southwestern PA. No grants to individuals, or for scholarships or endowment funds.

2175. 3 Rivers Connect, Pittsburgh, PA. $100,000, 2005. For Regional Education Technology Initiative, development and implementation of new ideas and programs in educational technology.

2176. 3 Rivers Connect, Pittsburgh, PA. $14,700, 2005. For Summer Programs at 3 Rivers Computer Clubhouse.

2177. Allegheny County Library Association, Pittsburgh, PA. $10,000, 2005. For Knowledge Connections, study to evaluate and make recommendations for improving services at libraries at Knowledge Connection sites in public housing projects.

2178. Carnegie Library of Homestead, Munhall, PA. $11,600, 2005. For Early Literacy Outreach, book exchange and story-telling program for Mon Valley early education programs.

2179. Carnegie Library of Homewood, Pittsburgh, PA. $10,650, 2005. For repairs to swimming pool.

2180. Carnegie Library of Pittsburgh, Pittsburgh, PA. $50,000, 2005. For BLAST School Program, to support activities of Carnegie Library in third grade classrooms in Pittsburgh public schools.

2181. Focus on Renewal Sto-Rox Neighborhood Corporation, McKees Rocks, PA. $15,000, 2005. For Youth Services Librarian in Sto-Rox.

2182. OASIS Institute, Pittsburgh, PA. $10,000, 2005. For Intergenerational Tutoring Program for elementary school students in Pittsburgh and Woodland Hills school districts.

2183. Penn Hills Library Foundation, Penn Hills, PA. $50,000, 2005. For capital campaign for new library in Penn Hills.

Howard Heinz Endowment

Limitations: Giving primarily directed to southwestern PA, although in certain cases support may be considered on a national or international basis. No grants to individuals.

2184. 3 Rivers Connect, Pittsburgh, PA. $250,000, 2004. For expansion of new data system.

2185. Americans for the Arts, DC. $15,000, 2004. For monograph, Public Art: An Essential Component of Creative Communities.

2186. Carnegie Library of Pittsburgh, Pittsburgh, PA. $50,000, 2004. For research and development of Environmental Health Initiative Information System.

2187. United Way of Allegheny County, Pittsburgh, PA. $700,000, 2004. For annual operating support of youth-serving agencies through United Way's Impact Fund and to connect United Way's provider and service data with Allegheny County's HumanServices.net online resource.

2188. Wireless Neighborhoods, Pittsburgh, PA. $200,000, 2004. For high speed non-profit network.

Vira I. Heinz Endowment

Limitations: Giving primarily directed to southwestern PA, although in certain cases support may be considered on a national or international basis. No grants to individuals.

2189. 3 Rivers Connect, Pittsburgh, PA. $300,000, 2004. For K-12 computer-based learning programs and operating support.

2190. Allegheny County Library Association, Pittsburgh, PA. $100,000, 2004. For business planning of area libraries.

2191. Carnegie Library of Pittsburgh, Pittsburgh, PA. $50,000, 2004. For Information for Action on Environmental Health, research and creation of cutting-edge, publicly accessible data system on toxins and human health.

Roy A. Hunt Foundation

Limitations: Giving primarily in the Boston, MA, and Pittsburgh, PA, areas, also in CA, ID, NH, ME, and OH. No grants to individuals.

2192. Carnegie Mellon University, Pittsburgh, PA. $50,000, 2006. For Hunt Library Fund in memory of Torrence M. Hunt.

2193. Carnegie Mellon University, Pittsburgh, PA. $10,000, 2006. For Annual Fund, Library Director's Discretionary Fund, and Athletics Department.

2194. Esalen Institute, Big Sur, CA. $12,000, 2006. For library/archives and gazebo school film.

2195. Global Footprint Network, Oakland, CA. $25,000, 2006. For general operating support.

2196. National Center for Family Philanthropy, DC. $10,000, 2006. For general operating support.

The Sidney Kimmel Foundation

2197. Survivors of the Shoah Visual History Foundation, Los Angeles, CA. $10,000, 2004.

McCune Foundation

Limitations: Giving primarily in southwestern PA, with emphasis on the Pittsburgh area. No grants to individuals, or for general operating support.

2198. Chartiers Valley Partnership, Carnegie, PA. $500,000, 2005. For capital campaign.

2199. Lebanese American University, New York, NY. $150,000, 2005. For Gibran Library.

2200. Pittsburgh Dance Alloy, Pittsburgh, PA. $35,000, 2005. For marketing initiative, equipment purchase, curriculum development and library.

Mellon Financial Corporation Fund

(formerly Mellon Financial Corporation Foundation)

Limitations: Giving primarily in areas of company operations, with emphasis on Boston, MA, and Philadelphia and Pittsburgh, PA. No support for fraternal or religious organizations, United Way agencies, or national organizations. No grants to individuals, or for emergency needs, debt reduction, endowments, equipment, land acquisition, scholarships, fellowships, research, publications, travel, conferences, continuing support, or specialized health campaigns or other highly specialized projects with little or no positive impact on communities; no loans.

2201. Carnegie Library of Pittsburgh, Pittsburgh, PA. $50,000, 2004.

Richard King Mellon Foundation

Limitations: Giving primarily in PA. No grants to individuals, or for fellowships or scholarships, or conduit organizations.

2202. 3 Rivers Connect, Pittsburgh, PA. $400,000, 2005. 2-year grant. For continued development of the Information Commons.

2203. Chartiers Valley Partnership, Carnegie, PA. $500,000, 2005. For capital campaign to restore and revitalize Andrew Carnegie Free Library and Music Hall facility.

2204. Manchester Craftsmens Guild, Pittsburgh, PA. $200,000, 2005. For income generating and archiving components of MCG Jazz.

2205. Pennsylvania Trolley Museum, Washington, PA. $25,000, 2005. For costs resulting from Hurricane Ivan, including archive restoration and streetcar repairs, and for deficit reduction.

The William Penn Foundation

Limitations: Giving limited to the Greater Philadelphia region. No support for sectarian religious activities, recreational programs, political lobbying or legislative activities, nonpublic schools, pass-through organizations, mental health or retardation treatment programs, or programs focusing on a particular disease, disability, or treatment for addiction, or profit-making enterprises; no support for private foundations. No grants to individuals, or for debt reduction, hospital capital projects, medical research, programs that replace lost government support, housing construction or rehabilitation, scholarships, or fellowships; no loans (except for program-related investments).

2206. Free Library of Philadelphia Foundation, Philadelphia, PA. $10,000, 2005. For Regional Foundation Center programming and outreach, print and electronic collections, and professional development.

2207. Haverford Township Free Library Association, Havertown, PA. $44,000, 2005. For retaining consultant to develop strategic plan.

2208. Philadelphia Museum of Art, Philadelphia, PA. $251,199, 2005. 2-year grant. Toward upgrading collaborative online public access catalogs of PACSCL member institutions, and creating virtual union member library catalog.

The Philadelphia Foundation

Limitations: Giving limited to Bucks, Chester, Delaware, Montgomery, and Philadelphia counties in southeastern PA, except for designated funds. No support for religious purposes; generally, low priority given to national organizations, government agencies, large budget agencies, public or private schools, or umbrella funding organizations. No grants to individuals (except for scholarships), or for annual or capital campaigns, building funds, land acquisition, endowment funds, research, publications, tours or trips, conferences, or deficit financing; no loans.

2209. Action AIDS, Philadelphia, PA. $10,000, 2005. For general operating support.

2210. Easttown Library, Berwyn, PA. $25,000, 2005. For Capital Campaign.

2211. HERS Foundation, Philadelphia, PA. $13,000, 2005. For general operating support.

2212. Media Tank, Philadelphia, PA. $10,000, 2005. For general operating support.

2213. Rosenbach Museum and Library, Philadelphia, PA. $50,000, 2005. For public education programs.

The Pittsburgh Foundation

Limitations: Giving from unrestricted funds limited to Pittsburgh and Allegheny County, PA. No support for sectarian purposes, private and parochial schools, or hospitals (from unrestricted funds). No grants to individuals (from unrestricted funds except for the Isabel P. Kennedy Award) or for annual campaigns, endowment funds, travel, operating budgets, fellowships, internships, awards, special events or research of a highly technical or specialized nature; no loans (except for program related investments).

2214. Allegheny County Library Association, Pittsburgh, PA. $50,000, 2005. To expand services to member libraries by strengthening local library Boards of Trustees to grow libraries.

2215. Carnegie Library of Pittsburgh, Pittsburgh, PA. $140,366, 2005. Toward construction of new Hill District library.

2216. OASIS Institute, Pittsburgh, PA. $75,000, 2005. To expand Intergenerational Tutoring Program in Pittsburgh Public Schools and Woodland Hills School District.

2217. Rodef Shalom Temple, Pittsburgh, PA. $12,000, 2005. For Freehof tapes for archives.

The PNC Foundation

(formerly PNC Bank Foundation)

Limitations: Giving primarily in Washington, DC, DE, IN, KY, MD, NJ, OH, PA, and VA. No support for churches or religious organizations. No grants to individuals, or for endowments, conferences, seminars, tickets, or advertising; no loans (except for program-related investments).

2218. Rostraver Public Library, Belle Vernon, PA. $10,000, 2005.

John Templeton Foundation

Limitations: Giving on a national and international basis. No grants to individuals, (except for awards chosen by trustees) or for scholarships, endowment funds, building funds, capital campaigns, or artistic productions; no loans.

2219. Friends of African Village Libraries, San Jose, CA. $10,000, 2005. For general support.

2220. Interreligious Information Center, New York, NY. $10,000, 2005. For Church and World - Media conference at Vatican.

Harry C. Trexler Trust

Limitations: Giving limited to Lehigh County, PA. No grants to individuals, or for endowment funds, research, scholarships, or fellowships; no loans.

2221. Allentown Public Library, Allentown, PA. $100,000, 2005. For operating support.

2222. Slatington Public Library, Slatington, PA. $10,000, 2005. Toward building improvements and additional lending resources.

2223. Southern Lehigh Public Library, Coopersburg, PA. $100,000, 2005. Toward new library building.

RHODE ISLAND

The Carter Family Charitable Trust

Limitations: Giving primarily in RI, with emphasis on Providence. No support for religious organizations. No grants to individuals.

2224. Providence Public Library, Providence, RI. $25,000, 2005. For educational programs.

The Champlin Foundations

Limitations: Giving primarily in RI. No support for churches (with few exceptions) or generally for daycare centers, housing, mental health counseling centers or senior centers. No grants to individuals; or for program or operating expenses, administrative facilities, equipment, books, films, videos, plays, or for multi-year grants.

2225. Ashaway Free Library, Ashaway, RI. $14,545, 2005. For new roof.

2226. Central Falls Free Public Library, Central Falls, RI. $149,643, 2005. For fire safety upgrades.

2227. Community College of Rhode Island, Warwick, RI. $100,000, 2005. For restoration of library collections at Knight, Flanagan, and Liston Campuses.

2228. Cooperating Libraries Automated Network (CLAN), Providence, RI. $591,585, 2005. For technology on behalf of public libraries and the CLAN office.

2229. East Providence Public Library, East Providence, RI. $17,500, 2005. To furnish Program Room and new Riverside branch.

2230. Foster Public Library, Foster, RI. $14,900, 2005. To replace roof.

2231. Jesse M. Smith Memorial Library, Harrisville, RI. $250,000, 2005. Toward construction of new library.

2232. Memorial and Library Association of Westerly, Westerly, RI. $150,000, 2005. Toward Save America's Treasure grant for improvements to Wilcox Park.

2233. Newport Public Library, Newport, RI. $15,000, 2005. Toward Self-Check Unit.

2234. North Kingstown Free Library, North Kingstown, RI. $32,500, 2005. Toward new boiler.

2235. North Providence Union Free Library, North Providence, RI. $18,500, 2005. For new circulation desk.

2236. Portsmouth Free Public Library, Portsmouth, RI. $50,000, 2005. Toward construction of new parking lot.

2237. Providence Athenaeum, Providence, RI. $139,000, 2005. Toward stucco and chimney restoration and waterproofing the building.

2238. Providence Public Library, Providence, RI. $193,000, 2005. For public elevators at Central Library.

2239. Providence Public Library, Providence, RI. $128,000, 2005. For chiller unit at Central Library.

2240. Providence Public Library, Providence, RI. $30,000, 2005. For carpet at Central and Olneyville Library.

2241. Providence Public Library, Providence, RI. $20,000, 2005. For computer room air conditioning at Central.

2242. Redwood Library and Athenaeum, Newport, RI. $50,000, 2005. Toward cost of shelving in new addition.

2243. Rhode Island Supreme Court, Providence, RI. $48,900, 2005. For technology upgrades at State Law Library at Licht Judicial Complex.

2244. South Kingstown Public Library, Peace Dale, RI. $26,400, 2005. To complete carpet replacement project at Peace Dale Library.

2245. Warwick Public Library, Warwick, RI. $11,500, 2005. To purchase new printer and associated software for photo library card system.

2246. West Warwick Public Library System, West Warwick, RI. $110,000, 2005. For new roof.

Citizens Charitable Foundation

Limitations: Giving limited to the New England area. No support for local affiliates of national organizations or labor, fraternal, veterans', sectarian, or public organizations. No grants to individuals, or for endowments, general operating support, research, annual campaigns, conferences or seminars, advertising or fundraising, debt reduction, or non-capital support for United Way member agencies; no loans.

2247. Boston Public Library, Boston, MA. $25,000, 2004. For general support for Homework Assistance Program (HAP).

2248. Boston Public Library Foundation, Boston, MA. $10,000, 2004. For general support.

2249. Exeter Public Library, Friends of, Exeter, RI. $18,000, 2004. For general support.

2250. John F. Kennedy Library Foundation, Boston, MA. $12,000, 2004. For general support.

2251. Providence Public Library, Providence, RI. $10,000, 2004. For general support.

CVS/pharmacy Charitable Trust, Inc.

(formerly CVS Charitable Trust, Inc.)
Limitations: Giving limited to areas of company operations.

2252. Providence Public Library, Providence, RI. $20,000, 2005. For program support.

Dorot Foundation

Limitations: Giving primarily in the U.S. and Israel. No support for acquisitions for museums or excavation phase of archaeological work. No grants for endowments, capital campaigns, equipment, debt reduction, consultants or technical assistance, or events.

2253. Hebrew University of Jerusalem, Orion Center for the Study of the Dead Sea Scrolls, Jerusalem, Israel. $25,000, 2005. For Web site project.

2254. Jewish National and University Library, Jerusalem, Israel. $66,667, 2005. To acquire and digitize materials for collection.

2255. Jewish Womens Archive, Brookline, MA. $150,000, 2005. For Women Who Dared, exhibition in gallery and on-line.

The Rhode Island Foundation

(also known as The Rhode Island Community Foundation)
Limitations: Giving through discretionary funds limited to RI. No support for religious organizations for sectarian purposes (except as specified by donors). No grants to individuals (except from Donor-Advised and Designated funds), or for endowment funds, research, hospital equipment, capital needs of health organizations, annual campaigns, deficit financing, or educational institutions for general operating expenses; no loans.

2256. Rhode Island Natural History Survey, Kingston, RI. $50,000, 2005. For Ecological Inventory, Monitoring, and Stewardship (EIMS) Program, providing ecological information and environmental management expertise and assisting with land stewardship and management.

2257. Rhode Island Natural History Survey, Kingston, RI. $45,000, 2005. For Rhode Island Rivers Council's work to improve state rivers and growing capacity of watershed councils.

The Textron Charitable Trust

Limitations: Giving on a national basis in areas of company operations. No grants to individuals (except for employee-related scholarships), or for endowments, land acquisition, debt reduction, or demonstration projects; no loans.

2258. Providence Public Library, Providence, RI. $83,333, 2004.

van Beuren Charitable Foundation, Inc.

Limitations: Giving primarily in Newport County, RI. No grants to individuals.

2259. Portsmouth Free Public Library, Portsmouth, RI. $25,000, 2005. For general operating support.

2260. Redwood Library and Athenaeum, Newport, RI. $501,000, 2005. For general support.

2261. Redwood Library and Athenaeum, Newport, RI. $250,000, 2005.

SOUTH CAROLINA

Gibbs Charitable Foundation

Limitations: Giving primarily in SC. No grants to individuals.

2262. United Way of the Piedmont, Spartanburg, SC. $15,229, 2005. For Imagination Library.

TENNESSEE

The Assisi Foundation of Memphis, Inc.

(formerly Assisi Foundation)

Limitations: Giving primarily in Memphis and Shelby County, TN.

2263. Center for Southern Folklore, Memphis, TN. $40,000, 2004. For multimedia archives.

2264. Grant Center, Memphis, TN. $50,000, 2004. For Program for Nonprofit Excellence.

2265. Grant Center, Memphis, TN. $50,000, 2004. For programming.

2266. Memphis/Shelby County Public Library, Foundation for the, Memphis, TN. $19,700, 2004. For Same Book, Same Time Reading Initiative.

2267. Partners in Public Education (PIPE), Memphis, TN. $30,000, 2004. For KIPP Academy Satellite Library.

2268. Shelby County Schools Education Foundation, Memphis, TN. $61,000, 2004. For library support.

Christy-Houston Foundation, Inc.

Limitations: Giving limited to Rutherford County, TN. No support for religious, political, or veterans' organizations or historical societies. No grants to individuals, operating expenses or endowments.

2269. Linebaugh Public Library, Murfreesboro, TN. $50,000, 2004. For matching grant for book mobile.

Community Foundation of Greater Memphis

Limitations: Giving limited to Crittenden County, AR, DeSoto, Marshall, Tate, and Tunica counties, MS, and Fayette, Shelby, and Tipton counties, TN. No grants to individuals (except for scholarships), or for endowments, capital or building funds, annual campaigns, code enforcement, or core operating costs; no loans.

2270. Grant Center, Memphis, TN. $10,000, 2005. For operating support.

2271. Memphis/Shelby County Public Library, Foundation for the, Memphis, TN. $10,000, 2005. For general operating support.

The HCA Foundation

(formerly Columbia/HCA Healthcare Foundation, Inc.)

Limitations: Giving primarily in middle TN. No support for political organizations, individual churches or schools, organizations established less than 3 years ago, or organizations involved with arts and culture, athletics, the environment or wildlife, or civic or international affairs. No grants to individuals, or for advertising or sponsorships, or social events or similar fundraising activities.

2272. Conexion Americas, Nashville, TN. $34,000, 2004. For new marketing initiative.

2273. Conexion Americas, Nashville, TN. $27,000, 2004. For continued operating support.

2274. Nashville Public Library Foundation, Nashville, TN. $25,000, 2004. For operating support of Bringing Books to Life initiative.

2275. Neighborhoods Resource Center, Nashville, TN. $15,000, 2004. For Neighborhood Information Services program.

2276. You Have the Power Know How to Use It, Nashville, TN. $10,000, 2004. For video documentary and resource guide on Methamphetamine.

Hyde Family Foundations

Limitations: Giving primarily in Memphis, TN. No support for political organizations. No grants to individuals.

2277. Charter School Resource Center of Tennessee, Memphis, TN. $50,000, 2004. For operating support.

2278. Charter School Resource Center of Tennessee, Memphis, TN. $25,000, 2004. For general operating support.

2279. Grant Center, Memphis, TN. $10,000, 2004. For Key Organization support.

2280. Grant Center, Memphis, TN. $10,000, 2004. For Program for Nonprofit Excellence.

The Lazarus Foundation, Inc.

Limitations: Giving primarily in Bristol, TN, and surrounding communities.

2281. Palm Beach Atlantic University, West Palm Beach, FL. $1,000,000, 2005. For Warren Library.

Plough Foundation

Limitations: Giving primarily in Shelby County, TN, with an emphasis on Memphis. No grants to individuals, and generally no grants for annual operating funds.

2282. Grant Center, Memphis, TN. $55,000, 2005. For general operating support.

TEXAS

Abell-Hanger Foundation

Limitations: Giving limited to TX, with emphasis within the Permian Basin. No grants to individuals, or for individual scholarships or fellowships; no loans.

2283. Odessa LINKS, Odessa, TX. $10,000, 2005. For unrestricted operating support.

2284. Permian Basin Petroleum Museum, Library and Hall of Fame, Midland, TX. $85,000, 2005. For unrestricted operating support.

2285. Permian Basin Petroleum Museum, Library and Hall of Fame, Midland, TX. $30,000, 2005. For property deed.

2286. Permian Basin Petroleum Museum, Library and Hall of Fame, Midland, TX. $15,000, 2005. To underwrite reprinting of Lovell Legacy paperback for museum's 30th anniversary special edition.

Amarillo Area Foundation, Inc.

Limitations: Giving limited to the Texas Panhandle region. No support for private or parochial schools, national, state, or local fundraising activities, or religious activities or programs that serve or appear to serve specific religious groups, or denominations. No grants to individuals (except for the scholarship program), or generally for operating budgets, annual campaigns, deficit financing, endowment funds, publications, conferences, travel, research projects, or historic preservation; no loans.

2287. Swisher County Archives and Museum Association, Tulia, TX. $10,000, 2005. To replace heating and air-conditioning units.

M. D. Anderson Foundation

Limitations: Giving primarily in TX, with emphasis on the Houston area. No grants to individuals, or for operating funds or endowments.

2288. Baylor College of Medicine, Houston, TX. $50,000, 2004. Toward Michael E. DeBakey Library and Museum.

2289. University of Houston-University Park, Houston, TX. $200,000, 2004. Toward expansion and renovation of M. D. Anderson Library and Honors College.

AT&T Foundation

(formerly SBC Foundation)

Limitations: Giving primarily in areas of company operations; giving also to statewide, regional, and national organizations. No support for religious organizations not of direct benefit to the entire community, fraternal, veterans', or labor organizations not of direct benefit to the entire community, individual K-12 schools or districts, political organizations, disease-specific organizations, religious schools, or discriminatory organizations. No grants to individuals (except for employee-related scholarships), or for hospital general operating support, capital campaigns, endowments, general operating support for United Way-supported organizations, advertising, ticket or dinner purchases, sports programs or events or cause-related marketing, or political activities; no product or service donations.

2290. Austin Public Library Foundation, Austin, TX. $10,000, 2005. For technology training for staff in new library information management system that will deliver better services to library going public.

2291. Benedictine College, Atchison, KS. $11,300, 2005. To install new wireless network in library which will facilitate learning by providing broader access to students, faculty, administrators and community members. wireless network will complete library as research center.

2292. Center for Information of Elgin, Elgin, IL. $11,455, 2005. To purchase computer hardware, software, equipment, and training.

2293. Charities Aid Foundation (UK), West Malling, England. $50,000, 2005. For AT&T CARES Program in Europe, Middle East, and Africa.

2294. Charities Aid Foundation (UK), West Malling, England. $15,000, 2005. For AT&T CARES support for Relay for Life programs outside U.S.

2295. Cleveland Clinic Foundation, Cleveland, OH. $211,600, 2005. To create Cleveland Clinic Heart Resource and Information Center that will use state-of-the-art technology to provide education regarding diagnosis and treatment to heart patients and their families.

2296. Dallas Public Library, Friends of the, Dallas, TX. $25,000, 2005. For computer hardware and data communication services to provide at-risk youth with computer training, homework help, and social network with community leaders, volunteers, local agencies, and peers providing positive life choices.

2297. Foundation Center, New York, NY. $12,500, 2005. For membership.

2298. Foundation Center, New York, NY. $12,500, 2005. For membership.

2299. Foundation for Technology Access, Petaluma, CA. $30,000, 2005. For Accessibility Training Center Online (ARTCO), which will be training program and online interactive resource center for community technology programs to increase their capacity to serve people with disabilities.

2300. Friends of the Historic Genesee Theater, Waukegan, IL. $15,000, 2005. To install touch-screen kiosks in local libraries of Lake County, IL communities who rarely go to the theater.

2301. Grandville Avenue Arts and Humanities, Grand Rapids, MI. $23,092, 2005. To automate library's catalog system in effort to increase computer skills of Hispanic youth and add new donor database management system to provide more efficiencies.

2302. Greenlights for Nonprofit Success, Austin, TX. $15,000, 2005. For more interactive website that includes free downloadable resource library of online nonprofit management tools to help nonprofit staff, boards, and volunteers build skills to be more effective.

2303. Harry S. Truman Library Institute for National and International Affairs, Independence, MO. $10,800, 2005. For video conferencing technology to connect Truman Library in Independence with Truman Center in Kansas City for educational programs for students, teachers, and public.

2304. Highland County District Library, Hillsboro, OH. $23,668, 2005. To implement wireless computer lab through joint partnership between Highland County Library and Senior Center with lab providing computer technology workshops to underserved residents in community.

2305. Indianapolis-Marion County Public Library Foundation, Indianapolis, IN. $11,000, 2005. For children's programs and initiatives.

2306. Information Center, Taylor, MI. $19,800, 2005. To purchase and implement mobile technology to streamline management of client information and assist with delivery of services to elderly and disabled clients.

2307. Library of Congress, DC. $100,000, 2005. For sponsorship of National Book Festival.

2308. Library of Congress, DC. $30,000, 2005. For sponsorship of National Book Festival.

2309. Library of Congress, DC. $20,000, 2005. For sponsorship of National Book Festival.

2310. Lyndon Baines Johnson Foundation, Austin, TX. $50,000, 2005. For Robert S. Strauss Center for International Security and Law.

2311. Milwaukee Public Library Foundation, Milwaukee, WI. $16,500, 2005. To integrate portable computer training lab with wireless capability to increase computer training classes to extend outreach efforts to underserved members of community.

2312. Monterey County Business Education Research Institute, Salinas, CA. $24,450, 2005. For Entrepreneurial Support Network and Knowledge Base project, which will serve small and medium business owners as clearinghouse for important resources that are necessary for success of economic development in county.

2313. National Organization on Fetal Alcohol Syndrome, DC. $10,000, 2005. For National Fetal Alcohol Spectrum Disorders Information and Resource Clearinghouse.

2314. Nonprofit Resource Center of Texas, San Antonio, TX. $30,000, 2005. For SBC Signature Seminar Series on key topics of interest to nonprofit leaders throughout Texas.

2315. OASIS Institute, Saint Louis, MO. $500,000, 2005. For National SBC Excelerator grant which will assist seniors in developing technology training capability skills at OASIS Centers around the country.

2316. Riverside Community On-Line, Riverside, CA. $20,000, 2005. For SmartRiverside Technology Incubator Project, which will provide services to budding technology entrepreneurs who will be housed in incubator.

2317. San Antonio Public Library Foundation, San Antonio, TX. $100,000, 2005. For Centennial Achievement Plan in celebration of Library's 100th birthday and for educational activities planned for centennial, including books for youth and children.

2318. San Antonio Public Library Foundation, San Antonio, TX. $50,000, 2005. To purchase improved technology and other materials as part of Raoul A. Cortez Branch Library Capital Campaign.

2319. Ted Stevens Foundation, Anchorage, AK. $20,000, 2005. To preserve of Senator Ted Stevens and programs to improve communications between Alaskans.

2320. Texas Book Festival, Austin, TX. $250,000, 2005. For Annual Texas Book Festival, reading and literacy project to provide grants to public libraries throughout state.

2321. University of Texas M. D. Anderson Cancer Center, Houston, TX. $200,000, 2005. For Telehealth Center providing clinical telemedicine services, distance education and multi-media instruction, and multi-purpose auditorium.

2322. Visiting Nurse Association of the Inland Counties, Riverside, CA. $15,000, 2005. For Point-of-Care Technology for Clinical Staff Telehealth program, which will provide electronic medical records system that allows clinicians to document and retrieve records in patient's home.

2323. White Pine Library Cooperative, Saginaw, MI. $38,176, 2005. To purchase software for shared database to be accessed by 19 rural libraries, including website development and staff and patron training to improve effectiveness of library services.

The Brown Foundation, Inc.

Limitations: Giving primarily in TX, with emphasis on Houston. No support for political organizations, private foundations, or religious organizations for religious purposes. No grants to individuals, or for operating deficits, debt retirement, testimonial dinners, marketing or fundraising events; no loans.

2324. American Friends of the British Museum, New York, NY. $50,000, 2005. For Lhasa Archives Project in Tibet.

2325. Marlin Public Library, Marlin, TX. $25,000, 2005. For Frank C. Oltorf Archival Collection.

2326. Sterling and Francine Clark Art Institute, Williamstown, MA. $25,000, 2005. For program support.

The Burnett Foundation

(formerly The Burnett-Tandy Foundation)
Limitations: Giving primarily in the Fort Worth, TX, area.

2327. Crime Prevention Resource Center, Fort Worth, TX. $50,000, 2004. For violence prevention program.

2328. George Bush Presidential Library Foundation, College Station, TX. $1,000,000, 2004. For library.

2329. Texas Wesleyan University, Fort Worth, TX. $250,000, 2004. For renovations for the Law Library.

C.I.O.S.

Limitations: Giving on a national basis. No grants to individuals.

2330. Hill House Austin, Austin, TX. $20,000, 2005. For operating support.

The Effie and Wofford Cain Foundation

Limitations: Giving primarily in TX. No grants to individuals or organizations on behalf of specific individuals.

2331. Texas Music Office, Austin, TX. $13,000, 2005. For program expenses and Texas Music Industry Directory.

The Gordon and Mary Cain Foundation

Limitations: Giving primarily in Houston, TX. No grants to individuals.

2332. Friends of Neighborhood Libraries, Houston, TX. $10,000, 2004. For expansion at Looscan Library.

Amon G. Carter Foundation

Limitations: Giving largely restricted to Fort Worth and Tarrant County, TX. No grants to individuals, or for ongoing operating budgets, deficit financing, publications, or conferences; no loans.

2333. Crime Prevention Resource Center, Fort Worth, TX. $40,000, 2004. For special program.

2334. Fort Worth Public Library Foundation, Fort Worth, TX. $175,000, 2004. For technology support.

2335. Mental Health Connection of Tarrant County, Fort Worth, TX. $25,000, 2004. For operating support.

Communities Foundation of Texas, Inc.

Limitations: Giving primarily in the Dallas, TX, area (for grants from unrestricted funds). No support for religious purposes from general fund or organizations which redistribute funds to other organizations. No grants to individuals (except for scholarships), or for continuing support, media projects or publications, deficit financing, endowment funds, fellowships, salaries, annual campaigns, or operational expenses of well-established organizations.

2336. Library of Congress, DC. $25,500, 2005.

2337. McComb Public Library, McComb, OH. $80,000, 2005.

2338. Wilkinson Center, Dallas, TX. $16,500, 2005.

The Dallas Foundation

Limitations: Giving limited to the City and County of Dallas, TX. No support for religious purposes from discretionary funds. No grants to individuals from discretionary funds, or for endowments, research, operating budgets, annual campaigns, debt retirement, or underwriting of fundraising events; generally no multi-year grants.

2339. Dallas Public Library, Friends of the, Dallas, TX. $10,000, 2005. For Express Yourself, Poetry Competition.

2340. Laura Bush Foundation for Americas Libraries, DC. $50,000, 2005. For general operating support.

2341. Laura Bush Foundation for Americas Libraries, DC. $32,000, 2005. For general operating support.

2342. Wilkinson Center, Dallas, TX. $25,000, 2005. For unrestricted support for CLIMB program.

The Michael and Susan Dell Foundation

Limitations: Giving on a local, regional, national and international basis. No support for medical research. No grants to individuals, or for fundraisers, sponsorships, or endowments.

2343. Austin Public Library Foundation, Austin, TX. $50,251, 2004. For Wired for Youth Cyberlifeguards.

Dodge Jones Foundation

Limitations: Giving primarily in Abilene, TX. No grants to individuals.

2344. Old Jail Art Center, Albany, TX. $32,500, 2004. For salary of archivist/ librarian.

The M. S. Doss Foundation, Inc.

Limitations: Giving primarily in the eastern NM and western TX area; giving limited to Gaines County, TX, for scholarships. No grants to individuals directly.

2345. El Progreso Library, Uvalde, TX. $25,000, 2005. For building renovations.

ExxonMobil Foundation

(formerly ExxonMobil Education Foundation)

Limitations: Giving primarily in Baldwin and Mobile counties, AL, Anchorage, Fairbanks, Juneau, and North Slope, AK, Santa Barbara County and Torrance, CA, Cortez and Rio Blanco County, CO, Washington, DC, LaGrange, GA, Joliet, IL, Kingman and Stevens County, KS, Baton Rouge, Chalmette, Grand Isle, Gueydan, and Kaplan, LA, Detroit, MI, Billings, MT, Clinton and Paulsboro, NJ, Lee County, NM, Rochester, NY, Akron, OH, Shawnee and Texas County, OK, Exton, PA, Baytown, Beaumont, Dallas, Fort Worth, Houston, Longview, Midland, Odessa, and Tyler, TX, San Juan County, UT, Fairfax County and northern VA, and Lincoln, Sublette, and Sweetwater counties, WY; giving also in developing countries. No support for political or religious organizations or youth sports organizations. No grants to individuals, or for institutional scholarship or fellowship programs, capital campaigns, land acquisition, equipment, renovation projects, endowments, athletics, or scholarships; no loans.

2346. Capital Research Center, DC. $50,000, 2005. For Green Watch Project.

2347. Foundation Center, New York, NY. $10,000, 2005. For General Operating Support.

2348. New England Forestry Foundation, Littleton, MA. $50,000, 2005. For Private Landowner Network.

2349. University of Massachusetts, School of Public Health, Amherst, MA. $150,000, 2005. For Biological Effects of Low-Level Exposure (BELLE) - Chemical Hormesis Database.

Leland Fikes Foundation, Inc.

Limitations: Giving primarily in the Dallas, TX, area. No grants to individuals; no loans.

2350. Janes Due Process, Austin, TX. $25,000, 2004. For toll-free legal hotline.

2351. National Center for Science Education, Oakland, CA. $60,000, 2004. For public information program.

The Fondren Foundation

Limitations: Giving primarily in TX, with emphasis on Houston. No grants to individuals, or for annual or operating fund drives.

2352. Houston Wilderness, Houston, TX. $150,000, 2005. For Houston Wilderness Nature Passport, Houston Wilderness Web site and Atlas of Biodiversity programs.

The Hamill Foundation

Limitations: Giving primarily in Houston, TX. No grants to individuals.

2353. Texas A & M Foundation, College Station, TX. $50,000, 2005. For scholarships and library collection.

2354. Texas Heart Institute Foundation, Houston, TX. $200,000, 2005. For operating support, research and Heart Information Center.

Hillcrest Foundation

Limitations: Giving limited to TX, with emphasis on Dallas County. No grants to individuals, or for endowment funds, scholarships, or fellowships; no loans.

2355. Fairhill School, Dallas, TX. $20,000, 2005. For shelving and books for library.

2356. Laura Bush Foundation for Americas Libraries, DC. $50,000, 2005. To update, extend, and diversify book and print collections of school libraries.

2357. Library of Graham, Graham, TX. $20,000, 2005. For renovations to expand Children's Division.

2358. Saint Johns Episcopal School, Dallas, TX. $100,000, 2005. To rebuild lower school facilities, Hillcrest Library, classrooms, labs, and technology.

2359. Tawakoni Area Public Library, West Tawakoni, TX. $20,000, 2005. To build new library and community center in southern Hunt County.

2360. University of Dallas, Irving, TX. $25,000, 2005. For Integrated Library System for library management and computer-based services.

Houston Endowment Inc.

Limitations: Giving primarily in Houston, TX; no grants outside the continental U.S. No support for religious organizations for religious purposes, or organizations that are the responsibility of the government. No grants to individuals (except for scholarships); or generally for fundraising activities including galas, grantmaking organizations or charities operated by service clubs, testimonial dinners, or advertising; or the purchase of uniforms, equipment or trips for school related organizations; no loans.

2361. Baylor College of Medicine, Houston, TX. $208,200, 2005. Toward distributing research results and providing educational information in English and Spanish to women with disabilities.

2362. Foundation Center, New York, NY. $22,500, 2005. Toward increasing awareness and understanding of philanthropy by providing information, education, and research services.

2363. Kelsey Research Foundation, Houston, TX. $25,000, 2005. Toward providing health information and disease management resources through computerized kiosks at Neighborhood Centers facilities.

2364. Knowbility, Austin, TX. $60,000, 2005. Toward designing barrier-free information technology and websites for people with disabilities.

2365. Philanthropic Research, Inc., Williamsburg, VA. $30,000, 2005. Toward GuideStar website, which provides public with data about nonprofit organizations.

2366. Rosenberg Library, Galveston, TX. $250,000, 2005. Toward repairing and restoring historic public library.

2367. Texas Council on Family Violence, Austin, TX. $200,000, 2005. Toward operating National Domestic Violence Hotline, providing training and technical assistance to staff at women's shelters in Texas, promoting exchange of information between service providers throughout state, and advocating for laws and policies that affect battered women and their children.

2368. W. Oscar Neuhaus Memorial Foundation, Bellaire, TX. $150,000, 2005. Toward Parent Resource Office, free resource and referral service that provides information about language and literacy developmental delays.

Helen Jones Foundation, Inc.

Limitations: Giving primarily in Lubbock, TX. No grants to individuals.

2369. Texas Tech University, College of Education, Lubbock, TX. $15,000, 2004. For autism library.

Kimberly-Clark Foundation, Inc.

Limitations: Giving primarily in areas of company operations; giving also to national organizations. No support for religious or political organizations. No grants to individuals (except for employee-related scholarships), or for sports or athletic activities; no loans.

2370. NatureServe, Arlington, VA. $10,000, 2005.

Kinder Foundation

(formerly Richard D. Kinder Foundation, Inc.)

Limitations: Giving primarily in TX. No grants to individuals.

2371. Save Looscan Library Now, Houston, TX. $25,000, 2005. For general support.

Robert J. Kleberg, Jr. and Helen C. Kleberg Foundation

Limitations: Giving on a national basis. No support for organizations limited by race or religion. No grants for endowments, or for normal operating functions.

2372. Valley Baptist Medical Foundation, Harlingen, TX. $500,000, 2004. For radiation center records system.

Albert & Bessie Mae Kronkosky Charitable Foundation

Limitations: Giving limited to Bandera, Bexar, Comal, and Kendall counties, TX. No support for religious or political activities, private or public education, or for economic development. No grants to individuals, scholarships, annual funds, or for galas and other events.

2373. Bandera County Library, Friends of, Bandera, TX. $50,000, 2004.

The Eugene McDermott Foundation

Limitations: Giving primarily in Dallas, TX. No grants to individuals.

2374. Dallas Public Library, Dallas, TX. $50,000, 2005. For programs.

2375. Laura Bush Foundation for Americas Libraries, DC. $50,000, 2005. For Expansion of School Libraries Across America program.

2376. University of Texas at Dallas, Richardson, TX. $31,000, 2005. For textiles for library.

John P. McGovern Foundation

Limitations: Giving primarily in TX, with emphasis on Houston; giving also in the Southwest. No grants to individuals.

2377. George Bush Presidential Library Foundation, College Station, TX. $15,000, 2005. For program support for McGovern Troubadours Endowment.

2378. Houston Academy of Medicine, Texas Medical Center Library, Houston, TX. $150,000, 2005. For John P. McGovern Historical Collections and Research Center Endowment Fund.

2379. Houston Academy of Medicine, Texas Medical Center Library, Houston, TX. $80,000, 2005. For archival support.

2380. Houston Academy of Medicine, Texas Medical Center Library, Houston, TX. $20,000, 2005. For John P. McGovern Endowment Challenge Grant.

2381. Houston Academy of Medicine, Trinity Medical Center Library, Houston, TX. $25,000, 2005. For John P. McGovern History of Medicine Collection.

2382. Houston Academy of Medicine, Trinity Medical Center Library, Houston, TX. $15,000, 2005. For unrestricted support of curator and director of the John P. McGovern Historical Collections and Research Center.

2383. Houston Public Library, Friends of the, Houston, TX. $10,000, 2005.

2384. McGill University, Friends of, Montreal, Canada. $10,000, 2005. For Friends of Osler Library.

2385. McGill University, Friends of, Montreal, Canada. $10,000, 2005. For unrestricted use for the Osler librarian.

2386. Medical Library Association, Chicago, IL. $10,000, 2005. For John P. McGovern Award Lectureship Endowment Fund.

2387. National Library of Medicine, Friends of the, DC. $12,500, 2005.

2388. National Library of Medicine, Friends of the, DC. $10,000, 2005. For AMIA Dinner, Health IT for States.

2389. Ronald Reagan Presidential Foundation, Simi Valley, CA. $10,000, 2005. For Nation Honors Nancy Reagan.

2390. Rosenberg Library, Friends of, Galveston, TX. $10,000, 2005.

2391. Texas Medical Center, Jesse H. Jones Library Building, Houston, TX. $142,510, 2005. For grant of property.

2392. University of Houston-University Park, Houston, TX. $10,000, 2005. For John P. McGovern Award for Library Staff Excellence Endowment Fund.

The Meadows Foundation, Inc.

Limitations: Giving limited to TX. No grants to individuals; generally, no grants for annual campaigns, fundraising events, professional conferences and symposia, travel expenses for groups to perform or compete outside of TX, or construction of churches and seminaries.

2393. Community Voice Mail National Office, Seattle, WA. $60,000, 2005. Toward start-up support to implement statewide voice mail system linking people in crisis and without phones to jobs, housing, and other support services.

2394. Greenlights for Nonprofit Success, Austin, TX. $91,000, 2005. 2-year grant. Toward establishing set of shared administrative functions for nonprofit organizations.

2395. Marlin Public Library, Marlin, TX. $25,000, 2005. 3-year grant. Toward constructing new library.

2396. Mental Health Association of Greater Dallas, Dallas, TX. $75,000, 2005. To conduct mental health survey of Katrina victims and provide referrals to mental health services.

2397. New Waverly Public Library, New Waverly, TX. $88,000, 2005. Toward construction of new library.

Paso del Norte Health Foundation

Limitations: Giving limited to the Paso del Norte Region, including eastern TX and southern NM. No support for political organizations. No grants to individuals, building/renovation, or for research.

2398. NAACP, Newark, NJ. $15,000, 2004. For Begin at Birth's Always Kids Miracle Hotline.

The Perot Foundation

Limitations: Giving primarily in TX.

2399. Library of Congress, DC. $15,000, 2005. For James Madison Council Fund which supports programs to publicize and make accessible collections of Library of Congress including publications, multimedia works, exhibitions, symposia, electronic projects and educational programs.

Sid W. Richardson Foundation

Limitations: Giving limited to TX, with emphasis on Fort Worth for the arts and human services, and statewide for health and education. No support for religious organizations. No grants to individuals, or for scholarships or fellowships; no loans (except for program-related investments).

2400. Crime Prevention Resource Center, Fort Worth, TX. $75,000, 2004. For general support for Safe City Fort Worth.

2401. Crime Prevention Resource Center, Fort Worth, TX. $40,000, 2004. For general support of Partnership for Change project.

2402. Texas Wesleyan University, School of Law, Fort Worth, TX. $250,000, 2004. Toward expansion of law school library.

Rockwell Fund, Inc.

Limitations: Giving primarily in Houston, TX. No grants to individuals or for medical or scientific research projects, underwriting benefits, dinners, galas, and fundraising special events, or mass appeal solicitations; grants primarily awarded on a year-to-year basis only.

2403. Bellville Public Library, Bellville, TX. $50,000, 2004. For renovations to library building.

2404. University of Houston-University Park, Houston, TX. $100,000, 2004. To expand and restore library and Honors College.

T. L. L. Temple Foundation

Limitations: Giving primarily in counties in TX constituting the East Texas Pine Timber Belt. No support for private foundations. No grants to individuals, or for deficit financing.

2405. Allan Shivers Library and Museum, Woodville, TX. $25,000, 2005. For renovations.

2406. Christian Information and Service Center, Lufkin, TX. $80,000, 2005. For general support.

2407. Christian Information and Service Center, Lufkin, TX. $35,000, 2005. For loading dock construction and clothing bins.

2408. Pineland, City of, Pineland, TX. $40,000, 2005. For Arthur Temple Senior Memorial Library.

2409. T.L.L. Temple Memorial Library and Archives, Diboll, TX. $298,417, 2005. For The History Center.

2410. T.L.L. Temple Memorial Library and Archives, Diboll, TX. $153,000, 2005. For general support.

Temple-Inland Foundation

Limitations: Giving primarily in areas of company operations. No grants to individuals (except for scholarships).

2411. T.L.L. Temple Memorial Library and Archives, Diboll, TX. $69,450, 2005.

Tenet Healthcare Foundation

Limitations: Giving on a national basis, with emphasis on areas of company operations. No support for political organizations or fraternal organizations. No grants to individuals (except for employee-related scholarships), or for travel expenses.

2412. Los Gatos Medical Resource Facility, Los Gatos, CA. $35,000, 2004. For general operating support.

2413. Los Gatos Medical Resource Facility, Los Gatos, CA. $10,000, 2004. For update of medical texbook collection.

Topfer Family Foundation

(formerly The Morton & Angela Topfer Family Foundation)

Limitations: Giving primarily in the greater metropolitan areas of Chicago, IL and Austin, TX. No support for political campaigns or purposes, academic or scientific research. No grants to individuals, advertising, dinner, gala, or raffle tickets, school fundraisers or events; no loans.

2414. Austin Public Library, Austin, TX. $15,000, 2004. For Storytime Connection for low-income neighborhoods in South and East Austin.

2415. Communities in Schools, Chicago, IL. $50,000, 2004. For new programs in schools, linking community resources to at-risk children and families.

2416. Communities in Schools - Central Texas, Austin, TX. $45,000, 2004. For Rodriguez Elementary program providing counseling and supportive guidance, health and human service referrals, parental involvement, and educational enhancement.

Valero Energy Foundation

(formerly Ultramar Diamond Shamrock Foundation)

Limitations: Giving primarily in areas of company operations, with emphasis on TX. No grants to individuals.

2417. Friends of Wilmington Branch Library, Wilmington, CA. $20,000, 2004. For fundraising activities.

2418. Nonprofit Resource Center, Rockville, MD. $10,000, 2004. For fundraising activities.

2419. San Antonio Public Library Foundation, San Antonio, TX. $20,000, 2004. For fundraising activities.

UTAH

George S. and Dolores Dore Eccles Foundation

Limitations: Giving primarily in the intermountain area, particularly UT. No support for private foundations or conduit organizations. No grants to individuals, or for endowment funds, contingencies, deficits, debt reduction, conferences, seminars, or medical research.

2420. Andrew S. Rowan Reading Room for the Blind, Salt Lake City, UT. $10,000, 2005. For general support of programs for visually impaired.

2421. College of Eastern Utah, Price, UT. $301,227, 2005. For in-kind gift of stock to help construct new Library/Health Sciences Building on the College of Eastern Utah San Juan campus.

2422. Community Health Connect, Provo, UT. $30,000, 2005. For general program support to alleviate costs of serving uninsured patients.

2423. Salt Lake City Public Library, Friends of the, Salt Lake City, UT. $30,000, 2005. For annual Dewey Lecture Series, offering monthly program featuring noted national and international experts.

2424. University of Utah, Salt Lake City, UT. $15,000, 2005. For J. William Marriott Library and to publish book, The Olpin Years, University of Utah history, 1946 to 1964.

2425. Utah Festival Opera Company, Logan, UT. $50,000, 2005. To expand orchestra pit in Ellen Eccles Theater and acquire property to be used to store library resources, scenery and sets, and instruments.

2426. Utah Valley State College, Orem, UT. $50,000, 2005. For general operating support of library.

VERMONT

Carl Gary Taylor Foundation for Children, Inc.

Limitations: Giving primarily in VT. No grants to individuals.

2427. Chateaugay Memorial Library, Chateaugay, NY. $30,000, 2005. For general support.

VIRGINIA

The Community Foundation Serving Richmond & Central Virginia

(formerly Greater Richmond Community Foundation)

Limitations: Giving limited to residents of metropolitan Richmond, the tri-cities area, including Hopewell, Colonial Heights, and Petersburg, and Chesterfield, Hanover, and Henrico counties, VA. No grants for annual campaigns, deficit financing, land acquisition, or building funds.

2428. George C. Marshall Research Foundation, Lexington, VA. $15,000, 2005. To expand Virginia Role Models Program, designed to enhance students' understanding of 20th century history and support character education for grades 6-8.

2429. Homeward: Richmonds Regional Response to Homelessness, Richmond, VA. $35,000, 2005. To expand Central Intake, program providing information about housing, health, and human services to people in crisis.

2430. Virginia Center for Healthy Communities, Richmond, VA. $10,000, 2005. For Virginia Atlas for Community Health, interactive Web site that is used to report and map community data. Grant made through Jenkins Foundation.

The Freedom Forum, Inc.

Limitations: Giving on a national and international basis.

2431. John F. Kennedy Library Foundation, Boston, MA. $10,000, 2004. For general support.

2432. Remnant Trust, Hagerstown, IN. $10,000, 2004. For general support.

Gannett Foundation, Inc.

(formerly Gannett Communities Fund/Gannett Co., Inc.)

Limitations: Giving primarily in areas of company daily newspaper and television station operations, including in the United Kingdom. No support for religious organizations, elementary or secondary schools (except for special initiatives not provided for by regular school budgets), fraternal, political, or veterans' organizations, athletic teams, bands, volunteer fire departments, or national or international organizations (except for journalism education/training grants). No grants to individuals (except for employee-related scholarships), or for endowments, multiple-year pledge campaigns, or medical or other research.

2433. Center for Governmental Research, Rochester, NY. $10,000, 2005. For provision of unbiased data to facilitate reporting on state and local governmental issues.

2434. Freestore/Foodbank, Cincinnati, OH. $10,000, 2005. For Emergency Client Services Center, providing Cincinnati's most vulnerable citizens with emergency food, housing/transportation assistance, clothing, access to health care, and referrals to other resources.

2435. Hawthorne Social Service Association, Indianapolis, IN. $10,000, 2005. For childcare, referrals, and basic social services, with Hispanic Services Coordinator providing case management for Spanish-speaking clients.

2436. Public Library of Des Moines Foundation, Des Moines, IA. $25,000, 2005. For campaign to support four libraries in Des Moines, funding new central and southeast regional library and targeting improvements to other branches.

2437. Washington County School District Foundation, Saint George, UT. $10,000, 2005. To purchase library books for new schools in area.

The Norfolk Foundation

Limitations: Giving limited to southeastern VA. No support for national or international organizations (except for those with offices in southeastern VA), or religious organizations for religious purposes, fraternal activities, hospitals and similar health care facilities, or projects normally the responsibility of the government. No grants to individuals (except for donor-designated scholarships), or for operating budgets, annual campaigns, endowment funds, fundraising events, ongoing operating support, scholarly research, travel, or deficit financing.

2438. Portsmouth Public Library, Friends of the, Portsmouth, VA. $10,325, 2004. To purchase security system for local history collection.

The Mary Morton Parsons Foundation

Limitations: Giving primarily in VA, with an emphasis on Richmond. No grants to individuals, or for debt reduction, endowments, research, or general operating expenses.

2439. Braille Circulating Library, Richmond, VA. $20,000, 2005. For annual fund.

Samberg Family Foundation

Limitations: Giving primarily in NY. No grants to individuals.

2440. Center for Jewish History, New York, NY. $100,000, 2004.

The Whitaker Foundation

Limitations: Giving limited to the U.S. and Canada. No support for sectarian religious purposes. No grants to individuals, or for deficit financing, annual campaigns, emergency funds, or endowment funds.

2441. Cleve J. Fredricksen Library, Harrisburg, PA. $10,000, 2004. For Regional Program grant for annual support.

2442. Cleve J. Fredricksen Library, Harrisburg, PA. $10,000, 2004. For Regional Program grant for annual support.

2443. Dauphin County Library System, Harrisburg, PA. $10,000, 2004. For Regional Program grant for annual support.

2444. Dauphin County Library System, Harrisburg, PA. $10,000, 2004. For Regional Program grant for annual support.

2445. Foundation Center, New York, NY. $10,000, 2004. For annual support.

2446. Foundation Center, New York, NY. $10,000, 2004. For annual support.

WASHINGTON

Marguerite Casey Foundation

(formerly Casey Family Grants Program)

Limitations: Giving primarily in four regions of the U.S.: CA; the Southwest, including the U.S./Mexico border; the deep south; the Midwest, beginning in Chicago, IL; and WA state. No support for religious purposes. No grants to individuals, or for capital campaigns, endowments, fundraising drives, litigation, or film and video production.

2447. California Child Care Resource and Referral Network, San Francisco, CA. $125,000, 2004. To help expand Parent Voices throughout California so organization can become statewide parent-driven movement to improve lives of California parents and their families.

2448. Childrens Defense Fund, DC. $125,000, 2004. To expand Working Families Benefits Initiative in southern states by training student and community members to conduct outreach and help more working families connect with all of their available benefits.

2449. Family Voices of California, San Francisco, CA. $75,000, 2004. To strengthen statewide parent advocacy and organizing.

2450. Georgia State University Research Foundation, Atlanta, GA. $150,000, 2004. To conduct participatory narrative evaluation of ACORN's Accelerated Income Redistribution Campaign.

2451. Miami Workers Center, Miami, FL. $135,000, 2004. To build grassroots organizing leadership capacity in Miami-Dade and connect with other low-income worker advocacy efforts at local, state, national and international levels.

2452. Texas Low Income Housing Information Service, Austin, TX. $40,000, 2004. To expand Border Low-Income Housing Coalition's education and organizing work around housing among low-income and immigrant families living along U.S./Mexico Border.

Ben B. Cheney Foundation

Limitations: Giving limited to portions of Del Norte, Humboldt, Lassen, Shasta, Siskiyou, and Trinity counties in CA, southern OR, particularly in the Medford area, Tacoma and Pierce County, and southwestern WA. No support for religious organizations for sectarian purposes. No grants to individuals, or for general operating budgets, basic research, endowment funds, conferences or seminars, book, film, or video production, or school-related tours, no loans.

2453. Pacific University, Forest Grove, OR. $50,000, 2005. To build new library.

Bill & Melinda Gates Foundation

(formerly William H. Gates Foundation)

Limitations: Giving on a national and international basis to support initiatives in health and learning; the foundation also supports community giving in the Pacific Northwest. No support for religious purposes. No grants to individuals.

2454. Alabama Public Library Service, Montgomery, AL. $46,350, 2005. To promote sustainability of public access computing in rural libraries.

2455. Alaska State Library, Juneau, AK. $33,650, 2005. To promote sustainability of public access computing in rural libraries.

2456. Albuquerque-Bernalillo County Library System, Albuquerque, NM. $159,000, 2005. 3-year grant. To provide sustainable public access computer hardware and software upgrades.

2457. Americans for Libraries Council, New York, NY. $770,386, 2005. 2.25-year grant. For opinion research and economic assessment tool to build knowledge for libraries and public access computing advocacy.

2458. Anne Arundel County Public Library, Annapolis, MD. $12,000, 2005. To provide sustainable public access computer hardware and software upgrades to previous grantees.

2459. Arizona State Library, Archives and Public Records, Phoenix, AZ. $25,950, 2005. 1.50-year grant. To promote sustainability of public access computing in rural libraries.

2460. Arkansas State Library, Little Rock, AR. $52,650, 2005. 1.50-year grant. To promote sustainability of public access computing in rural libraries.

2461. Arlington Public Library System, Arlington, TX. $33,000, 2005. To provide sustainable public access computer hardware and software upgrades.

2462. Atlanta-Fulton Public Library, Atlanta, GA. $180,000, 2005. 3-year grant. To provide sustainable public access computer hardware and software upgrades.

2463. Berks County Public Libraries, Reading, PA. $144,000, 2005. To provide sustainable public access computer hardware and software upgrades.

2464. Bucks County Free Library, Doylestown, PA. $72,000, 2005. To provide sustainable public access computer hardware and software upgrades.

2465. California State Library, Sacramento, CA. $82,050, 2005. 1.50-year grant. To promote sustainability of public access computing in rural libraries.

2466. Camden Free Public Library, Camden, NJ. $13,500, 2005. To provide sustainable public access computer hardware and software upgrades.

2467. Carbondale Public Library, Carbondale, IL. $12,000, 2005. To provide sustainable public access computer hardware and software upgrades.

2468. Council on Library and Information Resources, DC. $125,758, 2005. 2-year grant. For Access to Learning Award.

2469. Cumberland County Public Library and Information Center, Fayetteville, NC. $21,000, 2005. To provide sustainable public access computer hardware and software upgrades.

2470. Dallas Public Library, Dallas, TX. $136,500, 2005. 3-year grant. To provide sustainable public access computer hardware and software upgrades.

2471. Davenport Public Library, Davenport, IA. $13,500, 2005. To provide sustainable public access computer hardware and software upgrades.

2472. Dayton Metro Library, Dayton, OH. $60,000, 2005. 3-year grant. To provide sustainable public access computer hardware and software upgrades.

2473. DeKalb County Public Library, Decatur, GA. $84,000, 2005. 3-year grant. To provide sustainable public access computer hardware and software upgrades.

2474. Delaware Division of Libraries, Dover, DE. $12,450, 2005. 1.50-year grant. To promote sustainability of public access computing in rural libraries.

2475. Detroit Public Library, Detroit, MI. $252,000, 2005. 3-year grant. To provide sustainable public access computer hardware and software upgrades.

2476. EdSource, Mountain View, CA. $25,000, 2005. To raise public awareness about how California high schools could better prepare students for college and work.

2477. El Paso Public Library, El Paso, TX. $94,500, 2005. To provide sustainable public access computer hardware and software upgrades.

2478. Gary Public Library, Gary, IN. $24,000, 2005. To provide sustainable public access computer hardware and software upgrades.

2479. Genesee District Library, Flint, MI. $103,500, 2005. 3-year grant. To provide sustainable public access computer hardware and software upgrades.

2480. Georgia Office of Public Library Services, Atlanta, GA. $53,850, 2005. 1.50-year grant. To promote sustainability of public access computing in rural libraries.

2481. Greenville County Library, Greenville, SC. $58,500, 2005. To provide sustainable public access computer hardware and software upgrades.

2482. Haines Borough Public Library, Haines, AK. $13,670, 2005. 1.50-year grant. For general operating support, professional affinity membership fees, and conference costs.

2483. Harris County Public Library, Houston, TX. $78,000, 2005. To provide sustainable public access computer hardware and software upgrades.

2484. Hartford Public Library, Hartford, CT. $72,000, 2005. To provide sustainable public access computer hardware and software upgrades.

2485. Houston Public Library, Houston, TX. $315,000, 2005. To provide sustainable public access computer hardware and software upgrades.

2486. Illinois State Library, Springfield, IL. $133,050, 2005. To promote sustainability of public access computing in rural libraries.

2487. Indiana State Library, Indianapolis, IN. $65,250, 2005. 1.50-year grant. To promote sustainability of public access computing in rural libraries.

2488. Kansas State Library, Topeka, KS. $86,850, 2005. 1.50-year grant. To promote sustainability of public access computing in rural libraries.

2489. Las Vegas-Clark County Library District, Las Vegas, NV. $82,500, 2005. To provide sustainable public access computer hardware and software upgrades.

2490. Library of Virginia, Richmond, VA. $36,150, 2005. To promote sustainability of public access computing in rural libraries.

2491. Live Oak Public Libraries, Savannah, GA. $127,500, 2005. 3-year grant. To provide sustainable public access computer hardware and software upgrades.

2492. Louisville Free Public Library, Louisville, KY. $132,000, 2005. 3-year grant. To provide sustainable public access computer hardware and software upgrades.

2493. Maine State Library, Augusta, ME. $70,950, 2005. 1.50-year grant. To promote sustainability of public access computing in rural libraries.

2494. Maricopa County Library District, Phoenix, AZ. $75,000, 2005. To provide sustainable public access computer hardware and software upgrades.

2495. Massachusetts, Commonwealth of, Boston, MA. $79,050, 2005. 1.50-year grant. To promote sustainability of public access computing in rural libraries.

2496. Metropolitan Library System, Oklahoma City, OK. $90,000, 2005. To provide sustainable public access computer hardware and software upgrades.

2497. Minneapolis Public Library, Minneapolis, MN. $70,500, 2005. To provide sustainable public access computer hardware and software upgrades.

2498. Montana State Library, Helena, MT. $31,650, 2005. 1.50-year grant. To promote sustainability of public access computing in rural libraries.

2499. Nashville Public Library, Nashville, TN. $133,500, 2005. 3-year grant. To provide sustainable public access computer hardware and software upgrades.

2500. National Low Income Housing Coalition and Low Income Housing Information Service, DC. $25,000, 2005. For national summit on future of federal housing voucher program.

2501. Nebraska Library Commission, Lincoln, NE. $69,450, 2005. To promote sustainability of public access computing in rural libraries.

2502. New Mexico State Library, Santa Fe, NM. $22,650, 2005. To promote sustainability of public access computing in rural libraries.

2503. New York Public Library, New York, NY. $735,000, 2005. 3-year grant. To provide sustainable public access computer hardware and software upgrades.

2504. New York State Library, Albany, NY. $156,750, 2005. 1.50-year grant. To promote sustainability of public access computing in rural libraries.

2505. NewSchools Venture Fund, San Francisco, CA. $3,327,879, 2005. 3-year grant. To build Communities of Practice (share lessons, convene practitioners, and develop Web-based technology platform) and capture, codify, and share important intellectual capital to influence broader ecosystem.

2506. Norfolk Public Library, Norfolk, VA. $69,000, 2005. To provide sustainable public access computer hardware and software upgrades.

2507. Oakland Public Library, Oakland, CA. $147,000, 2005. 3-year grant. To provide sustainable public access computer hardware and software upgrades.

2508. Office of the Superintendent of Public Instruction, Olympia, WA. $1,200,000, 2005. 1.50-year grant. For automated real-time collection of student data from local district data systems to state data warehouse.

2509. Oklahoma Department of Libraries, Oklahoma City, OK. $51,150, 2005. To promote sustainability of public access computing in rural libraries.

2510. Omaha Public Library Foundation, Omaha, NE. $48,000, 2005. 2-year grant. To provide sustainable public access computer hardware and software upgrades.

2511. Online Computer Library Center (OCLC), Dublin, OH. $2,068,908, 2005. 3.25-year grant. For outreach program for Spanish-speaking patrons to increase use of public access computing in libraries.

2512. Online Computer Library Center (OCLC), Dublin, OH. $1,074,307, 2005. 3-year grant. To promote sustainable technology in rural libraries.

2513. Orange County Library System, Orlando, FL. $73,500, 2005. To provide sustainable public access computer hardware and software upgrades.

2514. Phoenix Public Library, Friends of the, Phoenix, AZ. $55,500, 2005. To provide sustainable public access computer hardware and software upgrades.

2515. Pioneer Multi-County Library System, Norman, OK. $79,500, 2005. To provide sustainable public access computer hardware and software upgrades.

2516. Riverside County Library System, Riverside, CA. $90,000, 2005. To provide sustainable public access computer hardware and software upgrades.

2517. Sacramento Public Library, Sacramento, CA. $96,000, 2005. 3-year grant. To provide sustainable public access computer hardware and software upgrades.

2518. San Antonio Public Library, San Antonio, TX. $151,500, 2005. 3-year grant. To provide sustainable public access computer hardware and software upgrades.

2519. San Bernardino County Library, San Bernardino, CA. $117,000, 2005. To provide sustainable public access computer hardware and software upgrades.

2520. San Diego Public Library, San Diego, CA. $144,000, 2005. To provide sustainable public access computer hardware and software upgrades.

2521. San Francisco Public Library, San Francisco, CA. $153,000, 2005. To provide sustainable public access computer hardware and software upgrades.

2522. San Jose Public Library, San Jose, CA. $78,000, 2005. 2-year grant. To provide sustainable public access computer hardware and software upgrades.

2523. Seattle Public Library Foundation, Seattle, WA. $94,500, 2005. To provide sustainable public access computer hardware and software upgrades.

2524. Seattle Public Library Foundation, Seattle, WA. $13,760, 2005. For general operating support.

2525. Sonoma County Library, Santa Rosa, CA. $21,000, 2005. To provide sustainable public access computer hardware and software upgrades.

2526. South Carolina State Library, Columbia, SC. $30,750, 2005. 1.50-year grant. To promote sustainability of public access computing in rural libraries.

2527. South Dakota State Library, Pierre, SD. $186,720, 2005. 3-year grant. For public access computing sustainability efforts in public libraries.

2528. Squaxin Island Museum Library and Research Center, Shelton, WA. $29,532, 2005. 2-year grant. For facilities for at-risk youth and community projects.

2529. Stanislaus County Free Library, Modesto, CA. $72,000, 2005. To provide sustainable public access computer hardware and software upgrades.

2530. State Library of Iowa, Des Moines, IA. $129,450, 2005. 1.50-year grant. To promote sustainability of public access computing in rural libraries.

2531. State Library of Ohio, Columbus, OH. $70,350, 2005. 1.50-year grant. To promote sustainability of public access computing in rural libraries.

2532. Stockton-San Joaquin County Public Library, Stockton, CA. $66,000, 2005. To provide sustainable public access computer hardware and software upgrades.

2533. Thomas B. Fordham Institute, DC. $497,639, 2005. 3-year grant. To inform public debate and advance academic achievement in Ohio charter schools by convening charter school leaders, producing research, and disseminating information on charter school issues.

2534. Timberland Regional Library, Olympia, WA. $93,000, 2005. To provide sustainable public access computer hardware and software upgrades.

2535. Tomas Rivera Policy Institute, Los Angeles, CA. $30,000, 2005. For messaging and dissemination strategies for College Knowledge Information Campaign for Latino students and their parents.

2536. Tucson-Pima Public Library, Tucson, AZ. $94,500, 2005. To provide sustainable public access computer hardware and software upgrades.

2537. Urban Libraries Council, Evanston, IL. $60,000, 2005. For building knowledge for libraries and public access computing advocacy through analysis of economic development impact of urban public libraries.

2538. Utah State Library Division, Salt Lake City, UT. $21,450, 2005. 1.50-year grant. To promote sustainability of public access computing in rural libraries.

2539. Ventura County Library, Ventura, CA. $52,500, 2005. To provide sustainable public access computer hardware and software upgrades.

2540. West Virginia Library Commission, Charleston, WV. $35,850, 2005. To promote sustainability of public access computing in rural libraries.

2541. Whatcom County Commission on Children and Youth, Bellingham, WA. $229,745, 2005. 3-year grant. For integrated client data management system for low-income families.

2542. Wichita Public Library, Wichita, KS. $54,000, 2005. 3-year grant. To provide sustainable public access computer hardware and software upgrades.

2543. William J. Clinton Presidential Foundation, Little Rock, AR. $750,000, 2005. For general operating support.

2544. William J. Clinton Presidential Foundation, Little Rock, AR. $750,000, 2005. For HIV/AIDS Initiative, to bring quality care and treatment to people living with HIV/AIDS and to improve health systems in resource-poor setting.

2545. William J. Clinton Presidential Foundation, New York, NY. $500,000, 2005. To facilitate summit of global leaders to identify solutions to some of world's most pressing problems.

2546. York County Library System, York, PA. $33,000, 2005. To provide sustainable public access computer hardware and software upgrades.

Medina Foundation

Limitations: Giving limited to the greater Puget Sound, WA, area, with emphasis on the counties of Grays Harbor, Island, Jefferson, King, Kitsap, Mason, Pacific, Pierce, San Juan, Skagit, and Snohomish. No support for public institutions. No grants to individuals, or for endowment funds, research, scholarships, or matching gifts.

2547. First Place, Seattle, WA. $60,000, 2004. For program support for Library and Information Systems Initiative.

Gary E. Milgard Family Foundation

(formerly Gary & Carol Milgard Family Foundation)

Limitations: Giving primarily in Pierce County and the greater Puget Sound, WA, area. No support for political organizations or religious organizations where funds would be used to further a religious purpose. No grants for deficit reduction.

2548. Pierce County Library Foundation, Tacoma, WA. $17,148, 2004. For Explorer Coast and Bilingual books.

M. J. Murdock Charitable Trust

Limitations: Giving primarily in the Pacific Northwest (AK, ID, MT, OR, and WA). No support for government programs; projects common to many organizations without distinguishing merit; sectarian or religious organizations whose principal activities are for the benefit of their own members. No grants to individuals, or for deficit financing, debt retirement, political activities, generally no grants for annual campaigns, general support, continuing support, endowments, or emergency funds; no loans.

2549. Foundation Center, New York, NY. $42,000, 2005. For public service programs for nonprofit sector.

2550. National Strategy Information Center, DC. $350,000, 2005. For U.S. Security Research to educate policymakers and young students.

2551. Peregrine Fund, Boise, ID. $270,000, 2005. For new web-based information project and expanded student education program to strengthen raptor conservation work worldwide.

The Norcliffe Foundation

(formerly The Norcliffe Fund)

Limitations: Giving in the Puget Sound region of WA, with emphasis in and around Seattle. No grants to individuals, or for deficit financing, matching gifts, or scholarships; no loans.

2552. Deming Library, Friends of the, Deming, WA. $20,000, 2005. To expand existing library.

2553. Seattle Public Library Foundation, Seattle, WA. $10,000, 2005.

The Seattle Foundation

Limitations: Giving limited to Seattle-King County, WA. No support for religious purposes. No grants to individuals, or for endowment funds, debt reduction, fundraising events, fundraising feasibility projects, conferences or seminars, film or video production, publications, or operating expenses for public or private elementary and secondary schools, colleges, and universities.

2554. Alliance for Education, Seattle, WA. $30,000, 2005. For Seattle School District to purchase elementary school library books.

2555. Child Care Resources, Seattle, WA. $43,500, 2005. For Leadership and Learning for Family, Friends and Neighbor Caregiving.

2556. Child Care Resources, Seattle, WA. $15,000, 2005. For general support.

2557. Child Care Resources, Seattle, WA. $10,000, 2005. For general support.

2558. Densho, Seattle, WA. $10,000, 2005. To help continue legacy.

2559. Greenwich Library, Greenwich, CT. $10,000, 2005. For Peterson Business Award Dinner.

2560. Huntington Library, Art Collections and Botanical Gardens, San Marino, CA. $10,000, 2005. For Society of Fellows.

2561. Our Ladys Dowry, San Antonio, TX. $147,500, 2005. For library finishes, fixtures, furniture and equipment, and lunchroom furniture.

2562. Seattle Public Library Foundation, Seattle, WA. $69,726, 2005. For general support.

2563. Seattle Public Library Foundation, Seattle, WA. $30,000, 2005. For Campaign for Seattle's Public Libraries Fund.

2564. Seattle Public Library Foundation, Seattle, WA. $20,000, 2005. For construction of new library branch in South Park.

2565. Seattle Public Library Foundation, Seattle, WA. $12,119, 2005. For general support.

2566. Seattle Public Library Foundation, Seattle, WA. $10,000, 2005. For general support.

2567. Women at Work, Pasadena, CA. $10,000, 2005. For general support.

The Wilburforce Foundation

Limitations: Giving primarily in the western U.S. and western Canada, particularly AK, AZ, NM, OR, UT, WA, WY, British Columbia, and the Yellowstone to Yukon region of U.S.-Canada. No support for schools or universities, or governmental agencies. No grants to individuals, or for fellowships or scholarships, endowment funds, operating budgets, or deficit financing or indirect costs; no loans.

2568. Earthworks, DC. $25,000, 2004. To ensure scientific research on mining is shared with government and corporate decision-makers.

2569. Environmental Working Group, DC. $150,000, 2004. For managing and publicizing online national mining atlas and database to support campaign for U.S. mining reform.

2570. Montana Environmental Information Center, Helena, MT. $50,000, 2004. For general support to protect biologically significant habitats in Montana by helping reform hard rock mining.

WEST VIRGINIA

The Daywood Foundation, Inc.

Limitations: Giving limited to Barbour, Greenbrier and Kanawha counties, WV. No grants to individuals, or for endowment funds, research, individual scholarships, or fellowships; no loans.

2571. Greenbrier County Library, Lewisburg, WV. $50,000, 2004. For capital campaign.

2572. Greenbrier County Library, Lewisburg, WV. $10,000, 2004. For program support.

Bernard McDonough Foundation, Inc.

Limitations: Giving primarily in WV. No support for religious organizations. No grants to individuals.

2573. Vienna Public Library, Vienna, WV. $10,000, 2004.

WISCONSIN

Helen Bader Foundation, Inc.

Limitations: Giving primarily in the greater Milwaukee, WI, area for education and economic development; giving locally and nationally for Alzheimer's disease and dementia; giving in Israel for early childhood development. No grants to individuals.

2574. Asset Builders of America, Madison, WI. $30,000, 2005. 2-year grant. For PAID - Payment Aggregation and Information Dissemination for Low-Income Families.

2575. Donors Forum of Wisconsin, Milwaukee, WI. $60,000, 2005. 3-year grant. For sustainability of operations and capacity building.

2576. Donors Forum of Wisconsin, Milwaukee, WI. $25,000, 2005. For Wisconsin EngAGEment Initiative, seeking to build awareness and increase support of aging issues among funders throughout the state.

2577. Donors Forum of Wisconsin, Milwaukee, WI. $10,000, 2005. For gathering of Social Enterprise Alliance.

2578. KESHER, Jerusalem, Israel. $50,000, 2005. 2-year grant. For information and counseling service for Arab families of children with special needs.

2579. Nonprofit Center of Milwaukee, Milwaukee, WI. $12,700, 2005. For 12 Step Club Leaders Conference.

2580. University of Wisconsin Foundation, Madison, WI. $14,000, 2005. For Wisconsin Alzheimer's Institute host a conference for affiliated dementia diagnostic clinics in June 2005 in effort to share information about current research.

2581. University of Wisconsin System, UW-Madison Center of Excellence in Family Service, Madison, WI. $10,000, 2005. For Medicaid Wisconsin Family Impact Seminar.

The Lynde and Harry Bradley Foundation, Inc.

Limitations: Giving primarily in Milwaukee, WI; giving also on a national and international basis. No support for strictly denominational projects. No grants to individuals (except for Bradley Prizes), or for endowment funds.

2582. Donors Forum of Wisconsin, Milwaukee, WI. $15,000, 2005. For Wisconsin Giving Initiative.

2583. Heartland Institute, Chicago, IL. $30,000, 2005. For School Reform News.

2584. Jamestown Foundation, DC. $20,000, 2005. For publications program.

2585. Manhattan Institute for Policy Research, New York, NY. $25,000, 2005. For PointofLaw.com web site.

2586. Milwaukee Public Library Foundation, Milwaukee, WI. $50,000, 2005. For general operating support.

2587. National Strategy Information Center, DC. $400,000, 2005. For general operating support and Special Project to Enhance U.S. Intelligence.

2588. National Strategy Information Center, DC. $250,000, 2005. For Arab Media project.

2589. School Choice Wisconsin, American Education Reform Council, Milwaukee, WI. $200,000, 2005. For general operating support.

Madison Community Foundation

Limitations: Giving limited to Dane County, WI. No support for religious organizations for religious purposes, health care services, including mental health, or substance abuse treatment. No grants to individuals, or for annual campaigns, endowment funds, debt retirement, short-term events (such as conferences, festivals, celebrations and fund raising functions), or scholarships; no capital grants to support ongoing maintenance.

2590. McFarland Library, Friends of, Madison, WI. $30,000, 2005. To expand library to promote lifelong learning for growing population.

2591. Rosemary Garfoot Public Library, Cross Plains, WI. $50,000, 2005. For Village of Cross Plains creation of environmentally friendly building, including teen area, parents' zone, and adult learning space.

Greater Milwaukee Foundation

(formerly Milwaukee Foundation)

Limitations: Giving primarily in Milwaukee, Ozaukee, Washington, and Waukesha, WI. No support for the general use of churches or for sectarian religious purposes, or for specific medical or scientific projects, except from components of the foundation established for such purposes. No grants to individuals (except for established awards), or for operating budgets, continuing support, annual campaigns, endowment funds, or deficit financing.

2592. Donors Forum of Wisconsin, Milwaukee, WI. $40,000, 2005. For Executive Transitions Initiative.

2593. Donors Forum of Wisconsin, Milwaukee, WI. $10,000, 2005. For Grantmakers in Aging Engagement Initiative.

2594. Donors Forum of Wisconsin, Milwaukee, WI. $10,000, 2005. For Community Foundation Division.

2595. Nonprofit Center of Milwaukee, Milwaukee, WI. $138,879, 2005. For resident engagement strategies in Making Connections.

2596. Nonprofit Center of Milwaukee, Milwaukee, WI. $40,000, 2005. For replacement of heating and cooling systems.

2597. Nonprofit Center of Milwaukee, Milwaukee, WI. $28,125, 2005. For Community Organizing.

2598. South Milwaukee Public Library, South Milwaukee, WI. $10,000, 2005. For installation of wireless computer system.

2599. University of Wisconsin Foundation, Milwaukee, WI. $200,000, 2005. For expansion of COMPASS Guide.

Northwestern Mutual Foundation

(formerly Northwestern Mutual Life Foundation)

Limitations: Giving primarily in the greater Milwaukee, WI, area. No grants to individuals.

2600. Donors Forum of Wisconsin, Milwaukee, WI. $10,000, 2005.

2601. Milwaukee Public Library Foundation, Milwaukee, WI. $50,000, 2005.

2602. Milwaukee Public Library Foundation, Milwaukee, WI. $50,000, 2005.

2603. Nonprofit Center of Milwaukee, Milwaukee, WI. $14,000, 2005.

Jane Bradley Pettit Foundation

(formerly Jane and Lloyd Pettit Foundation, Inc.)

Limitations: Giving primarily in the greater Milwaukee, WI, area. No grants to individuals.

2604. Donors Forum of Wisconsin, Milwaukee, WI. $10,000, 2004. For operating support.

Reiman Foundation, Inc.

(formerly Reiman Charitable Foundation, Inc.)

2605. Denver Public Library, Denver, CO. $10,000, 2004. For general operating support.

Siebert Lutheran Foundation, Inc.

Limitations: Giving primarily in WI. No grants to individuals, or for endowment funds, scholarships, or fellowships; no loans.

2606. Donors Forum of Wisconsin, Milwaukee, WI. $10,000, 2005. For Leadership Grant for operating support.

Wisconsin Energy Corporation Foundation, Inc.

(formerly Wisconsin Electric System Foundation, Inc.)

Limitations: Giving limited to areas of company operations in the Upper Peninsula, MI, area and WI. No support for political action or legislative advocacy organizations or veterans' or fraternal organizations. No grants to individuals, or for trips, tours, pageants, team or extra-curricular school events, or student exchange programs, programs whose primary purpose is the promotion of religious doctrine or tenets, or programs whose purpose is solely athletic in nature.

2607. Saint Ignace Public Library, Saint Ignace, MI. $12,500, 2005. For new library construction.

2608. Wisconsin Womens Health Foundation, Madison, WI. $25,000, 2005. For Dr. Judith Stitt Woman Faculty Scholarship.

WYOMING

The Andrew Allen Charitable Foundation

Limitations: Giving in the U.S., primarily in PA and WY. No grants to individuals.

2609. Free Library of Philadelphia, Philadelphia, PA. $10,000, 2005.

Homer A. & Mildred S. Scott Foundation

Limitations: Giving primarily within a 35-mile radius of Sheridan, WY and in specific areas of MT. No grants to individuals.

2610. Montana Child Care Resource and Referral Network, Missoula, MT. $15,000, 2005. For Montana Afterschool Network.

2611. Sheridan County Library Foundation, Sheridan, WY. $150,000, 2005. For Library Improvement Project.

The Wolf Creek Charitable Foundation

Limitations: Giving on a national basis. No support for religious or political organizations. No grants to individuals.

2612. Sheridan County Library Foundation, Sheridan, WY. $10,000, 2004. For general support.

Wyoming Community Foundation

Limitations: Giving primarily in WY. No grants to individuals (except for scholarships), or generally for block grants, capital campaigns, annual campaigns, or debt retirement.

2613. Crook County Library System, Sundance, WY. $25,000, 2005.

RECIPIENT INDEX

OASIS Institute, MO, 371, 1087, 1108-1118, 2315, 2167, 2182, 2216
Objective Reality Foundation, Russia, 1468
Occidental College, CA, 54
OCCUR Community Information Service, CA, 2060
Odessa LINKS, TX, 2283
Oelwein Public Library, IA, 760
Office of the Superintendent of Public Instruction, WA, 2508
Ohio Grantmakers Forum, OH, 1958, 1970, 1981-1983, 1990, 1993, 2002, 2003, 2008, 2013, 2025
Oklahoma Department of Libraries, OK, 2509
Oklahoma Garden Clubs, OK, 2029
Old Jail Art Center, TX, 2344
Old Town Library, ME, 812
Older Adult Service and Information Systems (OASIS), OH, 1971
Omaha Public Library, NE, 1127
Omaha Public Library Foundation, NE, 2510
OMG Center for Collaborative Learning, PA, 670, 1878
One Economy Corporation, DC, 109
Oneida Library, NY, 1138
Online Computer Library Center (OCLC), OH, 2511, 2512
Open Memory Civil Association-Human Rights Organizations Coordinated Action, Argentina, 1469
Open University, England, 201
Operation Truth, NY, 1732
Orange County Library System, FL, 2513
Orange County Museum of Art, CA, 1580
Oregon Child Care Resource and Referral Network, OR, 2086
Oregon Health Access Project, OR, 2087
Oregon Partnership, OR, 2051, 2088
Organic Center, RI, 1150
Organic Center for Education and Promotion, MA, 1151, 1152
Organisation for Economic Cooperation and Development, France, 202, 203
Orient Foundation, England, 1470
Otis Library, CT, 967
Our Lady of Lourdes School, MT, 1142
Our Ladys Dowry, TX, 2561
Ozark Christian College, MO, 564

P.E.F. Israel Endowment Funds, NY, 1798
Pace University Law School, NY, 1879
PACER Center, MN, 1049
Pacific University, OR, 2453
Pacifica Library Foundation, CA, 304
Pain Relief Network, NY, 1769
Palm Beach Atlantic University, FL, 2281
Palm Beach County Youth Symphony Orchestras, FL, 566
Palo Alto Medical Foundation for Health Care, Research and Education, CA, 305
Parent Information Center, NH, 1146
Parent Trust for Washington Children, WA, 1050
Park Street Foundation, NH, 1153, 1249
Partners in Public Education (PIPE), TN, 2267
Pasadena Public Library Foundation, CA, 150
Patrons Program, NY, 457
Patten Free Library, ME, 1523
Paul Robeson Foundation, NY, 1471
Peabody Memorial Library, ME, 813, 823
Pembroke Library Association, ME, 824
Peninsula Library Foundation, CA, 343
Penn Hills Library Foundation, PA, 2183
Pennsylvania Trolley Museum, PA, 2205
Pension Rights Center, DC, 697
Pere Marquette District Library, MI, 948
Peregrine Fund, ID, 2551
Permian Basin Petroleum Museum, Library and Hall of Fame, TX, 2284-2286
Peter G. Monnier Elementary School, MI, 1009
Petersburg, City of, AK, 13
Philadelphia Museum of Art, PA, 2208
Philanthropic Research, Inc., VA, 55, 122, 227, 257, 286, 360, 361, 580, 736, 1216, 1375, 1417, 1502, 1503, 1532, 2365
Philanthropy Roundtable, DC, 737

Phillips Theological Seminary, OK, 573
Phillips-Morrison Institute of California, CA, 490
Phoebe Apperson Hearst Library, SD, 1273
Phoenix Library, Friends of the, OR, 2073
Phoenix Public Library, Friends of the, AZ, 2514
Phoenixville Public Library, PA, 2134
Pierce County Library Foundation, WA, 2548
Pierpont Morgan Library, NY, 492, 1277, 1278, 1390, 1423, 1424, 1494, 1512, 1556, 1563, 1676, 1733-1735
Pikes Peak Library District Foundation, CO, 448-450
Pineland, City of, TX, 2408
Pioneer Multi-County Library System, OK, 2026, 2515
Pittsburgh Dance Alloy, PA, 2200
Pittsfield Public Library, ME, 814
Plainfield Public Library, Friends of the, NJ, 1158
Plains Medical Center, CO, 439
Poets House, NY, 1322, 1519, 1535, 1553, 1837
Politz Hebrew Academy of Northeast Philadelphia, PA, 2154
Polk County Library, Friends of, NC, 1939
Polytechnic University, NY, 462
Port Hueneme Library, Friends of, CA, 1250
Port Orford Public Library Foundation, OR, 2041, 2052
Port Washington Public Library, NY, 1736
Porter Memorial Library, ME, 815
Portsmouth Free Public Library, RI, 2236, 2259
Portsmouth Public Library, Friends of the, VA, 2438
Positive Wellness Alliance, NC, 1941
Prairie Grove Public Library, AR, 31
Prairie Rivers Network, IL, 649, 1044
Prevent Child Abuse, MT, 591
Princeton Public Library, NJ, 1394
Princeton University, NJ, 1513
Pro Mujer, NY, 1550
probono.net, NY, 1323
Project HOPE - People-to-People Health Foundation, VA, 1526
Project Inform, CA, 190, 344, 403, 451
Providence Athenaeum, RI, 2237
Providence Public Library, RI, 1251, 1737, 2224, 2238-2241, 2251, 2252, 2258
Providers Resource Clearinghouse, CO, 1084
PsychSource, GA, 597
Public Library of Charlotte and Mecklenburg County, Friends of the, NC, 1916
Public Library of Des Moines Foundation, IA, 404-406, 2004, 2436
Public Library of Nashville and Davidson County, Friends of the, TN, 2151
Public Library of Science, CA, 258, 287
Public Utility Law Project of New York, NY, 144
PUENTE Learning Center: People United to Enrich the Neighborhood Through Education, CA, 2125
Puerto Rico Department of Health, PR, 1195

Queens Borough Public Library, NY, 1286
Queens Council on the Arts, NY, 1738
Queens Library Foundation, NY, 458, 466, 1252, 1261, 1367, 1536, 1537, 1795, 1871
Queens Museum of Art, NY, 1287
Quogue Free Library, NY, 1739

Rachel Carson Council, MD, 841
Ramon Magsaysay Award Foundation, Philippines, 1805
Rauchholz Memorial Library, MI, 928
Ravenswood City School District, CA, 306
Ready Set Grow Passport Initiative, MI, 1003
Red Feather Lakes Community Library, CO, 445
Redwood City Library Foundation, CA, 307, 308
Redwood City School District, CA, 309
Redwood Library and Athenaeum, RI, 683-685, 968, 2242, 2260, 2261
Remnant Trust, IN, 2432
Research Foundation of the State University of New York, NY, 1196
Research Libraries Group, CA, 1642
Research, Action and Information Network for the Bodily Integrity of Women (RAINBO), NY, 558
Resources for Children with Special Needs, NY, 1299, 1385, 1538, 1679, 1740, 1741, 1786

Rex Healthcare, NC, 1929
Rhode Island Department of Health, RI, 1197
Rhode Island Natural History Survey, RI, 2256, 2257
Rhode Island Parent Information Network, RI, 855
Rhode Island Supreme Court, RI, 2243
Richard Nixon Library and Birthplace Foundation, CA, 76, 1742, 1842, 1872
Richmond County Community Support Center, NC, 1936
Richmond Memorial Library, NY, 1801
Richmond Public Library Foundation, VA, 1918, 2168
Right Side Foundation, IN, 717
Riverside Community On-Line, CA, 2316
Riverside County Library System, CA, 2516
Robin Hood Foundation, NY, 1407, 1408
Rochester Institute of Technology, NY, 164
Rockefeller University, NY, 1383, 1814
Rodef Shalom Temple, PA, 2217
Rogers Public Library Foundation, AR, 32, 33
Romanian Donors Forum, Romania, 994
Romare Bearden Foundation, NY, 1472
Ronald Reagan Presidential Foundation, CA, 105, 520, 898, 1093, 1134, 1398, 2126-2128, 2389
Rosemary Garfoot Public Library, WI, 2591
Rosenbach Museum and Library, PA, 2135, 2213
Rosenberg Library, TX, 2366
Rosenberg Library, Friends of, TX, 2390
Rostraver Public Library, PA, 2173, 2218
Roswell P. Flower Memorial Library, NY, 1997
Roswell Park Alliance Foundation, NY, 578
Rowan, City of, IA, 761
Royal Botanic Gardens, Kew, England, 259, 1643-1645
Rundel Library Foundation, NY, 1495, 1802
Russia Donors Forum, Russia, 671
Rutgers, The State University of New Jersey Foundation, NJ, 165
Rye Free Reading Room, NY, 1821

Sacramento Public Library, CA, 2517
Sacramento Public Library Foundation, CA, 407, 1081
Safe Harbor Retreat, CA, 891
Sage Ridge School, NV, 1143
Saint Athanasius School, NY, 1528
Saint Augustine College of South Africa, South Africa, 511
Saint Charles Borromeo Seminary, PA, 2155
Saint Edward, City of, NE, 1128
Saint Ignace Public Library, MI, 2607
Saint Johns Episcopal School, TX, 2358
Saint Johns University, MN, 1067
Saint Lawrence University, NY, 1646
Saint Louis County Library Foundation, MO, 1092, 2009
Saint Louis University, MO, 1088
Saint Mary School, NJ, 1260
Saint Mary-Collinwood School, OH, 1955
Saint Matthews Parish School, CA, 56
Saint Patricks Seminary, CA, 152
Saint Paul Jaycees Charitable Foundation, MN, 1068
Saint Paul Public Library, Friends of the, MN, 102, 1013, 1016, 1017, 1069, 1078
Saint Paul University, Canada, 2141
Salt Lake City Public Library, Friends of the, UT, 2423
Sampson Regional Medical Center, NC, 1930
San Antonio Public Library, TX, 2518
San Antonio Public Library Foundation, TX, 1917, 2317, 2318, 2419
San Bernardino County Library, CA, 2519
San Diego County Cancer Navigator, CA, 87
San Diego Public Library, CA, 191, 322, 2520
San Francisco Adult Day Services Network, CA, 176
San Francisco Performing Arts Library and Museum, CA, 204
San Francisco Public Library, CA, 2521
San Jose Public Library, CA, 2522
San Jose Public Library Foundation, CA, 123-125
San Marino Public Library Foundation, CA, 57
San Mateo County Library Joint Powers Authority, CA, 205, 206
San Mateo Public Library Foundation, CA, 310, 311
Santa Barbara County Education Office, CA, 1368

GEOGRAPHIC INDEX

INDONESIA
Combine Resource Institution 1440

IOWA
Clearfield Public Library 712
Columbus Community Civic Center Foundation 748
Coralville Public Library 775
Coralville Public Library Foundation 749
Cornell College 750
Council Bluffs Public Library 770
Davenport Public Library 751, 2471
Des Moines Public Library Foundation 774
Elberon Public Library 752
Friends of Burlington Public Library Foundation 753
Gibson Memorial Library 714
Hull Public Library 754
Humeston Public Library 755
Irwin, City of 771
Le Claire Community Library 766
Malvern Public Library 756
Marengo Public Library, Friends of the 757
Massena, Town of 758
Missouri Valley, City of 1126
Monroe Public Library, Friends of 759
National Czech and Slovak Museum and Library 767,
  776
Oelwein Public Library 760
Public Library of Des Moines Foundation 404-406,
  2004, 2436
Rowan, City of 761
Sigourney Public Library 762
Springville Memorial Library 763
State Library of Iowa 2530
University of Iowa 764
Waldorf College 765, 768, 769

IRELAND
Trinity College 166
University of Dublin 1656

ISRAEL
Hebrew University of Jerusalem 2253
Jewish National and University Library 171, 2254
Kav LaOved-Workers Hotline for the Protection of
  Workers Rights 1663
KESHER 2578

ITALY
Centro Studi Erbario Tropicale 1605

JAMAICA
Denbigh High School 2104
Glenmuir High School 2105

KANSAS
Benedictine College 2291
Christian Foundation Center of America 923
Johnson County Library Foundation 1058
Kansas Association of Child Care Resources and
  Referral Agencies 779, 781
Kansas Department of Health and Environment 1181
Kansas Health Institute 782, 783
Kansas State Library 2488
Unified School District No. 259 784
United Way of the Plains 785
Wichita Public Library 2542

KENTUCKY
Appalachian College Association 1590
Council of State Governments 1170, 1849
Help Office of Hancock County, Kentucky 2106
Kentucky Jobs with Justice 550
Library Foundation 746, 795, 2007
Louisville Free Public Library 2492
Louisville Free Public Library Foundation 786, 787,
  790, 791, 794
Thomas More College 2017
Trimble County Public Library 789

United Way, Metro 856, 857
University of Kentucky 793, 1262
University of Kentucky Research Foundation 1200

KENYA
AfriAfya 1807
African Medical and Research Foundation 1808
African Women and Child Information Network 1427,
  1428
Indigenous Information Network 1456
Thibitisha Trust 1476

LEBANON
Arab Network of NGOs for Development 1431
Assabil Association 1432

LOUISIANA
Chamber of Commerce, Greater Baton Rouge 797
East Baton Rouge Parish Public Library 798
Family Service of Greater Baton Rouge 799
Greater New Orleans Knowledge Works 796, 849
Keyes Foundation 801
Lake Charles Boston High School 320
Louisiana Family Recovery Corps 800
Louisiana Library Foundation 802
Louisiana Public Health Institute 1182
Louisiana State University and A & M College 1855
National Network of Public Health Institutes
  1189-1191

MAINE
Andover Public Library 583
Bagaduce Music Lending Library 820
Bangor Public Library 804
Berwick Library Association 821
Brown Memorial Library 805, 827
Brownfield Public Library 806
Camden Public Library 497-499
Caswell Public Library Association 822
Charlotte Hobbs Memorial Library 807
Cushing Public Library 500
CyberSeniors.org 828
Fulbright Academy of Science and Technology 1852
Hollis Center Library 808
Homeworks 835
Jeremiah Cromwell Disabilities Center 803, 911
John Curtis Free Library 809
Maine Center for Public Health 1183
Maine Department of Corrections 829
Maine Health Information Center 830
Maine Medical Center 831
Maine State Library 2493
MaineGeneral Health 832
New Portland Community Library 810
Northeast Harbor Library 811, 1731
Old Town Library 812
Patten Free Library 1523
Peabody Memorial Library 813, 823
Pembroke Library Association 824
Pittsfield Public Library 814
Porter Memorial Library 815
Stephen Phillips Memorial Library 504
Thompson Free Library 816
Veterans Memorial Library 817
Waldoboro Public Library 818, 825
William A. Farnsworth Library and Art Museum
  505-508, 826, 1772
Wiscasset Public Library 819

MARYLAND
Alban Institute 727
American Medical Informatics Association 1411
American Pain Foundation 133, 1046, 1047
Anne Arundel County Public Library 2458
Boys and Girls Club of Annapolis, Bywater 135
Chesapeake Center for Youth Development 837
Citizens Planning and Housing Association 839
Enoch Pratt Free Library 840, 847, 877, 1075, 1908
Foundation of the ARC of the United States 1160
Friends of the Library Montgomery County 2149

Harwood Institute for Public Innovation 579
Maryland Regional Practitioners Network for Fathers
  and Families 878, 1766
National Coalition for Cancer Survivorship 66, 104,
  725, 1163
New Inc./Fourth World Movement 852
Nonprofit Resource Center 2418
Rachel Carson Council 841
Southern Maryland Child Care Resource Center 1040
Talbot County Free Library 1255
University of Maryland Foundation 582
Village Learning Place 842, 861

MASSACHUSETTS
American Antiquarian Society 39, 1564, 1588, 1752
American Library in Paris USA Foundation 2113
Balfour Gold Dusters 881
Boston Athenaeum 882
Boston College 1846
Boston Public Library 2247
Boston Public Library Foundation 910, 1234, 2144,
  2248
Boston University 907, 1597
Burndy Library 459
Concord Free Public Library 1421
Education Development Center 1443
Education Resources Institute 469, 525, 740, 883,
  908
Five College Center for East Asian Studies 1490
General Hospital Corporation 1172
Girls Coalition of Boston 1306
Harvard College Library 1904
Harvard University 1509, 1615, 1784
Higher Education Resource Center 879, 1527
Ipswich Public Library 888
Jewish Womens Archive 843, 951, 1797, 2255
John F. Kennedy Library Foundation 889, 894, 2250,
  2431
Leveraging Investments in Creativity 1812
Massachusetts Affordable Housing Alliance 890,
  899, 909
Massachusetts Institute of Technology 198
Massachusetts, Commonwealth of 2495
Morse Institute Library 897
Nantucket Atheneum 121
National Yiddish Book Center 460, 912, 1206
New England Forestry Foundation 2348
Northeast Document Conservation Center 163,
  1567-1570, 1890
Organic Center for Education and Promotion 1151,
  1152
SATELLIFE 236
Social Law Library 892
Springfield Library and Museums Association 836
Sterling and Francine Clark Art Institute 1379, 1571,
  2326
University of Massachusetts 2349
Visual Resources Association 169
W G B H Educational Foundation 1770
Western Massachusetts Regional Library System
  893
Womens International Network Foundation 560
Worcester Public Library 880

MAURITIUS
University of Mauritius 215

MEXICO
Fideicomiso Fondo para la Biodiversidad (Trust Fund
  for Biodiversity) 1451
Mexican Center for Philanthropy 471, 958-960, 990
Mexican Commission for the Defense and Promotion
  of Human Rights 1459
Mexican Council for Popular Savings and Credit
  (COMACREP) 1460
University of the Americas Foundation, Puebla 1480

MICHIGAN
Alma Public Library 926
Chandler Park Academy - Greenfield 1004
Charlevoix Public Library 944

NIGERIA

NORTH CAROLINA

NORTH DAKOTA

OHIO

OKLAHOMA

Oklahoma Department of Libraries 2509
Oklahoma Garden Clubs 2029
Phillips Theological Seminary 573
Pioneer Multi-County Library System 2026, 2515
Tulsa Library Trust 2033, 2035, 2036

OREGON
211 Info 2081
Banks Community Library, Friends of the 2046
Birth to Three 2037
Cedar Mill Community Library Association of
    Washington County 1236
Creswell Public Library Foundation 2038, 2062
Curry Public Library District 2063
Disability Navigators 2064
Dora Sitkum Rural Fire Protection District 2065
Douglas County Library Foundation 2082
Elgin Public Library 2039
Elgin, City of 2066
Estacada Public Library 2093
Estacada Public Library Foundation 2040, 2067,
    2083
Forest Grove Library Foundation 2047
Harney County Library Foundation 2048
Independence Public Library, Friends of the 2084
Jackson County Library Services 2069
Jefferson County Library District 2070
Klamath County Library Foundation 2071
La Grande Community Library Foundation 2049
Lewis and Clark College 1052
Libraries of Eastern Oregon 2094
Library Foundation 2072, 2095
North Plains Public Library, Friends of the 2050,
    2085
Oregon Child Care Resource and Referral Network
    2086
Oregon Health Access Project 2087
Oregon Partnership 2051, 2088
Pacific University 2453
Phoenix Library, Friends of the 2073
Port Orford Public Library Foundation 2041, 2052
Siletz Valley Friends of the Library 2042, 2053
SMG Foundation 2089
Stayton Public Library Foundation 2043, 2054,
    2074, 2090
Sutherlin, City of 2044, 2075
Talent Library, Friends of the 2055, 2076
Tillamook County Library Foundation 2056, 2091
Trappist Abbey of Our Lady of Guadalupe 2077
Union County Library District 2078
Washington County Cooperative Library Services
    2079
Winston Area Community Partnership 2045, 2058,
    2092, 2096

PENNSYLVANIA
3 Rivers Connect 2175, 2176, 2184, 2189, 2202
Action AIDS 2209
Allegheny County Library Association 2142, 2177,
    2190, 2214
Allentown Public Library 2221
Arcadia University 1690
Athenaeum of Philadelphia 1505, 1506
Berks County Public Libraries 2463
Bethlehem Area Public Library 677
Biblical Theological Seminary 562
Bucks County Free Library 2464
Carnegie Library of Homestead 2178
Carnegie Library of Homewood 2179
Carnegie Library of Pittsburgh 2098, 2163, 2170,
    2171, 2180, 2186, 2191, 2201, 2215
Carnegie Library of Pittsburgh Foundation 2145
Carnegie Mellon University 2192, 2193
Chartiers Valley Partnership 2198, 2203
Chemical Heritage Foundation 252
Chester County Cares 2152
Cleve J. Fredricksen Library 2441, 2442
Dauphin County Library System 1757, 2443, 2444
Easttown Library 2210
Elkland Area Community Library 895
Episcopal Academy 2118

Exeter Community Library 2133
Focus on Renewal Sto-Rox Neighborhood Corporation
    2181
Free Library of Philadelphia 585, 2119, 2609
Free Library of Philadelphia Foundation 738, 1501,
    2148, 2206
Generations on Line 692
Haverford Township Free Library Association 2207
HERS Foundation 2211
Hughesville Public Library 2159
Institute for Research, Education, and Training in
    Addictions (IRETA) 589
Ligonier Valley Library 2172
Manchester Craftsmens Guild 2204
Media Tank 1458, 2212
Northumberland, Borough of 2160
OASIS Institute 2167, 2182, 2216
OMG Center for Collaborative Learning 670, 1878
Penn Hills Library Foundation 2183
Pennsylvania Trolley Museum 2205
Philadelphia Museum of Art 2208
Phoenixville Public Library 2134
Pittsburgh Dance Alloy 2200
Politz Hebrew Academy of Northeast Philadelphia
    2154
Rodef Shalom Temple 2217
Rosenbach Museum and Library 2135, 2213
Rostraver Public Library 2173, 2218
Saint Charles Borromeo Seminary 2155
Slatington Public Library 2222
Southern Lehigh Public Library 2223
Unemployment Information Center 2156
Union County Library System 2161
United States Catholic Conference 2111
United Way of Allegheny County 2187
University of Pennsylvania 1202
West End Library 2162
Westminster College 2174
Wireless Neighborhoods 2188
Wyoming Seminary 1213
York County Library System 2546

PERU
Centro Peruano de Audicion Lenguaje y Aprendizaje
    1541

PHILIPPINES
Health Action Information Network 281
Ramon Magsaysay Award Foundation 1805
University of the Philippines 1481

PUERTO RICO
Fundacion Luis Munoz Marin 611, 1161
Puerto Rico Department of Health 1195
University of the Sacred Heart 1166

RHODE ISLAND
Ashaway Free Library 2225
Brown University 43, 1696
Central Falls Free Public Library 2226
Community College of Rhode Island 2227
Cooperating Libraries Automated Network (CLAN)
    2228
East Providence Public Library 2229
Exeter Public Library, Friends of 2249
Foster Public Library 2230
Jesse M. Smith Memorial Library 2231
Memorial and Library Association of Westerly 586,
    2232
Newport Public Library 2233
North Kingstown Free Library 2234
North Providence Union Free Library 2235
Organic Center 1150
Portsmouth Free Public Library 2236, 2259
Providence Athenaeum 2237
Providence Public Library 1251, 1737, 2224,
    2238-2241, 2251, 2252, 2258
Redwood Library and Athenaeum 683-685, 968,
    2242, 2260, 2261
Rhode Island Department of Health 1197
Rhode Island Natural History Survey 2256, 2257

Rhode Island Parent Information Network 855
Rhode Island Supreme Court 2243
South Kingstown Public Library 2244
Warwick Public Library 2245
West Warwick Public Library System 2246

ROMANIA
Romanian Donors Forum 994

RUSSIA
Agency for Social Information 971
Center for Information Research 662
Charities Aid Foundation-Russia 2101
Objective Reality Foundation 1468
Russia Donors Forum 671
Saratov Legal Reform Project 672

SLOVAKIA
Slovak Donors Forum 995

SOUTH AFRICA
Centre for Higher Education Transformation Trust
    1312
Charities Aid Foundation-Southern Africa 977, 1438
Foundation for Library and Information Service
    Development 1315, 1612
Johannesburg, City of 1319
Nelson Mandela Foundation 1465
Saint Augustine College of South Africa 511
South African National Biodiversity Institute 1647
University of Cape Town 1652, 1653
University of KwaZulu-Natal 1657
University of the Western Cape 1482
University of the Witwatersrand 1660

SOUTH CAROLINA
Georgetown County Memorial Hospital 1927
Greenville County Library 2481
South Carolina State Library 2526
United Way of the Piedmont 2262
University of South Carolina Research Foundation
    1933, 1934

SOUTH DAKOTA
Phoebe Apperson Hearst Library 1273
Sinte Gleska University 1268
South Dakota State Library 2527
University of South Dakota 860

SPAIN
Instituto Educacion Secundaria Antonio Jose
    Cavanilles 2108

SWEDEN
Stiftelsen Studio Emad Eddin 1474
Swedish Museum of Natural History 1649

SWITZERLAND
Conservatoire et Jardin Botaniques 1606
Habitat International Coalition 1455

TANZANIA
Tropical Pesticides Research Institute 1650

TENNESSEE
Attachment Parenting International 593
Center for Southern Folklore 2263
Charter School Resource Center of Tennessee 2277,
    2278
Conexion Americas 2272, 2273
Grant Center 2264, 2265, 2270, 2279, 2280, 2282
Health and Education Research Operative Services
    (HEROS) 1517
Knox County Public Library, Friends of the 2016
Linebaugh Public Library 2269

SUBJECT INDEX

Deaf/hearing impaired, public affairs/government 1613

Denmark, international affairs/development 1445

Depression, children/youth 1891

Depression, electronic media/online services 1891

Depression, mentally disabled 1891

Depression, publication 1891

Developing countries, arts/culture/humanities 1526

Developing countries, community improvement/development 557, 1361, 1767

Developing countries, education 1619

Developing countries, environment 542, 972

Developing countries, health—general 236, 1526

Developing countries, health—specific diseases 236, 1526

Developing countries, international affairs/development 236, 1361, 1433, 1619, 1767

Developing countries, public affairs/government 236, 542, 557, 972, 1433, 1619

Developmentally disabled, centers & services 1160

Developmentally disabled, electronic media/online services 1160

Diagnostic imaging 2372

Disabilities, people with, arts/culture/humanities 1695

Disabilities, people with, civil rights 1049, 1952

Disabilities, people with, education 803, 823, 911, 940, 1146, 1695, 1740, 1952, 2078, 2299, 2304, 2311

Disabilities, people with, environment 903

Disabilities, people with, health—general 510, 635, 903, 1049, 2110, 2361

Disabilities, people with, health—specific diseases 2110

Disabilities, people with, housing/shelter 430

Disabilities, people with, human services—multipurpose 111, 372, 510, 739, 911, 919, 1146, 1299, 1385, 1538, 1679, 1740, 1741, 1786, 1952, 2064, 2299, 2306, 2361, 2364, 2449, 2578

Disabilities, people with, mental health/substance abuse 903, 919

Disabilities, people with, philanthropy/voluntarism 70

Disabilities, people with, public affairs/government 635, 2299, 2311

Disabilities, people with, safety/disaster relief 70, 510

Disasters, aging 70

Disasters, building/renovation 416, 1191, 2065

Disasters, children/youth 528, 799, 849

Disasters, collections management/preservation 2205

Disasters, debt reduction 2205

Disasters, disabilities, people with 70

Disasters, domestic resettlement 1042

Disasters, economically disadvantaged 799, 849, 1042, 2111

Disasters, electronic media/online services 1042, 1853

Disasters, faculty/staff development 798

Disasters, fire prevention/control 2065

Disasters, floods 2111

Disasters, Hurricane Katrina 528, 797-800, 848, 849, 1042, 1191, 1648, 1853, 2396

Disasters, preparedness/services 70, 416, 1190, 2205

Disasters, program evaluation 1190

Disasters, research 848, 2396

Disasters, seed money 1042

Dispute resolution 1353, 1879

Dispute resolution, income development 1879

Domestic violence, children/youth 1022, 2367

Domestic violence, crime/abuse victims 568, 943, 1022, 1211, 2367

Domestic violence, minorities 568

Domestic violence, women 568, 943, 1022, 1211, 2367

Drawing, collections acquisition 1512

Early childhood education, African Americans/Blacks 1034

Early childhood education, children 1367

Early childhood education, curriculum development 631

Early childhood education, economically disadvantaged 847, 955, 1034, 1282, 2112

Early childhood education, faculty/staff development 631, 643, 1061, 1066

Early childhood education, Hispanics/Latinos 2112

Early childhood education, immigrants/refugees 389, 1034

Early childhood education, infants/toddlers 389, 424, 631, 643, 847, 955, 1034, 1061, 1066, 1282, 1363, 1367, 2112, 2178

Early childhood education, minorities 389, 1282

Early childhood education, research 631, 1066

Eastern Europe, community improvement/development 979

Eastern Europe, environment 1888

Eastern Europe, international affairs/development 442, 980, 1888

Eastern Europe, philanthropy/voluntarism 442, 979, 985

Eastern Europe, public affairs/government 1888

Economic development 181, 333, 561, 582, 1451, 1460, 1488, 2312, 2537

Economic development, Asians/Pacific Islanders 1488

Economic development, children/youth 181

Economic development, economically disadvantaged 181, 1488

Economic development, electronic media/online services 561, 582, 2312

Economic development, immigrants/refugees 1488

Economic development, research 582, 1451

Economically disadvantaged, arts/culture/humanities 924, 945, 1428, 1458, 2204

Economically disadvantaged, civil rights 547, 1427, 1428, 1458, 1485, 1663

Economically disadvantaged, community improvement/development 181, 839, 844, 845, 849, 852, 854, 866, 963, 1333, 1342, 1348, 1349, 1356, 1361, 1372, 1454-1456, 1461, 1466, 1488, 1550, 1746, 1767, 2060, 2275

Economically disadvantaged, crime/courts/legal services 627, 679, 855, 900, 1323, 1399

Economically disadvantaged, education 109, 457, 837, 847, 853, 861, 879, 908, 914, 924, 945, 955, 978, 1034, 1078, 1281, 1282, 1284, 1340, 1360, 1407, 1408, 1488, 1527, 1664, 1870, 2079, 2112, 2125, 2147, 2177, 2204, 2267, 2296, 2301, 2304, 2311, 2414-2416

Economically disadvantaged, employment 77, 91, 247, 314, 550, 551, 570, 616, 838, 845, 890, 1340, 1663, 1673, 2156, 2448, 2451, 2567

Economically disadvantaged, environment 144, 543, 547, 1456

Economically disadvantaged, food/nutrition/agriculture 963, 1040, 1349, 1984, 2015, 2434

Economically disadvantaged, health—general 72, 87, 89, 91, 92, 94, 95, 173, 236, 335, 341, 547, 549, 687, 1040, 1051, 1176, 1205, 1284, 1427, 1428, 1441, 1666, 1667, 1807-1809, 1936, 1942, 1954, 2087, 2156, 2416, 2422, 2429, 2434

Economically disadvantaged, health—specific diseases 87, 236, 1666, 1667, 1940

Economically disadvantaged, housing/shelter 108, 144, 183, 353, 354, 363, 530, 624, 669, 890, 899-902, 909, 1042, 1073, 1076, 1455, 1813, 1816, 1876, 1911, 1914, 2156, 2452, 2500

Economically disadvantaged, human services—multipurpose 107, 181, 187, 220, 325, 352, 363, 394, 408, 551, 570, 645, 646, 799, 837, 845, 847, 852-855, 860-862, 909, 919, 955, 978, 1008, 1019, 1020, 1023, 1024, 1036, 1045, 1059, 1084, 1176, 1228, 1293, 1323, 1340, 1348, 1373, 1377, 1399, 1485, 1488, 1544, 1666, 1667, 1824, 1885, 1940, 2015, 2087, 2106, 2111, 2147, 2152, 2292, 2306, 2338, 2342, 2393, 2407, 2415, 2416, 2429, 2434, 2448, 2450, 2541, 2574, 2610

Economically disadvantaged, international affairs/development 236, 543, 866, 1333, 1340, 1342, 1348, 1349, 1356, 1361, 1372, 1427, 1428, 1454, 1456, 1550, 1767, 1809

Economically disadvantaged, membership benefit groups 695

Economically disadvantaged, mental health/substance abuse 799, 837, 919, 2416

Economically disadvantaged, philanthropy/voluntarism 1485

Economically disadvantaged, public affairs/government 72, 107, 109, 144, 183, 220, 236, 352, 408, 695, 838, 839, 1032, 1045, 1051, 1323, 1372, 1373, 1399, 1454, 1458, 1673, 2156, 2296, 2311, 2393, 2448, 2450, 2451

Economically disadvantaged, religion 2407

Economically disadvantaged, safety/disaster relief 799, 849, 1042, 2111

Economically disadvantaged, social sciences 860

Economically disadvantaged, youth development 2296, 2301

Economics 1159, 1335, 1350, 1858, 2098, 2457

Economics, curriculum development 1350

Economics, management development/capacity building 2098

Economics, research 2098

Education, administration/regulation 1884

Education, Africa 907, 1312, 1325, 1619, 1655, 2219

Education, African Americans/Blacks 743, 1596, 1626, 1979

Education, aging 269, 1525, 2078, 2167, 2182, 2216, 2315

Education, alumni groups 312, 345, 633, 1852

Education, Argentina 1469, 2097

Education, Asia 1470, 1486, 1487, 1490

Education, Asians/Pacific Islanders 1488

Education, association 467, 1106, 1297, 1642, 2094, 2177, 2190, 2386

Education, Austria 415

Education, awards/prizes/competitions 2386, 2389, 2468

Education, Azerbaijan 1763

Education, Bahamas 1397

Education, building/renovation 10, 57, 81, 237, 300, 417, 443, 513, 592, 606, 711, 723, 749, 753, 757, 759, 821, 837, 898, 916, 1037, 1060, 1063, 1082, 1121, 1136, 1156, 1158, 1527, 1618, 1745, 1920, 1938, 2038, 2040-2042, 2047-2050, 2052-2056, 2062, 2067, 2071, 2073, 2074, 2076, 2085, 2090, 2091, 2104, 2122, 2126, 2154, 2289, 2332, 2552, 2564, 2611

Education, Canada 160, 969, 1514, 2141, 2384, 2385

Education, capital campaigns 172, 182, 311, 324, 539, 822, 1043, 1058, 1120, 1210, 1671, 2082, 2095, 2183, 2198, 2436, 2563

Education, children 978, 1006, 1187, 1407, 1408, 1787, 2090, 2182

Education, children/youth 10, 110, 237, 239, 269, 296, 466, 539, 724, 837, 850, 851, 853, 856, 857, 910, 1017, 1078, 1139, 1146, 1307, 1320, 1336, 1364, 1368-1370, 1487, 1517, 1541, 1561, 1695, 1740, 1802, 1882, 1979, 2071, 2122, 2144, 2154, 2167, 2216, 2247, 2299, 2305, 2340, 2341, 2343, 2356, 2368, 2375, 2416

Education, Chile 1371, 1546, 1547

Education, China 1338, 1343, 1351-1353, 1357-1359, 1486, 1542

Education, China & Mongolia 2324

Education, collections acquisition 458, 1006, 1058, 1281, 1482, 2123, 2356

Education, collections management/preservation 1599

Education, community/cooperative 1336

Education, computer systems/equipment 16, 231, 350, 351, 722, 784, 790, 896, 2228, 2296, 2301, 2311, 2318, 2334

Education, conferences/seminars 203, 215, 328, 978, 2423

Education, continuing education 828, 1971, 2590

Education, crime/abuse victims 837

Education, curriculum development 199, 213, 214, 217, 631, 784, 1334, 1487, 1525, 1584, 1882

2502, 2504, 2505, 2509-2513, 2526, 2527,
2530, 2531, 2538, 2540, 2551, 2585
Electronic media/online services, religion 728, 2253
Electronic media/online services, safety/disaster
relief 1042, 1853
Electronic media/online services, science 193, 199,
213, 214, 258, 1479, 1585, 1593, 1594,
1598, 1605, 1606, 1623, 1631-1638,
1643-1645, 1647, 1649, 1650, 1652,
1656-1659, 1661, 1852, 1877
Electronic media/online services, social sciences
662, 693, 1443, 1597, 1797, 2253, 2585
Electronic media/online services, youth development
2296
Elementary school/education 20, 80, 137, 374,
453, 457, 675, 713, 718, 784, 949, 950, 978,
1006, 1407, 1408, 1698, 1955, 2180, 2182,
2352, 2358, 2416, 2554
Elementary school/education, aging 2182
Elementary school/education, building/renovation
137, 374, 1955, 2358
Elementary school/education, children 20, 137,
453, 457, 978, 1006, 1407, 1408, 1698,
2180, 2182, 2352, 2554
Elementary school/education, children/youth 675,
2416
Elementary school/education, collections acquisition
137, 675, 950, 1006, 2554
Elementary school/education, computer systems/
equipment 784, 1955, 2358
Elementary school/education, conferences/
seminars 978
Elementary school/education, curriculum
development 675, 784
Elementary school/education, economically
disadvantaged 457, 978, 1407, 1408, 2416
Elementary school/education, electronic media/
online services 2352
Elementary school/education, equipment 784, 949
Elementary school/education, faculty/staff
development 675
Elementary school/education, income development
1407
Elementary school/education, minorities 457, 2416
Elementary school/education, publication 2352
Elementary/secondary education 37, 56, 79, 90,
110, 194, 196, 199, 219, 296, 301, 334, 367,
368, 386, 468, 707, 726, 850, 927, 1017,
1062, 1078, 1142, 1154, 1260, 1318, 1336,
1364, 1368-1370, 1486, 1487, 1490, 1697,
1882, 1952, 2032, 2107, 2115, 2118, 2132,
2143, 2144, 2153, 2154, 2189, 2216, 2247,
2267, 2268, 2277, 2278, 2415, 2428, 2437,
2508, 2533, 2561
Elementary/secondary education, aging 2216
Elementary/secondary education, building/
renovation 56, 726, 927, 2107, 2115, 2118,
2132, 2154
Elementary/secondary education, children/youth 56,
90, 110, 296, 386, 707, 726, 850, 1017, 1062,
1078, 1260, 1318, 1336, 1364, 1368-1370,
1486, 1487, 1490, 1882, 1952, 2032, 2107,
2115, 2118, 2132, 2144, 2154, 2189, 2216,
2247, 2267, 2268, 2415, 2428, 2437
Elementary/secondary education, collections
acquisition 726, 1260, 2132, 2153, 2437
Elementary/secondary education, computer
systems/equipment 1260
Elementary/secondary education, conferences/
seminars 707
Elementary/secondary education, curriculum
development 199, 1487, 1882
Elementary/secondary education, disabilities,
people with 1952
Elementary/secondary education, economically
disadvantaged 1078, 2267, 2415
Elementary/secondary education, electronic media/
online services 79, 199, 1318
Elementary/secondary education, equipment 296,
726, 2032, 2153, 2561
Elementary/secondary education, faculty/staff
development 1260
Elementary/secondary education, infants/toddlers
301

Elementary/secondary education, minorities 301,
2267, 2415
Elementary/secondary education, research 368,
850
Elementary/secondary education, seed money 2153
Elementary/secondary education, youth 2143
Elementary/secondary school reform 38, 221, 329,
432, 1496, 1517, 1815, 2505, 2583, 2589
Elementary/secondary school reform, children/youth
1517
Elementary/secondary school reform, electronic
media/online services 221, 1815, 2505
Elementary/secondary school reform, minorities 329
Elementary/secondary school reform, program
evaluation 1517
Elementary/secondary school reform, publication
2583
Elementary/secondary school reform, research 1517
Elementary/secondary school reform, seed money
221
Elementary/secondary school reform, youth 329
Employment, aging 17
Employment, children/youth 845
Employment, computer systems/equipment 570,
722
Employment, conferences/seminars 531
Employment, economically disadvantaged 77, 91,
247, 314, 550, 551, 570, 616, 845, 1340,
1663, 1673, 2156, 2451, 2567
Employment, electronic media/online services 447,
1583
Employment, equal rights 447
Employment, Global programs 2451
Employment, homeless 1030
Employment, immigrants/refugees 1663
Employment, India 1340
Employment, information services 77, 247, 314,
399, 447, 531, 550, 551, 570, 616, 876, 1039,
1258, 1551, 1583, 1663, 1673, 2156, 2567
Employment, Israel 1663
Employment, Jamaica 2105
Employment, job counseling 531, 876, 1258, 1551
Employment, labor unions/organizations 550, 838,
890, 2448, 2451
Employment, LGBTQ 447
Employment, management development/capacity
building 570, 1663, 2105
Employment, management/technical aid 91, 2451
Employment, migrant workers 1663
Employment, minorities 550, 551, 570, 1663, 2451
Employment, public education 2156
Employment, publication 1673
Employment, research 2105
Employment, services 17, 77, 247, 314, 399, 616,
797, 800, 845, 1039, 2105, 2158, 2476, 2567
Employment, single parents 531, 876, 1258, 1551
Employment, training 722, 1030, 1340, 1834
Employment, women 247, 531, 550, 845, 876,
1258, 1340, 1551
Employment, youth 1834, 2105, 2476
Energy, economically disadvantaged 144
Energy, electronic media/online services 561
Energy, publication 142
Energy, seed money 139
Engineering 1159
Engineering school/education 1357-1359
Engineering school/education, curriculum
development 1357-1359
Engineering/technology 462, 1877
Engineering/technology, electronic media/online
services 1877
England, animals/wildlife 2131
England, arts/culture/humanities 1470, 1478,
1599, 2131
England, education 157, 201, 1470, 1498,
1599-1601, 1697, 2114, 2131
England, environment 259, 1637, 1638, 1643-1645
England, health—general 1437, 2099
England, health—specific diseases 1426, 1437
England, housing/shelter 2099
England, human services—multipurpose 1437
England, international affairs/development 976,
2293, 2294

England, philanthropy/voluntarism 112, 366, 440,
441, 614, 615, 698, 699, 886, 887, 976, 1214,
1217, 1291, 1292, 1400, 1402-1405, 1419,
1420, 1436, 1543, 1677, 1776, 1845, 2099
England, public affairs/government 201, 1470,
1478, 1600, 1637, 1638, 2099
England, recreation/sports/athletics 2294
England, science 259, 271, 1637, 1638,
1643-1645
Environment, Africa 1456, 1593, 1594, 1598, 1605,
1606, 1623, 1631-1638, 1643-1645, 1647,
1649, 1650, 1652, 1656-1659, 1661
Environment, Belgium 1634
Environment, Bolivia 256
Environment, Canada 1850
Environment, Caribbean 1857
Environment, children 2352
Environment, China 140-142
Environment, computer systems/equipment 253,
2191
Environment, conferences/seminars 1444, 1861
Environment, Developing countries 542, 972
Environment, disabilities, people with 903
Environment, Eastern Europe 1888
Environment, economically disadvantaged 144
Environment, electronic media/online services 278,
561, 1593, 1594, 1598, 1605, 1606, 1623,
1631-1638, 1643-1645, 1647, 1649, 1650,
1652, 1656-1659, 1661, 2346, 2348, 2352,
2569
Environment, endowments 1413
Environment, energy 139-144, 561, 1762
Environment, England 259, 1637, 1638, 1643-1645
Environment, forests 279, 465, 2348
Environment, formal/general education 148, 1154
Environment, France 1593, 1594, 1632, 1633,
1658, 1659
Environment, Germany 1598
Environment, Global programs 145, 253, 255, 259,
284, 285, 561, 863, 1272, 1413, 1848, 1850,
1855, 1857, 1860, 1861, 2195, 2346, 2370
Environment, global warming 561, 657, 1760, 1874
Environment, income development 1413, 1879
Environment, India 1444
Environment, information services 139-141, 144,
145, 253, 255, 259, 278, 279, 285, 433, 542,
553, 554, 561, 649, 841, 863, 903, 906, 922,
937, 972, 973, 981, 993, 996, 1119, 1269,
1413, 1444, 1593, 1594, 1598, 1605, 1606,
1623, 1631-1638, 1643-1645, 1647, 1649,
1650, 1652, 1656-1659, 1661, 1773-1775,
1848, 1850, 1855, 1857, 1860, 1861, 1879,
2195, 2256, 2346, 2348, 2352, 2370
Environment, Ireland 1656
Environment, Italy 1605
Environment, Kenya 1456
Environment, land resources 996, 1879, 2256,
2570
Environment, Lebanon 1431
Environment, management development/capacity
building 255, 285, 1413
Environment, management/technical aid 142, 256,
284, 993, 996, 1270, 2256, 2257
Environment, Mexico 1451
Environment, Middle East 1431
Environment, Namibia 1635
Environment, Native Americans/American Indians
552, 1761
Environment, natural resources 244, 255, 256, 278,
285, 287, 333, 337, 543, 547, 863, 906, 922,
1154, 1271, 1413, 1431, 1444, 1451, 1456,
1774, 1888, 2370, 2591
Environment, Netherlands 1661
Environment, Pakistan 543
Environment, Peru 256
Environment, plant conservation 259, 1593, 1594,
1598, 1605, 1606, 1623, 1631-1633,
1635-1638, 1643-1645, 1647, 1649, 1650,
1652, 1656-1659, 1661
Environment, pollution control 937
Environment, public education 414, 1298, 2352
Environment, public policy 561, 993, 996, 1044,
1874, 2569, 2570
Environment, publication 142, 906, 1774, 2352

Residential/custodial care, crime/abuse victims 2147, 2150
Residential/custodial care, curriculum development 2147
Residential/custodial care, economically disadvantaged 2147
Residential/custodial care, minorities 2147
Residential/custodial care, senior continuing care 690
Roman Catholic agencies & churches 2077
Roman Catholic agencies & churches, building/renovation 2077
Romania, philanthropy/voluntarism 994
Rural development 568, 963, 1456, 1807, 2348
Rural development, crime/abuse victims 568
Rural development, economically disadvantaged 963, 1456, 1807
Rural development, electronic media/online services 2348
Rural development, indigenous people 1456
Rural development, minorities 568
Rural development, women 568
Russia, arts/culture/humanities 1468, 1889
Russia, community improvement/development 2101
Russia, crime/courts/legal services 662, 672
Russia, education 1889
Russia, environment 1889
Russia, health—general 1354, 1437, 2099
Russia, health—specific diseases 1354, 1437
Russia, housing/shelter 2099
Russia, human services—multipurpose 1437
Russia, international affairs/development 662, 1354, 1889
Russia, philanthropy/voluntarism 615, 671, 971, 985, 1436, 2099
Russia, public affairs/government 662, 1468
Russia, social sciences 662, 672

Safety, aging 510
Safety, automotive safety 386
Safety, children/youth 386
Safety, disabilities, people with 510
Safety, education 510
Safety, equipment 510
Safety, faculty/staff development 510
Safety, Native Americans/American Indians 552
Safety, poisons 552
Safety, research 552
Safety/disasters, aging 70
Safety/disasters, disabilities, people with 70
Safety/disasters, electronic media/online services 1853
Safety/disasters, equal rights 70
Safety/disasters, information services 70, 1853
Safety/disasters, management/technical aid 1849
Scholarship funds, arts/culture/humanities 312, 868, 1472
Scholarship funds, education 312, 868, 1472, 1699, 2353
Scholarship funds, health—general 2608
Scholarship funds, philanthropy/voluntarism 541
Scholarships/financial aid 24, 469, 525, 883
Science 199, 258, 271, 287, 462, 1159, 1305, 1352, 1986, 2154, 2358
Science, administration/regulation 1861
Science, Africa 1593, 1594, 1598, 1605, 1606, 1623, 1631-1638, 1643-1645, 1647, 1649, 1650, 1652, 1656-1659, 1661
Science, Belgium 1634
Science, building/renovation 2154, 2358
Science, Canada 263, 1850
Science, Caribbean 1857
Science, children/youth 1986, 2154, 2351
Science, China 1352, 1357-1359
Science, computer systems/equipment 2358
Science, conferences/seminars 271, 1861
Science, curriculum development 199
Science, electronic media/online services 193, 199, 258, 1852
Science, England 259, 271, 1637, 1638, 1643-1645
Science, equal rights 1856
Science, fellowships 1352

Science, France 1593, 1594, 1632, 1633, 1658, 1659
Science, Germany 1598
Science, Global programs 253, 259, 262, 271, 1848, 1850, 1852, 1855, 1857, 1860, 1861
Science, India 1479
Science, information services 74, 193, 260, 262, 263, 271, 1852, 1859, 1874, 2059, 2109, 2351
Science, Ireland 1656
Science, Italy 1605
Science, management/technical aid 1860
Science, minorities 2109
Science, Namibia 1635
Science, Netherlands 1661
Science, public education 2351
Science, public policy 271
Science, research 193, 260, 262, 263, 1848, 1850, 2568
Science, seed money 1856
Science, South Africa 1647, 1652, 1657
Science, Sweden 1649
Science, Switzerland 1606
Science, Tanzania 1650
Science, Venezuela 1857
Science, women 74, 1856, 2059, 2109
Science, Zimbabwe 1636
Secondary school/education 59, 64, 418, 455, 456, 1283, 1334, 1346, 1480, 1755, 1973, 2104, 2105, 2116, 2476
Secondary school/education, building/renovation 59, 418, 456, 1973, 2104
Secondary school/education, collections acquisition 64
Secondary school/education, curriculum development 1334
Secondary school/education, electronic media/online services 1334, 1480
Secondary school/education, faculty/staff development 1480
Secondary school/education, girls 456
Secondary school/education, management development/capacity building 2105
Secondary school/education, minorities 456
Secondary school/education, research 2105
Secondary school/education, seed money 64
Secondary school/education, youth 59, 64, 418, 455, 1334, 1346, 2104, 2105, 2116, 2476
Senior continuing care, aging 690
Senior continuing care, research 690
Serbia, health—general 1051
Serbia, public affairs/government 1051
Single parents, employment 531, 876, 1258, 1551
Skin disorders 636
Skin disorders, collections acquisition 636
Slovakia, philanthropy/voluntarism 995
Smoking, research 831
Social entrepreneurship 1101, 1366, 2577
Social entrepreneurship, conferences/seminars 2577
Social entrepreneurship, electronic media/online services 1101
Social sciences 511, 666, 1201
Social sciences, Africa 907
Social sciences, aging 693
Social sciences, Argentina 1469
Social sciences, Asia 1486, 1487, 1490, 1597
Social sciences, Bolivia 256
Social sciences, China 1486
Social sciences, collections acquisition 511, 1509
Social sciences, collections management/preservation 1201, 1509
Social sciences, electronic media/online services 693, 2253
Social sciences, Europe 662
Social sciences, Global programs 262, 662, 1604, 1817, 1855, 2310
Social sciences, information services 693
Social sciences, interdisciplinary studies 1509, 2253
Social sciences, internship funds 693
Social sciences, Ireland 1350
Social sciences, Israel 2253
Social sciences, Italy 1509

Social sciences, Nigeria 666
Social sciences, Peru 256
Social sciences, Philippines 281
Social sciences, Poland 1335
Social sciences, research 1201
Social sciences, Russia 662, 672
Social sciences, South Africa 511
Social sciences, Southeast Asia 1581
Social sciences, United Kingdom 1094
Social work school/education 1525
Social work school/education, aging 1525
Social work school/education, curriculum development 1525
South Africa, arts/culture/humanities 511, 1465, 1660
South Africa, civil rights 1465, 1653
South Africa, community improvement/development 1438
South Africa, crime/courts/legal services 1653
South Africa, education 215, 511, 1312, 1315, 1319, 1465, 1482, 1612, 1653, 1660
South Africa, environment 1647, 1652, 1657
South Africa, international affairs/development 1465
South Africa, philanthropy/voluntarism 977, 1438
South Africa, public affairs/government 215, 1647, 1652, 1657, 1660
South Africa, science 1647, 1652, 1657
South Africa, social sciences 511
Southeast Asia, education 1581
Southeast Asia, health—general 1481
Southeast Asia, social sciences 1581
Soviet Union (Former), arts/culture/humanities 1889
Soviet Union (Former), education 1889
Soviet Union (Former), environment 1888, 1889
Soviet Union (Former), international affairs/development 1888, 1889
Soviet Union (Former), public affairs/government 1888
Spain, arts/culture/humanities 514
Spain, education 514, 2108
Speech/hearing centers 1541
Speech/hearing centers, children/youth 1541
Speech/hearing centers, deaf/hearing impaired 1541
Speech/hearing centers, equipment 1541
Student aid, education 1870
Student services/organizations 1147, 1881
Student services/organizations, collections acquisition 1881
Student services/organizations, curriculum development 1881
Student services/organizations, faculty/staff development 1881
Sub-Saharan Africa, education 1810
Sub-Saharan Africa, food/nutrition/agriculture 1810
Sub-Saharan Africa, public affairs/government 1810
Substance abuse, children/youth 1173, 2051
Substance abuse, film/video/radio 2276
Substance abuse, prevention 603, 2088
Substance abuse, program evaluation 1193
Substance abuse, publication 2276
Substance abuse, research 1193
Substance abuse, services 2027, 2051, 2276
Substance abuse, treatment 589, 1173, 1193
Substance abuse, youth 2088
Substance abusers, community improvement/development 1173
Substance abusers, education 589
Substance abusers, health—general 1173, 1193, 2030, 2051, 2276, 2313
Substance abusers, health—specific diseases 589, 1173, 2313
Substance abusers, mental health/substance abuse 589, 1173, 1193, 2027, 2051, 2088, 2276
Sweden, arts/culture/humanities 1474
Sweden, environment 1649
Sweden, public affairs/government 1649
Sweden, science 1649
Switzerland, community improvement/development 1455
Switzerland, environment 1606
Switzerland, housing/shelter 1455
Switzerland, public affairs/government 1606

FOUNDATIONS

The following is an alphabetical list of foundations appearing in this volume, including any geographic restrictions on the foundation's giving program. A full listing of geographic, program, and type of support limitations is provided with the full listing of each foundation's grants in Section 1. Please read these limitations carefully, as well as reading additional program and application information available in the foundation's report or other Foundation Center products, before applying for grant assistance. Foundations in bold face are among the 100 largest.

3M Foundation
3M Ctr., Bldg. 225-1S-23
St. Paul, MN 55144-1000 (651) 733-0144
FAX: (651) 737-3061; E-mail: cfkleven@mmm.com;
URL: http://www.3Mgiving.com
Limitations: Giving on a national and international basis in areas of company operations.

Abbott Laboratories Fund
100 Abbott Park Rd., D379/AP6D
Abbott Park, IL 60064-3500 (847) 937-7075
URL: http://www.abbott.com/global/url/content/ en_US/40.80:80/general_content/ General_Content_00070.htm
Limitations: Giving primarily in areas of company operations.

The Abell Foundation, Inc.
111 S. Calvert St., Ste. 2300
Baltimore, MD 21202-6174 (410) 547-1300
FAX: (410) 539-6579; E-mail: abell@abell.org;
URL: http://www.abell.org
Limitations: Giving limited to MD, with emphasis on Baltimore.
Publishes an annual or periodic report.

Abell-Hanger Foundation
P.O. Box 430
Midland, TX 79702 (432) 684-6655
FAX: (432) 684-4474; E-mail: AHF@abell-hanger.org;
URL: http://www.abell-hanger.org
Limitations: Giving limited to TX, with emphasis within the Permian Basin.
Publishes an annual or periodic report.

Louis and Anne Abrons Foundation, Inc.
437 Madison Ave.
New York, NY 10017 (212) 756-3376
Limitations: Giving primarily in the metropolitan New York, NY, area.

AEGON Transamerica Foundation
c/o Tax Dept.
4333 Edgewood Rd., N.E.
Cedar Rapids, IA 52499-3210
Limitations: Giving on a national basis, with emphasis on areas of company operations.

The Aflac Foundation, Inc.
1932 Wynnton Rd.
Columbus, GA 31999
FAX: (706) 320-2288; E-mail: fmedley@aflac.com

Limitations: Giving primarily in areas of company operations, with emphasis on the greater Atlanta, GA, area.

The Ahmanson Foundation
9215 Wilshire Blvd.
Beverly Hills, CA 90210 (310) 278-0770
URL: http://www.theahmansonfoundation.org
Limitations: Giving primarily in southern CA, with emphasis on the Los Angeles area.
Publishes an annual or periodic report.

Akron Community Foundation
345 W. Cedar St.
Akron, OH 44307-2407 (330) 376-8522
FAX: (330) 376-0202;
E-mail: acfmail@akroncommunityfdn.org;
URL: http://www.akroncommunityfdn.org
Limitations: Giving primarily in Summit County, OH.
Publishes an annual or periodic report.

Alabama Power Foundation, Inc.
600 N. 18th St.
P.O. Box 2641
Birmingham, AL 35291-0011 (205) 257-2508
FAX: (205) 257-1860; URL: http:// www.southerncompany.com/alpower/ foundation
Limitations: Giving limited to AL.
Publishes an annual or periodic report.

Alcoa Foundation
Alcoa Corporate Ctr.
201 Isabella St.
Pittsburgh, PA 15212-5858 (412) 553-2348
E-mail: alcoafoundation@alcoa.com; URL: http:// www.alcoa.com/global/en/community/ foundation.asp
Limitations: Giving on a national and international basis in areas of company operations; giving also to national and international organizations.
Publishes an annual or periodic report.

The George I. Alden Trust
370 Main St.
Worcester, MA 01608-1779 (508) 798-8621
FAX: (508) 791-6454;
E-mail: trustees@aldentrust.org; Additional tel.: (508) 798-8621, ext. 3303; URL: http:// www.aldentrust.org
Limitations: Giving limited to NY, NJ, PA and the six New England states.
Publishes an annual or periodic report.

The Andrew Allen Charitable Foundation
c/o Thomas N. Long
P.O. Box 87
Cheyenne, WY 82003
Limitations: Giving in the U.S., primarily in PA and WY.

Altman Foundation
521 5th Ave., 35th Fl.
New York, NY 10175 (212) 682-0970
FAX: (212) 682-1648; URL: http:// www.altmanfoundation.org
Limitations: Giving limited to NY, with emphasis on the boroughs of New York City.
Publishes an annual or periodic report.

Amarillo Area Foundation, Inc.
801 S. Fillmore, Ste. 700
Amarillo, TX 79101 (806) 376-4521
FAX: (806) 873-3656; E-mail: haf@aaf-hf.org;
Additional tel.: (806) 373-8353; Additional
E-mail: kathie@aaf-hf.org; URL: http:// www.aaf-hf.org
Limitations: Giving limited to the Texas Panhandle region.
Publishes an annual or periodic report.

American Express Foundation
World Financial Ctr.
200 Vesey St., 48th Fl.
New York, NY 10285-4804 (212) 640-5661
Application addresses: Greensboro, NC: Laura T. Rhodes, Sr. Community Affairs Specialist, Philanthropy and Media, M.C. NC-06-03-10, American Express Svc. Ctr., 7701 Airport Center Dr., Greensboro, NC 27409, Cultural Heritage: Cheryl G. Rosario, Mgr., Philanthropic Prog., M.C. NY-01-48-04, American Express Co., 3 World Financial Ctr., New York, NY 10285, Economic Independence: Terry Savage, Dir., Philanthropic Prog., M.C. NY-01-48-04 American Express Co., 3 World Financial Ctr., New York, NY 10285, Community Service: Angela C. Woods, Dir., Philanthropic Prog., M.C. NY-01-48-04, American Express Co., 3 World Financial Ctr., New York, NY 10285, Phoenix, AZ: JoEllen L. Lynn, Mgr., Community Affairs, M.C. AZ-08-01-08, American Express Svc. Ctr., 20022 N. 31st Ave., Phoenix, AZ 85027, Salt Lake City, UT: Dorothy Anderson, Mgr., Community Affairs, M.C. UT-02-03-10, American Express Svc. Ctr., 4315 S. 2700 W., Salt Lake City, UT 84184, South FL (Ft. Lauderdale and Miami): Stacey L. Orange, Dir., Public Affairs and Comms., M.C. FL-05-02-16A, American Express Svc. Ctr., 777 American Expwy., Fort Lauderdale, FL 33337;

URL: http://home3.americanexpress.com/corp/
giving_back.asp
Limitations: Giving on a national and international
basis, including in Asia, Canada, the Caribbean,
Europe, and Latin America, with emphasis on
Phoenix, AZ, South FL, New York, NY,
Greensboro, NC, and Salt Lake City, UT.

Amgen Foundation, Inc.
1 Amgen Center Dr., M.S. 28-1-B
Thousand Oaks, CA 91320-1799
(805) 447-4056
FAX: (805) 449-6757;
E-mail: amgenfoundation@amgen.com;
URL: http://www.amgen.com/citizenship/
foundation.html
Limitations: Giving primarily in areas of company
operations in CA, CO, PR, RI, and WA; giving also
to regional and national organizations.
Publishes an annual or periodic report.

Fred C. and Katherine B. Andersen Foundation
P.O. Box 80
Bayport, MN 55003 (651) 264-7355
Limitations: Giving on a national basis for higher
education, locally for all other areas.

M. D. Anderson Foundation
P. O. Box 2558
Houston, TX 77252-8037
Limitations: Giving primarily in TX, with emphasis on
the Houston area.

Anheuser-Busch Foundation
c/o Anheuser-Busch Cos., Inc.
1 Busch Pl.
St. Louis, MO 63118
URL: http://www.anheuser-busch.com/Citizenship/
default.htm
Limitations: Giving primarily in areas of company
operations.

The Annenberg Foundation
Radnor Financial Ctr., Ste. A-200
150 N. Radnor-Chester Rd.
Radnor, PA 19087 (610) 341-9066
FAX: (610) 964-8688;
E-mail: info@annenbergfoundation.org;
Additional address (CA office): Center West, Ste.
1605, 10877 Wilshire Blvd., Los Angeles, CA
90024, tel.: (310) 209-4560, FAX: (310)
209-1631; URL: http://
www.annenbergfoundation.org
Limitations: Giving nationally with preference for
southern CA, greater Philadelphia, PA, and New
York, NY; some unsolicited grants to the United
Kingdom, France, Africa and Asia.

Aon Foundation
200 E. Randolph St.
Chicago, IL 60601 (312) 381-3549
Limitations: Giving on a national basis.

The Eugene Applebaum Family Foundation
39400 Woodward Ave., Ste. 100
Bloomfield Hills, MI 48304
Limitations: Giving primarily in MI, and New York, NY;
some funding nationally.

The Applied Materials Foundation
c/o Mike O'Farrell
3050 Bowers Ave., M.S. 2033
Santa Clara, CA 95054
Limitations: Giving primarily in CA.

The Arcadia Foundation
105 E. Logan St.
Norristown, PA 19401-3058
Limitations: Giving limited to eastern PA organizations
whose addresses have zip codes beginning with
18 and 19.
Publishes an annual or periodic report.

Archstone Foundation
401 E. Ocean Blvd., Ste. 1000
Long Beach, CA 90802-4933 (562) 590-8655
FAX: (562) 495-0317;
E-mail: archstone@archstone.org; URL: http://
www.archstone.org
Limitations: Giving primarily in southern CA.
Publishes an annual or periodic report.

Arcus Foundation
402 E. Michigan Ave.
Kalamazoo, MI 49007 (269) 373-4373
E-mail: contact@arcusfoundation.org; New York
address: 119 W. 24th St., 9th Fl., New York, NY
10011, tel.: (212) 488-3000; URL: http://
www.arcusfoundation.org
Limitations: Giving on a national basis, with emphasis
on Kalamazoo, MI for some programs.
Publishes an annual or periodic report.

Arizona Community Foundation
2201 E. Camelback Rd., Ste. 202
Phoenix, AZ 85016 (602) 381-1400
FAX: (602) 381-1575;
E-mail: slandis@azfoundation.org; Additional tel.:
(800) 222-8221; Grant application E-mail:
grants@azfoundation.org; URL: http://
www.azfoundation.org
Limitations: Giving limited to AZ.
Publishes an annual or periodic report.

Arkansas Community Foundation, Inc.
700 S. Rock St.
Little Rock, AR 72202 (501) 372-1116
FAX: (501) 372-1166; E-mail: arcf@arcf.org;
Additional tel.: (888) 220-2723; Additional
E-mail: plile@arcf.org; Grant application E-mail:
cpatterson@arcf.org; URL: http://www.arcf.org
Limitations: Giving limited to AR.
Publishes an annual or periodic report.

The Assisi Foundation of Memphis, Inc.
515 Erin Dr.
Memphis, TN 38117
E-mail: jyoung@assisifoundation.org; URL: http://
www.assisifoundation.org/
Limitations: Giving primarily in Memphis and Shelby
County, TN.

AT&T Foundation
130 E. Travis, Ste. 350
San Antonio, TX 78205 (210) 351-2218
FAX: (210) 351-2599;
E-mail: sbcfdn@txmail.sbc.com; Additional tel.:
(800) 591-9663; URL: http://att.sbc.com/gen/
corporate-citizenship?pid=7736
Limitations: Giving primarily in areas of company
operations; giving also to statewide, regional,
and national organizations.

Avenir Foundation, Inc.
3280 Wadsworth Blvd., Ste. 280
Wheat Ridge, CO 80033-4633
Limitations: Giving on a national basis with emphasis
on CO, as well as in Vienna, Austria.

The AVI CHAI Foundation
1015 Park Ave.

New York, NY 10028 (212) 396-8850
FAX: (212) 396-8833; E-mail: info@avichina.org;
Additional address (Israel office): 31 Hanevlim,
95103 Jerusalem, tel.: (02) 624-3330, FAX: (02)
624-3310, E-mail: office@avichai.org.il;
URL: http://www.avichai.org
Limitations: Giving primarily in North America and
Israel.
Publishes an annual or periodic report.

Helen Bader Foundation, Inc.
233 N. Water St., 4th Fl.
Milwaukee, WI 53202 (414) 224-6464
FAX: (414) 224-1441; E-mail: info@hbf.org;
URL: http://www.hbf.org
Limitations: Giving primarily in the greater Milwaukee,
WI, area for education and economic
development; giving locally and nationally for
Alzheimer's disease and dementia; giving in
Israel for early childhood development.
Publishes an annual or periodic report.

The Earl & Doris Bakken Foundation
Hale Ku'e Plz., No. 207
73-5619 Kauhola St.
Kailua Kona, HI 96740 (808) 326-9171
FAX: (808) 326-9173; E-mail: buschg@hawaii.rr.com
Limitations: Giving primarily in HI, with some
emphasis on Kamuela.

L. G. Balfour Foundation
c/o Bank of America, N.A., Philanthropic
Management
100 Federal St., MA5-100-05-01
Boston, MA 02110 (617) 434-4846
Additional tel.: (617) 434-4941
Limitations: Giving primarily in New England, with
emphasis on Attleboro, MA.

George and Frances Ball Foundation
P.O. Box 1408
Muncie, IN 47308 (765) 741-5500
Additional address: 222 S. Mulberry St., Muncie, IN
47305; FAX: (765) 741-5518;
E-mail: jjpruis@iquest.net
Limitations: Giving primarily in Muncie and Delaware
County, IN.

The Baltimore Community Foundation
2 E. Read St., 9th Fl.
Baltimore, MD 21202 (410) 332-4171
FAX: (410) 837-4701; E-mail: questions@bcf.org;
Grant application E-mail: grants@bcf.org;
URL: http://www.bcf.org
Limitations: Giving primarily in Baltimore City and
Baltimore County, MD.
Publishes an annual or periodic report.

**The Bank of America Charitable Foundation,
Inc.**
101 S. Tryon St., NC1-002-33-77
Charlotte, NC 28255-0001
URL: http://www.bankofamerica.com/foundation/
index.cfm?template=fd_funding
Limitations: Giving limited to areas of major company
operations.

Baptist Community Ministries
400 Poydras St., Ste. 2950
New Orleans, LA 70130
E-mail: info@bcm.org; URL: http://www.bcm.org/
Limitations: Giving primarily in Jefferson, Orleans,
Plaquemines, St. Bernard, and St. Tammany
parishes, LA.
Publishes an annual or periodic report.

Barr Foundation
The Pilot House
Lewis Wharf
Boston, MA 02110 (617) 854-3500
FAX: (617) 854-3501;
E-mail: info@barrfoundation.org; URL: http://
www.barrfoundation.org
Limitations: Giving primarily in the greater Boston,
MA, area.

Baton Rouge Area Foundation
402 N. 4th St.
Baton Rouge, LA 70802 (225) 387-6126
FAX: (225) 387-6153; E-mail: jdavies@braf.org;
Additional tel.: (877) 387-6126; Grant
information E-mail: grantmaking@braf.org;
URL: http://www.braf.org
Limitations: Giving limited to the Baton Rouge, LA,
area, including East Baton Rouge, West Baton
Rouge, Livingston, Ascension, Iberville, Pointe
Coupee, East Feliciana, and West Feliciana
parishes.
Publishes an annual or periodic report.

Bauman Family Foundation, Inc.
c/o Jewett House
2040 S St. N.W.
Washington, DC 20009-1110 (202) 328-2040
Limitations: Giving on a national basis.

BB&T Charitable Foundation
P.O. Box 1547, M.C. 001-05-04-30
Winston-Salem, NC 27102-1547
FAX: (336) 733-0118;
E-mail: rodney.hughes@bbandt.com
Limitations: Giving primarily in areas of company
operations.

Norwin S. and Elizabeth N. Bean Foundation
c/o New Hampshire Charitable Foundation
37 Pleasant St.
Concord, NH 03301-4005
FAX: (603) 225-1700; E-mail: dvd@nhcf.org;
URL: http://www.nhcf.org
Limitations: Giving limited to Amherst and
Manchester, NH.
Publishes an annual or periodic report.

S. D. Bechtel, Jr. Foundation
P.O. Box 193809
San Francisco, CA 94119-3809 (415) 284-8572
FAX: (415) 284-8571;
E-mail: esb@fremontgroup.com
Limitations: Giving primarily in the San Francisco Bay
Area and northern CA.

Arnold and Mabel Beckman Foundation
100 Academy Dr.
Irvine, CA 92617 (949) 721-2222
FAX: (949) 721-2225; Mailing address: P.O. Box
13219 Newport Beach, CA 92658; E-mail (for
Kathlene Williams, Exec. Asst.):
k.williams@beckman-foundation.com;
URL: http://www.beckman-foundation.com
Limitations: Giving primarily in the U.S.

The J. L. Bedsole Foundation
P.O. Box 1137
Mobile, AL 36633 (251) 432-3369
FAX: (251) 432-1134;
E-mail: info@jlbedsolefoundation.org;
URL: http://www.jlbedsolefoundation.org
Limitations: Giving limited to Mobile, Baldwin, Clarke,
Monroe, and Washington counties, AL.

Beldon Fund
99 Madison Ave., 8th Fl.

New York, NY 10016 (800) 591-9595
FAX: (212) 616-5656; E-mail: info@beldon.org;
Additional tel.: (212) 616-5600; URL: http://
www.beldon.org
Limitations: Giving on a national basis.

Claude Worthington Benedum Foundation
1400 Benedum-Trees Bldg.
223 4th Ave.
Pittsburgh, PA 15222 (412) 288-0360
FAX: (412) 288-0366; E-mail: info@benedum.org;
URL: http://www.benedum.org
Limitations: Giving limited to southwestern PA and
WV.
Publishes an annual or periodic report.

Israel Henry Beren Charitable Trust
P.O. Box 20380
Wichita, KS 67208
Limitations: Giving primarily in NY; some giving also
in Israel.

H. N. & Frances C. Berger Foundation
P.O. Box 13390
Palm Desert, CA 92255-3390 (760) 341-5293
Limitations: Giving primarily in CA.

Berkshire Taconic Community Foundation
271 Main St., Ste. 3
Great Barrington, MA 01230-1972
(413) 528-8039
FAX: (413) 528-8158;
E-mail: info@berkshiretaconic.org; Additional tel.:
(413) 528-8039; Grant inquiry E-mail:
maeve@berkshiretaconic.org; URL: http://
www.berkshiretaconic.org
Limitations: Giving limited to northwest Litchfield
County, CT, Berkshire County, MA, and Columbia
County and northeast Dutchess County, NY.
Publishes an annual or periodic report.

Best Buy Children's Foundation
7601 Penn Ave. S.
Richfield, MN 55423-3645
FAX: (612) 292-4001; Application address: P.O. Box
9448, Minneapolis, MN 55440-9448;
URL: http://www.bestbuy.com/
communityrelations
Limitations: Giving on a national basis.

F. R. Bigelow Foundation
600 5th St. Ctr.
55 E. 5th St.
St. Paul, MN 55101-1797 (651) 224-5463
FAX: (651) 224-8123; E-mail: inbox@frbigelow.org;
URL: http://www.frbigelow.org
Limitations: Giving limited to the Greater St. Paul, MN,
metropolitan area, which includes; Ramsey,
Washington, and Dakota counties, with a
particular emphasis on serving people who live
and work in the city of St. Paul.
Publishes an annual or periodic report.

Bing Fund Corporation
990 N. Sierra St.
Reno, NV 89503
Limitations: Giving on a national basis.

The Blandin Foundation
100 N. Pokegama Ave.
Grand Rapids, MN 55744 (218) 326-0523
FAX: (218) 327-1949;
E-mail: bfinfo@blandinfoundation.org; Additional
tel.: (877) 882-2257; URL: http://
www.blandinfoundation.org
Limitations: Giving limited to rural areas of MN;
scholarships limited to graduates of an Itasca

County, Hill City, or Remer, Blackduck, or
Northome, MN, high school.

The Arthur M. Blank Family Foundation
3223 Howell Mill Rd, N.W.
Atlanta, GA 30327 (404) 367-2100
FAX: (404) 367-2059; E-mail: kday@ambfo.com;
URL: http://www.blankfoundation.org
Limitations: Giving primarily in Maricopa County, AZ,
Atlanta, GA, and Beaufort County, SC.
Publishes an annual or periodic report.

The Jacob and Hilda Blaustein Foundation, Inc.
10 E. Baltimore St., Ste. 1111
Baltimore, MD 21202-1630 (410) 347-7201
E-mail: info@blaufund.org; URL: http://
www.blaufund.org/foundations/
jacobandhilda_f.html
Limitations: Giving primarily in MD (no local projects
outside Baltimore, MD); giving also in Israel.

The Bodman Foundation
767 3rd Ave., 4th Fl.
New York, NY 10017-2023 (212) 644-0322
FAX: (212) 759-6510;
E-mail: main@achelis-bodman-fnds.org;
URL: http://www.foundationcenter.org/
grantmaker/achelis-bodman/
Limitations: Giving primarily in northern NJ and New
York, NY.

Boehringer Ingelheim Cares Foundation, Inc.
900 Ridgebury Rd.
Ridgefield, CT 06877
URL: http://us.boehringer-ingelheim.com/about/
philanthropy/philanthropy.html
Limitations: Giving primarily in northern Fairfield
County, CT.

Boettcher Foundation
600 17th St., Ste. 2210 S.
Denver, CO 80202-5422 (303) 534-1937
E-mail: grants@boettcherfoundation.org; Additional
e-mails: scholarships@Boettcherfoundation.org
and info@Boettcherfoundation.org; URL: http://
www.boettcherfoundation.org/
Limitations: Giving limited to CO.
Publishes an annual or periodic report.

Booth Ferris Foundation
c/o JPMorgan Chase Bank, N.A.
345 Park Ave., 4th Fl., NY1-N040
New York, NY 10154 (212) 464-2487
FAX: (212) 464-2305; URL: http://
foundationcenter.org/grantmaker/boothferris/
Limitations: Giving limited to the New York, NY,
metropolitan area for the arts, K-12 education,
and civic and urban affairs; a broader geographic
scope for higher education.
Publishes an annual or periodic report.

Boston Foundation, Inc.
75 Arlington St.,10th Fl.
Boston, MA 02116 (617) 338-1700
FAX: (617) 338-1604; E-mail: info@tbf.org; Additional
E-mails: david.trueblood@tbf.org and
cld@tbf.org; URL: http://www.tbf.org
Limitations: Giving from discretionary funds limited to
the greater Boston, MA, area.
Publishes an annual or periodic report.

The Bothin Foundation
1660 Bush St., Ste. 300
San Francisco, CA 94109 (415) 561-6540
FAX: (415) 561-6477; E-mail: esloan@pfs-llc.net;
URL: http://www.pfs-llc.net/bothin/index.html

Limitations: Giving primarily in CA, with emphasis on San Francisco, Marin, Sonoma and San Mateo counties.
Publishes an annual or periodic report.

BP Foundation, Inc.
4101 Winfield Rd., M.C. 1W
Warrenville, IL 60555-3521
URL: http://www.bp.com/subsection.do?
    categoryId=9004440&contentId=7009902
Limitations: Giving on a national and international basis.

The Lynde and Harry Bradley Foundation, Inc.
1241 N. Franklin Pl.
Milwaukee, WI 53202-2901 (414) 291-9915
FAX: (414) 291-9991; URL: http://
    www.bradleyfdn.org
Limitations: Giving primarily in Milwaukee, WI; giving also on a national and international basis.
Publishes an annual or periodic report.

Bradley-Turner Foundation, Inc.
P.O. Box 140
Columbus, GA 31902 (706) 571-6040
Limitations: Giving primarily in GA, with emphasis on Columbus.

Otto Bremer Foundation
445 Minnesota St., Ste. 2250
St. Paul, MN 55101-2107 (651) 227-8036
FAX: (651) 312-3665; E-mail: obf@ottobremer.org;
    Additional tel.: (888) 291-1123; URL: http://
    www.ottobremer.org
Limitations: Giving limited to organizations whose beneficiaries are residents of MN, MT, ND and WI with preference given to those in regions served by Bremer Banks.

The Bristol-Myers Squibb Foundation, Inc.
c/o Fdn. Coord.
345 Park Ave., 43rd Fl.
New York, NY 10154
E-mail for Distinguished Achievement Awards:
    daa_admin@bms.com; URL: http://
    www.bms.com/aboutbms/founda/data
Limitations: Giving on a national and international basis, including in Africa, with emphasis on Wallingford, CT, Evansville, IN, New Brunswick, Princeton, and Skillman, NJ, and Buffalo and Syracuse, NY.

Broad Foundation
10900 Wilshire Blvd., 12th Fl.
Los Angeles, CA 90024-6532 (310) 954-5050
FAX: (310) 954-5051;
    E-mail: info@broadfoundation.org; E-mail for grant information: grants@broadfoundation.org; URL: http://www.broadfoundation.org/
Limitations: Giving on a national basis.
Publishes an annual or periodic report.

Eli & Edythe L. Broad Foundation
10900 Wilshire Blvd., 12th Fl.
Los Angeles, CA 90024-6532
For Broad Medical Research Prog.: tel.: (310)
    954-5091, FAX: (310) 954-5092;
    E-mail: info@broadmedical.org; URL: http://
    www.broadmedical.org
Publishes an annual or periodic report.

The Brown Foundation, Inc.
2217 Welch Ave.
Houston, TX 77019 (713) 523-6867
FAX: (713) 523-2917;
    E-mail: bfi@brownfoundation.org; Application address: P.O. Box 130646, Houston, TX

77219-0646; URL: http://
    www.brownfoundation.org
Limitations: Giving primarily in TX, with emphasis on Houston.
Publishes an annual or periodic report.

Eva L. and Joseph M. Bruening Foundation
1422 Euclid Ave., Ste. 627
Cleveland, OH 44115-1952 (216) 621-2632
FAX: (216) 621-8198; URL: http://
    www.fmscleveland.com/bruening
Limitations: Giving limited to the Cuyahoga, OH.
Publishes an annual or periodic report.

Martin Bucksbaum Family Foundation
P.O. Box 498
Ankeny, IA 50021-0498
Limitations: Giving primarily in IA and NY.

Temple Hoyne Buell Foundation
1666 S. University Blvd., Ste. B
Denver, CO 80210 (303) 744-1688
FAX: (303) 744-1601;
    E-mail: info@buellfoundation.org; URL: http://
    www.buellfoundation.org
Limitations: Giving only in CO.
Publishes an annual or periodic report.

The Susan Thompson Buffett Foundation
222 Kiewit Plz.
Omaha, NE 68131
E-mail: scholarships@stbfoundation.org; Tel. for
    scholarship information: (402) 943-1383
Limitations: Giving on a national basis; scholarships awarded only to residents in NE.

Burlington Northern Santa Fe Foundation
5601 W. 26th St.
Cicero, IL 60804 (708) 924-5615
Limitations: Giving limited to areas of company operations in the Midwest, North, Northwest, Southeast, Southwest, and West.

The Burnett Foundation
801 Cherry St., Unit 16
Fort Worth, TX 76102-6881 (817) 877-3344
Limitations: Giving primarily in the Fort Worth, TX, area.

Fritz B. Burns Foundation
4001 W. Alameda Ave., Ste. 203
Burbank, CA 91505-4338 (818) 840-8802
Limitations: Giving primarily in the Los Angeles, CA, area.

Burroughs Wellcome Fund
21 T. W. Alexander Dr.
P.O. Box 13901
Research Triangle Park, NC 27709-3901
    (919) 991-5100
FAX: (919) 991-5160; E-mail: info@bwfund.org;
    Contact info. for Russ Campbell III tel.: (919)
    991-5119; Fax: (919) 991-5179, E-mail:
    rcampbell@bwfund.org; URL: http://
    www.bwfund.org
Limitations: Giving limited to the U.S. and Canada.
Publishes an annual or periodic report.

Bush Foundation
E-900 First National Bank Bldg.
332 Minnesota St.
St. Paul, MN 55101 (651) 227-0891
FAX: (651) 297-6485;
    E-mail: info@bushfoundation.org; URL: http://
    www.bushfoundation.org
Limitations: Giving primarily in MN, ND, and SD.

Publishes an annual or periodic report.

J. E. & Z. B. Butler Foundation, Inc.
825 3rd Ave., 40th Fl.
New York, NY 10022
Limitations: Giving primarily in New York, NY.

The Byrne Foundation, Inc.
3 Laramie Rd.
P.O. Box 599
Etna, NH 03750 (603) 643-4555
Limitations: Giving primarily in NH, NY, and VT.

The C.E. and S. Foundation, Inc.
1650 National City Twr.
Louisville, KY 40202 (502) 583-0546
FAX: (502) 583-7648; URL: http://
    www.cesfoundation.com
Limitations: Giving primarily in Louisville, KY.
Publishes an annual or periodic report.

C.I.O.S.
P.O. Box 20815
Waco, TX 76702
Limitations: Giving on a national basis.

The Morris and Gwendolyn Cafritz Foundation
1825 K St. N.W., Ste. 1400
Washington, DC 20006 (202) 223-3100
FAX: (202) 296-7567;
    E-mail: info@cafritzfoundation.org; URL: http://
    www.cafritzfoundation.org
Limitations: Giving limited to the Washington, DC, area and the immediate surrounding counties in MD and VA, specifically Prince George and Montgomery counties, MD, and Arlington and Fairfax counties, and the city of Alexandria, VA.
Publishes an annual or periodic report.

The Effie and Wofford Cain Foundation
4131 Spicewood Springs Rd., Ste. A-1
Austin, TX 78759 (512) 346-7490
Limitations: Giving primarily in TX.

The Gordon and Mary Cain Foundation
8 Greenway Plz., Ste. 702
Houston, TX 77046
Limitations: Giving primarily in Houston, TX.

The Louis Calder Foundation
175 Elm St.
New Canaan, CT 06840 (203) 966-8925
FAX: (203) 966-5785; E-mail: admin@calderfdn.org;
    URL: http://www.louiscalderfdn.org
Limitations: Giving primarily in the greater New York, NY, metropolitan area and surrounding areas.
Publishes an annual or periodic report.

California Community Foundation
445 S. Figueroa St., Ste. 3400
Los Angeles, CA 90071 (213) 413-4130
FAX: (213) 383-2046; E-mail: info@ccf-la.org;
    URL: http://www.calfund.org
Limitations: Giving limited to Los Angeles County, CA.
Publishes an annual or periodic report.

The California Endowment
1000 N. Alameda St.
Los Angeles, CA 90012 (800) 449-4149
FAX: (213) 928-8801;
    E-mail: questions@calendow.org; URL: http://
    www.calendow.org
Limitations: Giving primarily in CA.
Publishes an annual or periodic report.

The California Wellness Foundation
6320 Canoga Ave., Ste. 1700
Woodland Hills, CA 91367-7111 (818) 702-1900
FAX: (818) 702-1999; E-mail: tcwf@tcwf.org; Branch
Office address: 575 Market St., Ste. 1850, San
Francisco, CA 94105, tel.: (415) 908-3000, FAX:
(415) 908-3001; URL: http://www.tcwf.org
Limitations: Giving limited to CA; national
organizations providing services in CA are also
considered.
Publishes an annual or periodic report.

The Cannon Foundation, Inc.
P.O. Box 548
Concord, NC 28026-0548 (704) 786-8216
URL: http://www.thecannonfoundationinc.org
Limitations: Giving primarily in NC, with emphasis on
the Cabarrus County area.

**The Capital Group Companies Charitable
Foundation**
11100 Santa Monica Blvd., 9th Fl.
Los Angeles, CA 90025-3384
Limitations: Giving on a national and internationl
basis.

Capitol Federal Foundation
700 S. Kansas Ave., Ste. 517
Topeka, KS 66603 (785) 270-6040
Limitations: Giving limited to major metropolitan
areas of central and northeastern KS.

The Cargill Foundation
P.O. Box 5626
Minneapolis, MN 55440-5626 (952) 742-4311
FAX: (952) 742-7224; URL: http://www.cargill.com/
about/citizenship/foundation.htm
Limitations: Giving primarily in Minneapolis, MN, and
its western suburbs.

The Carls Foundation
333 W. Fort St., Ste. 1940
Detroit, MI 48226 (313) 965-0990
FAX: (313) 965-0547; URL: http://www.carlsfdn.org
Limitations: Giving primarily in MI.
Publishes an annual or periodic report.

Carnegie Corporation of New York
437 Madison Ave.
New York, NY 10022 (212) 371-3200
FAX: (212) 754-4073; URL: http://www.carnegie.org
Limitations: Giving primarily for U.S. projects,
although some grants are made to selected
countries in Sub-Saharan Africa through the
International Development Program.
Publishes an annual or periodic report.

E. Rhodes & Leona B. Carpenter Foundation
c/o Joseph A. O'Connor, Jr., Morgan, Lewis &
Bockius
1735 Market St., Ste. 3420
Philadelphia, PA 19103-2921 (215) 979-3222
Limitations: Giving primarily in areas east of the
Mississippi River.

The Carson Family Charitable Trust
c/o U.S. Trust
114 W. 47th St.
New York, NY 10036
Limitations: Giving primarily in New York, NY.

The Carter Family Charitable Trust
P.O. Box 41119
Providence, RI 02940-1119
Limitations: Giving primarily in RI, with emphasis on
Providence.

Amon G. Carter Foundation
201 Main St., Ste. 1945
Fort Worth, TX 76102 (817) 332-2783
FAX: (817) 332-2787; E-mail: jrobinson@agcf.org;
Application address: P.O. Box 1036, Fort Worth,
TX 76101; URL: http://www.agcf.org/
Limitations: Giving largely restricted to Fort Worth and
Tarrant County, TX.

Roy J. Carver Charitable Trust
202 Iowa Ave.
Muscatine, IA 52761-3733 (563) 263-4010
FAX: (563) 263-1547; E-mail: info@carvertrust.org;
URL: http://www.carvertrust.org
Limitations: Giving primarily in IA.

The Case Foundation
1720 N St. N.W.
Washington, DC 20036 (202) 467-5788
FAX: (202) 775-9161;
E-mail: info@casefoundation.org; URL: http://
www.casefoundation.org
Limitations: Giving in the U.S. and abroad.

The Annie E. Casey Foundation
701 St. Paul St.
Baltimore, MD 21202 (410) 547-6600
FAX: (410) 547-6624; E-mail: webmail@aecf.org;
URL: http://www.aecf.org
Limitations: Giving on a national basis.

Marguerite Casey Foundation
1300 Dexter Ave. N., Ste. 115
Seattle, WA 98109-3542 (206) 691-3134
FAX: (206) 286-2725; E-mail: info@caseygrants.org;
TTY: (206) 273-7395; URL: http://
www.caseygrants.org/
Limitations: Giving primarily in four regions of the
U.S.: CA; the Southwest, including the U.S./
Mexico border; the deep south; the Midwest,
beginning in Chicago, IL; and WA state.
Publishes an annual or periodic report.

Harold K. L. Castle Foundation
146 Hekili St., Ste. 203
Kailua, HI 96734 (808) 263-7073
FAX: (808) 262-6918;
E-mail: jfry@castlefoundation.org; URL: http://
www.castlefoundation.org
Limitations: Giving limited to HI with priority given to
Windward Oahu.

Caterpillar Foundation
100 N.E. Adams St.
Peoria, IL 61629-1480 (309) 675-4464
URL: http://www.cat.com/foundation
Limitations: Giving primarily in areas of company
operations.

Central New York Community Foundation, Inc.
500 S. Salina St., Ste. 428
Syracuse, NY 13202 (315) 422-9538
FAX: (315) 471-6031; E-mail: peggy@cnycf.org;
URL: http://www.cnycf.org
Limitations: Giving limited to Onondaga and Madison
counties, NY, for general grants; giving in a wider
area for Donor-Advised funds.
Publishes an annual or periodic report.

The Champlin Foundations
300 Centerville Rd., Ste. 300S
Warwick, RI 02886-0226 (401) 736-0370
FAX: (401) 736-7248; URL: http://
www.foundationcenter.org/grantmaker/
champlin
Limitations: Giving primarily in RI.

Publishes an annual or periodic report.

Chartwell Charitable Foundation
1999 Ave. of the Stars, Ste. 3050
Los Angeles, CA 90067-4613 (310) 556-7600
Limitations: Giving primarily in CA and NY.

Chase Foundation
10 S. Dearborn, IL1-0308
Chicago, IL 60603 (312) 732-8133
Application address: 10 S. Dearborn, IL1-0356,
Chicago, IL 60603
Limitations: Giving primarily in areas of company
operations in AZ, DE, IL, MI, OH, and WI, with
emphasis on the metropolitan Chicago, IL, area.

The Chatlos Foundation, Inc.
P.O. Box 915048
Longwood, FL 32791-5048 (407) 862-5077
E-mail: info@chatlos.org; URL: http://
www.chatlos.org

CHC Foundation
P.O. Box 1644
Idaho Falls, ID 83403 (208) 522-2368
Limitations: Giving limited to southeastern ID.

Ben B. Cheney Foundation
3110 Ruston Way, Ste. A
Tacoma, WA 98402-5307 (253) 572-2442
E-mail: info@benbcheneyfoundation.org; URL: http://
www.benbcheneyfoundation.org
Limitations: Giving limited to portions of Del Norte,
Humboldt, Lassen, Shasta, Siskiyou, and Trinity
counties in CA, southern OR, particularly in the
Medford area, Tacoma and Pierce County, and
southwestern WA.
Publishes an annual or periodic report.

The Chicago Community Trust
111 E. Wacker Dr., Ste. 1400
Chicago, IL 60601 (312) 616-8000
FAX: (312) 616-7955; E-mail: info@cct.org; TDD:
(312) 856-1703; Grant inquiries E-mail:
grants@cct.org; URL: http://www.cct.org
Limitations: Giving primarily in Cook County and the
adjacent 5 counties of northeastern, IL.
Publishes an annual or periodic report.

Chichester duPont Foundation, Inc.
3120 Kennett Pike
Wilmington, DE 19807-3052 (302) 658-5244
Limitations: Giving primarily in DE and MD.

Christy-Houston Foundation, Inc.
1296 Dow St.
Murfreesboro, TN 37130 (615) 898-1140
Limitations: Giving limited to Rutherford County, TN.

The Greater Cincinnati Foundation
200 W. 4th St.
Cincinnati, OH 45202-2602 (513) 241-2880
FAX: (513) 852-6886;
E-mail: info@greatercincinnatifdn.org; Grant
application E-mail:
penningtonk@greatercincinnatifdn.org;
URL: http://www.greatercincinnatifdn.org
Limitations: Giving limited to southeastern IN,
northern KY, and the greater Cincinnati, OH area.
Publishes an annual or periodic report.

The Cinnabar Foundation
P.O. Box 5088
Helena, MT 59604 (406) 449-2795

E-mail: cinnabar@mt.net; Application address: 219 Vawter St., Helena, MT 59601; FAX: (406) 449-9985; E-mail: cinnabar@mt.net
Limitations: Giving limited to MT and the Yellowstone area.
Publishes an annual or periodic report.

Cisco Systems Foundation
170 W. Tasman Dr.
San Jose, CA 95134-1706
E-mail: ciscofoundation@cisco.com; E-mail for product donations: dicountech_cisco@techsoup.org; URL: http://www.cisco.com/go/foundation
Limitations: Giving primarily in CA.
Publishes an annual or periodic report.

Citigroup Foundation
850 3rd Ave., 13th Fl.
New York, NY 10022-6211   (212) 559-9163
FAX: (212) 793-5944;
  E-mail: citigroupfoundation@citigroup.com;
  URL: http://www.citigroupfoundation.org
Limitations: Giving on a national and international basis, with emphasis on areas of company operations.
Publishes an annual or periodic report.

Citizens Charitable Foundation
c/o Citizens Bank of Rhode Island
1 Citizens Plz.
Providence, RI 02903   (401) 456-7287
Limitations: Giving limited to the New England area.

The Edna McConnell Clark Foundation
415 Madison Ave., 10th Fl.
New York, NY 10017   (212) 551-9100
FAX: (212) 421-9325; E-mail: info@emcf.org;
  Additional E-mail (for Albert Chung): achung@emcf.org; URL: http://www.emcf.org
Limitations: Giving on a national basis.
Publishes an annual or periodic report.

Robert Sterling Clark Foundation, Inc.
135 E. 64th St.
New York, NY 10021   (212) 288-8900
FAX: (212) 288-1033; URL: http://www.rsclark.org
Limitations: Giving primarily in New York State for the Public Institutions Program and in New York City for the Cultural Program; giving nationally for reproductive freedom and arts advocacy projects.
Publishes an annual or periodic report.

The Clark Foundation
1 Rockefeller Plz., 31st Fl.
New York, NY 10020-2102
Limitations: Giving primarily in Cooperstown, NY and New York City; scholarships restricted to students residing in the Cooperstown, NY, area.

The Cleveland Foundation
1422 Euclid Ave., Ste. 1300
Cleveland, OH 44115-2001   (216) 861-3810
FAX: (216) 861-1729;
  E-mail: grantsmgmt@clevefdn.org; TTY: (216) 861-3806; URL: http://www.clevelandfoundation.org
Limitations: Giving limited to the greater Cleveland, OH, area, with primary emphasis on Cleveland, Cuyahoga, Lake, and Geauga counties, unless specified by donor.
Publishes an annual or periodic report.

Allen Whitehill Clowes Charitable Foundation, Inc.
320 N. Meridian St., Ste. 811

Indianapolis, IN 46204   (317) 955-0138
Limitations: Giving primarily in central IN.

Cogswell Benevolent Trust
1001 Elm St.
Manchester, NH 03101-1828   (603) 622-4013
Limitations: Giving primarily in NH (90 percent of funding limited to NH).

Naomi and Nehemiah Cohen Foundation
P.O. Box 30100
Bethesda, MD 20824   (301) 652-2230
FAX: (301) 652-2260; E-mail: nncf@starpower.net
Limitations: Giving primarily in Washington, DC, and Israel.

Sam L. Cohen Foundation
P.O. Box 1123
Portland, ME 04104   (207) 871-5600
FAX: (207) 871-9043; E-mail: nbrain@maine.rr.com;
  URL: http://www.samlcohenfoundation.org
Limitations: Giving primarily in southern ME.

The Collins Foundation
1618 S.W. 1st Ave., Ste. 505
Portland, OR 97201-5706   (503) 227-7171
FAX: (503) 295-3794;
  E-mail: information@collinsfoundation.org;
  URL: http://www.collinsfoundation.org
Limitations: Giving limited to OR, with emphasis on Portland.
Publishes an annual or periodic report.

The Colorado Trust
1600 Sherman St.
Denver, CO 80203-1604   (303) 837-1200
FAX: (303) 839-9034;
  E-mail: Carol@coloradotrust.org; Additional tel.: (888) 847-9140; URL: http://www.coloradotrust.org
Limitations: Giving limited to CO.
Publishes an annual or periodic report.

The Columbus Foundation and Affiliated Organizations
1234 E. Broad St.
Columbus, OH 43205-1453   (614) 251-4000
FAX: (614) 251-4009;
  E-mail: tcfinfo@columbusfoundation.org;
  Additional E-mail: rbiddisc@columbusfoundation.org; URL: http://www.columbusfoundation.org
Limitations: Giving limited to central OH.
Publishes an annual or periodic report.

The Comcast Foundation
1500 Market St.
E. Tower, 33rd Fl.
Philadelphia, PA 19102
URL: http://www.comcast.com/InTheCommunity/foundation/foundation.html
Limitations: Giving primarily in areas of company operations.

Comerica Foundation
c/o Comerica Inc.
P.O. Box 75000, M.C. 3390
Detroit, MI 48275-3390   (313) 222-7356
FAX: (313) 222-5555; Application addresses: Michigan: Michigan Comerica Corp. Contribs. Mgr., M.C. 3390, P.O. Box 75000, Detroit, MI 48275-3390, West Division: Comerica Corp. Contribs. Mgr., M.C. 4805, 333 W. Santa Clara St., San Jose, CA 95113, Dallas, TX, area: Comerica Corp. Contribs. Mgr., M.C. 6500, P.O. Box 650282, Dallas, TX 75265-0282, Houston,

TX, area: Comerica Corp. Contribs. Mgr., M.C. 6623, P.O. Box 4167, Houston, TX 77210-4167, Florida: Randy Nobles, Comerica Corp. Contribs. Mgr., M.C. 5172, 1800 Corporate Blvd. N.W., Boca Raton, FL 33431-7394; URL: http://www.comerica.com/vgn-ext-templating/v/index.jsp?vgnextoid=374970d75d994010VgnVCM100000 4502a8c0RCRD
Limitations: Giving in areas of company operations, with emphasis on MI.
Publishes an annual or periodic report.

The Commonwealth Fund
1 E. 75th St.
New York, NY 10021-2692   (212) 606-3800
FAX: (212) 606-3500; E-mail: cmwf@cmwf.org;
  URL: http://www.cmwf.org
Limitations: Giving on a national basis.
Publishes an annual or periodic report.

Communities Foundation of Texas, Inc.
5500 Caruth Haven Ln.
Dallas, TX 75225-8146   (214) 750-4222
FAX: (214) 750-4210; E-mail: Jcook@cftexas.org;
  Grant application E-mail: LParks@cftexas.org;
  URL: http://www.cftexas.org
Limitations: Giving primarily in the Dallas, TX, area (for grants from unrestricted funds).
Publishes an annual or periodic report.

Community Foundation for Greater Atlanta, Inc.
50 Hurt Plz., Ste. 449
Atlanta, GA 30303   (404) 688-5525
FAX: (404) 688-3060; E-mail: info@atlcf.org;
  Additional E-mail: grants@atlcf.org (for grant guidelines and grant orientation session registration); URL: http://www.atlcf.org
Limitations: Giving limited to the 23-county metropolitan area of Atlanta, GA.
Publishes an annual or periodic report.

Community Foundation for Monterey County
2354 Garden Rd.
Monterey, CA 93940   (831) 375-9712
FAX: (831) 375-4731; E-mail: info@cfmco.org;
  Additional Address: 945 S. Main, Ste. 205, Salinos, CA 93901; Additional E-mails: jackie@cfmco.org and jeff@cfmco.org;
  URL: http://www.cfmco.org
Limitations: Giving primarily in Monterey County, CA.
Publishes an annual or periodic report.

Community Foundation for Muskegon County
425 W. Western Ave., Ste. 200
Muskegon, MI 49440   (231) 722-4538
FAX: (231) 722-4616; E-mail: info@cffmc.org; Grant application E-mail: aboezaart@cffmc.org;
  URL: http://www.cffmc.org
Limitations: Giving limited to Muskegon County, MI.
Publishes an annual or periodic report.

Community Foundation for Palm Beach and Martin Counties, Inc.
700 S. Dixie Hwy., Ste. 200
West Palm Beach, FL 33401   (561) 659-6800
FAX: (561) 832-6542; E-mail: info@cfpbmc.org;
  Additional tel.: (888) 853-4438; Grant application E-mail: lraybin@cfpbmc.org;
  URL: http://www.yourcommunityfoundation.org
  Additional URL: http://www.cfpbmc.org
Limitations: Giving primarily in Palm Beach and Martin counties, FL.
Publishes an annual or periodic report.

Community Foundation for Southeast
Michigan
333 W. Fort St., Ste. 2010
Detroit, MI 48226 (313) 961-6675
FAX: (313) 961-2886; E-mail: cfsem@cfsem.org;
    URL: http://www.cfsem.org
Limitations: Giving limited to southeast MI.
Publishes an annual or periodic report.

**The Community Foundation for the National
Capital Region**
1201 15th St. N.W., Ste. 420
Washington, DC 20005 (202) 955-5890
FAX: (202) 955-8084; E-mail: tfreeman@cfncr.org;
    Tel. for grant applications: (202) 955-5890, ext.
    119; E-mail for grant applications:
    areid@cfncr.org; URL: http://www.cfncr.org
Limitations: Giving limited to the Washington, DC,
    Prince George's and Montgomery counties, MD,
    and northern VA.
Publishes an annual or periodic report.

The Community Foundation in Jacksonville
121 W. Forsyth St., Ste. 900
Jacksonville, FL 32202 (904) 356-4483
FAX: (904) 356-7910; E-mail: jherrin@jaxcf.org;
    Additional E-mails: jzell@jaxcf.org and
    nwaters@jaxcf.org; Grant application E-mail:
    applications@jaxcf.org; URL: http://
    www.jaxcf.org
Limitations: Giving primarily in northeastern FL,
    including Baker, Clay, Duval, Nassau and St.
    Johns counties.
Publishes an annual or periodic report.

The Community Foundation of Greater Lorain
County
1865 N. Ridge Rd. E., Ste. A
Lorain, OH 44055 (440) 277-0142
FAX: (440) 277-6955;
    E-mail: foundation@peoplewhocare.org;
    Additional tel.: (440) 323-4445; Additional
    E-mail: info@peoplewhocare.org; URL: http://
    www.peoplewhocare.org
Limitations: Giving limited to Huron County and Lorain
    County, OH, and immediate vicinity.
Publishes an annual or periodic report.

Community Foundation of Greater Memphis
1900 Union Ave.
Memphis, TN 38104 (901) 728-4600
FAX: (901) 722-0010; E-mail: gsmith@cfgm.org; Tel.
    for scholarships: (901) 722-0054; E-mail for
    grants and scholarships: mwolowicz@cfgm.org;
    URL: http://www.cfgm.org
Limitations: Giving limited to Crittenden County, AR,
    DeSoto, Marshall, Tate, and Tunica counties,
    MS, and Fayette, Shelby, and Tipton counties,
    TN.
Publishes an annual or periodic report.

The Community Foundation of Sarasota
County, Inc.
P.O. Box 49587
Sarasota, FL 34230-6587 (941) 955-3000
FAX: (941) 952-1951;
    E-mail: info@sarasota-foundation.org; Office
    address: 2635 Fruitville Rd., Sarasota, FL
    34237; Grant application tel.: (941) 556-7152;
    Grant inquiry E-mail:
    wendy@sarasota-foundation.org; URL: http://
    www.sarasota-foundation.org
Limitations: Giving primarily in Sarasota County, FL,
    and surrounding communities.
Publishes an annual or periodic report.

Community Foundation of Western
Massachusetts
1500 Main St., Ste. 2300
P.O. Box 15769
Springfield, MA 01115 (413) 732-2858
FAX: (413) 733-8565;
    E-mail: wmass@communityfoundation.org;
    Additional E-mail:
    kfaerber@communityfoundation.org; Grant
    information E-mail:
    grants@communityfoundation.org; URL: http://
    www.communityfoundation.org
Limitations: Giving limited to western MA, including
    Franklin County, Hampden County, and
    Hampshire County.
Publishes an annual or periodic report.

The Community Foundation of Western North
Carolina, Inc.
The BB&T Bldg., Ste. 1600
1 W. Pack Sq., P.O. Box 1888
Asheville, NC 28802 (828) 254-4960
FAX: (828) 251-2258; E-mail: dollar@cfwnc.org;
    Additional E-mail: sandlin@cfwnc.org;
    URL: http://www.cfwnc.org
Limitations: Giving limited to Avery, Buncombe,
    Burke, Cherokee, Clay, Graham, Haywood,
    Henderson, Jackson, Macon, Madison,
    McDowell, Mitchell, Polk, Rutherford, Swain,
    Transylvania, and Yancey counties, NC.
Publishes an annual or periodic report.

The Community Foundation Serving Richmond
& Central Virginia
7501 Boulders View Dr., Ste. 110
Richmond, VA 23225 (804) 330-7400
FAX: (804) 330-5992; E-mail: info@tcfrichmond.org;
    Additional E-mail: doman@tcfrichmond.org; Grant
    application E-mails: shallett@tcfrichmond.org
    and esummerfield@tcfrichmond.org;
    URL: http://www.tcfrichmond.org
Limitations: Giving limited to residents of
    metropolitan Richmond, the tri-cities area,
    including Hopewell, Colonial Heights, and
    Petersburg, and Chesterfield, Hanover, and
    Henrico counties, VA.
Publishes an annual or periodic report.

Community Foundation Silicon Valley
60 S. Market St., Ste. 1000
San Jose, CA 95113-1000 (408) 278-2200
FAX: (408) 278-0280; E-mail: info@cfsv.org;
    Additional E-mails: phero@cfsv.org and
    lbarrera@cfsv.org; Community Investment Grant
    E-mail: mmccray@cfsv.org; URL: http://
    www.cfsv.org
Limitations: Giving primarily in Santa Clara and
    southern San Mateo counties, CA.
Publishes an annual or periodic report.

Compton Foundation, Inc.
255 Shoreline Dr., Ste. 540
Redwood City, CA 94065 (650) 508-1181
FAX: (650) 508-1191;
    E-mail: info@comptonfoundation.org;
    URL: http://www.comptonfoundation.org
Limitations: Giving on an international basis to
    U.S.-based organizations for projects in Mexico,
    Central America, and Sub-Saharan Africa and on
    a national basis for programs in peace and
    population and the environment. Other funding
    limited to areas where board members reside:
    primarily San Francisco, Marin, and Santa Clara
    counties, CA.

ConAgra Foods Foundation
1 ConAgra Dr., CC-304
Omaha, NE 68102-5001

URL: http://www.conagrafoods.com/company/
    corporate_responsibility/foundation/index.jsp
Limitations: Giving on a national basis in areas of
    company operations, with emphasis on NE.

The William F. Connell Charitable Trust
c/o Lynch, Brewer, Hoffman & Sands, LLP
101 Federal St., 22nd Fl.
Boston, MA 02110
Limitations: Giving primarily in MA.

Connelly Foundation
1 Tower Bridge, Ste. 1450
West Conshohocken, PA 19428 (610) 834-3222
FAX: (610) 834-0866; E-mail: info@connellyfdn.org;
    URL: http://www.connellyfdn.org
Limitations: Giving primarily in Philadelphia, and
    surrounding counties of Bucks, Chester,
    Delaware and Montgomery, PA and Camden, NJ.

The Jon S. Corzine Foundation
c/o BCRS Assocs., LLC
100 Wall St., 11th Fl.
New York, NY 10017
Limitations: Giving primarily in NJ.

S. H. Cowell Foundation
120 Montgomery St., Ste. 2570
San Francisco, CA 94104 (415) 397-0285
FAX: (415) 986-6786; URL: http://www.shcowell.org
Limitations: Giving limited to northern CA.
Publishes an annual or periodic report.

Credit Suisse Americas Foundation
1 Madison Ave., 6th Fl.
New York, NY 10010-3629 (212) 325-2389
E-mail: annemarie.fell@csfb.com; Additional tel.:
    (212) 325-2000; URL: http://www.csfb.com/
    about_csfb/company_information/foundation/
    index.shtml
Limitations: Giving primarily in areas of company
    operations, with emphasis on New York, NY.

Arie and Ida Crown Memorial
222 N. LaSalle St., Ste. 2000
Chicago, IL 60601-1109 (312) 236-6300
Limitations: Giving primarily in metropolitan Chicago,
    IL.

Crystal Trust
P.O. Box 39
Montchanin, DE 19710-0039 (302) 651-0533
Limitations: Giving primarily in DE, with emphasis on
    Wilmington.

Lewis B. & Dorothy Cullman Foundation, Inc.
c/o Lewis B. Cullman
767 3rd Ave., 36th Fl.
New York, NY 10017 (212) 751-6655
Limitations: Giving primarily in NY.

The Nathan Cummings Foundation
475 10th Ave., 14th Fl.
New York, NY 10018 (212) 787-7300
FAX: (212) 787-7377;
    E-mail: info@nathancummings.org; URL: http://
    www.nathancummings.org
Limitations: Giving primarily in the U.S. and Israel.
Publishes an annual or periodic report.

CVS/pharmacy Charitable Trust, Inc.
1 CVS Dr.
Woonsocket, RI 02895
URL: http://www.cvs.com/corpInfo/community/
    charitable_mission.html

Limitations: Giving limited to areas of company operations.

D & DF Foundation
1 Maritime Plz., Ste. 1400
San Francisco, CA 94111
Limitations: Giving primarily in San Francisco, CA.

Dade Community Foundation, Inc.
200 S. Biscayne Blvd., Ste. 505
Miami, FL 33131-2343 (305) 371-2711
FAX: (305) 371-5342;
    E-mail: ruth.shack@dadecommunityfoundation.o
    rg; Additional E-mails:
    Charisse.grant@dadecommunityfoundation.org,
    Betty.alonso@dadecommunityfoundation.org,
    and
    Todd.weeks@dadecommunityfoundation.org;
    URL: http://www.dadecommunityfoundation.org
Limitations: Giving limited to Miami-Dade County, FL.
Publishes an annual or periodic report.

DaimlerChrysler Corporation Fund
CIMS: 485-10-94
1000 Chrysler Dr.
Auburn Hills, MI 48326-2766 (248) 512-2502
FAX: (248) 512-2503; E-mail: mek@dcx.com;
    URL: http://www2.daimlerchrysler.com/
    dccfund/
Limitations: Giving primarily in areas of company
    operations in Wittman, AZ, Irvine, CA, Englewood,
    CO, Newark, DE, Washington, DC, Orlando, FL,
    Belvidere and Lisle, IL, Indianapolis and Kokomo,
    IN, Elkridge, MD, Detroit, MI, Fenton, MO,
    Syracuse and Tappan, NY, Perrysburg, Toledo,
    and Twinsburg, OH, and Addison, TX, Kenosha,
    WI; giving also to regional and national
    organizations.
Publishes an annual or periodic report.

The Dallas Foundation
900 Jackson St., Ste. 150
Dallas, TX 75202 (214) 741-9898
FAX: (214) 741-9848;
    E-mail: info@dallasfoundation.org; Additional
    E-mail: mjalonick@dallasfoundation.org; Grant
    request E-mail:
    sfuldnasso@dallasfoundation.org; URL: http://
    www.dallasfoundation.org
Limitations: Giving limited to the City and County of
    Dallas, TX.
Publishes an annual or periodic report.

The Dana Foundation
745 5th Ave., Ste. 900
New York, NY 10151-0799 (212) 223-4040
FAX: (212) 317-8721; E-mail: danainfo@dana.org;
    URL: http://www.dana.org
Limitations: Giving on a national basis.
Publishes an annual or periodic report.

The Danforth Foundation
1 Metropolitan Sq.
211 N. Broadway, Ste. 2390
St. Louis, MO 63102 (314) 588-1900
Limitations: Giving limited to the metropolitan St.
    Louis, MO, area.
Publishes an annual or periodic report.

The Daniel Foundation of Alabama
820 Shades Creek Pkwy., Ste. 1200
Birmingham, AL 35209
Limitations: Giving primarily in the southeastern U.S.,
    with emphasis on AL.
Publishes an annual or periodic report.

Daniels Fund
101 Monroe St.
Denver, CO 80206 (720) 941-4422
FAX: (720) 941-4182;
    E-mail: pdroege@danielsfund.org; General tel.:
    (303) 393-7220; Toll free tel.: (877) 791- 4726;
    General contact e-mail:
    contact@danielsfund.org; URL: http://
    www.danielsfund.org
Limitations: Giving primarily in CO, with emphasis on
    Denver; funding also in NM, WY and UT with a
    limited basis nationally.
Publishes an annual or periodic report.

The Shelby Cullom Davis Foundation
3 Bethesda Metro Ctr., Ste. 118
Bethesda, MD 20814 (301) 961-4000
FAX: (301) 961-4001;
    E-mail: scdf@scdfoundation.org; URL: http://
    www.scdfoundation.org
Limitations: Giving on a national basis.

The Arthur Vining Davis Foundations
225 Water St., Ste. 1510
Jacksonville, FL 32202-5185 (904) 359-0670
FAX: (904) 359-0675;
    E-mail: arthurvining@bellsouth.net; URL: http://
    www.avdfdn.org/
Limitations: Giving limited to the U.S. and its
    possessions and territories.
Publishes an annual or periodic report.

The Daywood Foundation, Inc.
1600 Bank One Ctr.
Charleston, WV 25301 (304) 345-8900
Application address: 1500 Bank One Ctr., Charleston,
    WV 25301, tel.: (304) 343-4841
Limitations: Giving limited to Barbour, Greenbrier and
    Kanawha counties, WV.

The Ira W. DeCamp Foundation
c/o JPMorgan Private Bank, Global Foundations
    Group
345 Park Ave., 4th Fl.
New York, NY 10154
FAX: (212) 464-2305; E-mail (for Lisa Philp):
    Philp_lisa@jpmorgan.com; URL: http://
    foundationcenter.org/grantmaker/decamp/
Limitations: Giving primarily in the New York City
    metropolitan area.

John Deere Foundation
1 John Deere Pl.
Moline, IL 61265 (309) 748-7960
FAX: (309) 748-7953;
    E-mail: bustlejohnw@johndeere.com;
    URL: http://www.deere.com/en_US/compinfo/
    csr/community/found.html
Limitations: Giving primarily in areas of company
    operations in IL, IA, NC, and WI.

The 1994 Charles B. Degenstein Foundation
c/o Mellon Bank, N.A.
P.O. Box 185
Pittsburgh, PA 15230-0185
Application address: c/o Sidney Apfelbaum, 43 S. 5th
    St., Sunbury, PA 17801-2896, tel.: (570)
    286-9421
Limitations: Giving within a 75-mile radius of Sunbury,
    PA.

Dekko Foundation, Inc.
P.O. Box 548
Kendallville, IN 46755-0548 (260) 347-1278
FAX: (260) 347-7103;
    E-mail: dekko@dekkofoundation.org;
    URL: http://www.dekkofoundation.org

Limitations: Giving primarily in Limestone County, AL;
    Clarke, Decatur, Lucas, Ringgold, and Union
    counties, IA; and DeKalb, Kosciousko, LaGrange,
    Noble, Steuben, and Whitley counties, IN.
Publishes an annual or periodic report.

Beatrice P. Delany Charitable Trust
c/o JPMorgan Chase Bank, N.A.
P.O. Box 6089
Newark, DE 19714-6089
Application address: c/o JPMorgan Chase Bank, N.A.,
    345 Park Ave., 8th Fl., New York, NY 10154
Limitations: Giving primarily in the metropolitan
    Chicago, IL, area.

The Michael and Susan Dell Foundation
P.O. Box 163867
Austin, TX 78716-3867
URL: http://www.msdf.org/
Limitations: Giving on a local, regional, national and
    international basis.

The Denver Foundation
950 S. Cherry St., Ste. 200
Denver, CO 80246-2662 (303) 300-1790
FAX: (303) 300-6547;
    E-mail: information@denverfoundation.org; Grant
    application E-mail: jsharp@denverfoundation.org;
    URL: http://www.denverfoundation.org
Limitations: Giving limited to Adams, Arapahoe,
    Boulder, Broomfield, Denver, Douglas, and
    Jefferson counties, CO.
Publishes an annual or periodic report.

Deutsche Bank Americas Foundation
60 Wall St., NYC60-2110
New York, NY 10005-2858 (212) 250-0555
URL: http://www.community.db.com/
Limitations: Giving on a national basis in areas of
    company operations and in Canada and Latin
    America.
Publishes an annual or periodic report.

The Richard and Helen DeVos Foundation
P.O. Box 230257
Grand Rapids, MI 49523-0257 (616) 643-4700
Limitations: Giving primarily in central FL and western
    MI.

Irene Diamond Fund
800 3rd Ave., Ste. 2700
New York, NY 10022
Limitations: Giving primarily in NY.

The Dibner Fund, Inc.
P.O. Box 7575
Wilton, CT 06897 (203) 761-9904
FAX: (203) 761-9989; E-mail: info@dibnerfund.org;
    URL: http://www.dibnerfund.org
Limitations: Giving primarily in CT, MA, and NY, some
    national and international giving.

Dillon Foundation
P.O. Box 537
Sterling, IL 61081 (815) 626-9000
Limitations: Giving primarily in the Sterling, IL, area.

Geraldine R. Dodge Foundation, Inc.
163 Madison Ave., 6th Fl.
P.O. Box 1239
Morristown, NJ 07962-1239 (973) 540-8442
FAX: (973) 540-1211; E-mail: info@grdodge.org;
    URL: http://www.grdodge.org
Limitations: Giving primarily in NJ, with support for the
    arts and local humane groups limited to NJ, and
    support for other local projects limited to the

Morristown-Madison area; some giving to national organizations.
Publishes an annual or periodic report.

Dodge Jones Foundation
P.O. Box 176
Abilene, TX 79604-0176 (325) 673-6429
Limitations: Giving primarily in Abilene, TX.

Carrie Estelle Doheny Foundation
707 Wilshire Blvd., Ste. 4960
Los Angeles, CA 90017-9843 (213) 488-1122
FAX: (213) 488-1544;
E-mail: peggy@dohenyfoundation.org;
URL: http://www.dohenyfoundation.org
Limitations: Giving primarily in the Los Angeles, CA, area.
Publishes an annual or periodic report.

Dominion Foundation
625 Liberty Ave.
Pittsburgh, PA 15222-3197 (412) 690-1430
FAX: (412) 690-7608; E-mail for Dominion Educational Partnership:
educational_grants@dom.com; URL: http://www.dom.com/about/community/foundation/index.jsp
Limitations: Giving on a national basis in areas of company operations.

The William H. Donner Foundation
60 E. 42nd St., Ste. 1560
New York, NY 10165 (212) 949-0404
FAX: (212) 949-6022; E-mail: dfeeney@donner.org;
Additional tel.: (212) 949-5213; URL: http://www.donner.org
Limitations: Giving on a national basis.

Dorot Foundation
439 Benefit St.
Providence, RI 02903 (401) 351-8866
FAX: (401) 351-4975; E-mail: info@dorot.org;
URL: http://www.dorot.org
Limitations: Giving primarily in the U.S. and Israel.

The M. S. Doss Foundation, Inc.
P.O. Box 1677
Seminole, TX 79360-1677 (915) 758-2770
Limitations: Giving primarily in the eastern NM and western TX area; giving limited to Gaines County, TX, for scholarships.

The Dow Chemical Company Foundation
2030 Dow Ctr.
Midland, MI 48674
URL: http://www.dow.com/about/corp/social/social.htm
Limitations: Giving primarily in areas of company operations.

The Herbert H. and Grace A. Dow Foundation
1018 W. Main St.
Midland, MI 48640-4292 (989) 631-3699
FAX: (989) 631-0675;
E-mail: info@hhdowfoundation.org; URL: http://www.hhdowfoundation.org
Limitations: Giving limited to MI, with emphasis on Midland County.
Publishes an annual or periodic report.

Joseph Drown Foundation
1999 Ave. of the Stars, Ste. 2330
Los Angeles, CA 90067 (310) 277-4488
FAX: (310) 277-4573; E-mail: staff@jdrown.org;
URL: http://www.jdrown.org
Limitations: Giving primarily in Los Angeles, CA.

Doris Duke Charitable Foundation
650 5th Ave., 19th Fl.
New York, NY 10019 (212) 974-7000
FAX: (212) 974-7590; Additional tel.: (212) 974-7100; URL: http://www.ddcf.org
Limitations: Giving on a national basis.

The Duke Endowment
100 N. Tryon St., Ste. 3500
Charlotte, NC 28202-4012 (704) 376-0291
FAX: (704) 376-9336; E-mail: cperleins@tde.org;
URL: http://www.dukeendowment.org
Limitations: Giving limited to NC and SC.
Publishes an annual or periodic report.

Jessie Ball duPont Fund
1 Independent Dr., Ste. 1400
Jacksonville, FL 32202-5011 (904) 353-0890
FAX: (904) 353-3870;
E-mail: contactus@dupontfund.org; Additional tel.: (800) 252-3452; Additional e-mails: smagill@dupontfund.org (for Sherry P. Magill), jbennett@dupontfund.org (for Jo Ann P. Bennett), sdouglass@dupontfund.org (for Sally Douglass), ekingjr.@dupontfund.org (for Edward King), and sgreene@dupontfund.org (for Sharon Greene); URL: http://www.dupontfund.org/
Limitations: Giving primarily in the South, especially DE, FL, and VA.
Publishes an annual or periodic report.

Dyson Foundation
25 Halcyon Rd.
Millbrook, NY 12545 (845) 677-0644
FAX: (845) 677-0650; E-mail: info@dyson.org;
URL: http://www.dysonfoundation.org
Limitations: Giving primarily in Dutchess County, NY, and organizations providing services in Dutchess County; limited grants to other Mid-Hudson Valley counties. National and other grants on a solicited basis.
Publishes an annual or periodic report.

E.ON U.S. Foundation
220 W. Main St.
Louisville, KY 40202
FAX: (502) 627-3629; Application address: P.O. Box 32030, Louisville, KY 40232; URL: http://www.lgeenergy.com/foundation/default.asp
Limitations: Giving primarily in areas of company operations in KY.

Earhart Foundation
2200 Green Rd., Ste. H
Ann Arbor, MI 48105
Publishes an annual or periodic report.

The Eaton Charitable Fund
c/o Eaton Corp.
1111 Superior Ave.
Cleveland, OH 44114-2584 (216) 523-4944
FAX: (216) 479-7013;
E-mail: barrydoggett@eaton.com; URL: http://www.eaton.com/NASApp/cs/ContentServer?pagename=EatonCom%2FPage%2FEC_T_ArticleFull&c=Page&cid=1007421140590
Limitations: Giving on a national and international basis in areas of company operations.
Publishes an annual or periodic report.

George S. and Dolores Dore Eccles Foundation
79 S. Main St., 12th Fl.
Salt Lake City, UT 84111 (801) 246-5340
FAX: (801) 350-3510; E-mail: gse@gseccles.org;
URL: http://www.gsecclesfoundation.org

Limitations: Giving primarily in the intermountain area, particularly UT.

Eden Hall Foundation
600 Grant St., Ste. 3232
Pittsburgh, PA 15219 (412) 642-6697
FAX: (412) 642-6698; URL: http://www.edenhallfdn.org
Limitations: Giving limited to southwestern PA.

The Educational Foundation of America
35 Church Ln.
Westport, CT 06880-3515 (203) 226-6498
E-mail: efa@efaw.org; Letter of inquiry E-mail: loi@efaw.org; URL: http://www.efaw.org
Limitations: Giving limited to the U.S.
Publishes an annual or periodic report.

The Eisner Foundation, Inc.
9401 Wilshire Blvd., Ste. 760
Beverly Hills, CA 90212 (310) 777-3640
FAX: (310) 777-3644; URL: http://www.eisnerfoundation.org
Limitations: Giving limited to Los Angeles and Orange counties, CA.

El Pomar Foundation
10 Lake Cir.
Colorado Springs, CO 80906 (719) 633-7733
FAX: (719) 577-5702; Additional tel.: (800) 554-7711; URL: http://www.elpomar.org
Limitations: Giving limited to CO.
Publishes an annual or periodic report.

The Ellison Foundation
c/o David L. Babson Co.
1 Memorial Dr.
Cambridge, MA 02142-1300
Limitations: Giving primarily in MA.

Emerson Charitable Trust
8000 W. Florissant Ave.
P.O. Box 4100
St. Louis, MO 63136 (314) 553-2000
Limitations: Giving primarily in areas of company operations.

Energy Foundation
1012 Torney Ave., No. 1
San Francisco, CA 94129 (415) 561-6700
FAX: (415) 561-6709; E-mail: energyfund@ef.org;
URL: http://www.ef.org
Limitations: Giving limited to the U.S. and China.
Publishes an annual or periodic report.

The Charles Engelhard Foundation
c/o Engelhard Hanovia, Inc.
Olympic Twrs.
645 5th Ave., Ste. 712
New York, NY 10022 (212) 935-2433
Limitations: Giving primarily on a national basis.

Englander Foundation, Inc.
740 Park Ave.
New York, NY 10021 (212) 841-4148
Limitations: Giving primarily in the metropolitan New York, NY, area.

English-Bonter-Mitchell Foundation
c/o National City Bank
110 W. Berry St.
Fort Wayne, IN 46802-2316
Limitations: Giving primarily in Fort Wayne, IN.

Enterprise Rent-A-Car Foundation
600 Corporate Park Dr.
St. Louis, MO 63105 (314) 512-5000
FAX: (314) 512-4754; URL: http://
aboutus.enterprise.com/what_we_believe/
our_foundation.html
Limitations: Giving on a national and international
basis in areas of company operations, including
in Canada and the United Kingdom.

ExxonMobil Foundation
5959 Las Colinas Blvd.
Irving, TX 75039-2298 (972) 444-1104
URL: http://www.exxonmobil.com/community
Limitations: Giving primarily in Baldwin and Mobile
counties, AL, Anchorage, Fairbanks, Juneau, and
North Slope, AK, Santa Barbara County and
Torrance, CA, Cortez and Rio Blanco County, CO,
Washington, DC, LaGrange, GA, Joliet, IL,
Kingman and Stevens County, KS, Baton Rouge,
Chalmette, Grand Isle, Gueydan, and Kaplan, LA,
Detroit, MI, Billings, MT, Clinton and Paulsboro,
NJ, Lee County, NM, Rochester, NY, Akron, OH,
Shawnee and Texas County, OK, Exton, PA,
Baytown, Beaumont, Dallas, Fort Worth,
Houston, Longview, Midland, Odessa, and Tyler,
TX, San Juan County, UT, Fairfax County and
northern VA, and Lincoln, Sublette, and
Sweetwater counties, WY; giving also in
developing countries.
Publishes an annual or periodic report.

Richard M. Fairbanks Foundation, Inc.
9292 N. Meridan St., Ste. 304
Indianapolis, IN 46260 (317) 846-7111
FAX: (317) 844-0167; E-mail (for Betsy Bikoff):
Bikoff@rmfairbanksfoundation.org; URL: http://
www.rmfairbanksfoundation.org
Limitations: Giving primarily in greater Indianapolis,
IN.

The Sherman Fairchild Foundation, Inc.
5454 Wisconsin Ave., Ste. 1205
Chevy Chase, MD 20815 (301) 913-5990
Limitations: Giving on a national basis.

Fannie Mae Foundation
4000 Wisconsin Ave., N.W.
N. Tower, Ste. 1
Washington, DC 20016-2804 (202) 274-8057
FAX: (202) 274-8100;
E-mail: grants@fanniemaefoundation.org;
Application addresses: James A. Johnson
Community Fellowship Prog.: Wendy New, Dir.,
Policy and Leadership Devel., 4000 Wisconsin
Ave., N.W., N. Tower, Ste. 1, Washington, DC
20016-2804, tel.: (202) 274-8043, FAX: (202)
274-8101, E-mail:
wnew@fanniemaefoundation.org, Maxwell
Awards of Excellence Prog.: Maxwell Awards of
Excellence, c/o Christine Tucker, Mgr., Policy and
Leadership Devel., 4000 Wisconsin Ave., N.W.,
N. Tower, Ste. 1, Washington, DC 20016-2804,
tel.: (202) 274-8044, E-mail:
ctucker@fanniemaefoundation.org; Contact for
Fannie Mae Foundation Fellowship Program at
the Kennedy School of Government: Wendy New,
Dir., Policy and Leadership Devel., tel.: (202)
274-8043, FAX: (202) 274-8101, E-mail:
wnew@fanniemaefoundation.org; Tel. for Fannie
Mae Foundation Innovations in American
Government Award in Affordable Housing: (800)
722-0074; E-mail for Fannie Mae Foundation
Innovations in American Government Award in
Affordable Housing:
webmaster@innovationsaward.harvard.edu;
URL: http://www.fanniemaefoundation.org
Limitations: Giving on a national basis, with emphasis
on Washington, DC.
Publishes an annual or periodic report.

Joseph and Bessie Feinberg Foundation
505 N. Lake Shore Dr., Ste. 1005
Chicago, IL 60611
Limitations: Giving primarily in IL.

Fidelity Foundation
82 Devonshire St., S2
Boston, MA 02109-3614 (617) 563-6806
URL: http://www.fidelityfoundation.org
Limitations: Giving on a national basis and in Canada,
with emphasis on areas of company operations,
including Northern KY, Boston and Marlborough,
MA, Merrimack, NH, Jersey City, NJ, lower
Manhattan, NY, NC, Cincinnati, OH, Smithfield,
RI, Dallas, Fort Worth, and northern TX, Salt Lake
City, UT, and Toronto, Canada.

The Fifth Third Foundation
c/o Fifth Third Bank
38 Fountain Square Plz., M.D. 1090CA
Cincinnati, OH 45263 (513) 534-7001
Limitations: Giving primarily in areas of company
operations, with emphasis on the Cincinnati, OH,
area.
Publishes an annual or periodic report.

V. O. Figge and Elizabeth Kahl Figge Charitable
Foundation
326 W. 3rd St, Ste. 714
Davenport, IA 52801 (563) 336-8902
Limitations: Giving primarily in IA.

Leland Fikes Foundation, Inc.
500 N. Akard St., Ste. 1919
Dallas, TX 75201-3322 (214) 754-0144
Limitations: Giving primarily in the Dallas, TX, area.

First Data Western Union Foundation
6200 S. Quebec St., Ste. 370AU
Greenwood Village, CO 80111 (303) 967-6606
FAX: (303) 967-6492;
E-mail: luella.dangelo@firstdata.com; Application
address for organizations located outside the
U.S.: Ellen Y. Brown, Sr. Prog. Dir., 6200 S.
Quebec St., Ste. 370AU, Greenwood Village, CO
80111, tel.: (303) 967-6535; Additional tel.:
(303) 967-6305; URL: http://
www.firstdatawesternunion.org
Limitations: Giving on a national and international
basis in areas of company operations, with
emphasis on the metropolitan Denver, CO, area,
Coral Springs and Hollywood, FL, Hagerstown,
MD, Omaha, NE, Melville, NY, Houston, TX, and
in China, India, and Mexico.
Publishes an annual or periodic report.

First Interstate BancSystem Foundation, Inc.
490 N. 31st St., Ste. 300
Billings, MT 59101 (406) 255-5393
Limitations: Giving primarily in areas of company
operations in MT and WY.

FirstEnergy Foundation
76 S. Main St.
Akron, OH 44308 (330) 761-4246
URL: http://www.firstenergycorp.com/community
Limitations: Giving primarily in areas of company
operations in NJ, OH, and PA.

Flight Attendant Medical Research Institute,
Inc.
201 S. Biscayne Blvd., Ste. 1310
Miami, FL 33131 (305) 379-7007
FAX: (305) 577-0005; E-mail: ekress@famri.org;
URL: http://www.famri.org
Limitations: Giving on a national basis.

Flora Family Foundation
2121 Sand Hill Rd., Ste. 123
Menlo Park, CA 94025 (650) 233-1335
FAX: (650) 233-1340; E-mail: info@florafamily.org;
URL: http://www.florafamily.org

The Fondren Foundation
P.O. Box 2558
Houston, TX 77252-8037 (713) 216-4513
Limitations: Giving primarily in TX, with emphasis on
Houston.

The Ford Family Foundation
1600 N.W. Stewart Pkwy.
Roseburg, OR 97470 (541) 957-5574
FAX: (541) 957-5720; E-mail: info@tfff.org;
URL: http://www.tfff.org
Limitations: Giving primarily in rural OR, with special
interest in Douglas and Coos counties; giving
also in Siskiyou County, CA.

The Ford Foundation
320 E. 43rd St.
New York, NY 10017 (212) 573-5000
FAX: (212) 351-3677;
E-mail: office-secretary@fordfound.org;
URL: http://www.fordfound.org
Limitations: Giving on an international basis,
including the U.S., Africa and the Middle East,
Asia, Russia, Latin America and the Caribbean.
Publishes an annual or periodic report.

Ford Motor Company Fund
1 American Rd.
P.O. Box 1899
Dearborn, MI 48126-2798 (313) 248-4745
FAX: (313) 594-7001; E-mail: fordfund@ford.com;
Additional tel.: (888) 313-0102; URL: http://
www.ford.com/go/fordfund
Limitations: Giving primarily in areas of company
operations, with emphasis on southeastern MI.
Publishes an annual or periodic report.

Forest City Enterprises Charitable Foundation,
Inc.
1100 Terminal Tower
50 Public Sq., Ste. 1100
Cleveland, OH 44113 (216) 621-6060
Limitations: Giving primarily in OH.

Foundation for Child Development
145 E. 32nd St., 14th Fl.
New York, NY 10016-6055
FAX: (212) 213-5897;
E-mail: inforequest@fcd-us.org; URL: http://
www.fcd-us.org
Limitations: Giving limited to research and policy
grants related to foundation focus and restricted
to the U.S.
Publishes an annual or periodic report.

Foundation for the Carolinas
217 S. Tryon St.
Charlotte, NC 28202 (704) 973-4500
FAX: (704) 973-4599; E-mail: infor@fftc.org;
Additional tel.: (800) 973-7244; Additional
E-mail: djonas@fftc.org; URL: http://www.fftc.org
Limitations: Giving primarily to organizations serving
the citizens of NC and SC, with emphasis on the
greater Charlotte, NC, region.
Publishes an annual or periodic report.

The Freedom Forum, Inc.
1101 Wilson Blvd.
Arlington, VA 22209-2248 (703) 528-0800

FAX: (703) 284-3770;
E-mail: news@freedomforum.org; URL: http://
www.freedomforum.org
Limitations: Giving on a national and international
basis.
Publishes an annual or periodic report.

Freeman Foundation
c/o The Rockefeller Trust Company
30 Rockefeller Plz.
New York, NY 10112 (212) 649-5853
E-mail: freemanfoundation@hjsimmons.com;
Application address: 499 Tabor Hill Road, Stowe,
VT 05672
Limitations: Giving primarily in VT for conservation and
environment grants; Asian studies grants are
awarded nationally.
Publishes an annual or periodic report.

The Ella West Freeman Foundation
P.O. Box 13218
New Orleans, LA 70185-3218 (504) 895-1984
FAX: (504) 895-1988; E-mail: info@ellawest.org;
URL: http://www.ellawest.org
Limitations: Giving primarily in the greater New
Orleans, LA, area.

Fremont Area Community Foundation
4424 W. 48th St.
P.O. Box B
Fremont, MI 49412 (231) 924-5350
FAX: (231) 924-5391; E-mail: info@tfacf.org;
Additional FAX: (231) 924-7637; Additional
E-mails: echerin@tfacf.org and
gzerlaut@tfacf.org; URL: http://www.tfacf.org
Limitations: Giving primarily in Newaygo County, MI.
Publishes an annual or periodic report.

Frey Foundation
40 Pearl St. N.W., Ste. 1100
Grand Rapids, MI 49503-3028 (616) 451-0303
FAX: (616) 451-8481; E-mail: contact@freyfdn.org;
URL: http://www.freyfdn.org
Limitations: Giving primarily in Emmet, Charlevoix,
and Kent counties, MI.
Publishes an annual or periodic report.

Charles A. Frueauff Foundation, Inc.
3 Financial Ctr.
900 S. Shackleford, Ste. 300
Little Rock, AR 72211 (501) 219-1410
URL: http://www.frueauffoundation.com
Limitations: Giving limited to the U.S. with emphasis
on east of the Rockies, the South, and Northeast.

Lloyd A. Fry Foundation
120 S. LaSalle St., Ste. 1950
Chicago, IL 60603-3419 (312) 580-0310
FAX: (312) 580-0980;
E-mail: usong@fryfoundation.org; URL: http://
www.fryfoundation.org
Limitations: Giving generally limited to Chicago, IL.
Publishes an annual or periodic report.

Gannett Foundation, Inc.
7950 Jones Branch Dr.
McLean, VA 22107
FAX: (703) 854-2167;
E-mail: isimpson@gannett.com; URL: http://
www.gannettfoundation.org
Limitations: Giving primarily in areas of company daily
newspaper and television station operations,
including in the United Kingdom.
Publishes an annual or periodic report.

The GAR Foundation
50 S. Main St.
P.O. Box 1500
Akron, OH 44309-1500 (330) 643-0201
FAX: (330) 252-5584; E-mail: GAR@bdblaw.com;
Temporary relocation address: 3875 Embassy
Pkwy., Ste. 250 Akron, OH 44333; Additional
E-mail: RBriggs@BDBlaw.com; URL: http://
www.garfdn.org
Limitations: Giving primarily in the Akron-Summit
County area and secondarily in Cuyahoga, Stark,
Medina, Portage and Wayne counties, OH.

John Jewett & Helen Chandler Garland
Foundation
P.O. Box 550
Pasadena, CA 91102-0550
Limitations: Giving primarily in CA, with emphasis on
southern CA.

Gates Family Foundation
3575 Cherry Creek N. Dr., Ste. 100
Denver, CO 80209 (303) 722-1881
FAX: (303) 316-3038;
E-mail: info@gatesfamilyfoundation.org;
URL: http://www.gatesfamilyfoundation.org
Limitations: Giving limited to CO, with emphasis on
the Denver area, except for foundation-initiated
grants.
Publishes an annual or periodic report.

Bill & Melinda Gates Foundation
P.O. Box 23350
Seattle, WA 98102 (206) 709-3100
FAX: (206) 709-3180;
E-mail: info@gatesfoundation.org; URL: http://
www.gatesfoundation.org
Limitations: Giving on a national and international
basis to support initiatives in health and learning;
the foundation also supports community giving in
the Pacific Northwest.
Publishes an annual or periodic report.

GE Foundation
3135 Easton Tpke.
Fairfield, CT 06828-0001 (203) 373-3216
FAX: (203) 373-3029; E-mail: gefoundation@ge.com;
URL: http://www.gefoundation.com
Limitations: Giving on a national and international
basis, with emphasis on areas of company
operations.

The Carl Gellert and Celia Berta Gellert
Foundation
1169 Market St., Ste. 808
San Francisco, CA 94103 (415) 255-2829
URL: http://www.gellertfoundation.org/
Limitations: Giving limited to the nine counties of the
greater San Francisco Bay Area, CA, (Alameda,
Contra Costa, Marin, Napa, San Francisco, San
Mateo, Santa Clara, Solano and Sonoma).

General Mills Foundation
P.O. Box 1113
Minneapolis, MN 55440
FAX: (763) 764-4114; URL: http://
www.generalmills.com/corporate/commitment/
foundation.aspx
Limitations: Giving primarily in areas of major
company operations.
Publishes an annual or periodic report.

Georgia-Pacific Foundation, Inc.
133 Peachtree St. N.E.
Atlanta, GA 30303 (404) 652-4182
FAX: (404) 749-2754; URL: http://www.gp.com/
center/community/index.html

Limitations: Giving limited to areas of company
operations.

Wallace Alexander Gerbode Foundation
111 Pine St., Ste. 1515
San Francisco, CA 94111-5602 (415) 391-0911
FAX: (415) 391-4587; E-mail: info@gerbode.org;
URL: http://www.foundationcenter.org/
grantmaker/gerbode/
Limitations: Giving primarily to programs directly
affecting residents of Alameda, Contra Costa,
Marin, San Francisco, and San Mateo counties in
CA, and HI.
Publishes an annual or periodic report.

The Rollin M. Gerstacker Foundation
P.O. Box 1945
Midland, MI 48641-1945 (989) 631-6097
Limitations: Giving primarily in MI; giving also in OH.
Publishes an annual or periodic report.

The Ann and Gordon Getty Foundation
1 Embarcadero Ctr., Ste. 1050
San Francisco, CA 94111-3600
Limitations: Giving primarily in CA, with emphasis on
the San Francisco Bay Area.

J. Paul Getty Trust
1200 Getty Ctr. Dr., Ste. 800
Los Angeles, CA 90049-1685 (310) 440-7320
FAX: (310) 440-7703; URL: http://www.getty.edu
Limitations: Giving on an international basis.
Publishes an annual or periodic report.

Gibbs Charitable Foundation
P.O. Box 1727
Spartanburg, SC 29304-1727
Limitations: Giving primarily in SC.

Gilder Foundation, Inc.
1775 Broadway
New York, NY 10019
Limitations: Giving primarily in NY.

Gilhousen Family Foundation
599 High Tower Rd.
Bozeman, MT 59718 (406) 586-2517
E-mail: foundation.admin@gilhousen.net; Tel. for
Patti A. Guptill: (503) 643-4183
Limitations: Giving primarily in Gallatin County, MT.

The Gill Foundation
2215 Market St.
Denver, CO 80205 (303) 292-4455
FAX: (303) 292-2155;
E-mail: info@gillfoundation.org; Additional toll
free tel.: (888) 530-4455; Additional contact inf.
(for Gay & Lesbian Fund for Colorado): 315 E.
Costilla St., Colorado Springs, CO 80903, toll
free tel.: (800) 964-5643, tel.: (719) 473-4455,
FAX: (719) 473-2254, E-mail: info@gayand
lesbianfund.org; URL: http://
www.gillfoundation.org
Limitations: Giving primarily to national and state-wide
organizations.
Publishes an annual or periodic report.

Gleason Foundation
P.O. Box 22970
Rochester, NY 14692-2970 (585) 241-4030
FAX: (585) 241-4099;
E-mail: gf@gleasonfoundation.org
Limitations: Giving primarily in Monroe County, NY.

Eugene and Marilyn Glick Foundation
Corporation
P.O. Box 40177
Indianapolis, IN 46240
Limitations: Giving primarily in Indianapolis, IN.

Lisa and Douglas Goldman Fund
1 Daniel Burnham Ct., Ste. 330C
San Francisco, CA 94109-5460 (415) 771-1717
FAX: (415) 771-1797; URL: http://
foundationcenter.org/grantmaker/goldman/
Limitations: Giving primarily in the San Francisco Bay
Area, CA.

Publishes an annual or periodic report.

Richard and Rhoda Goldman Fund
P.O. Box 29924
211 Lincoln Blvd.
San Francisco, CA 94129 (415) 345-6300
FAX: (415) 345-9686; URL: http://
www.goldmanfund.org
Limitations: Giving primarily in the San Francisco Bay
Area, CA, and Israel. Giving nationally and
internationally in the areas of population and the
environment.

Publishes an annual or periodic report.

Horace W. Goldsmith Foundation
375 Park Ave., Ste. 1602
New York, NY 10152
Limitations: Giving primarily in AZ, MA, and New York,
NY.

The Gottesman Fund
1818 N St. N.W., Ste. 700
Washington, DC 20036 (202) 785-2727
Limitations: Giving primarily in NY.

Gottstein Family Foundation
c/o B. J. Gottstein
550 W. 7th Ave., Ste. 1540
Anchorage, AK 99501-3567

The Florence Gould Foundation
c/o Cahill Gordon & Reindel LLP
80 Pine St.
New York, NY 10005 (212) 701-3400
Limitations: Giving primarily in the U.S. and France.

The Grable Foundation
650 Smithfield St., Ste. 240
Pittsburgh, PA 15222 (412) 471-4550
FAX: (412) 471-2267; E-mail: grable@grablefdn.org;
URL: http://www.grablefdn.org/
Limitations: Giving primarily in southwestern PA.

Publishes an annual or periodic report.

Philip L. Graham Fund
c/o The Washington Post Co.
1150 15th St. N.W.
Washington, DC 20071 (202) 334-6640
FAX: (202) 334-4498;
E-mail: plgfund@washpost.com
Limitations: Giving primarily in the metropolitan
Washington, DC, area.

Grand Rapids Community Foundation
161 Ottawa Ave. N.W., Ste. 209-C
Grand Rapids, MI 49503-2757 (616) 454-1751
FAX: (616) 454-6455;
E-mail: grfound@grfoundation.org; Grant inquiry
tel.: (616) 454-1751, ext. 123, and E-mail:
apuckett@grfoundation.org; URL: http://
www.grfoundation.org
Limitations: Giving limited to Kent County, MI.

Publishes an annual or periodic report.

Grand Victoria Foundation
200 W. Monroe St., Ste. 2530
Chicago, IL 60606 (312) 609-0200
FAX: (312) 658-0738;
E-mail: nancyf@grandvictoriafdn.org; Application
address for Elgin Grantworks: 60 S. Grove Ave.,
Elgin, IL 60120, tel.: (847) 289-8575, FAX: (847)
289-8576; Additional E-mail:
info@grandvictoriafdn.org; URL: http://
www.grandvictoriafdn.org
Limitations: Giving limited to IL, with emphasis on the
Chicago metropolitan area, Elgin, and southern
Cook, DeKalb, DuPage, Kane, Kendall, Lake,
McHenry, Winnebago, and Will counties.

William T. Grant Foundation
570 Lexington Ave., 18th Fl.
New York, NY 10022-6837 (212) 752-0071
FAX: (212) 752-1398; E-mail: info@wtgrantfdn.org;
URL: http://www.wtgrantfoundation.org
Limitations: Giving on a national basis; giving limited
to NY, NJ, and CT for youth service grants.

Publishes an annual or periodic report.

The Greenwall Foundation
420 Lexington Ave., Ste. 2500
New York, NY 10170 (212) 679-7266
FAX: (212) 679-7269; E-mail: admin@greenwall.org;
URL: http://www.greenwall.org
Limitations: Giving primarily in New York, NY, for arts
and humanities; giving nationally for bioethics.

The Gruss-Lipper Family Foundation
c/o Grusso & Co.
667 Madison Ave.
New York, NY 10021-8029
Limitations: Giving on a national basis and in Israel.

Henry L. Guenther Foundation
2029 Century Park E., Ste. 4392
Los Angeles, CA 90067 (310) 785-0658
Limitations: Giving primarily in southern CA.

The George Gund Foundation
1845 Guildhall Bldg.
45 Prospect Ave. W.
Cleveland, OH 44115-1018 (216) 241-3114
FAX: (216) 241-6560; E-mail: info@gundfdn.org;
URL: http://www.gundfdn.org
Limitations: Giving primarily in northeastern OH and
the greater Cleveland, OH, area.

Publishes an annual or periodic report.

Miriam and Peter Haas Fund
201 Filbert St., 5th Fl.
San Francisco, CA 94133-3238 (415) 296-9249
FAX: (415) 296-8842; E-mail: mphf@mphf.org;
E-mail: gmeagher@mphf.org
Limitations: Giving primarily in San Francisco, CA;
early childhood, direct service component is
limited to San Francisco.

Publishes an annual or periodic report.

Walter and Elise Haas Fund
1 Lombard St., Ste. 305
San Francisco, CA 94111 (415) 398-4474
URL: http://www.haassr.org
Limitations: Giving primarily in San Francisco and
Alameda County, CA; Jewish Life grants are
awarded throughout the Bay Area.

Publishes an annual or periodic report.

Evelyn and Walter Haas, Jr. Fund
1 Market, Landmark, Ste. 400

Publishes an annual or periodic report.

San Francisco, CA 94105 (415) 856-1400
FAX: (415) 856-1500; E-mail: guidelines@haasjr.org;
URL: http://www.haasjr.org
Limitations: Giving primarily in San Francisco and
Alameda counties, CA.

Hall Family Foundation
P.O. Box 419580, Dept. 323
Kansas City, MO 64141-6580
FAX: (816) 274-8547; URL: http://
www.hallfamilyfoundation.org
Limitations: Giving limited to greater Kansas City, MO.

Publishes an annual or periodic report.

The Hall-Perrine Foundation, Inc.
115 3rd St., S.E., Ste. 803
Cedar Rapids, IA 52401-1222
Limitations: Giving limited to Linn County, IA.

The Hamill Foundation
1160 Dairy Ashford, Ste. 250
Houston, TX 77079-3014 (281) 556-9581
FAX: (281) 556-0456;
E-mail: cread_hamill@sbcglobal.net
Limitations: Giving primarily in Houston, TX.

The Hamilton-White Foundation
P.O. Box 9969
San Diego, CA 92169
URL: http://www.hamiltonwhitefoundation.org
Limitations: Giving primarily in San Diego, CA.

The John K. & Luise V. Hanson Foundation
P.O. Box 450
Forest City, IA 50436
Limitations: Giving primarily in north central IA.

Harman Family Foundation
1101 Pennsylvania Ave. N.W.
Washington, DC 20004
Limitations: Giving primarily in Los Angeles, CA,
Washington, DC, MD, and New York, NY.

Gladys and Roland Harriman Foundation
c/o Brown Brothers Harriman Trust Co., LLC
140 Broadway, 4th Fl.
New York, NY 10005
Limitations: Giving on a national basis.

The Irving Harris Foundation
191 N. Wacker Dr., Ste. 1500
Chicago, IL 60606

Hartford Foundation for Public Giving
85 Gillett St.
Hartford, CT 06105 (860) 548-1888
FAX: (860) 524-8346; E-mail: hfpg2@hfpg.org;
Additional E-mail: RPorth@hfpg.org; URL: http://
www.hfpg.org
Limitations: Giving limited to the Greater Hartford, CT,
area.

Publishes an annual or periodic report.

The John A. Hartford Foundation, Inc.
55 E. 59th St., 16th Fl.
New York, NY 10022 (212) 832-7788
FAX: (212) 593-4913; E-mail: mail@jhartfound.org;
URL: http://www.jhartfound.org
Limitations: Giving primarily on a national basis.

Publishes an annual or periodic report.

Hawaii Community Foundation
1164 Bishop St., Ste. 800
Honolulu, HI 96813 (808) 537-6333

FAX: (808) 521-6286; E-mail: info@hcf-hawaii.org;
Additional tel.: (888) 731-3863; Scholarship
inquiry E-mail: scholarships@hcf-hawaii.org;
URL: http://
www.hawaiicommunityfoundation.org
Limitations: Giving limited to HI.
Publishes an annual or periodic report.

Charles Hayden Foundation
140 Broadway, 51st Fl.
New York, NY 10005 (212) 785-3677
FAX: (212) 785-3689; E-mail: fdn@chf.org; Boston
Office: c/o Grants Mgmt. Assocs., 77 Summer
St., 8th Fl., Boston, MA 02110, tel.: (617)
426-7080, ext. 306; URL: http://
www.charleshaydenfoundation.org
Limitations: Giving limited to the metropolitan Boston,
MA, and the metropolitan New York, NY areas
(including the cities of Newark, Jersey City, and
Paterson, NJ).

The HCA Foundation
1 Park Plz., Building 1, 4th Fl. E.
Nashville, TN 37203 (615) 344-2390
FAX: (615) 344-5722;
E-mail: lois.abrams@hcahealthcare.com;
URL: http://www.hcacaring.org/
Limitations: Giving primarily in middle TN.

Healthcare Georgia Foundation, Inc.
50 Hurt Plz, Ste. 1100
Atlanta, GA 30303 (404) 653-0990
FAX: (404) 577-8386;
E-mail: info@healthcaregeorgia.org; URL: http://
www.healthcaregeorgia.org/
Limitations: Giving limited to GA.
Publishes an annual or periodic report.

The Hearst Foundation, Inc.
Hearst Twrs.
300 W. 57th St., 26th Fl.
New York, NY 10019-3741 (212) 586-5404
FAX: (212) 586-1917; Address for applicants from
west of the Mississippi River: c/o Paul I. Dinovitz,
V.P. and Western Dir., 90 New Montgomery St.,
Ste. 1212, San Francisco, CA 94105, tel.: (415)
543-0400; URL: http://www.hearstfdn.org/
Limitations: Giving limited to the U.S. and its
territories.

Howard Heinz Endowment
30 Dominion Twr.
625 Liberty Ave.
Pittsburgh, PA 15222-3115 (412) 281-5777
FAX: (412) 281-5788; E-mail: info@heinz.org;
URL: http://www.heinz.org
Limitations: Giving primarily directed to southwestern
PA, although in certain cases support may be
considered on a national or international basis.
Publishes an annual or periodic report.

Vira I. Heinz Endowment
30 Dominion Twr.
625 Liberty Ave.
Pittsburgh, PA 15222-3115 (412) 281-5777
FAX: (412) 281-5788; E-mail: info@heinz.org;
URL: http://www.heinz.org
Limitations: Giving primarily directed to southwestern
PA, although in certain cases support may be
considered on a national or international basis.
Publishes an annual or periodic report.

Heritage Mark Foundation
P.O. Box 980
East Lansing, MI 48826-0980
Limitations: Giving on a national basis.

The F. B. Heron Foundation
100 Broadway, 17th Fl.
New York, NY 10005
URL: http://www.heronfdn.org
Limitations: Giving primarily in Appalachia; CA;
Chicago, IL; MI; Kansas City, MO; Twin Cities,
MN; the Mississippi Delta; NC; NJ; New York, NY;
and TX.
Publishes an annual or periodic report.

Herrick Foundation
150 W. Jefferson Ave., Ste. 2500
Detroit, MI 48226
Limitations: Giving primarily in MI; giving also in the
New York Metropolitan area, Washington, DC, IN,
MS, OH, OK, TN, and WI.

The William and Flora Hewlett Foundation
2121 Sand Hill Rd.
Menlo Park, CA 94025 (650) 234-4500
FAX: (650) 234-4501; URL: http://www.hewlett.org
Limitations: Giving limited to the San Francisco Bay
Area, CA, for family and community development
programs; performing arts primarily limited to the
Bay Area.
Publishes an annual or periodic report.

The Highland Street Connection
463 Worcester Rd., Ste. 403
Framingham, MA 01701 (508) 820-1151
FAX: (508) 820-1152;
E-mail: info@highlandstreet.org; URL: http://
www.highlandstreet.org
Limitations: Giving primarily in MA.

Hillcrest Foundation
c/o Bank of America, N.A.
P.O. Box 830241
Dallas, TX 75283-1041 (214) 209-1965
Limitations: Giving limited to TX, with emphasis on
Dallas County.

Conrad N. Hilton Foundation
100 W. Liberty St., Ste. 840
Reno, NV 89501
FAX: (310) 556-2301;
E-mail: cnhf@hiltonfoundation.org; Additional
address (Los Angeles office): 10100 Santa
Monica Blvd., No. 1000, Los Angeles, CA 90067;
URL: http://www.hiltonfoundation.org
Publishes an annual or periodic report.

HMSA Foundation
P.O. Box 860
818 Ke'eaumoku St.
Honolulu, HI 96808-0860 (808) 948-5585
FAX: (808) 948-6860; URL: http://
www.hmsafoundation.org
Limitations: Giving primarily in Honolulu, HI.

Mildred V. Horn Foundation
South Highway 53, Ste. 3, PMB 2028
La Grange, KY 40031-9119 (502) 895-2622
Limitations: Giving primarily in KY (for homeless
shelters and education) and historic homes open
to the public in KY, IL, IN, MO, OH, TN, VA, and
WV.

Houston Endowment Inc.
600 Travis, Ste. 6400
Houston, TX 77002-3000 (713) 238-8100
FAX: (713) 238-8101;
E-mail: info@houstonendowment.org;
URL: http://www.houstonendowment.org
Limitations: Giving primarily in Houston, TX; no grants
outside the continental U.S.

Publishes an annual or periodic report.

The R. D. & Joan Dale Hubbard Foundation
P.O. Box 2498
Ruidoso, NM 88345 (505) 258-5919
Limitations: Giving primarily in CA, KS, NM, OK, and
TX.
Publishes an annual or periodic report.

Hudson-Webber Foundation
333 W. Fort St., Ste. 1310
Detroit, MI 48226-3149 (313) 963-7777
FAX: (313) 963-2818;
E-mail: HWF@hudson-webber.org; URL: http://
www.hudson-webber.org
Limitations: Giving primarily in the city of Detroit, and
the tri-county Wayne, Oakland, and Macomb area
of southeastern MI.

The Humana Foundation, Inc.
500 W. Main St.
Louisville, KY 40202 (502) 580-3613
FAX: (502) 580-1256; E-mail: bwright@humana.com;
URL: http://www.humanafoundation.org
Limitations: Giving on a national and international
basis in areas of company operations, with
emphasis on Louisville, KY.

Jaquelin Hume Foundation
600 Montgomery St., Ste. 2800
San Francisco, CA 94111 (415) 705-5115
Limitations: Giving to organizations with a national
impact.

Roy A. Hunt Foundation
1 Bigelow Sq., Ste. 630
Pittsburgh, PA 15219-3030 (412) 281-8734
FAX: (412) 255-0522; E-mail: info@rahuntfdn.org;
URL: http://www.rahuntfdn.org
Limitations: Giving primarily in the Boston, MA, and
Pittsburgh, PA, areas, also in CA, ID, NH, ME, and
OH.

The Hyams Foundation, Inc.
50 Federal St., 9th Fl.
Boston, MA 02110 (617) 426-5600
FAX: (617) 426-5696;
E-mail: info@hyamsfoundation.org; Additional
e-mail for questions regarding application
process: sperry@hyamsfoundation.org;
URL: http://www.hyamsfoundation.org
Limitations: Giving primarily in Boston and Chelsea,
MA.
Publishes an annual or periodic report.

The Hyde and Watson Foundation
31-F Mountain Blvd.
Warren, NJ 07059 (908) 753-3700
FAX: (908) 753-0004;
E-mail: hydeandwatson@yahoo.com;
URL: http://foundationcenter.org/grantmaker/
hydeandwatson
Limitations: Giving is focused in the five boroughs of
New York, NY, and Essex, Union and Morris
counties in NJ. No giving outside the U.S.
Publishes an annual or periodic report.

Hyde Family Foundations
17 W. Pontotoc Ave., Ste. 200
Memphis, TN 38103 (901) 685-3400
FAX: (901) 683-3147;
E-mail: info@hydefamilyfoundations.org;
URL: http://www.hydefamilyfoundations.org
Limitations: Giving primarily in Memphis, TN.

Illinois Tool Works Foundation
3600 W. Lake Ave.
Glenview, IL 60025-5811   (847) 724-7500
FAX: (847) 657-4505; E-mail: mmallahan@itw.com;
    URL: http://www.itw.com/itw_foundation.html
Limitations: Giving primarily in areas of company
    operations, with emphasis on Chicago, IL.

Inasmuch Foundation
210 Park Ave., Ste. 3150
Oklahoma City, OK 73102   (405) 604-5292
FAX: (405) 604-0297;
    E-mail: nancy.woodson@inasmuchfoundation.org
    ; URL: http://www.inasmuchfoundation.org
Limitations: Giving primarily in Colorado Springs, CO,
    and OK.

Independence Community Foundation
182 Atlantic Ave.
Brooklyn, NY 11201   (718) 722-2300
FAX: (718) 722-5757; E-mail: inquiries@icfny.org;
    URL: http://www.icfny.org
Limitations: Giving primarily in Nassau, New York,
    Suffolk, and Westchester counties, NY, and
    Bergen, Essex, Hudson, Middlesex, Monmouth,
    Ocean, and Union counties, NJ.

Intel Foundation
5200 N.E. Elam Young Pkwy., AG6-601
Hillsboro, OR 97124-6497
FAX: (503) 456-1539;
    E-mail: intel.foundation@intel.com; URL: http://
    www.intel.com/community/index.htm
Limitations: Giving primarily in Phoenix, AZ, Folsom
    and Santa Clara, CA, Colorado Springs, CO,
    Hudson, MA, Albuquerque, NM, Portland, OR,
    Austin, TX, Riverton, UT, and Dupont, WA; giving
    also to national organizations.

Iowa West Foundation
25 Main Pl., Ste. 550
Council Bluffs, IA 51503   (712) 309-3003
FAX: (712) 322-2267;
    E-mail: grantinfo@iowawestfoundation.org;
    URL: http://www.iowawestfoundation.org
Limitations: Giving primarily in southwest IA and the
    Council Bluffs, Omaha, NE, area.
Publishes an annual or periodic report.

The James Irvine Foundation
575 Market St., Ste. 3400
San Francisco, CA 94105   (415) 777-2244
FAX: (415) 777-0869; Southern CA office: 865 S.
    Figueroa St., Ste. 2308, Los Angeles, CA
    90017-5430, tel.: (213) 236-0552, FAX: (213)
    236-0537; URL: http://www.irvine.org
Limitations: Giving limited to CA.
Publishes an annual or periodic report.

The J & L Foundation
2602 Grassland Dr.
Louisville, KY 40299-2524
Limitations: Giving primarily in Louisville, KY.

Janirve Foundation
1 N. Pack Sq., Ste. 416
Asheville, NC 28801   (828) 258-1877
FAX: (828) 258-1837;
    E-mail: janirve@charterinternet.com
Limitations: Giving primarily in western NC.
Publishes an annual or periodic report.

The Jeld-Wen Foundation
317 S.W. Alder St., Ste. 1100
Portland, OR 97204

Application address: P.O. Box 1329, Klamath Falls,
    OR 97601, tel.: (541) 882-3451
Limitations: Giving primarily in areas of company
    operations in AZ, FL, IA, KY, NC, OR, SD, and WA.

Jerome Foundation
400 Sibley St., Ste. 125
St. Paul, MN 55101-1928   (651) 224-9431
FAX: (651) 224-3439; E-mail: info@jeromefdn.org;
    Toll-free tel.: (800) 995-3766 (MN and New York
    City only); URL: http://www.jeromefdn.org
Limitations: Giving limited to MN and New York, NY.

**Johnson & Johnson Family of Companies
Contribution Fund**
1 Johnson & Johnson Plz.
New Brunswick, NJ 08933   (732) 524-3255
URL: http://www.jnj.com/community/contributions/
    index.htm

Christian A. Johnson Endeavor Foundation
1060 Park Ave.
New York, NY 10128-1033   (212) 534-6620

The Robert Wood Johnson Foundation
Rte. 1 and College Rd. E.
P.O. Box 2316
Princeton, NJ 08543-2316   (888) 631-9989
E-mail: mail@rwjf.org; URL: http://www.rwjf.org
Limitations: Giving limited to the U.S.
Publishes an annual or periodic report.

**The James M. Johnston Trust for Charitable
and Educational Purposes**
2 Wisconsin Cir., Ste. 600
Chevy Chase, MD 20815   (301) 907-0135
Limitations: Giving primarily in Washington, DC, and
    NC.

The Fletcher Jones Foundation
523 W. 6th St., Ste. 301
Los Angeles, CA 90014   (213) 943-4646
FAX: (213) 943-4648; URL: http://
    www.fletcherjonesfdn.org
Limitations: Giving primarily in CA.
Publishes an annual or periodic report.

Helen Jones Foundation, Inc.
P.O. Box 53665
Lubbock, TX 79453
Application address: 4608 89th St., Lubbock, TX
    79424, tel.: (806) 794-8899
Limitations: Giving primarily in Lubbock, TX.

The Joyce Foundation
70 W. Madison St., Ste. 2750
Chicago, IL 60602   (312) 782-2464
FAX: (312) 782-4160; E-mail: info@joycefdn.org;
    URL: http://www.joycefdn.org
Limitations: Giving primarily in the Great Lakes region,
    including IA, IL, IN, MI, MN, OH, and WI; limited
    number of environment grants made in Canada;
    culture grants restricted to the metropolitan
    Chicago, IL, area.
Publishes an annual or periodic report.

The JPMorgan Chase Foundation
270 Park Ave.
New York, NY 10017   (212) 270-6000
E-mail: jpmorgan.chase.grants@jpmchase.com;
    URL: http://www.jpmorganchase.com/grants
Limitations: Giving on a national basis in areas of
    company operations; giving also to U.S.-based
    international organizations active in areas of
    company operations abroad.

Max Kade Foundation, Inc.
6 E. 87th St., 5th Fl.
New York, NY 10128-0505   (646) 672-4354
Limitations: Giving primarily in the U.S. and Europe.

Kahle/Austin Foundation
c/o B. Kahle
513B Simonds Loop
San Francisco, CA 94129
Limitations: Giving primarily in San Francisco, CA.

Kalamazoo Community Foundation
151 S. Rose St., Ste. 332
Kalamazoo, MI 49007-4775   (269) 381-4416
FAX: (269) 381-3146; E-mail: info@kalfound.org;
    Additional E-mails: dgardiner@kalfound.org and
    sspringgate@kalfound.org; URL: http://
    www.kalfound.org
Limitations: Giving generally limited to Kalamazoo
    County, MI.
Publishes an annual or periodic report.

Kansas Health Foundation
309 E. Douglas
Wichita, KS 67202-3405   (316) 262-7676
FAX: (316) 262-2044; E-mail: info@khf.org; Additional
    tel.: (800) 373-7681; E-mail (for Nancy
    Claassen): nclaassen@khf.org; URL: http://
    www.kansashealth.org
Limitations: Giving limited to KS.
Publishes an annual or periodic report.

The J. M. Kaplan Fund, Inc.
261 Madison Ave., 19th Fl.
New York, NY 10016   (212) 767-0630
FAX: (212) 767-0639; E-mail: info@jmkfund.org;
    Application address for Furthermore Grants in
    Publishing program:, c/o Ann Birckmayer, Prog.
    Assoc., P.O. Box 667, Hudson, NY 12534; tel.:
    (518) 828-8900; URL: http://www.jmkfund.org
Limitations: Giving primarily in New York City, NY;
    cross-borders of North America; and worldwide.
Publishes an annual or periodic report.

The Kaplen Foundation
P.O. Box 792
Tenafly, NJ 07670
Limitations: Giving primarily in NJ, with some
    emphasis on Englewood. Some giving also in NY.

Ewing Marion Kauffman Foundation
4801 Rockhill Rd.
Kansas City, MO 64110-2046   (816) 932-1000
FAX: (816) 932-1100; E-mail: info@kauffman.org;
    URL: http://www.kauffman.org
Limitations: Giving limited to the U.S., with emphasis
    on the bi-state metropolitan Kansas City area
    (KS/MO) for K-12 education initiatives focused
    on math and science.
Publishes an annual or periodic report.

Muriel McBrien Kauffman Foundation
4801 Rockhill Rd.
Kansas City, MO 64110
Limitations: Giving primarily in Kansas City, MO, and
    New York, NY.

The Hugh Kaul Foundation
P.O. Box 11426
Birmingham, AL 35202   (205) 326-5382
Limitations: Giving limited to Jefferson, Clay and
    Coosa counties, and the greater metropolitan
    Birmingham, AL, area.

Anna Maria & Stephen Kellen Foundation, Inc.
1345 Ave. of the Americas, 44th Fl.

New York, NY 10105
Limitations: Giving primarily in New York, NY.

W. K. Kellogg Foundation
1 Michigan Ave. E.
Battle Creek, MI 49017-4058 (269) 968-1611
FAX: (269) 968-0413; URL: http://www.wkkf.org
Limitations: Giving primarily in the U.S., Latin America
and the Caribbean, and the South African
countries of Botswana, Lesotho, Malawi, South
Africa, Swaziland, Zimbabwe and Mozambique.
Publishes an annual or periodic report.

Kellogg's Corporate Citizenship Fund
1 Kellogg Sq.
Battle Creek, MI 49016-3599 (616) 961-2000
Limitations: Giving primarily in areas of company
operations.

William T. Kemper Foundation
922 Walnut, Ste. 200
Kansas City, MO 64106-1809 (816) 234-2112
Limitations: Giving primarily in the Midwest with
emphasis on MO and surrounding areas.

Key Foundation
127 Public Sq., 7th Fl.
M.C. OH-01-27-0705
Cleveland, OH 44114-1306 (216) 689-5458
FAX: (216) 689-3865;
E-mail: key_foundation@keybank.com; Additional
tel.: (216) 689-4465; Additional FAX: (216)
689-5444; URL: http://www.key.com/html/
A-12.html
Limitations: Giving primarily in areas of company
operations in AK, CO, FL, ID, IN, ME, MI, NY, OH,
OR, UT, VT, and WA.

Peter Kiewit Foundation
8805 Indian Hills Dr., Ste. 225
Omaha, NE 68114 (402) 344-7890
Limitations: Giving limited to Rancho Mirage, CA,
western IA, NE, and Sheridan, WY; college
scholarships available to graduating seniors in
NE.
Publishes an annual or periodic report.

Kimberly-Clark Foundation, Inc.
351 Phelps Dr.
Irving, TX 75038-6507
URL: http://www.kimberly-clark.com/aboutus/
kc_foundation.asp
Limitations: Giving primarily in areas of company
operations; giving also to national organizations.

The Sidney Kimmel Foundation
1650 Arch St., 22nd Fl.
Philadelphia, PA 19103-2097 (215) 977-2538
FAX: (215) 977-2644;
E-mail: mkamens@wolfblock.com; URL: http://
www.kimmel.org

Kinder Foundation
P.O. Box 130776
Houston, TX 77219-0776
Limitations: Giving primarily in TX.

Stephen and Tabitha King Foundation, Inc.
49 Florida Ave.
Bangor, ME 04401 (207) 990-2910
FAX: (207) 990-2975;
E-mail: info@stkfoundation.org; URL: http://
www.stkfoundation.org
Limitations: Giving limited to ME.

F. M. Kirby Foundation, Inc.
17 DeHart St.
P.O. Box 151
Morristown, NJ 07963-0151 (973) 538-4800
URL: http://www.foundationcenter.org/grantmaker/
kirby
Limitations: Giving primarily in Raleigh-Durham, NC,
Morris County, NJ, and eastern PA.

Robert J. Kleberg, Jr. and Helen C. Kleberg
Foundation
700 N. St. Mary's St., Ste. 1200
San Antonio, TX 78205 (210) 271-3691
Limitations: Giving on a national basis.
Publishes an annual or periodic report.

The Esther A. & Joseph Klingenstein Fund, Inc.
787 7th Ave., 6th Fl.
New York, NY 10019-6016 (212) 492-6181
FAX: (212) 492-7007;
E-mail: kathleen.pomerantz@klingenstein.com;
URL: http://www.klingfund.org

The John W. Kluge Foundation
15004 Sunflower Ct.
Rockville, MD 20853-1748 (301) 929-9340

John S. and James L. Knight Foundation
Wachovia Financial Ctr., Ste. 3300
200 S. Biscayne Blvd.
Miami, FL 33131-2349 (305) 908-2600
FAX: (305) 908-2698; Additional tel. for publication
requests: (305) 908-2629; E-mail:
publications@knightfdn.org, or
web@knightfdn.org; URL: http://
www.knightfdn.org
Limitations: Giving limited to projects serving the 26
communities where the Knight brothers
published newspapers for Community Initiatives
Program and local grants: Long Beach and San
Jose, CA, Boulder, CO, Boca Raton, Bradenton,
Miami, and Tallahassee, FL, Columbus, Macon,
and Milledgeville, GA, Fort Wayne and Gary, IN,
Wichita, KS, Lexington, KY, Detroit, MI, Duluth
and St. Paul, MN, Biloxi, MS, Charlotte, NC,
Grand Forks, ND, Akron, OH, Philadelphia and
State College, PA, Columbia and Myrtle Beach,
SC, and Aberdeen, SD; international for
Journalism.
Publishes an annual or periodic report.

The Kohlberg Foundation, Inc.
111 Radio Cir.
Mount Kisco, NY 10549
FAX: (914) 241-1195; E-mail: dehaan@kfound.org
Limitations: Giving primarily in the U.S., with
emphasis on CA and MA; giving also in Baja CA,
Mexico.
Publishes an annual or periodic report.

Koret Foundation
33 New Montgomery St., Ste. 1090
San Francisco, CA 94105-4526
FAX: (415) 882-7775;
E-mail: koret@koretfoundation.org; URL: http://
www.koretfoundation.org
Limitations: Giving limited to the Bay Area counties of
San Francisco, Alameda, Contra Costa, Marin,
Santa Clara, and San Mateo, CA; giving also in
Israel.
Publishes an annual or periodic report.

Henry R. Kravis Foundation, Inc.
c/o KKR & Co.
9 W. 57th St.
New York, NY 10019 (212) 750-8300

The Kresge Foundation
3215 W. Big Beaver Rd.
Troy, MI 48084 (248) 643-9630
FAX: (248) 643-0588; E-mail: info@kresge.org;
URL: http://www.kresge.org
Publishes an annual or periodic report.

Samuel H. Kress Foundation
174 E. 80th St.
New York, NY 10021 (212) 861-4993
FAX: (212) 628-3146; E-mail: lisa@shkf.org;
URL: http://www.kressfoundation.org
Limitations: Giving primarily in the U.S. and Europe.
Publishes an annual or periodic report.

Albert & Bessie Mae Kronkosky Charitable
Foundation
112 E. Pecan, Ste. 830
San Antonio, TX 78205 (210) 475-9000
FAX: (210) 354-2204;
E-mail: kronfndn@kronkosky.org; Additional tel.:
(888) 309-9001; URL: http://www.kronkosky.org
Limitations: Giving limited to Bandera, Bexar, Comal,
and Kendall counties, TX.
Publishes an annual or periodic report.

Lannan Foundation
313 Read St.
Santa Fe, NM 87501-2628 (505) 986-8160
FAX: (505) 986-8195; E-mail: info@lannan.org;
Additional contact information (for Ruth Simms):
FAX: (505) 954-5143, E-mail: ruth@lannan.org;
URL: http://www.lannan.org
Limitations: Giving on a national basis.

Forrest C. Lattner Foundation, Inc.
777 E. Atlantic Ave., Ste. 317
Delray Beach, FL 33483-5352 (561) 278-3781
FAX: (561) 278-3167; E-mail: lattner@bellsouth.net;
URL: http://www.lattnerfoundation.org
Limitations: Giving primarily in San Francisco, CA,
Palm Beach County, FL, Atlanta, GA, Wichita, KS,
Philadelphia, PA, Westerly, RI, and Dallas, TX.

Lavelle Fund for the Blind, Inc.
80 Maiden Ln., Ste. 1207
New York, NY 10038 (212) 668-9801
FAX: (212) 668-9803;
E-mail: afisher@lavellefund.org; URL: http://
foundationcenter.org/grantmaker/lavellefund/
Limitations: Giving primarily in the New York City
metropolitan area.

The Lazarus Foundation, Inc.
340 Edgemont Ave., Ste. 500
Bristol, TN 37620
Limitations: Giving primarily in Bristol, TN, and
surrounding communities.

Tom and Frances Leach Foundation, Inc.
1720 Burnt Boat Dr.
P.O. Box 1136
Bismarck, ND 58502-1136 (701) 255-0479
URL: http://www.leachfoundation.org
Limitations: Giving primarily in ND, particularly in
Bismarck and Mandan, and the upper Midwest.
Publishes an annual or periodic report.

The Lennar Foundation, Inc.
c/o Lennar Corp.
700 N.W. 107th Ave., Ste. 400
Miami, FL 33172 (305) 229-6400
Limitations: Giving primarily in Miami, FL.

The Fred A. Lennon Charitable Trust
29425 Chagrin Blvd., Ste. 201
Cleveland, OH 44122-4602
Limitations: Giving primarily in OH, with emphasis on
Cleveland.

Libra Foundation
3 Canal Plz.
P.O. Box 17516
Portland, ME 04112-8516 (207) 879-6280
FAX: (207) 879-6281; URL: http://
www.librafoundation.org
Limitations: Giving limited to ME.
Publishes an annual or periodic report.

Lied Foundation Trust
3907 W. Charleston Blvd.
Las Vegas, NV 89102 (702) 878-1559
Limitations: Giving primarily in NE and Las Vegas, NV.

Eli Lilly and Company Foundation
Lilly Corporate Ctr., D.C. 1627
Indianapolis, IN 46285
URL: http://www.lilly.com/products/access/
foundation.html
Limitations: Giving on a national and international
basis, with emphasis on areas of company
operations, including Indianapolis, IN.

Lilly Endowment Inc.
2801 N. Meridian St.
P.O. Box 88068
Indianapolis, IN 46208-0068 (317) 924-5471
FAX: (317) 926-4431; URL: http://
www.lillyendowment.org
Limitations: Giving limited to IN, with emphasis on
Indianapolis, for community development
projects (including the arts, preservation, capital
building funds, operating funds, and social
services). Education funding focused principally
on Indiana under invitational grant programs.
National giving in religion, philanthropic studies,
leadership education, and selected higher
education initiatives, principally to increase
educational opportunities for minorities.
Publishes an annual or periodic report.

Lincoln Financial Group Foundation
1300 S. Clinton St.
P.O. Box 7863
Fort Wayne, IN 46801-7863 (260) 455-3879
FAX: (260) 455-4004; E-mail: skemmish@lnc.com;
URL: http://www.lfg.com/lfg/ipc/abt/cgv/
index.html
Limitations: Giving limited to areas of company
operations, with emphasis on Hartford, CT,
Schaumburg and the Chicago, IL, area, Fort
Wayne, IN, Portland, ME, Omaha, NE, Concord,
NH, Greensboro, NC, Philadelphia, PA, and
London, United Kingdom.

The John M. Lloyd Foundation
11777 San Vicente Blvd., Ste. 745
Los Angeles, CA 90049 (310) 622-1050
FAX: (310) 622-1070; E-mail: info@johnmlloyd.org;
URL: http://www.johnmlloyd.org/jml_home.html
Limitations: Giving on a worldwide basis.

Lockheed Martin Corporation Foundation
6801 Rockledge Dr.
Bethesda, MD 20817
Limitations: Giving primarily in areas of company
operations.

The Thomas J. Long Foundation
2950 Buskirk Ave., Ste. 160
Walnut Creek, CA 94597 (925) 944-3800

Limitations: Giving primarily in northern CA and HI.

Longwood Foundation, Inc.
100 W. 10th St., Ste. 1109
Wilmington, DE 19801
Limitations: Giving primarily in DE and southern
Chester County, PA.

Leon Lowenstein Foundation, Inc.
126 E. 56th St., 28th Fl.
New York, NY 10022 (212) 319-0670
Limitations: Giving primarily in the metropolitan New
York, NY, area.

LSR Fund
c/o The Rockefeller Trust Co.
30 Rockefeller Plz., Rm. 5600
New York, NY 10112
Limitations: Giving on a national basis.

The Henry Luce Foundation, Inc.
111 W. 50th St., Ste. 4601
New York, NY 10020 (212) 489-7700
FAX: (212) 581-9541; E-mail: hlf@hluce.org;
URL: http://www.hluce.org
Limitations: Giving on a national and international
basis; international activities limited to East and
Southeast Asia.

Lucent Technologies Foundation
600 Mountain Ave., Rm. 6F4
Murray Hill, NJ 07974 (908) 582-7906
E-mail: foundation@lucent.com; Application address
for Graduate Research Fellowships: Bell Labs
Graduate Research Fellowship Prog., Scholarship
Management Svcs., Scholarship America, Inc., 1
Scholarship Way, P.O. Box 297, St. Peter, MN
56082, E-mail: coopgraduate@lucent.com; Tel.
for Conqueror of the Hill: (908) 582-7436; E-mail
for Conqueror of the Hill: lucentcoh@lucent.com;
URL: http://www.lucent.com/social/foundation/
home.html
Limitations: Giving on a national and international
basis, with emphasis on areas of company
operations.

Lumina Foundation for Education, Inc.
P.O. Box 1806
Indianapolis, IN 46206-1806 (317) 951-5300
FAX: (317) 951-5063; URL: http://
www.luminafoundation.org
Limitations: Giving on a national basis.
Publishes an annual or periodic report.

Ann and Robert H. Lurie Foundation
2 N. Riverside Plz., Ste. 1500
Chicago, IL 60606 (312) 466-3997
Limitations: Giving primarily in Chicago, IL, and MI.

The M & T Charitable Foundation
1 Fountain Plz., 12th Fl.
Buffalo, NY 14203
Limitations: Giving on a national basis, with emphasis
on Washington, DC, DE, MD, NY, PA, and WV.

**John D. and Catherine T. MacArthur
Foundation**
140 S. Dearborn St., Ste. 1200
Chicago, IL 60603-5285 (312) 726-8000
FAX: (312) 920-6258;
E-mail: 4answers@macfound.org; TDD: (312)
920-6285; URL: http://www.macfound.org
Limitations: Giving on a national and international
basis, with emphasis on Chicago, IL.
Publishes an annual or periodic report.

Josiah Macy, Jr. Foundation
44 E. 64th St.
New York, NY 10021 (212) 486-2424
FAX: (212) 644-0765;
E-mail: jmacyinfo@josiahmacyfoundation.org;
URL: http://www.josiahmacyfoundation.org
Publishes an annual or periodic report.

Madison Community Foundation
2 Science Ct.
P.O. Box 5010
Madison, WI 53705-0010 (608) 232-1763
FAX: (608) 232-1772;
E-mail: frontdesk@madisoncommunityfoundation
.org; Additional E-mail:
acasey@madisoncommunityfoundation.org;
Grant application E-mail:
tlinfield@madisoncommunityfoundation.org;
URL: http://
www.madisoncommunityfoundation.org
Limitations: Giving limited to Dane County, WI.
Publishes an annual or periodic report.

The Maine Community Foundation, Inc.
245 Main St.
Ellsworth, ME 04605 (207) 667-9735
FAX: (207) 667-0447; E-mail: info@mainecf.org;
Additional tel.: (877) 700-6800; Portland mailing
address: 1 Monument Way, Ste. 200, P.O. Box
7380, Portland, ME 04101, tel.: (207)
761-2440, fax: (207) 773-8832; Grant
information E-mail: ptaylor@mainecf.org;
URL: http://www.mainecf.org
Limitations: Giving limited to ME.
Publishes an annual or periodic report.

Maine Health Access Foundation
150 Capitol St., Ste. 4
Augusta, ME 04330 (207) 620-8266
FAX: (207) 620-8269; E-mail: wwolf@mehaf.org;
Toll-free tel.: (866) 848-9210; URL: http://
www.mehaf.org
Limitations: Giving primarily in ME.
Publishes an annual or periodic report.

The Marcus Foundation, Inc.
1266 W. Paces Ferry Rd., No. 615
Atlanta, GA 30327-2306 (404) 240-7700
Limitations: Giving primarily in Atlanta, GA.

Marin Community Foundation
5 Hamilton Landing, Ste. 200
Novato, CA 94949 (415) 464-2500
FAX: (415) 464-2555; E-mail: info@marincf.org;
URL: http://www.marincf.org
Limitations: Giving from Buck Trust limited to Marin
County, CA; other giving on a national and
international basis with emphasis on the San
Francisco Bay Area.
Publishes an annual or periodic report.

The Marisla Foundation
412 N. Coast Hwy., PMB 359
Laguna Beach, CA 92651 (949) 494-0365
Limitations: Giving primarily on the West Coast of the
U.S. (including Baja, CA), HI, and the Western
Pacific for the environment; funding for women
limited to Los Angeles and Orange County, CA.

The J. Willard and Alice S. Marriott Foundation
Marriott Dr.
Washington, DC 20058
Limitations: Giving primarily in Washington, DC.

The G. Harold & Leila Y. Mathers Charitable
Foundation
118 N. Bedford Rd., Ste. 203
Mount Kisco, NY 10549-2555 (914) 242-0465
FAX: (914) 242-0665;
E-mail: admin@mathersfoundation.org;
Additional e-mail (for James H. Handelman):
jh@mathersfoundation.org; URL: http://
www.mathersfoundation.org
Limitations: Giving on a national basis.

Mathile Family Foundation
6450 Sand Lake Rd., Ste. 100
Dayton, OH 45414 (937) 264-4607
FAX: (937) 264-4805;
E-mail: angela.hayes@cymi.com; Application
address: P.O. Box 13615, Dayton, OH
45413-0615
Limitations: Giving primarily in the Dayton and
Montgomery County, OH, areas.
Publishes an annual or periodic report.

The May Department Stores Foundation
611 Olive St.
St. Louis, MO 63101 (314) 342-6299
FAX: (314) 342-4461;
E-mail: mayfoundation@may-co.com;
URL: http://www2.mayco.com/common/
com_index.jsp
Limitations: Giving on a national basis in areas of
company operations; giving also to national
organizations.

The MBNA Foundation
1100 N. King St.
Wilmington, DE 19884-0723
Tel. for Cleveland Excellence in Education Grants:
(216) 545-8000, (800) 410-6262, ext. 58000;
Tel. for Cleveland Scholars Prog.: (216)
545-4178, (800) 410-6262, ext. 54178; Tel. for
Community Donations: (302) 432-5205, (800)
205-8877, option 3; Tel. for Delaware Excellence
in Education Grants and Helen F. Graham
Grants: (302) 432-5288, (800) 205-8877, option
1; Tel. for Delaware Scholars Prog. and HBCU
Scholarship Prog.: (302) 432-4800, option 2,
(800) 205-8877, option 2; Tel. for Maine
Excellence in Education Grants: (800) 386-6262,
ext. 65886; Tel. for Maine Scholars Prog.: (800)
386-6262, ext. 65878; E-mail for Helen F.
Graham Grants: grahamgrants@mbna.com;
E-mail for Maine Excellence in Education
Grants: mainegrants@mbna.com; URL: http://
www.mbnafoundation.org
Limitations: Giving primarily in areas of company
operations, with emphasis on DE, ME, and OH.

B. C. McCabe Foundation
8152 Painter Ave., Ste. 201
Whittier, CA 90602 (562) 696-1433
Limitations: Giving primarily in CA.

The McConnell Foundation
P.O. Box 492050
Redding, CA 96049-2050 (530) 226-6200
FAX: (530) 226-6210;
E-mail: info@mcconnellfoundation.org;
URL: http://www.mcconnellfoundation.org
Limitations: Giving limited to Shasta, Trinity, Modoc,
Tehema and Siskiyou counties, CA; and Nepal.
Publishes an annual or periodic report.

McCune Charitable Foundation
345 E. Alameda St.
Santa Fe, NM 87501-2229
FAX: (505) 983-7887; E-mail: info@nmmccune.org;
URL: http://www.nmmccune.org
Limitations: Giving limited to NM.

McCune Foundation
750 6 PPG Pl.
Pittsburgh, PA 15222 (412) 644-8779
FAX: (412) 644-8059; E-mail: info@mccune.org;
URL: http://www.mccune.org
Limitations: Giving primarily in southwestern PA, with
emphasis on the Pittsburgh area.
Publishes an annual or periodic report.

The Eugene McDermott Foundation
3808 Euclid Ave.
Dallas, TX 75205-3102 (214) 521-2924
Limitations: Giving primarily in Dallas, TX.

Bernard McDonough Foundation, Inc.
311 4th St.
Parkersburg, WV 26101 (304) 424-6280
FAX: (304) 424-6281; URL: http://
www.mcdonoughfoundation.org/
Limitations: Giving primarily in WV.

John P. McGovern Foundation
2211 Norfolk St., Ste. 900
Houston, TX 77098-4044 (713) 661-4808
Limitations: Giving primarily in TX, with emphasis on
Houston; giving also in the Southwest.

McGregor Fund
333 W. Fort St., Ste. 2090
Detroit, MI 48226-3134 (313) 963-3495
FAX: (313) 963-3512;
E-mail: info@mcgregorfund.org; URL: http://
www.mcgregorfund.org
Limitations: Giving primarily in the metropolitan
Detroit, MI, area, including Wayne, Oakland, and
Macomb counties.
Publishes an annual or periodic report.

The MCJ Foundation
310 South St.
Morristown, NJ 07960 (973) 540-1946

The McKnight Foundation
710 S. 2nd St., Ste. 400
Minneapolis, MN 55401 (612) 333-4220
FAX: (612) 332-3833; E-mail: info@mcknight.org;
URL: http://www.mcknight.org
Limitations: Giving limited to organizations in MN,
especially the seven-county Twin Cities, MN,
area, except for programs in the environment,
international aid, and research.
Publishes an annual or periodic report.

MDU Resources Foundation
P.O. Box 5650
Bismarck, ND 58506-5650 (701) 530-1085
FAX: (701) 222-7607; URL: http://www.mdu.com/
the_vision/vision_foundation.htm
Limitations: Giving primarily in areas of company
operations.
Publishes an annual or periodic report.

The Meadows Foundation, Inc.
Wilson Historic District
3003 Swiss Ave.
Dallas, TX 75204-6049 (214) 826-9431
FAX: (214) 827-7042; E-mail: grants@mfi.org;
Additional tel.: (800) 826-9431; URL: http://
www.mfi.org
Limitations: Giving limited to TX.
Publishes an annual or periodic report.

Medina Foundation
1300 Norton Bldg.
801 2nd Ave., 13th Fl.

Seattle, WA 98104 (206) 652-8783
FAX: (206) 652-8791;
E-mail: info@medinafoundation.org; Additional
tel.: (206) 652-8783; URL: http://
www.medinafoundation.org
Limitations: Giving limited to the greater Puget Sound,
WA, area, with emphasis on the counties of Grays
Harbor, Island, Jefferson, King, Kitsap, Mason,
Pacific, Pierce, San Juan, Skagit, and
Snohomish.

The Medtronic Foundation
710 Medtronic Pkwy.
Minneapolis, MN 55432-5604 (763) 505-2639
FAX: (763) 505-2648; URL: http://
www.medtronic.com/foundation
Limitations: Giving primarily in areas of company
operations, with emphasis on Phoenix and
Tempe, AZ, Goleta, Northridge, Santa Ana, and
Santa Rosa, CA, Louisville and Parker, CO,
Warsaw, IN, Danvers and the Twin Cities-Seven
County metro, MN, area, Humacao and Villalba,
PR, Memphis, TN, and Redmond, WA; giving also
to national and international organizations active
in areas of company operations.
Publishes an annual or periodic report.

Mellon Financial Corporation Fund
1 Mellon Ctr., Ste. 1830
Pittsburgh, PA 15258-0001
URL: http://www.mellon.com/aboutmellon/
communityinvolvement/
charitablegivingprogram.html
Limitations: Giving primarily in areas of company
operations, with emphasis on Boston, MA, and
Philadelphia and Pittsburgh, PA.
Publishes an annual or periodic report.

The Andrew W. Mellon Foundation
140 E. 62nd St.
New York, NY 10021 (212) 838-8400
FAX: (212) 223-2778; URL: http://www.mellon.org
Limitations: Giving on a national basis.
Publishes an annual or periodic report.

Richard King Mellon Foundation
1 Mellon Ctr.
500 Grant St., 41st Fl., Ste. 4106
Pittsburgh, PA 15219-2502 (412) 392-2800
FAX: (412) 392-2837; URL: http://fdncenter.org/
grantmaker/rkmellon
Limitations: Giving primarily in PA.
Publishes an annual or periodic report.

The Melville Charitable Trust
160 Federal St., 8th Fl.
Boston, MA 02110 (617) 338-2590
FAX: (617) 338-2591; E-mail: mct@tpi.org;
URL: http://www.melvilletrust.org
Limitations: Giving primarily in CT.
Publishes an annual or periodic report.

The Merck Company Foundation
1 Merck Dr., WS 1A-17
P.O. Box 100
Whitehouse Station, NJ 08889-0100
(908) 423-2042
FAX: (908) 423-1987; Contact for PPPI: Heather
Richmond, Coord., tel.: (908) 423-4820;
URL: http://www.merck.com/cr/
company_profile/philanthropy_at_merck/
the_merck_company_foundation/home.html
Limitations: Giving on a national and international
basis in areas of company operations.
Publishes an annual or periodic report.

The John Merck Fund
47 Winter St., 7th Fl.
Boston, MA 02108
FAX: (617) 556-4130; E-mail: info@jmfund.org;
  URL: http://www.jmfund.org
Limitations: Giving on a national basis in the areas of
  reproductive health, the environment, and job
  opportunities; giving in Latin America in the area
  of human rights.

Merrill Lynch & Co. Foundation, Inc.
c/o Merrill Lynch & Co., Inc.
100 Union Ave.
Cresskill, NJ 07626   (201) 871-0350
FAX: (212) 236-3821;
  E-mail: philant7@exchange.ml.com; Application
  address: c/o Global Philanthropy and Community
  Rels., 2 World Financial Ctr., 5th Fl., New York,
  NY 10281; URL: http://community.ml.com/
  index.asp?id=66319_67036
Limitations: Giving to national and international
  organizations.

Mertz Gilmore Foundation
218 E. 18th St.
New York, NY 10003-3694   (212) 475-1137
FAX: (212) 777-5226; E-mail: info@mertzgilmore.org;
  URL: http://www.mertzgilmore.org
Limitations: Giving on a national basis with some
  emphasis on the New York City Program.

Messengers of Healing Winds Foundation
P.O. Box 32360
Santa Fe, NM 87594-2360
Limitations: Giving primarily in the lake region of
  northwest IA, FL, SD, Santa Fe, NM, and the
  Southwest. Giving on a national basis for
  environmental concerns.

MetLife Foundation
27-01 Queens Plz. N.
Long Island City, NY 11101   (212) 578-6272
URL: http://www.metlife.org
Limitations: Giving on a national basis.

Eugene and Agnes E. Meyer Foundation
1400 16th St. N.W., Ste. 360
Washington, DC 20036   (202) 483-8294
FAX: (202) 328-6850; E-mail: meyer@meyerfdn.org;
  URL: http://www.meyerfoundation.org
Limitations: Giving limited to the metropolitan
  Washington, DC, area, including Montgomery,
  Prince George's, Calvert, Charles, and St. Mary's
  counties in suburban MD and Arlington, Fairfax,
  Loudoun, Prince William and Stafford counties,
  and the cities of Alexandria, Falls Church,
  Manassas, and Manassas Park in northern VA.
Publishes an annual or periodic report.

Meyer Memorial Trust
425 N.W. 10th Ave., Ste. 400
Portland, OR 97209   (503) 228-5512
E-mail: mmt@mmt.org; URL: http://www.mmt.org
Limitations: Giving primarily in OR and Clark County,
  WA.

Gary E. Milgard Family Foundation
1701 Commerce St.
Tacoma, WA 98402   (253) 274-0121
FAX: (253) 274-0478; URL: http://
  www.garymilgardfamilyfoundation.org
Limitations: Giving primarily in Pierce County and the
  greater Puget Sound, WA, area.

Paul and Irma Milstein Foundation
335 Madison Ave., Ste. 1500
New York, NY 10017   (212) 708-0280

Limitations: Giving primarily in New York, NY.

Greater Milwaukee Foundation
1020 N. Broadway, Ste. 112
Milwaukee, WI 53202   (414) 272-5805
FAX: (414) 272-6235;
  E-mail: info@greatermkefdn.org; Additional
  address: N16 W23250 Stoneridge Dr., Ste. 6,
  Waukesha, WI 53188, tel.: (262) 522-8350, FAX:
  (262) 544-9301; Additional E-mail:
  cgraham@greatermkefdn.org; URL: http://
  www.greatermilwaukeefoundation.org
Limitations: Giving primarily in Milwaukee, Ozaukee,
  Washington, and Waukesha, WI.
Publishes an annual or periodic report.

The Minneapolis Foundation
800 IDS Ctr.
80 S. Eighth St.
Minneapolis, MN 55402   (612) 672-3878
FAX: (612) 672-3846;
  E-mail: e-mail@mplsfoundation.org; Community
  grants E-mail: grants@mplsfoundation.org;
  Connection grants tel: (612) 672-3863, E-mail:
  rhybben@mplsfoundation.org; URL: http://
  www.MinneapolisFoundation.org;
  Additional URL: http://www.mplsfoundation.org
Limitations: Giving limited to MN, with emphasis on
  organizations in the Twin Cities metropolitan
  region.
Publishes an annual or periodic report.

The Ambrose Monell Foundation
c/o Fulton, Rowe, & Hart
1 Rockefeller Plz., Ste. 301
New York, NY 10020-2002
FAX: (212) 245-1863;
  E-mail: info@monellvetlesen.org; URL: http://
  www.monellvetlesen.org/
Publishes an annual or periodic report.

Monterey Fund, Inc.
c/o Bear Stearns & Co.
1 Metrotech Ctr. N., 9th Fl.
Brooklyn, NY 11201
Publishes an annual or periodic report.

Gordon and Betty Moore Foundation
The Presidio of San Francisco
P.O. Box 29910
San Francisco, CA 94129-0910   (415) 561-7700
FAX: (415) 561-7707; E-mail: info@moore.org;
  Additional E-mail: grantprocessing@moore.org;
  URL: http://www.moore.org/
Limitations: Giving on a worldwide basis, with some
  focus on the San Francisco Bay Area, CA, for
  selected projects.

Morgan Stanley Foundation
c/o Community Affairs
1633 Broadway, 20th Fl.
New York, NY 10019   (212) 537-1400
FAX: (646) 519-5460;
  E-mail: whatadifference@morganstanley.com;
  URL: http://www.morganstanley.com/about/
  inside/community.html
Limitations: Giving primarily in areas of company
  operations, with emphasis on the Phoenix, AZ,
  Los Angeles and San Francisco, CA, Wilmington,
  DE, Chicago, IL, Baltimore, MD, New York, NY,
  Columbus, OH, Philadelphia, PA, Dallas and
  Houston, TX, and Salt Lake City, UT, metropolitan
  areas; giving also to national organizations.

Moriah Fund
1 Farragut Sq. S.
1634 I St. N.W., Ste. 1000

Washington, DC 20006   (202) 783-8488
FAX: (202) 783-8499; E-mail: info@moriahfund.org;
  Additional E-mail: proposals@moriahfund.org;
  Requests in Israel: Don Futterman, Beilenson
  St., No. 3, Apt. 1, Kfar Saba, Israel 44350;
  URL: http://www.moriahfund.org/index.htm
Limitations: Giving nationally and internationally,
  including Israel and Latin America, specifically
  Guatemala; giving primarily in Washington, DC for
  poverty program.

Charles Stewart Mott Foundation
c/o Office of Proposal Entry
Mott Foundation Bldg.
503 S. Saginaw St., Ste. 1200
Flint, MI 48502-1851   (810) 238-5651
FAX: (810) 766-1753; E-mail: info@mott.org;
  Additional E-mail: publications@mott.org;
  URL: http://www.mott.org
Limitations: Giving nationally and to emerging
  countries in Central and Eastern Europe, Russia,
  and South Africa.
Publishes an annual or periodic report.

Ruth Mott Foundation
111 E. Court St., Ste. 3C
Flint, MI 48502-1649   (810) 233-0170
FAX: (810) 233-7022; E-mail: rmf@rmfdn.org; E-mail
  (for Joy Murray): jmurray@rmfdn.org; URL: http://
  www.ruthmottfoundation.org
Limitations: Giving primarily in Genesee County and
  Flint, MI.

M. J. Murdock Charitable Trust
703 Broadway, Ste. 710
Vancouver, WA 98660   (360) 694-8415
FAX: (360) 694-1819; Mailing address: P.O. Box
  1618, Vancouver, WA 98668; URL: http://
  www.murdock-trust.org
Limitations: Giving primarily in the Pacific Northwest
  (AK, ID, MT, OR, and WA).
Publishes an annual or periodic report.

Dan Murphy Foundation
P.O. Box 711267
Los Angeles, CA 90071   (213) 623-3120
Limitations: Giving primarily in Los Angeles, CA.

The Murphy Foundation
Union Bldg.
El Dorado, AR 71730-6133
Application address: c/o Brett Williamson, 200 N.
  Jefferson, Ste. 400, El Dorado, AR 71730,
  tel.: (870) 862-4961
Limitations: Giving primarily in southern AR for grants
  to organizations; giving limited to the southern AR
  area for educational grants.

The Nash Family Foundation, Inc.
25 W. 45th St., Ste. 1400
New York, NY 10036   (212) 221-9491
FAX: (212) 221-9487; E-mail: info@nashff.org;
  Additional E-mail: judith@nashff.org; URL: http://
  www.nashfamilyfoundation.org
Limitations: Giving primarily in New York, NY and
  Israel.

Nationwide Foundation
1 Nationwide Plz., 1-22-05
Columbus, OH 43215-2220   (614) 249-4310
Additional tel.: (614) 249-0039; URL: http://
  www.nationwide.com/nw/about-us/
  community-involvement/investing-in-people/
  index.htm?WT.svl=3#Nationwide%20Foundation
Limitations: Giving primarily in areas of company
  operations, with emphasis on OH, including
  Columbus.

NCC Charitable Foundation
c/o National City Bank
1900 E. 9th St., LOC 2157
Cleveland, OH 44114 (216) 222-2994
E-mail: joanne.clark@nationalcity.com; Additional
E-mail: bruce.mccrodden@nationalcity.com;
URL: http://www.nationalcity.com/about/
commurelations/default.asp
Limitations: Giving primarily in IL, IN, KY, MI, OH, and
PA, with emphasis on OH.

The New Hampshire Charitable Foundation
37 Pleasant St.
Concord, NH 03301-4005 (603) 225-6641
FAX: (603) 225-1700; E-mail: info@nhcf.org; Grant
inquiry E-mail: grants_info@nhcf.org;
NHCF-Piscataqua Region application address:
446 Market St., Portsmouth, NH 03801;
NHCF-Upper Valley Region application address:
16 Buck Rd., Hanover, NH 03755-2700;
URL: http://www.nhcf.org
Limitations: Giving in the Lakes, Manchester,
Monadnock, Nashua, North Country, Piscataqua,
and Upper Valley regions in NH.
Publishes an annual or periodic report.

The New Mexico Community Foundation
343 E. Alameda St.
Santa Fe, NM 87501 (505) 820-6860
FAX: (505) 820-7860; E-mail: nmcf@nmcf.org;
Additional address: 303 Roma N.W., Ste. 400,
Albuquerque, NM 87102, tel.: (505) 821-6735;
URL: http://www.nmcf.org
Limitations: Giving limited to NM, with emphasis on
rural communities.
Publishes an annual or periodic report.

The New York Community Trust
909 Third Ave., 22nd Fl.
New York, NY 10022 (212) 686-0010
FAX: (212) 532-8528;
E-mail: info@nycommunitytrust.org; Additional
E-mail: las@nyct-cfi.org; Grant application E-mail:
grants@nycommunitytrust.org; URL: http://
www.nycommunitytrust.org
Limitations: Giving limited to the metropolitan New
York, NY, area.
Publishes an annual or periodic report.

New York Foundation
350 5th Ave., No. 2901
New York, NY 10118-2996
URL: http://www.nyf.org/
Limitations: Giving limited to local programs in the
New York, NY, metropolitan area.
Publishes an annual or periodic report.

New York Life Foundation
51 Madison Ave., Ste. 604
New York, NY 10010-1655 (212) 576-7341
URL: http://www.newyorklifefoundation.org
Limitations: Giving primarily in New York and
Westchester County, NY; giving also to national
organizations serving two or more of the following
cities and regions: Tampa, FL, Atlanta, GA,
Minneapolis, MN, Clinton/Hunterdon counties
and Morris/Parsippany counties, NJ, Cleveland,
OH, Dallas, TX, and the Gulf Coast region.
Publishes an annual or periodic report.

The New York Times Company Foundation, Inc.
229 W. 43rd St., 10 Fl.
New York, NY 10036-3959 (212) 556-1091
FAX: (212) 556-4450; URL: http://
www.nytimes.com/scholarship
http://www.nytco.com/foundation

Limitations: Giving primarily in areas of company
operations, with emphasis on the New York, NY,
metropolitan area.
Publishes an annual or periodic report.

Samuel I. Newhouse Foundation, Inc.
c/o Paul Scherer & Co. LLP
335 Madison Ave., 9th Fl.
New York, NY 10017

NIKE Foundation
1 Bowerman Dr.
Beaverton, OR 97005-6453 (888) 448-6453
E-mail: nike.foundation@nike.com; URL: http://
www.nike.com/nikebiz/nikefoundation/
home.jhtml
Limitations: Giving on an international basis, with
emphasis on Bangladesh, Brazil, China, Ethiopia,
and Zambia; giving also to national organizations.

The Samuel Roberts Noble Foundation, Inc.
2510 Sam Noble Pkwy.
P.O. Box 2180
Ardmore, OK 73402 (580) 223-5810
Additional tel.: (866) 223-5810; URL: http://
www.noble.org
Limitations: Giving primarily in the Southwest, with
emphasis on OK.
Publishes an annual or periodic report.

The Norcliffe Foundation
999 3rd Ave., Ste. 1006
Seattle, WA 98104 (206) 682-4820
FAX: (206) 682-4821;
E-mail: arline@thenorcliffefoundation.com;
URL: http://www.thenorcliffefoundation.com/
Limitations: Giving in the Puget Sound region of WA,
with emphasis in and around Seattle.

The Norfolk Foundation
1 Commercial Pl., Ste 1410
Norfolk, VA 23510-2103 (757) 622-7951
FAX: (757) 622-1751;
E-mail: info@norfolkfoundation.org; Additional
E-mails: alight@norfolkfoundation.org and
ldavis@norfolkfoundation.org; URL: http://
www.norfolkfoundation.org
Limitations: Giving limited to southeastern VA.
Publishes an annual or periodic report.

The Kenneth T. and Eileen L. Norris Foundation
11 Golden Shore, Ste. 450
Long Beach, CA 90802 (562) 435-8444
FAX: (562) 436-0584; E-mail: grants@ktn.org;
Additional e-mail: accordino@ktn.org;
URL: http://www.norrisfoundation.org
Limitations: Giving primarily in southern CA.
Publishes an annual or periodic report.

Northwest Area Foundation
c/o Karl N. Stauber
60 Plato Blvd. E., Ste. 400
St. Paul, MN 55107 (651) 224-9635
FAX: (651) 225-7701; E-mail: info@nwaf.org;
URL: http://www.nwaf.org
Limitations: Giving limited to IA, ID, MN, MT, ND, OR,
SD, and WA.
Publishes an annual or periodic report.

Northwestern Mutual Foundation
720 E. Wisconsin Ave.
Milwaukee, WI 53202 (414) 665-2904
E-mail: nmfoundation@northwesternmutual.com;
URL: http://www.nmfn.com/tn/aboutnet—
nm_fd_intro

Limitations: Giving primarily in the greater Milwaukee,
WI, area.

Peter Norton Family Foundation
225 Arizona, Ste. 350
Santa Monica, CA 90401 (310) 576-7700
Limitations: Giving primarily in southern CA for
human/social services; giving on a national basis
for arts-related grants.

Jessie Smith Noyes Foundation, Inc.
6 E. 39th St., 12th Fl.
New York, NY 10016-0112 (212) 684-6577
FAX: (212) 689-6549; E-mail: noyes@noyes.org;
URL: http://www.noyes.org
Limitations: Giving limited to the U.S.
Publishes an annual or periodic report.

I. A. O'Shaughnessy Foundation, Inc.
332 Minnesota St., Ste. W 1271
St. Paul, MN 55101-1330 (651) 222-2323
FAX: (651) 222-3638;
E-mail: iaoshaughnessyFD@Qwest.net;
URL: http://www.iaoshaughnessyfdn.org
Limitations: Giving limited to the U.S., with emphasis
on areas where foundation directors live.

Oakwood Foundation Charitable Trust
P.O. Box 4200
Tupelo, MS 38803 (662) 840-3322
Limitations: Giving primarily in MS.

The Offield Family Foundation
400 N. Michigan Ave., Rm. 407
Chicago, IL 60611
Limitations: Giving primarily in AZ, CA, the Chicago, IL,
area and MI.

Open Society Institute
400 W. 59th St.
New York, NY 10019 (212) 548-0600
FAX: (212) 548-4600; URL: http://www.soros.org
Limitations: Giving on a national and international
basis.
Publishes an annual or periodic report.

The Oregon Community Foundation
1221 S.W. Yamhill, Ste. 100
Portland, OR 97205 (503) 227-6846
FAX: (503) 274-7771; E-mail: info@ocf1.org;
URL: http://www.ocf1.org
Limitations: Giving limited to OR.
Publishes an annual or periodic report.

Osteopathic Heritage Foundations
1500 Lake Shore Dr., Ste. 230
Columbus, OH 43204-3800 (614) 737-4370
FAX: (614) 737-4371; E-mail: heritage@ohf-ohio.org;
Toll-free tel.: (866) 737-4370; URL: http://
www.osteopathicheritage.org/
Limitations: Giving primarily in the following OH
counties: Athens, Delaware, Fairfield, Fayette,
Franklin, Hocking, Jackson, Knox, Licking,
Madison, Meigs, Morgan, Perry, Pickaway, Ross,
Union, Vinton, and Washington.

The Overbrook Foundation
122 E. 42nd St., Ste. 2500
New York, NY 10168-2500 (212) 661-8710
FAX: (212) 661-8664;
E-mail: contact@overbrookfoundation.org;
URL: http://www.overbrook.org
Limitations: Giving primarily in New York, NY.

PacifiCare Health Systems Foundation
5995 Plaza Dr., M.S. CY20-326
Cypress, CA 90630 (714) 825-5233
Application address: P.O. Box 25186, Santa Ana, CA 92799
Limitations: Giving limited to areas of company operations in AZ, CA, CO, NV, OK, OR, TX, and WA.
Publishes an annual or periodic report.

The David and Lucile Packard Foundation
300 2nd St., Ste. 200
Los Altos, CA 94022 (650) 948-7658
E-mail: inquiries@packard.org; URL: http://www.packard.org
Limitations: Giving for the arts and community development primarily in Los Altos and Santa Clara, San Mateo, Santa Cruz, and Monterey counties, CA; Pueblo, CO, and national giving for child health and development; national and international giving for population, conservation, and science.
Publishes an annual or periodic report.

The Packard Humanities Institute
300 2nd St.
Los Altos, CA 94022
URL: http://www.packhum.org
Limitations: Giving primarily in CA.

Park Foundation, Inc.
P.O. Box 550
Ithaca, NY 14851
Limitations: Giving limited to the eastern U.S., primarily in central NY, Washington, DC, and North Carolina.

The Mary Morton Parsons Foundation
901 E. Cary St., Ste. 1404
Richmond, VA 23219-4037
Limitations: Giving primarily in VA, with an emphasis on Richmond.

The Ralph M. Parsons Foundation
1055 Wilshire Blvd., Ste. 1701
Los Angeles, CA 90017-5600 (213) 482-3185
FAX: (213) 482-8878; URL: http://www.parsonsfoundation.org
Limitations: Giving limited to Los Angeles County, CA, with the exception of some grants for higher education.

Paso del Norte Health Foundation
1100 N. Stanton, Ste. 510
El Paso, TX 79902 (915) 544-7636
FAX: (915) 544-7713; E-mail: apauli@pdnhf.org; URL: http://www.pdnhf.org
Limitations: Giving limited to the Paso del Norte Region, including eastern TX and southern NM.
Publishes an annual or periodic report.

Frank E. Payne and Seba B. Payne Foundation
c/o Bank of America, N.A.
231 S. LaSalle St.
Chicago, IL 60697 (312) 828-1785
Limitations: Giving primarily in Bethlehem, PA.

Peninsula Community Foundation
1700 S. El Camino Real, Ste. 300
San Mateo, CA 94402-3049 (650) 358-9369
FAX: (650) 358-9817; E-mail: inquiry@pcf.org; Grant application E-mails: ellen@pcf.org or grants@pcf.org; URL: http://www.pcf.org
Limitations: Giving limited to San Mateo County and northern Santa Clara County, CA.
Publishes an annual or periodic report.

The William Penn Foundation
2 Logan Sq., 11th Fl.
100 N. 18th St.
Philadelphia, PA 19103-2757 (215) 988-1830
FAX: (215) 988-1823;
E-mail: moreinfo@williampennfoundation.org;
URL: http://www.williampennfoundation.org
Limitations: Giving limited to the Greater Philadelphia region.
Publishes an annual or periodic report.

Irene W. & C. B. Pennington Foundation
2237 S. Acadian Thruway, Ste. 601
Baton Rouge, LA 70808 (225) 383-3412
FAX: (225) 381-0128; Additional tel. for Lori Bertman: (225) 338-9386, E-mail: lori@penningtonfamilyfoundation.org;
URL: http://www.penningtonfamilyfoundation.org
Limitations: Giving limited to communities within or near Baton Rouge, LA.

The PepsiCo Foundation, Inc.
c/o Dir., Corp. Contribs.
700 Anderson Hill Rd.
Purchase, NY 10577 (914) 253-3153
URL: http://www.pepsico.com/PEP_Citizenship/Contributions/index.cfm
Limitations: Giving on a national basis.

Perelman Family Foundation
c/o Mafco Holdings
35 E. 62nd St.
New York, NY 10021
Limitations: Giving on a national basis.

The Perot Foundation
P.O. Box 269014
Plano, TX 75026 (972) 788-3000
Limitations: Giving primarily in TX.

Jane Bradley Pettit Foundation
c/o Cook & Franke
660 E. Mason St., 5th Fl.
Milwaukee, WI 53202 (414) 227-1266
URL: http://www.jbpf.org
Limitations: Giving primarily in the greater Milwaukee, WI, area.

Pfaffinger Foundation
316 W. Second St., Ste. PH-C
Los Angeles, CA 90012 (213) 680-7460
Limitations: Giving limited to Los Angeles and Orange counties, CA, for charitable institutions.

The Pfizer Foundation, Inc.
235 E. 42nd St.
New York, NY 10017 (212) 733-4250
URL: http://www.pfizer.com/pfizer/subsites/philanthropy/index.jsp

The Carl and Lily Pforzheimer Foundation, Inc.
950 Third Ave., 30th Fl.
New York, NY 10022

The Philadelphia Foundation
1234 Market St., Ste. 1800
Philadelphia, PA 19107-3794 (215) 563-6417
FAX: (215) 563-6882;
E-mail: parkow@philafound.org; URL: http://www.philafound.org
Limitations: Giving limited to Bucks, Chester, Delaware, Montgomery, and Philadelphia counties in southeastern PA, except for designated funds.

The Jay and Rose Phillips Family Foundation
10 2nd St., N.E., Ste. 200
Minneapolis, MN 55413 (612) 623-1654
FAX: (612) 623-1653;
E-mail: phillipsfnd@phillipsfnd.org; Additional tel. (for Dana Jensen, Grants Mgr.): (612) 623-1652;
URL: http://www.phillipsfnd.org
Limitations: Giving primarily in the Twin Cities metropolitan, MN, area.
Publishes an annual or periodic report.

The Picower Foundation
9 W. 57th St., Ste. 3800
New York, NY 10019 (212) 935-9860
FAX: (212) 223-4361; E-mail for Gina Verdibello: gverdibello@picower.com
Limitations: Giving on a national basis, primarily in southeast FL and the Northeast.

The Pincus Family Fund
466 Lexington Ave.
New York, NY 10017 (212) 878-9291
Limitations: Giving primarily in NY.

The Pinkerton Foundation
610 5th Ave., Ste. 316
New York, NY 10020 (212) 332-3385
FAX: (212) 332-3399;
E-mail: pinkfdn@pinkertonfdn.org; URL: http://www.thepinkertonfoundation.org
Limitations: Giving primarily in New York, NY.

The Virginia G. Piper Charitable Trust
6720 N. Scottsdale Rd., Ste. 350
Scottsdale, AZ 85253 (480) 948-5853
FAX: (480) 348-1316; E-mail: info@pipertrust.org; URL: http://www.pipertrust.org
Limitations: Giving primarily in Maricopa County, AZ.
Publishes an annual or periodic report.

The Pittsburgh Foundation
5 PPG Pl., Ste. 250
Pittsburgh, PA 15222-5414 (412) 391-5122
FAX: (412) 391-7259; E-mail: email@pghfdn.org; Grant application E-mail: trueheartw@pghfdn.org; URL: http://www.pittsburghfoundation.org
Limitations: Giving from unrestricted funds limited to Pittsburgh and Allegheny County, PA.
Publishes an annual or periodic report.

Plough Foundation
6410 Poplar Ave., Ste. 710
Memphis, TN 38119
FAX: (901) 761-6186; E-mail: Masson@plough.org
Limitations: Giving primarily in Shelby County, TN, with an emphasis on Memphis.

The PNC Foundation
249 5th Ave., 20th Fl.
1 PNC Plz.
Pittsburgh, PA 15222 (412) 762-7076
FAX: (412) 705-3584;
E-mail: foundations@pncbank.com; URL: http://www.pnccommunityinvolvement.com/PNCFoundation.htm
Limitations: Giving primarily in Washington, DC, DE, IN, KY, MD, NJ, OH, PA, and VA.

Carl and Eloise Pohlad Family Foundation
60 S. 6th St., Ste. 3900
Minneapolis, MN 55402 (612) 661-3910
FAX: (612) 661-3715;
E-mail: info@pohladfamilygiving.org; Additional E-mail: rpeterson@pohladfamilygiving.org;
URL: http://www.pohladfamilygiving.org

Limitations: Giving primarily in Minneapolis and St. Paul, MN.
Publishes an annual or periodic report.

Polk Bros. Foundation, Inc.
20 W. Kinzie St., Ste. 1110
Chicago, IL 60610-4600 (312) 527-4684
FAX: (312) 527-4681; E-mail: info@polkbrosfdn.org;
    URL: http://www.polkbrosfdn.org/
Limitations: Giving primarily in Chicago, IL.
Publishes an annual or periodic report.

Wayne L. Prim Foundation
P.O. Box 12219
Zephyr Cove, NV 89448-4219 (775) 588-7300
Limitations: Giving primarily in CA and NV.

Prince Charitable Trusts
303 W. Madison St., Ste. 1900
Chicago, IL 60606 (312) 419-8700
FAX: (312) 419-8558;
    E-mail: srobison@prince-trusts.org; Additional
    address: Prince Charitable Trusts, 816
    Connecticut Ave. N.W., Washington, DC 20006,
    Tel.: (202) 728-0646, FAX: (202) 466-4726,
    E-mail: info@princetrusts.org (DC office);
    URL: http://www.foundationcenter.org/
    grantmaker/prince/
Limitations: Giving limited to local groups in
    Washington, DC, Chicago, IL, and RI, with
    emphasis on Aquidneck Island.

Principal Financial Group Foundation, Inc.
711 High St.
Des Moines, IA 50392-0150 (515) 247-7227
FAX: (515) 246-5475;
    E-mail: murphy.jodi@principal.com; URL: http://
    www.principal.com/about/giving
Limitations: Giving limited to Des Moines, IA, and
    areas of company operations in Phoenix, AZ,
    Middletown, CT, Wilmington, DE, Cedar Falls,
    Mason City, Ottumwa, and Pella, IA, Indianapolis,
    IN, Grand Island, NE, Spokane, WA, and
    Appleton, WI.

The Procter & Gamble Fund
2 Procter & Gamble Pl.
Cincinnati, OH 45202 (513) 983-2173
FAX: (513) 983-2147; E-mail: pgfund.im@pg.com;
    URL: http://www.pg.com/company/
    our_commitment/community.jhtml
Limitations: Giving on a national basis, with emphasis
    on areas of company operations.

The Prudential Foundation
Prudential Plz.
751 Broad St., 15th Fl.
Newark, NJ 07102-3777 (973) 802-4791
E-mail: community.resources@prudential.com;
    URL: http://www.prudential.com/
    productsAndServices/0,1474,intPageID%
    253D1440%2526blnPrinterFriendly%
    253D0,00.html
Limitations: Giving primarily in areas of company
    operations, with emphasis on Phoenix, AZ, Los
    Angeles, CA, Jacksonville, FL, Atlanta, GA,
    Minneapolis, MN, Newark, NJ, Philadelphia, PA,
    and Houston, TX.
Publishes an annual or periodic report.

Public Welfare Foundation, Inc.
1200 U St. N.W.
Washington, DC 20009-4443 (202) 965-1800
FAX: (202) 265-8851;
    E-mail: reviewcommittee@publicwelfare.org;
    URL: http://www.publicwelfare.org

Limitations: Giving is generally limited to the U.S.
    (more than 90 percent).
Publishes an annual or periodic report.

Publix Super Markets Charities
3300 Publix Corporate Pkwy.
Lakeland, FL 33811 (863) 680-5250
Application address: P.O. Box 407, Lakeland, FL
    33802-0407
Limitations: Giving primarily in AL, FL, GA, SC, and TN.

Nina Mason Pulliam Charitable Trust
135 N. Pennsylvania St., Ste. 1200
Indianapolis, IN 46204 (317) 231-6075
FAX: (317) 231-9208; E-mail: mprice@nmpct.org;
    Application address for Arizona organizations:
    2201 E. Camelback Rd., Ste. 600B, Phoenix, AZ
    85016, tel.: (602) 955-3000, FAX: (602)
    955-8029; URL: http://
    www.ninapulliamtrust.org
Limitations: Giving primarily in Phoenix, AZ, and
    Indianapolis, IN.
Publishes an annual or periodic report.

Raskob Foundation for Catholic Activities, Inc.
P.O. Box 4019
Wilmington, DE 19807-0019 (302) 655-4440
FAX: (302) 655-3223; URL: http://www.rfca.org
Limitations: Giving to domestic and international
    programs affiliated with the Roman Catholic
    church.

Rasmuson Foundation
301 W. Northern Lights Blvd., Ste. 400
Anchorage, AK 99503 (907) 297-2700
FAX: (907) 297-2770;
    E-mail: rasmusonfdn@rasmuson.org;
    URL: http://www.rasmuson.org
Limitations: Giving limited to AK.

V. Kann Rasmussen Foundation
c/o Wilmer Cutler Pickering Hale and Dorr LLP
60 State St.
Boston, MA 02109 (617) 526-6610
FAX: (617) 526-5000;
    E-mail: mkaplantrustee@vkrf.org; Additional
    address: c/o Wilmer Cutler Pickering Hale and
    Dorr, LLP, 399 Park Ave., New York, NY, 10022,
    tel.: (212) 937-7272, FAX: (212) 230-8888;
    URL: http://www.vkrf.org/

Nell J. Redfield Foundation
1755 E. Plumb Ln., Ste. 212
Reno, NV 89502 (775) 323-1373
Application address: P.O. Box 61, Reno, NV 89504
Limitations: Giving primarily in northern NV.

Michael Reese Health Trust
20 N. Wacker Dr., Ste. 760
Chicago, IL 60606 (312) 726-1008
FAX: (312) 726-2797;
    E-mail: programs@healthtrust.net; URL: http://
    www.healthtrust.net
Limitations: Giving limited to the metropolitan
    Chicago, IL, area with emphasis on the city of
    Chicago.

Reiman Foundation, Inc.
115 S. 84th St., No. 221
Milwaukee, WI 53214 (414) 456-0600
FAX: (414) 456-0606;
    E-mail: reimanfoundation@hexagoninc.com;
    URL: http://www.reimanfoundation.org

The Reinberger Foundation
27600 Chagrin Blvd., No. 355

Cleveland, OH 44122 (216) 292-2790
FAX: (216) 292-4466;
    E-mail: reinbergerfound@aol.com; URL: http://
    foundationcenter.org/grantmaker/reinberger/
Limitations: Giving primarily in Columbus and
    northeast OH.

The Retirement Research Foundation
8765 W. Higgins Rd., Ste. 430
Chicago, IL 60631-4170 (773) 714-8080
FAX: (773) 714-8089; E-mail: info@rrf.org; Additional
    E-mail (for Marilyn Hennessy): hennessy@rrf.org;
    URL: http://www.rrf.org
Limitations: Giving limited to the Midwest (IA, IL, IN,
    KY, MO, WI) and FL for direct service projects not
    having the potential of national impact.

Charles H. Revson Foundation, Inc.
55 E. 59th St., 23rd Fl.
New York, NY 10022-1112 (212) 935-3340
FAX: (212) 688-0633;
    E-mail: info@revsonfoundation.org
Limitations: Giving primarily in New York, NY.

Kate B. Reynolds Charitable Trust
128 Reynolda Village
Winston-Salem, NC 27106-5123
    (336) 723-1456
FAX: (336) 723-7765; E-mail: Karen@kbr.org;
    Additional tel. (for Karen Yoak Lewis, Dir.,
    Admin.): (336) 721-2273; URL: http://
    www.kbr.org
Limitations: Giving limited to NC; social welfare grants
    limited to Winston-Salem and Forsyth County;
    health care giving, statewide.
Publishes an annual or periodic report.

Donald W. Reynolds Foundation
1701 Village Center Cir.
Las Vegas, NV 89134 (702) 804-6000
FAX: (702) 804-6099;
    E-mail: generalquestions@dwrf.org; URL: http://
    www.dwreynolds.org
Limitations: Giving primarily in AR, NV, and OK for
    capital and planning grants. Giving nationally for
    cardiovascular clinic research and geriatrics
    training of physicians, and business journalism.

Z. Smith Reynolds Foundation, Inc.
147 S. Cherry St., Ste. 200
Winston-Salem, NC 27101-5287
    (336) 725-7541
FAX: (336) 725-6069; E-mail: info@zsr.org; Additional
    tel.: (800) 443-8319; URL: http://www.zsr.org
Limitations: Giving limited to NC.
Publishes an annual or periodic report.

The Rhode Island Foundation
1 Union Station
Providence, RI 02903 (401) 274-4564
FAX: (401) 331-8085; Artist grants E-mail:
    celliott@rifoundation.org; URL: http://
    www.rifoundation.org
Limitations: Giving through discretionary funds limited
    to RI.
Publishes an annual or periodic report.

Smith Richardson Foundation, Inc.
60 Jesup Rd.
Westport, CT 06880 (203) 222-6222
FAX: (203) 222-6282; URL: http://www.srf.org
Limitations: Giving limited to U.S.-based
    organizations only.
Publishes an annual or periodic report.

Sid W. Richardson Foundation
309 Main St.

Fort Worth, TX 76102 (817) 336-0494
FAX: (817) 332-2176; URL: http://
www.sidrichardson.org
Limitations: Giving limited to TX, with emphasis on
Fort Worth for the arts and human services, and
statewide for health and education.
Publishes an annual or periodic report.

The Riley Foundation
4518 Poplar Springs Dr.
Meridian, MS 39305 (601) 481-1430
FAX: (601) 481-1434;
E-mail: info@rileyfoundation.org; URL: http://
www.rileyfoundation.org
Limitations: Giving limited to Meridian, and
Lauderdale County, MS.

Rochester Area Community Foundation
500 East Ave.
Rochester, NY 14607-1912 (585) 271-4100
FAX: (585) 271-4292; E-mail: edoherty@racf.org;
Grant application E-mail: mhartmann@racf.org;
URL: http://www.racf.org
Limitations: Giving limited to Genesee, Livingston,
Monroe, Ontario, Orleans, and Wayne counties,
NY, except for donor-designated funds.
Publishes an annual or periodic report.

Rockefeller Brothers Fund, Inc.
437 Madison Ave., 37th Fl.
New York, NY 10022-7001 (212) 812-4200
FAX: (212) 812-4299; E-mail: info@rbf.org; E-mail for
annual report: anreport@rbf.org; URL: http://
www.rbf.org
Limitations: Giving on a national basis, and in Central
and Eastern Europe, East and Southeast Asia,
and South Africa.
Publishes an annual or periodic report.

The Rockefeller Foundation
420 5th Ave.
New York, NY 10018-2702 (212) 869-8500
URL: http://www.rockfound.org
Limitations: Giving primarily in Africa, North America,
and Southeast Asia.
Publishes an annual or periodic report.

The Winthrop Rockefeller Foundation
308 E. 8th St.
Little Rock, AR 72202-3999 (501) 376-6854
FAX: (501) 374-4797;
E-mail: programstaff@wrfoundation.org;
URL: http://www.wrockefellerfoundation.org
Limitations: Giving limited to AR, or for projects that
benefit AR.
Publishes an annual or periodic report.

Rockwell Collins Charitable Corporation
400 Collins Rd., N.E., M.S. 124-302
Cedar Rapids, IA 52498-0001
FAX: (319) 295-9374;
E-mail: cmdietz@rockwellcollins.com; Additional
E-mail:
communityrelations@rockwellcollins.com;
URL: http://www.rockwellcollins.com/about/
community/charitable_giving/
charitable_corporation/index.html
Limitations: Giving on a national and international
basis in areas of company operations, with
emphasis on Pomona, San Jose, and Tustin, CA,
Melbourne, FL, IA, Portland, OR, and Richardson,
TX.

Rockwell Fund, Inc.
770 S. Post Oak Ln., Ste. 525
Houston, TX 77056 (713) 629-9022

FAX: (713) 629-7702; E-mail (for Judy Ahlgrim):
jahlgrim@rockfund.org; URL: http://
www.rockfund.org
Limitations: Giving primarily in Houston, TX.

Frederick P. & Sandra P. Rose Foundation
200 Madison Ave., 5th Fl.
New York, NY 10016
Limitations: Giving primarily in New York, NY.

Murray & Sydell Rosenberg Foundation
75 Montebello Rd.
Suffern, NY 10901
Limitations: Giving primarily in NY, NJ, and Israel.

Arthur Ross Foundation, Inc.
c/o Anchin Block & Anchin, LLP
1375 Broadway
New York, NY 10018 (212) 737-7311
Limitations: Giving primarily in NY.

Helena Rubinstein Foundation, Inc.
477 Madison Ave., 7th Fl.
New York, NY 10022-5802 (212) 750-7310
URL: http://www.helenarubinsteinfdn.org
Limitations: Giving primarily in New York, NY.

Saint Luke's Foundation of Cleveland, Ohio
4208 Prospect Ave.
Cleveland, OH 44103 (216) 431-8010
FAX: (216) 431-8015;
E-mail: dzeman@saintlukesfoundation.org;
URL: http://www.saintlukesfoundation.org/
Limitations: Giving primarily in Cleveland and
Cuyahoga counties, OH.
Publishes an annual or periodic report.

The Saint Paul Foundation, Inc.
55 5th St. E., Ste. 600
St. Paul, MN 55101-1797 (651) 224-5463
FAX: (651) 224-8123;
E-mail: inbox@saintpaulfoundation.org;
Additional tel.: (800) 875-6167; Additional
E-mails: ckr@saintpaulfoundation.org and
lmh@saintpaulfoundation.org; URL: http://
saintpaulfoundation.org
Limitations: Giving limited to Dakota, Ramsey, and
Washington counties in the metropolitan Saint
Paul, MN, area.

Samberg Family Foundation
3101 Wilson Blvd., Suite 220
Arlington, VA 22201
Telephone for Jerry Levine: (703) 351-9405
Limitations: Giving primarily in NY.

The Fan Fox and Leslie R. Samuels
Foundation, Inc.
350 5th Ave., Ste. 4301
New York, NY 10118 (212) 239-3030
FAX: (212) 239-3039; E-mail: info@samuels.org;
URL: http://www.samuels.org
Limitations: Giving limited to New York, NY.

The San Diego Foundation
2508 Historic Decatur Rd., Ste. 200
San Diego, CA 92106 (619) 235-2300
FAX: (619) 239-1710; E-mail: info@sdfoundation.org;
Additional tel.: (858) 385-1595 (for North
County); URL: http://www.sdfoundation.org
Limitations: Giving primarily in the greater San Diego,
CA, region.
Publishes an annual or periodic report.

The San Francisco Foundation
225 Bush St., Ste. 500
San Francisco, CA 94104-4224 (415) 733-8500
FAX: (415) 477-2783; E-mail: rec@sff.org; Intent to
Apply E-mail: apps@sff.org; URL: http://
www.sff.org
Limitations: Giving limited to the San Francisco Bay
Area, CA, counties of Alameda, Contra Costa,
Marin, San Francisco, and San Mateo.
Publishes an annual or periodic report.

The Sandy River Charitable Foundation
349 Voter Hill Rd.
Farmington, ME 04938
FAX: (207) 779-1901;
E-mail: info@srcfoundation.org; URL: http://
www.srcfoundation.org
Limitations: Giving on an international and national
basis, (particularly Board/staff areas), with a
special emphasis on ME.

Santa Barbara Foundation
15 E. Carrillo St.
Santa Barbara, CA 93101 (805) 963-1873
FAX: (805) 966-2345;
E-mail: cslosser@sbfoundation.org; URL: http://
www.sbfoundation.org
Limitations: Giving limited to Santa Barbara County,
CA.
Publishes an annual or periodic report.

Sara Lee Foundation
c/o Direct Grants Prog.
3 First National Plz.
Chicago, IL 60602-4260
URL: http://www.saraleefoundation.org
Limitations: Giving primarily in areas of company
operations, with emphasis on the greater
metropolitan Chicago, IL, area.
Publishes an annual or periodic report.

Scaife Family Foundation
West Tower, Ste. 903
777 So. Flagler Dr.
West Palm Beach, FL 33401 (561) 659-1188
URL: http://www.scaifefamily.org
Limitations: Giving on a national basis.
Publishes an annual or periodic report.

The Scherman Foundation, Inc.
16 E. 52nd St., Ste. 601
New York, NY 10022-5306 (212) 832-3086
FAX: (212) 838-0154; E-mail: info@scherman.org;
URL: http://www.scherman.org
Limitations: Giving in NY and nationally in all areas,
except for the arts and social welfare, which are
primarily in New York City.
Publishes an annual or periodic report.

Dr. Scholl Foundation
1033 Skokie Blvd., Ste. 230
Northbrook, IL 60062 (847) 559-7430
URL: http://www.drschollfoundation.com
Limitations: Giving primarily in the U.S., with some
emphasis on the Chicago, IL area.

The Schumann Center for Media and
Democracy, Inc.
33 Park St.
Montclair, NJ 07042 (973) 783-6660
Limitations: Giving on a national basis.

Charles and Helen Schwab Foundation
1650 S. Amphlett Blvd., No. 300
San Mateo, CA 94402-2516 (650) 655-2410

FAX: (650) 655-2411;
E-mail: info@schwabfoundation.org; URL: http://
www.schwabfoundation.org
Limitations: Giving primarily in CA.

Homer A. & Mildred S. Scott Foundation
P.O. Box 2007
Sheridan, WY 82801-2007
FAX: (307) 672-1443; E-mail: lmavrakis@fib.com
Limitations: Giving primarily within a 35-mile radius of
Sheridan, WY and in specific areas of MT.

Scripps Howard Foundation
P.O. Box 5380
312 Walnut St., 28th Fl.
Cincinnati, OH 45201 (513) 977-3035
FAX: (513) 977-3800; E-mail: clabes@scripps.com;
Contact for Roy W. Howard National Reporting
Competition, Internships, and Top 10
Scholarship: Sue Porter, V.P., Progs., tel.: (800)
888-3000, E-mail: porters@scripps.com; Contact
for Jack R. Howard Fellowships in International
Journalism: Josh Friedman, Dir., Intl. Prog.,
Columbia Graduate School of Journalism, E-mail:
jf125@columbia.edu; Additional tel.: (513)
997-3048, (800) 888-3847; URL: http://
foundation.scripps.com/foundation/
Limitations: Giving on a national basis, with emphasis
on areas of company operations.
Publishes an annual or periodic report.

The Seattle Foundation
1200 5th Ave., Ste. 1300
Seattle, WA 98101-3151 (206) 622-2294
FAX: (206) 622-7673;
E-mail: info@seattlefoundation.org; Grant
information E-mails:
grantmaking@seattlefoundation.org and
ceil@seattlefoundation.org; URL: http://
www.seattlefoundation.org
Limitations: Giving limited to Seattle-King County, WA.
Publishes an annual or periodic report.

The Seaver Institute
11611 San Vicente Blvd., Ste. 545
Los Angeles, CA 90049 (310) 979-0298
E-mail: vsd@theseaverinstitute.org
Limitations: Giving on a national basis.

The Peter Jay Sharp Foundation
545 Madison Ave., 11th Fl.
New York, NY 10022 (212) 397-6060
Limitations: Giving primarily in New York, NY.

The Shubert Foundation, Inc.
234 W. 44th St.
New York, NY 10036 (212) 944-3777
FAX: (212) 944-3767; URL: http://
www.shubertfoundation.org
Limitations: Giving limited to the U.S.
Publishes an annual or periodic report.

SI Bank & Trust Foundation
260 Christopher Ln., Ste. 3B
Staten Island, NY 10314 (718) 697-2831
FAX: (718) 697-3180; URL: http://www.sibtf.org
Limitations: Giving only in Staten Island, NY.

Siebert Lutheran Foundation, Inc.
2600 N. Mayfair Rd., Ste. 390
Wauwatosa, WI 53226-1392 (414) 257-2656
FAX: (414) 257-1387;
E-mail: contactus@siebertfoundation.org;
URL: http://www.siebertfoundation.org
Limitations: Giving primarily in WI.
Publishes an annual or periodic report.

Marty and Dorothy Silverman Foundation
830 3rd Ave., 6th Fl.
New York, NY 10022 (212) 832-9170
Limitations: Giving primarily in NY.

William E. Simon Foundation, Inc.
140 E. 45th St., Ste. 14D
New York, NY 10017 (212) 661-8366
FAX: (212) 661-9450; URL: http://
www.wesimonfoundation.org
Limitations: Giving on a national basis, with emphasis
on New York, NY, and Los Angeles and the San
Francisco Bay Area, CA.

The Simons Foundation
101 Fifth Ave., 5th Fl.
New York, NY 10003
E-mail: admin@simonsfoundation.org; URL: http://
www.simonsfoundation.org
Publishes an annual or periodic report.

Simpson PSB Fund
P.O. Box 359
Lafayette, CA 94549-0359 (925) 284-7048
Limitations: Giving primarily in CA.

The Skillman Foundation
100 Talon Centre Dr., Ste. 100
Detroit, MI 48207 (313) 393-1185
FAX: (313) 393-1187; E-mail: mailbox@skillman.org;
URL: http://www.skillman.org
Limitations: Giving primarily in southeastern MI, with
emphasis on metropolitan Detroit, and Macomb,
Oakland, and Wayne counties.
Publishes an annual or periodic report.

Skirball Foundation
767 5th Ave., 50th Fl.
New York, NY 10153 (212) 832-8500
Limitations: Giving primarily in CA.

The Skoll Foundation
250 University Ave., Ste. 200
Palo Alto, CA 94301 (650) 331-1031
FAX: (650) 331-1033;
E-mail: grants@skollfoundation.org; URL: http://
www.skollfoundation.org/
Publishes an annual or periodic report.

Alan B. Slifka Foundation, Inc.
477 Madison Ave., 8th Fl.
New York, NY 10022-5802 (212) 303-9408
E-mail: programofficer@halcyonllc.com
Limitations: Giving primarily in NY.

Alfred P. Sloan Foundation
630 5th Ave., Ste. 2550
New York, NY 10111-0242 (212) 649-1649
FAX: (212) 757-5117; URL: http://www.sloan.org
Publishes an annual or periodic report.

The Smart Family Foundation
74 Pin Oak Ln.
Wilton, CT 06897-1329 (203) 834-0400
Limitations: Giving on a national basis.

George D. Smith Fund, Inc.
900 3rd Ave.
New York, NY 10022 (212) 895-2000
Limitations: Giving primarily in CA and UT.

Y & H Soda Foundation
2 Theater Sq., Ste. 211
Orinda, CA 94563-3346 (925) 253-2630

FAX: (925) 253-1814;
E-mail: info@yhsodafoundation.org; URL: http://
www.yhsodafoundation.org
Limitations: Giving limited to Alameda and Contra
Costa counties, CA.

Southern Oklahoma Memorial Foundation
P.O. Box 1409
Ardmore, OK 73402-1409 (580) 226-0700
FAX: (580) 226-0223;
E-mail: Lapulliam@sbcglobal.net
Limitations: Giving limited to OK organizations within
a 50-mile radius of Ardmore.
Publishes an annual or periodic report.

C. D. Spangler Foundation, Inc.
P.O. Box 36007
Charlotte, NC 28236-6007
Limitations: Giving primarily in NC.

The Spencer Foundation
625 N. Michigan Ave., Ste. 1600
Chicago, IL 60611 (312) 337-7000
FAX: (312) 337-0282;
E-mail: information@spencer.org; URL: http://
www.spencer.org
Limitations: Giving on a national and international
basis.
Publishes an annual or periodic report.

The Speyer Family Foundation, Inc.
45 Rockefeller Plz., 7th Fl.
New York, NY 10022
Limitations: Giving primarily in New York, NY.

St. Paul Travelers Foundation
385 Washington St., M.C. 514D
St. Paul, MN 55102 (651) 310-7757
FAX: (651) 310-2327; Additional contact: Shary
Kempainen, E-mail:
shkempai@stpaultravelers.com; URL: http://
www.stpaultravelers.com/about/community/
index.html
Limitations: Giving primarily in areas of significant
company operations, with emphasis on the Twin
Cities, MN; giving also to national organizations.

Stark Community Foundation
400 Market Ave., N. Ste. 200
Canton, OH 44702-2107 (330) 454-3426
FAX: (330) 454-5855; E-mail: jbower@starkcf.org;
Additional E-mail: cmlazer@starkcf.org;
URL: http://www.starkcommunityfoundation.org
Limitations: Giving limited to Stark County, OH.
Publishes an annual or periodic report.

The Starr Foundation
399 Park Ave., 17th Fl.
New York, NY 10022 (212) 909-3600
FAX: (212) 750-3536; Additional tel.: (212)
909-3611; URL: http://
www.starrfoundation.org/
Limitations: Giving primarily on a national and
international basis, with emphasis on New York
City, NY nationally and emphasis on Asia
internationally.

State Farm Companies Foundation
1 State Farm Plz.
Bloomington, IL 61710 (309) 766-2161
FAX: (309) 766-2314;
E-mail: kristy.funk.cm3n@statefarm.com;
Additional E-mail: home.sf-foundation.
494b00@statefarm.com; URL: http://
www.statefarm.com/foundati/foundati.htm
Limitations: Giving on a national basis and in Canada.

State Street Foundation
c/o Community Affairs Div.
225 Franklin St., 12th Fl.
Boston, MA 02110-2884   (617) 664-1937
E-mail: epsilvoy@statestreet.com; URL: http://
   www.statestreet.com/company/
   community_affairs/global_philanthropy/
   overview.html
Limitations: Giving on a national and international
   basis, with emphasis on the greater Boston, MA,
   area.

Steelcase Foundation
P.O. Box 1967, CH-4E
Grand Rapids, MI 49501-1967
FAX: (616) 475-2200;
   E-mail: sbroman@steelcase.com; URL: http://
   www.steelcase.com/na/
   steelcase_foundation_ourcompany.aspx?
   f=18486
Limitations: Giving limited to areas of company
   operations, with emphasis on Athens, AL, City of
   Industry, CA, Grand Rapids, MI, and Markham,
   Canada.
Publishes an annual or periodic report.

Stockman Family Foundation Trust
1041 Matador Ave. S.E.
Albuquerque, NM 87123   (505) 296-7057
Limitations: Giving primarily in NM.

Levi Strauss Foundation
1155 Battery St.
San Francisco, CA 94111   (415) 501-3577
FAX: (415) 501-6575; E-mail: lsf@levi.com;
   Application address for Syringe Access Fund:
   Stuart C. Burden, Dir., Community Affairs, The
   Americas, 1155 Battery St., San Francisco, CA
   94111, E-mail: syringeaccess@levi.com;
   URL: http://www.levistrauss.com/Citizenship/
   LeviStraussFoundation.aspx
Limitations: Giving on a national and international
   basis, with emphasis on areas of company
   operations.

Stuart Foundation
50 California St., Ste. 3350
San Francisco, CA 94111-4735   (415) 393-1551
FAX: (415) 393-1552;
   E-mail: info@stuartfoundation.org; URL: http://
   www.stuartfoundation.org
Limitations: Giving primarily in CA and WA.

The Sunshine Lady Foundation, Inc.
P.O. Box 1074
Morehead City, NC 28557-1074   (252) 240-2788
URL: http://www.sunshineladyfdn.org
Limitations: Giving on a national basis.

Surdna Foundation, Inc.
330 Madison Ave., 30th Fl.
New York, NY 10017-5001   (212) 557-0010
FAX: (212) 557-0003; E-mail: request@surdna.org;
   URL: http://www.surdna.org
Limitations: Giving on a national basis.
Publishes an annual or periodic report.

Ann and Bill Swindells Charitable Trust
1211 S.W. 5th Ave., Ste. 2340
Portland, OR 97204-3723   (503) 222-0689
FAX: (503) 222-0726; E-mail: cdehart@ipns.com;
   URL: http://www.swindellstrust.org
Limitations: Giving primarily in OR.

Carl Gary Taylor Foundation for Children, Inc.
P.O. Box 785
Newport, VT 05855-0785

Application address: c/o Carl Taylor, 337 Union St.,
   Newport, VT 05855, tel.: (802) 334-5085
Limitations: Giving primarily in VT.

TD Banknorth Charitable Foundation
P.O. Box 9540
1 Portland Sq.
Portland, ME 04112-9540   (207) 828-7558
E-mail: julie.mcquillan@tdbanknorth.com; Additional
   tel.: (207) 756-6947; URL: http://
   www.tdbanknorth.com/community/
   charitable_foundation.html
Limitations: Giving limited to CT, MA, ME, NH, NY, and
   VT.

The Teagle Foundation
10 Rockefeller Plz., Rm. 920
New York, NY 10020-1903   (212) 373-1970
E-mail: mbray@teaglefoundation.org; URL: http://
   www.teaglefoundation.org/intro.htm
Limitations: Giving limited to the U.S. No grants to
   community organizations outside New York City.
   No grants to U.S. organizations for foreign
   programmatic activities.
Publishes an annual or periodic report.

T. L. L. Temple Foundation
109 Temple Blvd., Ste. 300
Lufkin, TX 75901
Limitations: Giving primarily in counties in TX
   constituting the East Texas Pine Timber Belt.

Temple-Inland Foundation
1300 S. Mopac Expwy.
Austin, TX 78749   (936) 829-1721
Limitations: Giving primarily in areas of company
   operations.

John Templeton Foundation
300 Conshohocken State Rd., Ste. 500
West Conshohocken, PA 19428   (610) 941-2828
FAX: (610) 825-1730; E-mail: info@templeton.org;
   URL: http://www.templeton.org
Limitations: Giving on a national and international
   basis.
Publishes an annual or periodic report.

Tenet Healthcare Foundation
13737 Noel Rd., Ste. 100
Dallas, TX 75240   (469) 893-6502
FAX: (469) 893-2605;
   E-mail: foundation@tenethealth.com;
   URL: http://www.tenethealth.com/TenetHealth/
   TenetFoundation
Limitations: Giving on a national basis, with emphasis
   on areas of company operations.
Publishes an annual or periodic report.

The Textron Charitable Trust
c/o Textron Inc.
40 Westminster St.
Providence, RI 02903
URL: http://www.textron.com/profile/
   community.html
Limitations: Giving on a national basis in areas of
   company operations.

Eugene V. & Clare E. Thaw Charitable Trust
P.O. Box 2422
Santa Fe, NM 87504-2422   (505) 982-7023
FAX: (505) 982-7027; E-mail: (for Sherry Thompson):
   sherryt@thawtrust.org
Limitations: Giving on a national basis.

Tiger Foundation
101 Park Ave., 48th Fl.

New York, NY 10178   (212) 984-2565
FAX: (212) 949-9778;
   E-mail: info@tigerfoundation.org; URL: http://
   www.tigerfoundation.org
Limitations: Giving primarily in New York, NY.

Timken Foundation of Canton
200 Market Ave. N., Ste. 210
Canton, OH 44702   (330) 452-1144
Limitations: Giving primarily in local areas of Timken
   Co. domestic operations in Torrington, and
   Watertown, CT; Cairo, Dahlonega, and Sylvania,
   GA; Bucyrus, Canton, Eaton, New Philadelphia,
   and Wooster, OH; Ashboro, Columbus, and
   Lincolnton, NC; Keene, and Lebanon, NH;
   Latrobe, PA; Honea Path, Walhalla, Clinton,
   Union, and Gaffney, SC; Altavista, VA; and
   Mascot and Pulaski, TN. Giving also in local areas
   in Brazil, Canada, China, Czech Republic, France,
   Germany, Great Britain, India, Italy, Poland,
   Romania, and South Africa where Timken Co. has
   manufacturing facilities.

Tisch Foundation, Inc.
655 Madison Ave.
New York, NY 10021-8087   (212) 521-2930
Limitations: Giving primarily in NY.

Topfer Family Foundation
5000 Plz. on the Lake, Ste. 170
Austin, TX 78746
FAX: (512) 329-6462;
   E-mail: info@topferfoundation.org; URL: http://
   www.topferfamilyfoundation.org
Limitations: Giving primarily in the greater
   metropolitan areas of Chicago, IL and Austin, TX.

Harry C. Trexler Trust
33 S. 7th St., Ste. 205
Allentown, PA 18101-2406   (610) 434-9645
Limitations: Giving limited to Lehigh County, PA.

Triad Foundation, Inc.
P.O. Box 4440
Ithaca, NY 14852   (607) 257-1133
Limitations: Giving primarily in FL, NC, and NY.

Triangle Community Foundation
4813 Emperor Blvd., Ste. 130
P.O. Box 12834
Research Triangle Park, NC 27709
   (919) 474-8370
FAX: (919) 941-9208; E-mail: info@trianglecf.org;
   Additional E-mails: krystin@trianglecf.org and
   cathy@trianglecf.org; URL: http://
   www.trianglecf.org
Limitations: Giving limited to Chatham, Durham,
   Orange, and Wake counties, NC.
Publishes an annual or periodic report.

Trinity Foundation
P.O. Box 7008
Pine Bluff, AR 71611-7008
Limitations: Giving primarily in central AR.

The Trust for Mutual Understanding
30 Rockefeller Plz., Rm. 5600
New York, NY 10112   (212) 632-3405
FAX: (212) 632-3409; E-mail: tmu@tmuny.org;
   URL: http://www.tmuny.org
Limitations: Giving for exchanges between the U.S.
   and the countries of Central and Eastern Europe,
   primarily the Czech Republic, Hungary, Poland,
   Russia, and Slovakia. Support is also provided,
   to a lesser extent, for exchanges involving
   Albania, Belarus, Bosnia and Herzegovina,
   Bulgaria, Croatia, Georgia, Macedonia, Moldova,

Mongolia, Romania, Serbia and Montenegro, Slovenia, and Ukraine.
Publishes an annual or periodic report.

Tulsa Community Foundation
7020 S. Yale, Ste. 220
Tulsa, OK 74136 (918) 494-8823
FAX: (918) 494-9826; E-mail: Info@TulsaCF.org;
Additional E-mail: plakin@tulsacf.org;
URL: http://www.tulsacf.org
Limitations: Giving limited to northeastern OK through discretionary funds; donor-advised giving is nationwide.

The Turner Foundation
4 W. Main St., Ste. 800
Springfield, OH 45502 (937) 325-1300
FAX: (937) 325-0100;
E-mail: questions@hmturnerfoundation.org;
URL: http://www.hmturnerfoundation.org
Limitations: Giving primarily in Springfield and Clark County, Ohio.

Turrell Fund
21 Van Vleck St.
Montclair, NJ 07042-2358 (973) 783-9358
FAX: (973) 783-9283; E-mail: turrell@turrellfund.org;
URL: http://foundationcenter.org/grantmaker/turrell/
Limitations: Giving limited to Essex, Union, Hudson and Passaic counties, NJ, and VT.
Publishes an annual or periodic report.

U.S. Bancorp Foundation, Inc.
BC-MN-H21B
800 Nicollet Mall, 21st Fl.
Minneapolis, MN 55402 (612) 303-4000
FAX: (612) 303-0787; URL: http://www.usbank.com/cgi_w/cfm/about/community_relations/charit_giving.cfm
Limitations: Giving primarily in AR, AZ, CA, CO, ID, IA, IL, IN, KS, KY, MN, MO, MT, ND, NE, NV, OH, OR, SD, TN, UT, WA, WI, and WY.
Publishes an annual or periodic report.

UBS Foundation U.S.A.
800 Harbor Blvd.
Weehawken, NJ 07086
Limitations: Giving primarily in NY.

UniHealth Foundation
800 Wilshire Blvd., Ste. 1300
Los Angeles, CA 90017 (213) 630-6500
FAX: (213) 630-6509;
E-mail: Webadmin@unihealthfoundation.org;
URL: http://www.unihealthfoundation.org/
Limitations: Giving primarily in CA in the following areas: San Fernando and Santa Clarita Valley, Westside and Downtown Los Angeles, San Gabriel Valley, and Long Beach and Orange County.
Publishes an annual or periodic report.

Unilever United States Foundation
c/o Unilever United States, Inc., Tax Dept.
700 Sylvan Ave.
Englewood Cliffs, NJ 07632 (201) 894-2236
Limitations: Giving primarily in areas of company operations.

Union Pacific Foundation
1400 Douglas St., Stop 1560
Omaha, NE 68179 (402) 544-5600
E-mail: upf@up.com; URL: http://www.up.com/found
Limitations: Giving on a national basis in areas of company operations.

The UPS Foundation
55 Glenlake Pkwy., N.E.
Atlanta, GA 30328 (404) 828-6374
FAX: (404) 828-7435; URL: http://www.community.ups.com/philanthropy/main.html
Limitations: Giving on a national basis and in Canada and Mexico; giving also to statewide, regional, and national organizations.
Publishes an annual or periodic report.

Valero Energy Foundation
1 Valero Way
P.O. Box 696000
San Antonio, TX 78269-6000
E-mail: letitia.rutan@valero.com; URL: http://www.valero.com/Community/
Limitations: Giving primarily in areas of company operations, with emphasis on TX.

The Valley Foundation
16450 Los Gatos Blvd., Ste. 210
Los Gatos, CA 95032-5594 (408) 358-4545
FAX: (408) 358-4548; E-mail: admin@valley.org;
E-mail for Ervie L. Smith, Exec. Dir.:
ervie@valley.org; URL: http://www.valley.org
Limitations: Giving limited to Santa Clara County, CA.
Publishes an annual or periodic report.

Wayne & Gladys Valley Foundation
1939 Harrison St., Ste. 510
Oakland, CA 94612-3532 (510) 466-6060
FAX: (510) 466-6067; E-mail: info@wgvalley.org;
URL: http://foundationcenter.org/grantmaker/wgvalley/
Limitations: Giving primarily in Alameda and Contra Costa counties, CA.
Publishes an annual or periodic report.

van Ameringen Foundation, Inc.
509 Madison Ave.
New York, NY 10022-5501 (212) 758-6221
URL: http://www.vanamfound.org/
Limitations: Giving primarily in metropolitan New York, NY, and Philadelphia, PA.
Publishes an annual or periodic report.

Jay and Betty Van Andel Foundation
3133 Orchard Vista Dr. S.E.
Grand Rapids, MI 49546
Limitations: Giving primarily in MI, with some emphasis on Grand Rapids.

van Beuren Charitable Foundation, Inc.
P.O. Box 4098
Middletown, RI 02842 (401) 846-8167
FAX: (401) 849-6859; E-mail: vbcfdn@aol.com;
URL: http://www.vbcf.net
Limitations: Giving primarily in Newport County, RI.
Publishes an annual or periodic report.

Verizon Foundation
1 Verizon Way
Basking Ridge, NJ 07920
FAX: (212) 840-6988;
E-mail: verizon.foundation@verizon.com;
URL: http://foundation.verizon.com
Limitations: Giving on a national basis and in PR, the Dominican Republic, and Venezuela.

Victoria Foundation, Inc.
946 Bloomfield Ave., 2nd Fl.
Glen Ridge, NJ 07028 (973) 748-5300
FAX: (973) 748-0016;
E-mail: info@victoriafoundation.org; URL: http://www.victoriafoundation.org

Limitations: Giving limited to greater Newark, NJ; environmental grants limited to NJ.
Publishes an annual or periodic report.

Vulcan Materials Company Foundation
P.O. Box 385014
Birmingham, AL 35238-5014 (205) 298-3222
E-mail: giving@vmcmail.com; URL: http://www.vulcanmaterials.com/social.asp?content=vulcan
Limitations: Giving on a national basis in areas of company operations.
Publishes an annual or periodic report.

Sue and Edgar Wachenheim Foundation
3 Manhattanville Rd.
Purchase, NY 10577-2116
Limitations: Giving primarily in NY.

Waitt Family Foundation
P.O. Box 1948
La Jolla, CA 92038-1948 (858) 551-4839
FAX: (858) 551-6871;
E-mail: grants@waittfoundation.org; Application address: c/o Siouxland Chapter, P.O. Box 1397, North Sioux City, SD 57049, tel.: (605) 232-9929; FAX: (605) 232-9486; URL: http://www.waittfoundation.org/
Limitations: Giving primarily in the tri-state Siouxland region of IA, NE, and SD, and San Diego, CA.

Wal-Mart Foundation
702 S.W. 8th St.
Bentonville, AR 72716-0150 (800) 530-9925
FAX: (479) 273-6850; URL: http://www.walmartfoundation.org
Limitations: Giving primarily in areas of company operations.

The Wallace Foundation
5 Penn Plz., 7th Fl.
New York, NY 10001 (212) 251-9700
FAX: (212) 679-6990;
E-mail: info@wallacefoundation.org; URL: http://www.wallacefoundation.org
Limitations: Giving on a national basis.
Publishes an annual or periodic report.

Wallace Genetic Foundation, Inc.
4910 Massachusetts Ave., Ste. 221
Washington, DC 20016 (202) 966-2932
FAX: (202) 966-3370;
E-mail: president@wallacegenetic.org;
URL: http://www.wallacegenetic.org

Wallace Global Fund
1990 M St. N.W., Ste. 250
Washington, DC 20036 (202) 452-1530
FAX: (202) 452-0922; E-mail (for Tina Kroll-Guerch): tkroll@wgf.org; URL: http://www.wgf.org
Limitations: Giving on an international basis.

Wallis Foundation
1880 Century Park E., Ste. 950
Los Angeles, CA 90067 (310) 286-9777
Limitations: Giving primarily in CA.

Walton Family Foundation, Inc.
P.O. Box 2030
Bentonville, AR 72712 (479) 464-1570
FAX: (479) 464-1580; URL: http://www.wffhome.com
Limitations: Giving primarily in AR, with emphasis on the Mississippi River's delta region of AR and MS.

Charles B. Wang Foundation
Park 80 W., Plz. 2
Saddle Brook, NJ 07663
Limitations: Giving primarily in NY.

The Andy Warhol Foundation for the Visual Arts
65 Bleecker St., 7th Fl.
New York, NY 10012 (212) 387-7555
FAX: (212) 387-7560; URL: http://
www.warholfoundation.org

Wasserman Foundation
12100 W. Olympic Blvd., Ste. 400
Los Angeles, CA 90064 (310) 407-0200
FAX: (310) 882-4601; URL: http://
www.wassermanfoundation.org
Limitations: Giving primarily in CA.

The Raymond John Wean Foundation
P.O. Box 760
Warren, OH 44482-0760 (330) 394-5600
FAX: (330) 394-5601; E-mail: info@rjweanfdn.org;
Additional address: 108 Main Ave. S.W., Ste.
1005, Warren, OH, 44481-1058; URL: http://
www.rjweanfdn.org
Limitations: Giving primarily in Allegheny County, PA,
and northeast OH, with emphasis on Cuyahoga,
Mahoning, and Trumbull counties.

Wege Foundation
P.O. Box 6388
Grand Rapids, MI 49516-6388 (616) 957-0480
Limitations: Giving primarily in greater Kent County,
MI, with emphasis on the Grand Rapids area.
Publishes an annual or periodic report.

**The Harry and Jeanette Weinberg Foundation,
Inc.**
7 Park Center Ct.
Owings Mills, MD 21117-4200
URL: http://www.hjweinbergfoundation.org
Limitations: Giving on a national basis.

Weingart Foundation
1055 W. 7th St., Ste. 3050
Los Angeles, CA 90017-2305 (213) 688-7799
FAX: (213) 688-1515; E-mail: info@weingartfnd.org;
URL: http://www.weingartfnd.org
Limitations: Giving limited to 7 southern CA counties;
Los Angeles, Kern, Orange, Santa Barbara,
Riverside, San Bernadino, and Ventura.
Publishes an annual or periodic report.

Welfare Foundation, Inc.
100 W. 10th St., Ste. 1109
Wilmington, DE 19801
Limitations: Giving limited to DE and southern Chester
County, PA.

The Wells Fargo Foundation
550 California St., 7th Fl.
San Francisco, CA 94104 (415) 396-5947
Additional address: 333 S. Grand Ave., E2064-200,
Los Angeles, CA 90071, tel.: (888) 886-1785;
Application address for Wells Fargo Housing
Foundation: Kimberly Jackson, Exec. Dir., Wells
Fargo Housing Fdn., MAC N9305-192, 90 S. 7th
St., Minneapolis, MN 55479, tel.: (612)
667-2146; URL: http://www.wellsfargo.com/
donations
Limitations: Giving primarily in areas of company
operations; giving on a national basis for the
Wells Fargo Housing Foundation.

WEM Foundation
P.O. Box 5628

Minneapolis, MN 55440-9300 (952) 742-7544
Limitations: Giving primarily in MN.

The Margaret L. Wendt Foundation
40 Fountain Plz., Ste. 277
Buffalo, NY 14202-2220 (716) 855-2146
Limitations: Giving primarily in Buffalo and western
NY.

The Whitaker Foundation
1700 N. Moore St., Ste. 2200
Arlington, VA 22209 (703) 528-2430
E-mail: info@whitaker.org; URL: http://
www.whitaker.org
Limitations: Giving limited to the U.S. and Canada.
Publishes an annual or periodic report.

E. L. Wiegand Foundation
Wiegand Ctr.
165 W. Liberty St., Ste. 200
Reno, NV 89501 (775) 333-0310
Limitations: Giving primarily in NV and adjoining
western states, including AZ, ID, OR, UT and WA;
public affairs grants given primarily in
Washington, DC, and New York, NY.

Malcolm Hewitt Wiener Foundation, Inc.
c/o The Millburn Corporation
66 Vista Dr.
Greenwich, CT 06830

The Wilburforce Foundation
3601 Fremont Ave. N., Ste. 304
Seattle, WA 98103 (206) 632-2325
FAX: (206) 632-2326; E-mail: grants@wilburforce.org;
Additional address (Montana office): P.O. Box
296, Bozeman, MT 59771-0296, tel.: (406)
586-9796, FAX: (406) 586-3076, E-mail:
jennifer@wilburforce.org; Additional tel.: (800)
201-0148 (Seattle office), (800) 317-8180
(Montana office); URL: http://
www.wilburforce.org
Limitations: Giving primarily in the western U.S. and
western Canada, particularly AK, AZ, NM, OR, UT,
WA, WY, British Columbia, and the Yellowstone
to Yukon region of U.S.-Canada.

The Robert W. Wilson Charitable Trust
c/o Robert W. Wilson
520 83rd St., Ste. 1R
Brooklyn, NY 11209
Limitations: Giving primarily in NY.

The Winnick Family Foundation
9355 Wilshire Blvd., 4th Floor
Beverly Hills, CA 90210
Limitations: Giving in the U.S., with strong emphasis
on CA and NY.

The Norman and Rosita Winston Foundation,
Inc.
c/o John O'Neil, Paul Weiss et. al.
1285 Ave. of the Americas
New York, NY 10019-6064 (212) 373-3000
Limitations: Giving in the U.S., with emphasis on
national and local organizations in NY.

Wisconsin Energy Corporation Foundation, Inc.
231 W. Michigan St., Rm. P423
Milwaukee, WI 53203-0001 (414) 221-2107
FAX: (414) 221-2412;
E-mail: patti.mcnew@we-energies.com;
URL: http://www.wec-foundation.com/
Limitations: Giving limited to areas of company
operations in the Upper Peninsula, MI, area and
WI.

The Wolf Creek Charitable Foundation
c/o PNC Bank
1122 Soldier Creek Rd.
Wolf, WY 82844
Limitations: Giving on a national basis.

Wood-Claeyssens Foundation
P.O. Box 30586
Santa Barbara, CA 93130-0586
Limitations: Giving limited to Santa Barbara and
Ventura counties, CA.

Robert W. Woodruff Foundation, Inc.
50 Hurt Plz., Ste. 1200
Atlanta, GA 30303 (404) 522-6755
FAX: (404) 522-7026; E-mail: fdns@woodruff.org;
URL: http://www.woodruff.org
Limitations: Giving primarily in GA, with emphasis on
the metropolitan Atlanta area.

Wyoming Community Foundation
313 S. 2nd St.
Laramie, WY 82070 (307) 721-8300
FAX: (307) 721-8333; E-mail: wcf@wycf.org;
Additional tel.: (866) 708-7878; Grant
application E-mail: samin@wycf.org; URL: http://
www.wycf.org
Limitations: Giving primarily in WY.
Publishes an annual or periodic report.

Xcel Energy Foundation
414 Nicollet Mall
Minneapolis, MN 55401 (612) 215-5317
FAX: (612) 215-4522;
E-mail: john.pacheco-jr@xcelenergy.com;
Additional E-mail: foundation@xcelenergy.com;
URL: http://www.xcelenergy.com/XLWEB/CDA/
0,3080,1-1-1_4359_4842-922-0_0_0-0,00.htm
l
Limitations: Giving on a national basis, with emphasis
on areas of company operations.

Yawkey Foundation II
990 Washington St.
Dedham, MA 02026-6716 (781) 329-7470
URL: http://www.yawkeyfoundation.org
Limitations: Giving primarily in MA, with emphasis on
the greater metropolitan Boston area.

Yum! Brands Foundation
c/o Mary Nixon
1900 Colonel Sanders Ln., L-1365
Louisville, KY 40213-1964
Application address: 1441 Gardiner Ln., Louisville, KY
40213-5910; URL: http://www.yum.com/
responsibility/foundation.asp
Limitations: Giving on a national basis, with some
emphasis on Louisville, KY.

The Anne and Henry Zarrow Foundation
401 S. Boston, Ste. 900
Tulsa, OK 74103-4012 (918) 295-8004
FAX: (918) 295-8049; E-mail: (for Jeanne Gillert):
jgillert@zarrow.com; URL: http://
www.zarrow.com/ahz.htm
Limitations: Giving primarily in the Tulsa, OK, area.